CW00552628

Dispute Resolution in the Energy Sector

A Practitioner's Handbook

Consulting Editor **Ronnie King**

Consulting editor
Ronnie King

Publisher
Sian O'Neill

Editors
Carolyn Boyle, Jo Moore, Jeremy White

Marketing manager
Alan Mowat

Production
Natalie Clarke

Publishing directors
Guy Davis, Tony Harriss, Mark Lamb

Dispute Resolution in the Energy Sector: A Practitioner's Handbook
is published by
Globe Law and Business
Globe Business Publishing Ltd
New Hibernia House
Winchester Walk
London SE1 9AG
United Kingdom
Tel +44 20 7234 0606
Fax +44 20 7234 0808
Web www.globelawandbusiness.com

Printed by CPI Group (UK) Ltd, Croydon, CR0 4YY

ISBN 978-1-905783-62-5

Dispute Resolution in the Energy Sector: A Practitioner's Handbook
© 2012 Globe Business Publishing Ltd

DISCLAIMER
This publication is intended as a general guide only. The information and opinions which it contains are not intended to be a comprehensive study, nor to provide legal advice, and should not be treated as a substitute for legal advice concerning particular situations. Legal advice should always be sought before taking any action based on the information provided. The publishers bear no responsibility for any errors or omissions contained herein.

Table of contents

Introduction

Ronnie King
Ashurst LLP

This book is concerned with commercial disputes in the energy sector. It is intended for use by corporate counsel and commercial personnel of oil and gas companies and other companies in the energy sector. The contributors are drawn from 10 of the world's leading energy law firms. A number are well known to me from disputes going back over 20 years; Liz Tout of SNR Denton and Ted Greeno and his colleague Caroline Kehoe of Herbert Smith are particularly frequent opponents of my partner Tim Reid and myself at Ashurst.

Half a dozen or more London-headquartered law firms have dedicated energy sector dispute teams, with a number of partners spending all or most of their time working for industry clients. This gives an indication of the extent to which energy companies find themselves in, or on the verge of, disputes. Statistics compiled by the International Chamber of Commerce regularly report that between 10% and 15% of all arbitrations administered by them concern oil and gas. The International Centre for Settlement of Investment Disputes reports that as at early 2012, 25% of investor claims relate to oil, gas or mining and 13% to electric power or other energy.

The high-value nature of energy sector disputes means that legal and arbitral costs often represent an insignificant proportion of the amount at stake. Happily, however, and consistent with other business sectors, most disputes are resolved privately, through either negotiation or mediation, so that the case law discussed in the book is the exception rather than the rule.

Certain chapters deal with particular types of dispute resolution mechanism (eg, arbitration and expert determination). Other chapters discuss issues which commonly give rise to disputes, such as the chapter on contract pricing disputes and that on joint venture disputes, by Elie Kleiman of Freshfields Bruckhaus Deringer.

Many readers will be familiar with Tim Martin through his work at the Association of International Petroleum Negotiators; he provides an analysis of the development of case law in relation to oil and gas disputes and the development of discernable customs and practices applicable to those industries (what is sometimes called the 'lex petrolea').

There are also contributions from corporate counsel. David Isenegger at Centrica writes on dispute avoidance and risk management, as seen from his position as corporate counsel; while Drazen Petkovich of Crescent Petroleum has provided a chapter on international boundary disputes.

Should your company find itself in dispute, the authors hope that you will find useful information and ideas within this book.

I conclude by recording my thanks to my partner, Mark Clarke, for his assistance in bringing this project to conclusion. All involved in the book are indebted to Sian O'Neill of Globe Law and Business – first for the idea behind the book, and second for her patience and perseverance with us in successfully completing the project.

Ronnie King is a partner in the dispute resolution department of Ashurst LLP and heads the international arbitration group. He has considerable experience of multi-jurisdictional litigation and arbitration in the power and energy sectors.

Mr King is a fellow of the Chartered Institute of Arbitrators and is recognised as a leading practitioner in the field of arbitration, commercial litigation and energy law in the Chambers *and* Legal 500 *independent guides, which have described him as "a leader in energy litigation" and "almost peerless" for energy disputes.*

Drafting effective dispute resolution clauses

Mark Clarke
Jessica Neuberger
Ashurst LLP

1. Dispute resolution drafting as a risk management tool

When negotiating transaction documents, dispute resolution is rarely at the forefront of the contracting parties' minds. However, given the international scope and complexity of energy industry contracts, disputes frequently arise. When they do, the dispute resolution clause, together with the governing law clause, provides the basic rules of engagement. Any contract negotiator must view dispute resolution clauses in this light when sitting down to negotiations. Simply because they are at the end of a contract by custom does not mean that they should be relegated to the end of the list of important provisions.

Providing for effective dispute resolution in the transaction documents goes a long way to both avoiding the escalation of disputes and resolving disputes in a manner which best protects a party's commercial interests. Having a dispute resolution policy in place which sets out an organisation's approach to the drafting of these clauses is therefore integral to good risk management.

In this chapter we look at the different options available for dispute resolution and the considerations that should be taken into account when formulating a dispute resolution policy or drafting a dispute resolution clause.

2. The governing law clause

The choice of governing law applies to the contract as a whole, regulating the parties' rights and obligations. It is when disputes arise that governing law is most commonly invoked – hence the importance of this choice to the formulation of a dispute resolution mechanism. Confusion and uncertainties can arise when governing law and the dispute resolution procedure are dealt with in the same clause. As a matter of best practice, these should be dealt with separately.

When negotiating the governing law clause, there are two issues to consider:
- which law to choose; and
- the scope of the clause.

2.1 Choice of law

Energy industry contracts often involve parties from different jurisdictions. Therefore, the choice of governing law may require a degree of negotiation, each party preferring the laws with which it is most familiar. A recent survey confirmed that English law is the most commonly used for international oil and gas contracts, having been selected by 40% of respondents (followed by New York law

(17%)).[1] The dominance of English as the international business language is a pragmatic reason for choosing one of these two jurisdictions.

There are other reasons for preferring English law, and the list below provides a guide to choosing the governing law:

- English law is largely settled and predictable – principles of English law have developed over an extended period through case law. As commercial realities have changed through the centuries, this case law has been refined and adapted to suit. As a result, there tends to be a greater degree of certainty as to how contracts will be interpreted by the courts than in civil law jurisdictions.
- It is flexible and commercial – it seeks to uphold the freedom of the parties to contract as they see fit.
- It is suited to oil and gas agreements. The existence of significant case law on issues arising under commonly used oil and gas agreements means that parties can better predict how a court will interpret the agreement.
- English law imposes no obligation of good faith and restricts the ability of parties to evade contractual obligations (eg, by invocation of the doctrine of hardship found in many civil law jurisdictions).

The drafting of standard form contracts is significantly more straightforward when a common law jurisdiction is chosen. As the Association of International Petroleum Negotiators (AIPN) notes in its model form international operating agreement guidance notes, a number of additional drafting issues arise where a civil law jurisdiction is chosen. These include issues of operator agency, limitation on the liability of the operator, the distinction between legal and beneficial interests, mandatory pre-emption rights and *force majeure*.

Parties may also want their relationship to be governed by a law other than that of a country – for example, *lex mercatoria* (ie, merchant law). If that is the case, the dispute resolution provision should refer disputes to arbitration, as many courts (including all EU courts) will not recognise a choice of law other than that of a country.[2]

2.2 Scope of the clause

Whatever law is chosen, parties should ensure that the governing law clause is widely drafted so that it covers both contractual and non-contractual issues arising in respect of the contract. Otherwise, if a dispute arises relating to pre-contract representations or negotiations, a party could argue that a different law from that of the contract applies. In the European Union at least, courts generally will give effect to the parties' choice of governing law for non-contractual disputes.[3] Clear wording

---

1   The 2010 International Arbitration Survey: Choices in International Arbitration conducted by the School of International Arbitration at Queen Mary, University of London.

2   In *Shamil Bank of Bahrain EC v Beximco Pharmaceuticals Ltd (No 1)* [2004] EWCA Civ 19 the English Court of Appeal confirmed that under European conflict of law principles (the Rome Convention and Rome I Regulation), it is not open to the parties to select a non-national system of law (eg, *Sharia*) as the governing law of a contract.

3   Regulation (EC) No 864/2007 of the European Parliament and of the Council of July 11 2007 on the law applicable to non-contractual obligations (Rome II).

indicating the parties' intentions is all that is required. The following specimen clause is drafted on this basis.

This agreement, and any dispute, controversy, proceedings or claim of whatever nature arising out of or in any way relating to this agreement or its formation (including any non-contractual disputes or claims), shall be governed by and construed in accordance with English law.

3.   Dispute resolution: general principles

3.1   Clarity

The dispute resolution clause should be clearly drafted and unambiguous. Courts will generally endeavour to give effect to the parties' agreement on how they wish to resolve their disputes, but if the agreement is unclear because the clause has been poorly drafted, the parties could find themselves in a different forum from that chosen. Clarity is particularly important in lengthy complicated dispute resolution clauses that provide for a variety of dispute resolution mechanisms.

3.2   Umbrella clause

In transactions involving several agreements and where the aim is for all disputes to follow the same dispute process, it is sensible to draft an 'umbrella' clause which can then be incorporated by reference into each agreement or attached as a schedule. In addition to ensuring consistency between the agreements, it avoids the difficulties of ensuring that all of the dispute resolution clauses work back to back. In certain circumstances, it may be preferable for the parties to negotiate a separate, standalone umbrella agreement to which they are all party and which sets out the procedure by which disputes will be resolved.

3.3   Ensure that the process works

This is particularly important where a dispute resolution clause has several steps and refers different types of dispute to different forums. It is important that the parties ensure that all of the mechanisms work together, the process is clear and there are no gaps through which a dispute could fall. For example, if particular technical disputes are to be resolved by an expert and all other disputes are to be referred to arbitration, the parties should ensure that the definition of 'dispute' in the arbitration clause is widely drafted so as to catch all other possible disputes.

3.4   Inclusion of non-binding dispute resolution mechanism

All contracts must provide for a final and binding dispute resolution procedure, usually litigation or arbitration. However, as both are expensive and time consuming, contracting parties are increasingly adapting their dispute resolution clauses to include procedures aimed at encouraging resolution of the dispute before it reaches that stage. These alternative dispute resolution (ADR) procedures are particularly suited to long-term contracts, where the efficient and relatively amicable resolution of disputes can ensure the preservation of relationships. The other benefit of including these 'stepped' or 'tiered' clauses is that they put negotiation on the agenda, thereby avoiding a perception of weakness if ADR is suggested following the emergence of a dispute.

The drafting of these clauses varies significantly, from simple clauses to complex procedures. The AIPN international operating agreement, for example, offers a menu of optional dispute resolution methods which parties can select. The mechanisms commonly used in tiered clauses include the following:

- Structured negotiations – these are negotiations which can take place at varying levels within a corporation so that there is an attempt to resolve the dispute at management level, failing which it is escalated to senior management and on to board level if necessary.
- Mediation – this is the most common form of ADR. The mediator (a neutral person) facilitates a settlement between the parties by suggesting ways in which a satisfactory compromise could be achieved.

A typical tiered dispute resolution procedure might take a form similar to that set out in the flowchart in Figure 1 below. Often, contracts will provide for different steps to be taken depending on the nature of the dispute. So, for example, a dispute over quantum may be subject to a multi-step procedure as set out at Figure 1 and a legal dispute may be directly referred to mediation.

Figure 1

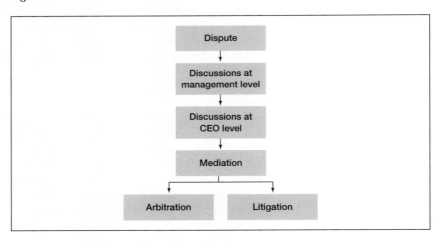

Tiered clauses work best when drafted to suit the particular transaction. Shorter-form clauses are often used as they are easier to draft. However, although broadly drafted clauses allow the parties to tailor the procedure to the dispute when it arises, they also increase the potential for delay and are less likely to be enforceable. When parties are drafting a detailed clause which provides for different procedures depending on the type of dispute, they should also include a 'catch-all' provision so that if a dispute does not fall within a specified category of dispute, a default procedure or forum is provided for.

(a) ***Drafting issues***

When parties are drafting a tiered dispute resolution clause, the key principles that should be considered are as follows:

- There should be a clear process.
- It must be apparent whether the process or parts thereof are to be mandatory. Some jurisdictions (including England) may enforce the parties' agreement to refer their disputes to an ADR process before they can commence litigation or arbitration proceedings. This may not be what the parties intended and, if not, it is important that this be reflected in the drafting. If the parties agree that mediation should be mandatory, they should ensure that there is an exception so that proceedings can be commenced if a party would be prejudiced by any delay – for example, where limitation is an issue and any delay would result in a claim becoming time barred. This is particularly important where the final destination for disputes is arbitration, as the tribunal may not have jurisdiction until the mediation process has been completed. The specimen clause below has been drafted on this basis.
- It must be clear when the process is triggered, as this will make it harder for a party to avoid the process and also reduce the potential for tactical delays.
- The clause should incorporate a timeframe. This is particularly important where there are several steps. The drafting should ensure that it is clear when one stage ends and another begins. The common approach is to provide for a structured time scale for when the various steps are to take place and to make it clear when the time period for each stage ends.
- Individuals with specific roles (eg, a mediator) must be readily identifiable, but the parties should avoid identifying a specific individual who may be unable to act or unavailable. Common practice is to refer to a body or institution as the appointing body in respect of such individuals. The parties should therefore always check that the specified organisation exists and that it has the ability to appoint an individual to the role in question.

A key advantage of a tiered dispute resolution clause is that it can be tailored to the particular circumstances of the transaction. Such clauses are therefore not boilerplate. Several bodies and institutions – including the AIPN, the International Court of Arbitration of the International Chamber of Commerce (ICC), the London Court of International Arbitration (LCIA) and the Centre for Effective Dispute Resolution (CEDR) – provide a menu of options on their websites. The following specimen clause is a short and straightforward tiered clause which illustrates the drafting points made above. It has been drafted on the basis that mediation is mandatory and that the dispute will ultimately be resolved by arbitration, although the arbitration part of the clause has not been included:

If any dispute arises out of or in connection with this Agreement, including any question regarding its existence, validity, formation or termination, senior representatives of the parties with authority to settle the dispute will, on receipt of a written request from one party to the other, enter into negotiations and attempt to resolve the dispute.

If the dispute is not resolved within [ ] days of the written request, the parties may attempt to settle it by mediation in accordance with [specify the mediation procedure if adopting one]. The mediation process is initiated once a party gives notice in writing to the other party(ies) to the dispute requesting a mediation ("ADR notice"). If agreement cannot be reached on the identity of the mediator, the mediator will be nominated by [specify the appointing body].

No party may commence an arbitration in relation to any dispute arising out of this agreement until it has attempted to settle the dispute by mediation and either the mediation has terminated or the other party has failed to participate in the mediation, provided that the right to issue proceedings is not prejudiced by a delay.

If the dispute is not settled by mediation within [ ] days of the ADR notice, the dispute shall be referred to and finally resolved by arbitration.

3.5 Where and how is a dispute to be ultimately resolved?

Regardless of the dispute resolution mechanism adopted, a contract needs to provide for a final means of determining a dispute which is binding on the parties. This provides ultimate certainty for the parties. However, because it is final in nature, choosing the forum in which the parties wish the dispute to be resolved requires careful advanced planning. The principal binding dispute resolution mechanisms are:

- litigation;
- arbitration; and
- expert determination.

Typically, however, the parties will decide between litigation and arbitration, with many international oil and gas disputes being referred to arbitration. That said, expert determination is increasing in popularity as a forum for resolving discrete technical disputes. It is therefore common for a dispute resolution clause to refer disputes on discrete technical issues to expert determination and all other disputes to arbitration (or litigation). This section focuses on what parties should consider when deciding upon their final dispute resolution mechanism and the drafting issues related to their dispute resolution clauses.

(a) Selecting your forum: litigation v arbitration

Historically, litigation was perceived as lengthy and expensive, and arbitration was perceived as offering a relatively efficient and cost-effective alternative. These advantages have disappeared over time and arbitration is now generally recognised as being as expensive and time consuming as litigation.

Nevertheless, a number of key questions remain which parties should consider when deciding which forum is more appropriate:

- Is confidentiality important? In court proceedings, hearings are heard in public in all but exceptional circumstances. In addition, key documents, such as statements of case filed by parties to proceedings and judgments, are generally available to the public without restriction. By contrast, arbitration is a private process, proceedings are not usually open to the public and awards can generally be kept confidential.

- Is enforceability likely to be an issue? More often than not, the parties to energy contracts will be domiciled in different jurisdictions or key assets may be held in different jurisdictions, in which case enforceability is more likely to be an issue. As a general rule, arbitral awards are a great deal easier to enforce than judgments secured through litigation. The New York Convention,[4] which has been ratified by 146 of the 193 members of the United Nations, has put in place a detailed regime for the reciprocal enforcement of awards which is far more comprehensive than the patchy international recognition of the court judgments made by a particular jurisdiction. Notable exceptions to the current signatories of the New York Convention include Iraq, Angola, Libya and Sierra Leone. As a general rule, if a party needs to enforce an English court judgment in another EU member state or Commonwealth country, enforcement is straightforward.[5] If, however, enforcement would be outside of these jurisdictions, arbitration is the preferable option.
- What is more important: certainty and speed or the right to appeal a decision? This is very much a commercial decision, as it must be decided what is more important: finality/certainty or the opportunity to appeal if a party is not satisfied with a decision. There are only very restricted circumstances in which arbitral awards can be challenged (eg, serious irregularity or lack of jurisdiction). In certain jurisdictions there may be scope for an appeal on an error of law. Consequently, parties can rely on certainty and a relatively speedy resolution to the dispute, by contrast with litigation, where multiple appeals may be possible.
- Is flexibility required? Arbitration is not governed by court rules. While it is common to elect for the arbitration to be governed by the rules of an arbitral institution, this is not essential. It is possible for the parties to agree to a procedure that is tailored to their circumstances, and certain very costly stages of litigation (eg, the disclosure of relevant documents) can be avoided or reduced in scale significantly.
- Is independence/neutrality important? This will depend largely on the jurisdiction being considered for litigation. There may well be legitimate concerns over the independence of certain courts if one party is domiciled in that jurisdiction (particularly if the party is a state entity). For this reason, it is often preferable to choose arbitration in cross-border contracts, as the parties can choose a neutral seat (see below) and tribunal.
- What type of decision maker(s) do the parties want and do the parties want

4 The New York Convention on the Recognition and Enforcement of Foreign Arbitral Awards 1958.
5 The Brussels I Regulation 2001 (Council Regulation (EC) No 44/2001 of December 22 2000 on jurisdiction and the recognition and enforcement of judgments in civil and commercial matters) provides for automatic recognition and enforcement of court judgements between EU member states. The Lugano Convention 1988 (Convention of September 16 1988 on jurisdiction and the enforcement of judgments in civil and commercial matters) provides for automatic recognition and enforcement between EU member states and European Free Trade Association states (Iceland, Norway and Switzerland, but not Lichtenstein). Reciprocal enforcement in most Commonwealth countries is provided for by the Administration of Justice Act 1920 and the Foreign Judgements (Reciprocal Enforcement Act) 1933.

to be able to choose their decision maker(s)? Generally, the quality of English High Court judges is very high and the judgments given are to a very high standard. On the other hand, in arbitration it is possible to select specialists in the relevant field, meaning that the arbitrators may have better expertise than a judge. However, where a panel of arbitrators may be selected by the parties, the quality of the tribunal may be more variable. This issue is of particular import, given the limited scope for appeal in arbitration. However, the counterargument is that many parties will feel more comfortable having an element of control over the identity of the arbitrators, which would not be possible in litigation.

- Are there connected contracts and/or multiple parties? Litigation permits the joinder of all relevant parties to the dispute, allowing all aspects of a dispute to be resolved in one hearing. It also allows the consolidation of related actions where, for example, they arise under related contracts. In contrast, arbitration is a creature of contract, so an arbitral tribunal has jurisdiction over only those parties which have entered into the arbitration agreement and there is no automatic right of joinder or consolidation. Where joinder or consolidation issues are likely to arise (eg, in a complex project with multiple parties and contracts), an umbrella arbitration agreement is recommended to ensure that all parties are contractually bound to adhere to the same dispute resolution mechanism; otherwise, there would be a risk of parallel proceedings and inconsistent outcomes. Such agreements need to be carefully considered and drafted.

4. Litigation: drafting issues to consider

Litigation is provided for by including a jurisdiction clause which clearly identifies the national court or courts to which the parties want to submit their disputes. Failure to include a jurisdiction clause will result in the court determining the dispute being decided by reference to rules of private international law. This is likely to cause uncertainty and can also lead to additional costs and delays in progressing any proceedings.

The drafting of a jurisdiction clause is straightforward. The issues that the parties need to consider are as follows:

- Which jurisdiction to submit disputes to – this will depend on the nature of the contract and the parties. Factors to consider include:
  - where the parties are domiciled (ie, convenience);
  - preferred judicial systems; and
  - enforcement – where are the assets held and can the chosen jurisdiction's judgments be enforced in the jurisdiction(s) where those assets are held?
- Whether the jurisdiction clause is to be exclusive, non-exclusive or a hybrid of the two – exclusive clauses require the parties to submit to the exclusive jurisdiction of a particular court or courts. These clauses offer certainty and greater protection against proceedings being commenced in a different court. With non-exclusive clauses, both parties agree that a particular court has jurisdiction, but that they can still refer a dispute to another court that has

jurisdiction. Non-exclusive clauses offer greater flexibility, but run the risk of parallel proceedings, particularly where one of the parties is domiciled outside of the European Union. Hybrid clauses, which are common in loan agreements, restrict one party (eg, the borrower) to suing in a particular court, while the other party (the lender) retains the right to bring proceedings in any court of competent jurisdiction (eg, wherever the borrower's assets are located).

- The scope of the clause – if the parties want to refer all conceivable disputes to litigation, the jurisdiction clause will need to be drafted widely to avoid arguments over whether a particular dispute falls within the scope of the clause. The specimen clause below contains appropriate wording.
- Additional protection – if a party is concerned that its counterparty may commence proceedings elsewhere in breach of an exclusive jurisdiction clause, it should consider adding an undertaking not to commence proceedings elsewhere or an indemnity in respect of costs incurred as a result of the breach.

A suitable specimen clause is as follows:

Each party irrevocably agrees that the courts of England shall have [non-]exclusive jurisdiction to hear and decide any dispute arising out of or in connection with this Agreement or its formation or validity.

5.   Arbitration: drafting issues to consider

In referring disputes to arbitration, the parties agree to be bound by the decision of one or more arbitrators whose award is legally enforceable. In choosing arbitration, the parties are opting to have their dispute resolved privately instead of going to court.

Unlike in litigation, the jurisdiction of an arbitral tribunal depends on the parties' agreement to arbitrate. Therefore, it is crucial that the agreement to arbitrate be properly drafted. A poorly drafted arbitration clause can lead to a number of unattractive consequences, such as:

- triggering expensive and time-consuming satellite litigation over the meaning and effect of the arbitration agreement;
- jeopardising a party's chances of successfully enforcing the award; or
- directing a party to the courts of a particular jurisdiction it had intended to avoid by agreeing to arbitration in the first place.

Once the parties have decided on arbitration as the appropriate forum, a number of key issues need to be addressed in the drafting of the arbitration agreement.

5.1   Where should the arbitration take place?

This is also known as the 'seat' of the arbitration. Choice of seat is very important, as the seat determines:

- which procedural law will apply to the arbitration – so, for example, if the seat is in London, the Arbitration Act 1996 will apply;

- whether the dispute is arbitrable in that country – that is, whether the subject matter is something over which the local courts reserve exclusive jurisdiction (eg, matters relating to crime) so that it cannot be submitted to arbitration;
- whether the courts of the seat will intervene in the arbitration;
- the possibility of the arbitral award being challenged or appealed; and
- the enforceability of the arbitral award – the seat identifies the 'nationality' of the award for the purpose of enforcement under the New York Convention.

As a general rule, in choosing the seat, contracting parties should look at both the legislation enacted in the particular jurisdiction relating to arbitration and the attitude of the national courts towards arbitration generally. For this reason, popular seats include England, France, Sweden, Singapore, Switzerland, Hong Kong and New York. These jurisdictions are recognised as arbitration friendly and their courts have limited scope to interfere with the arbitral process.

5.2 What type of arbitration should be used: *ad hoc* or institutional?

Arbitrations must be conducted under arbitral rules and the clause should specify which rules should be used. However, before parties decide on which rules to incorporate, they have to decide whether *ad hoc* or institutional arbitration is preferred.

Ad hoc arbitration is arbitration which the parties manage themselves. No arbitral institution oversees the process or supervises the conduct of the arbitrators and the parties. The parties can draw up the arbitral rules themselves, but as this is time-consuming and expensive, usual practice is either to leave the rules to the discretion of the arbitrators or to adopt rules specially written for *ad hoc* arbitration. The most popular rules governing arbitration are the United Nations Commission on International Trade Law (UNCITRAL) Rules.[6]

Institutional arbitration entails the supervision of the arbitral process by an institution. The parties can choose an arbitral institution whose rules can simply be incorporated into the arbitration clause by reference. Such rules are expressly formulated for arbitrations conducted under the administration of the relevant institution.

There are factors in favour, and against, each approach:

- A good *ad hoc* arbitration can be tailored specifically to a dispute, after the dispute arises. The parties can frame their own methodology for resolving the issues between them. However, if there is significant tactical advantage to one party in insisting on one element (eg, multiple arbitrators or disclosure), this benefit may be lost. The parties may disagree about how best to proceed, leading to delays.
- Conversely, *ad hoc* arbitrations are more susceptible to obstructive parties

---

6   The United Nations Commission on International Trade Law Arbitration Rules. These were revised in 2010, following the popularity of the previous version of the rules, which dated from 1976. Note that UNCITRAL does not act as an arbitral institution.

that seek to frustrate the arbitration proceedings (although once an arbitrator or tribunal is appointed, there is much less scope for this). Institutional arbitration is better suited to avoiding such tactics.

- Costs may be harder to control in *ad hoc* arbitration. By contrast, leading institutions such as the ICC and the LCIA provide schedules of fees which enable parties to estimate how much the proceedings will cost.
- The reputation of a leading arbitration institution may make it easier to enforce an arbitral award in certain jurisdictions. Both the ICC and the LCIA have significant name recognition globally, lending authority to any award issued in their names.

Contract negotiators often favour institutional arbitration. It provides a 'safety net' in the event of anything going wrong, such as a difficult party refusing to participate in the process. In addition, the comfort provided by the oversight of an institution is likely to make the arbitration exercise more certain and less stressful. That said, as with any aspect of the dispute resolution procedure, circumstances may dictate a different approach. Thus, many of the disadvantages of *ad hoc* arbitration are less of a consideration in contracts between sophisticated, substantial contractual parties with long-term aligned interests, such as major oil and gas companies.

5.3   Institutional arbitration: choosing the institution

There are numerous institutions to choose from, including:

- the American Arbitration Association (AAA) and its international body, the International Centre for Dispute Resolution (ICDR);
- the Hong Kong International Arbitration Centre (HKIAC);
- the ICC;
- the LCIA;
- the Singapore International Arbitration Centre (SIAC); and
- the Stockholm Chamber of Commerce (SCC).

All of these have advantages and disadvantages when compared with one another, although there is increasingly little distinction between the leading institutions. Parties are often influenced by differences in the rules themselves, sometimes by familiarity and sometimes by their opinion of the international acceptability or reputation of a given institution and/or its cost and speed.

The choice of seat often dictates which institution is chosen. Arbitration institutions at or near the seat of arbitration are usually best placed to appoint the best arbitrators in that location. This helps to reduce costs and increase efficiency in the arbitral process. It is also convenient to have an institution with an office in or near the same time zone as the arbitration hearing. Consequently, a frequent choice for English practitioners is the LCIA Rules, with the ICC Rules for Europe/Middle-East arbitration and SIAC or HKIAC for arbitration in Asia proving popular. Where neutrality is a particular issue, the fallback position is often the ICC because it is perceived to be the most 'international' arbitration institution.

5.4   Choosing your arbitrators

It is desirable for parties to specify the number of arbitrators. Usually, an arbitration is heard by one or three arbitrators; for obvious reasons, an even number of arbitrators should be avoided. Arbitration will be less expensive and involve less delay if the parties provide for a sole arbitrator. However, appointing a sole arbitrator is riskier, as only one person makes the award and there are usually very limited grounds of appeal. In high-value international contracts, it is more usual to provide for the appointment of three arbitrators.

The clause could be drafted so that the number of arbitrators depends on the value of the claim, ensuring more efficient and cost-effective resolution of lower-value disputes. Alternatively, contracting parties may prefer to leave the issue of number of arbitrators to be determined once it is known what the actual dispute involves. That way, the parties are better able to determine whether the dispute is suitable for a sole arbitrator, as value is not always a good guide to suitability. In addition, having a specified limit may encourage parties to artificially 'fix' the claim (either above or below the threshold), which may not be helpful. The disadvantage is that this may be difficult to agree once the parties are in dispute, and so could add delay to the process and increase costs.

Where the tribunal is to consist of three arbitrators, the procedure usually adopted is for each party to nominate an arbitrator and for a 'neutral' third arbitrator (the chairman) to be appointed either by agreement between the two party-nominated arbitrators or, failing that, by the supervising institution.

If *ad hoc* arbitration is used, it is important to specify a mechanism for the appointment of arbitrators in default of appointment by the parties. This is done by nominating a third-party authority to make the appointment. A number of authorities offer an appointing service, including most of the arbitral institutions, even if their arbitral rules are not being used. This is not required where an institutional clause is used, as default appointment by the arbitral institution will be provided for in the relevant rules.

It is possible for parties to specify the qualifications that an arbitrator should have. Qualifications should be defined carefully; too narrow a definition may make it impossible to identify an available arbitrator, while too wide a definition may give rise to satellite disputes or a finding that the appointed tribunal had no jurisdiction to act. Often, the most important quality for an arbitrator is familiarity with arbitration process and procedure, rather than the specific industry in which the dispute has arisen. It is also not advisable for parties to specify a named arbitrator, because if such person were unable or unwilling to act when a dispute arose, the arbitration clause would be incapable of being performed.

Under most institutional rules, the right to appoint an arbitrator is lost in a multi-party situation, unless specific provision is made in the arbitration clause. Therefore, if the parties anticipate that any dispute will involve multiple parties and provision has been made for all such parties to be joined in the same arbitration, consideration should be given as to how the appointment mechanism will work and it may be sensible to leave the appointment to the arbitral institution chosen.

5.5 Language

The parties should specify the language of the arbitration, as this will be the language of the written and oral submissions and any hearings. The language of the arbitration should normally be the language of the contract, since there will often be issues of contractual interpretation. Specifying the language in the clause will avoid time-consuming arguments over what the language should be once a dispute arises.

5.6 Excluding rights of appeal

In most jurisdictions there are only limited grounds on which an arbitration award can be appealed. Parties can exclude (as far as is permitted by the laws of the relevant jurisdiction) the right to appeal on a point of law, in order to ensure that the award is final and binding. This is the case as a matter of English law. Institutional rules may already provide for this,[7] but if not, or if the arbitration is *ad hoc*, the parties will need to consider whether they want to achieve greater finality by excluding rights of appeal. If they do, express provision must be made in the arbitration clause itself. Stating that the award is to be final, binding and conclusive will not suffice.[8]

5.7 Confidentiality

If confidentiality is considered to be important, an express confidentiality agreement should be included, along with a remedy for breach of the same. Although in England, confidentiality of the arbitration proceedings and the award is implied both during the arbitration and in any related court proceedings, there are exceptions. The procedural law of the seat, together with any applicable rules, determines whether and to what extent confidentiality provisions apply and should always be checked. If in doubt, it is safer to include an express confidentiality agreement in the clause.

5.8 Specimen clause

The advantage of arbitration is that the procedure can be tailored to suit the transaction. However, where parties have chosen institutional arbitration, the usual policy is to adapt the specimen clause provided by the particular institution (as available on the various institutions' websites). Industry bodies such as the AIPN also provide specimen clauses. *Ad hoc* clauses will often be more difficult to draft, particularly where the parties have agreed a bespoke procedure. If using the UNCITRAL Rules, the drafting principles are similar to when using an institutional clause, save for the need to add an appointing authority.

The specimen clause below follows the usual principles of the institutional clauses. It contains only the essential elements required and is recommended only as a starting point for a more sophisticated and bespoke clause:

Any dispute arising out of or in connection with this contract, including any question regarding its existence, validity, formation or termination, shall be referred to and finally resolved by arbitration by [one/three] arbitrators under the [specify Rules of institution or UNCITRAL Rules], which Rules are deemed to be incorporated by reference

---

7   For example, both the LCIA and ICC Rules exclude rights of appeal as permitted by law.
8   *Shell Egypt West Manzala GmbH v Dana Gas Egypt Ltd* [2009] EWHC 2097 (Comm).

into this clause. The seat, or legal place, of arbitration shall be [City and/or Country] and the language of the arbitration shall be [ ]. [The appointing authority shall be [ ].][9]

6. Expert determination

Expert determination is a form of alternative dispute resolution whereby the parties to a contract ask an independent expert to give a binding decision on a dispute. It is an attractive alternative for settling disputes involving single issues and technical rather than legal questions, because it allows the parties to turn to an expert for the answer, rather than a judge or arbitrator. If done properly, expert determination can provide a cheap, fast and informal means of determining an issue.

Consequently, expert determination has an established and increasing role in the energy sector and is frequently used in commodity sales contracts. A typical example of when expert determination would be appropriate is in a long-term contract where an expert is required to assess whether industrial plant machinery has met the relevant criteria, or whether a seller is entitled to terminate a long-term gas sales agreement because it is no longer economic for gas to be produced from a designated field.

Parties must appreciate, however, that the decision to refer disputes to expert determination is binding and the courts will usually hold parties to their agreement. Parties should therefore ensure that they refer only appropriate disputes to an expert.

6.1 Key characteristics

In order to understand how to draft an expert determination clause, it is important to understand the key characteristics of expert determination:

- Creature of contract – expert determination clauses operate wholly on a contractual basis. The parties can choose whom they want to deal with the relevant issue, which can be a significant advantage where the dispute requires knowledge of complicated technical issues. The exact confines of the expert's authority can be delineated by agreement between the parties without interference from the courts.
- No legislative background – in contrast to arbitration, expert determination is not backed up by statute. While this may make the process quicker and more efficient, the downside is that as the expert's remit is entirely dependent on the contract granting him authority, he has no residual powers beyond those expressly granted by the contracting parties.
- Privacy – whereas proceedings before a court take place in the public domain, parties to an expert determination can maintain the privacy of their contractual relationship.
- Finality – the expert's decision may be challenged on only a limited number of grounds. These include fraud or partiality on the part of the expert, or where the expert has failed to answer the question put to him by the parties in a material way. This greater certainty in the finality of the outcome, and the attendant advantages in terms of cost and speed, is one of the advantages

---

9   To be included if *ad hoc*.

of expert determination. Paradoxically, it is also one of the greatest pitfalls: if the expert gets it wrong, the parties may be stuck with the decision.

- Enforceability – this issue is frequently cited as one of the principal drawbacks of expert determination in comparison to litigation or arbitration. Unlike a court judgment or an arbitration award, there is no direct method of enforcing an expert's determination. A successful party is required to bring a claim before the court on the basis of the unsuccessful party's breach of contract in failing to comply with the determination. This process can add substantially to the difficulty and time involved in expert determination.
- Procedure – because an expert's remit is entirely dependent on contractual provisions, there are no rules of procedure and process to fall back on. The clause will need to incorporate the procedural rules that are to apply.

6.2   General drafting considerations
Many of the pitfalls associated with expert determination can be avoided by careful, bespoke drafting. Of all dispute resolution clauses, an expert determination clause requires the most care and tailoring to the specific circumstances. We have therefore not included a specimen clause, but have set out the key points to address in order to avoid the pitfalls:

- Act as expert – where an expert determination clause is used, it is important that the clause expressly states that the expert is to act as expert in order to avoid confusion with other methods of dispute resolution such as arbitration.
- Appointment of the expert – an expert should possess expertise and technical knowledge relevant to the dispute. However, it is not advisable to name a specific individual, but rather to specify the field of expertise and provide that the parties will try to agree on the identity of the expert. Failing such an agreement, the clause should provide for appointment by an appropriate professional institution. Checks should be made that the institution exists and is willing to appoint an expert. If not, the courts are unable to assist in appointing one.
- Finality and grounds for challenge – it is important to expressly state that the expert's decision is to be final, but consideration will need to be given as to whether the parties want the ability to challenge a decision of the expert on certain grounds. The mere fact that the expert has made a mistake is not grounds to challenge his decision. As such, it is common practice for parties to agree that an expert's decision is binding except in the case of manifest error.
- Procedure – as previously mentioned, expert determination is a process governed by contract and ideally the procedure should be set out in the clause; otherwise, it will need to be established at the time the dispute arises. However, once there is a dispute, agreement between the parties is more difficult to achieve and parties can become obstructive, slowing down the process and adding costs. Parties can avoid this issue by setting out a detailed procedure in the clause. The alternative is to agree that the expert can set the procedure, but this leaves the parties with no control over the timetable.

- Costs – unless provided for in the clause or the expert's terms of reference, the expert will have no power to make costs awards. The drafting will therefore have to deal specifically with powers such as including a power to award costs against the losing party and, if appropriate, referring costs matters to an independent costs draftsman, for example.
- Confidentiality – the parties may also want to include in the expert determination clause a provision relating to confidentiality. However, such a provision may be displaced by statutory or regulatory requirements.

7.   Other considerations

Whatever forum for dispute resolution is chosen, contracting parties should also consider whether they need to provide for an address for service and whether the contract requires a sovereign immunity waiver clause.

7.1   Address for service

An address for service clause sets out where or how proceedings are to be served in the event that a dispute arises. They are especially important if disputes are to be resolved in the English High Court and one or more of the parties resides outside the jurisdiction (ie, England and Wales). If not included, considerable time can be lost in ensuring that valid service is effected outside the jurisdiction once a dispute has arisen. Where arbitration is the chosen forum, an address for service within the jurisdiction is not essential, but is recommended for practical purposes so that both parties know where they are to serve proceedings in the event that a dispute arises. It is also useful in the event that applications have to be made to the court of the seat in support of the arbitration.

7.2   Sovereign immunity

If one of the parties is a state or state entity, then a waiver of sovereign immunity clause is required in order to ensure that any judgment or arbitration award can be enforced.

8.   Conclusion

The inclusion of an effective dispute resolution clause is essential to the proper functioning of a contract. The optimal approach will vary, depending on the type of contract and the identity of the counterparty, but the options should always be carefully evaluated, since selecting the right mechanism can go a long way to avoiding the escalation of disputes and protecting a party's commercial interests.

International arbitration

Peter Edworthy
Ronnie King
Ashurst LLP

1. Introduction

Over the course of the 20th century, the commercial world became international in every sense of the word, and no other industry reflects this globalisation better than the energy sector. It is as common to find a major Nigerian oil company contracting with a large French exploration organisation as it is to find an English construction firm dealing with a Russian power plant owner, or a Chinese state-owned enterprise setting up a joint venture with a Chilean mining company.

The oil industry illustrates why energy disputes need a dispute resolution procedure that takes into account the international flavour of commerce. Historically, oil-rich countries may not have had the technology, capital and management skills to find and extract oil and the major corporations had greater power to insist on disputes being resolved in the courts of the home nations. The creation of the Organisation of the Petroleum Exporting Countries in the 1960s allowed petrostates to start their own state-backed national oil companies to take charge of reserves, and the sector has seen the emergence of the likes of Saudi Aramco, National Iranian Oil Company and Kuwait Oil Company as dominant players in the industry. This shift in the balance of power means that the international community is operating on a markedly more level playing field.

In addition to securing a neutral venue, choosing arbitration creates greater opportunities for the enforcement of awards than can be obtained in relation to national court litigation. The reason for this is the enforcement framework provided by the New York Convention on the Recognition and Enforcement of Foreign Arbitral Awards 1958 (see below). Parties can select arbitrators with expertise in the relevant industry or subject matter of the underlying commercial contract; they can choose the language in which the proceedings will be conducted. Arbitration also offers greater procedural flexibility compared with court proceedings, and is generally private and confidential; disputes can be resolved faster because the possibility of appeals is limited, and sometimes the costs can be lower.

Therefore, parties regularly demand dispute resolution procedures that recognise the international context of their industries and do not favour one party over another. Submitting disputes to the national courts of either party can now be an unpalatable option for both sides. The public forum of court litigation may also prove undesirable in the competitive world of energy, where commercial terms need to be kept secret.

Redfern and Hunter note that "there is now a consensus in the business community that arbitration is the principal method of resolving international disputes".[1] States have modernised their arbitration laws to accommodate this growing trend and parties are including arbitration clauses in high-value contracts with increasing regularity.

The International Chamber of Commerce Court of Arbitration (ICC) received:

- 529 requests for arbitration in 1999, involving 1,354 parties from 107 different countries and territories and arbitrators from 57 different countries;
- 593 requests for arbitration in 2006, involving 1,613 parties from 125 different countries and territories and arbitrators from 71 different countries; and
- 793 requests for arbitration in 2010, involving 2,145 parties from 140 different countries and territories and arbitrators from 73 different countries.[2]

2. Arbitration in the energy sector

Arbitration is the dispute resolution mechanism of choice in the energy sector. Parties regularly include arbitration clauses in joint venture agreements, joint operating agreements, production sharing contracts, construction contracts and commodity export contracts. The Association of International Petroleum Negotiators also has arbitration as the standard form of dispute resolution in all of its main standard agreements, including:

- the Study and Bid Group Agreement 2006;
- the Farm-Out Agreement 2004;
- the Joint Operating Agreement 2002;
- the Unitisation and Unit Operating Agreement;
- the Gas Sales Agreement; and
- the Gas Transfer Agreement.

In addition to any contractual rights to arbitration, bilateral investment treaties (and multilateral investment treaties) provide investors in contracting nations with the opportunity to bring an arbitration against a state (or state entity) for any acts that breach the agreement to protect investments in that state by investors from the counter-signatory state.

Claims relating to project management have also been referred to arbitration. In ICC Case 11663 a company had failed to pay cash calls and to provide letters of credit on time or in the correct form to the oil ministry of the country in which the oil exploration and production project was being carried out.[3] Its counterparties in the shared management agreement and participation agreement successfully sought a declaration that it had forfeited its interest in the project as a result.

In *Joint Venture Yashlar v Government of Turkmenistan* a joint venture partner claimed (unsuccessfully) that its partner's drilling of two exploratory wells was so

---

1   *Redfern and Hunter on International Arbitration*, Redfern, Hunter et al (2009), p 439.
2   Facts and Figures on ICC Arbitration – 1999, 2006 and 2010 Statistical Reports at www.iccwbo.org.
3   ICC Case 11663 of 2003, Final Award on Jurisdiction (cited in Thomas CC Childs, "The continuing development of customary law relating to international oil and gas exploration and production", *The Journal of World Energy Law & Business Advance Access*, August 5 2011).

incompetent that it constituted a repudiation of the joint venture agreement.[4] The tribunal was also asked to consider whether the contract had been frustrated by macroeconomic and geopolitical changes which made it impossible for the joint venture to sell gas on the international markets.

3. What is international arbitration?

3.1 Key aspects

Arbitration is a consensual and binding procedure for resolving disputes. It serves as an alternative, rather than a supplement, to litigation through the courts and provides autonomy to the parties over all aspects of the proceedings. As the parties control the manner in which the dispute will be resolved, they are free to agree on the law that will govern the arbitration, the venue of the hearing, the procedural rules (if any) that will guide them through the dispute and, importantly, the identity of the individual or individuals who will decide on the dispute.

As arbitration is consensual, it arises only out of an agreement between the parties that a particular dispute will be resolved by arbitration rather than through the courts. Typically, that agreement may be contained in the main contract (eg, the joint operating agreement, the production sharing contract and the engineering, procurement and construction contract). More rarely, after a dispute has arisen the parties may agree to refer that particular dispute to arbitration.

Once the parties have agreed to refer disputes to arbitration, they cannot unilaterally withdraw their consent. Furthermore, an arbitration agreement will survive termination of the contract in which it is contained so that if that contract comes to an end, the right to arbitrate any dispute that arises from that contract will still exist.[5]

The terms of the arbitration agreement are critical and most national arbitration laws require the arbitration agreement to be in writing in order to ensure certainty of those terms.[6] This reflects the fact that the terms of the arbitration, in relation to both the procedure and the choice of law, derive from the parties' agreement, and therefore those terms must be clearly defined. In particular, an arbitration agreement should make clear which national laws will govern the substance and procedure of the dispute and identify which procedural rules (if any) the parties wish to adopt.

The effectiveness of arbitration depends largely on the willingness of the courts to accept the parties' decision to refer their dispute to arbitration. As a result, 146

---

4   *Joint Venture Yashlar v Government of Turkmenistan*, ICC Case 9151, Interim Award, June 8 1999 (cited in Thomas CC Childs, "The continuing development of customary law relating to international oil and gas exploration and production", *The Journal of World Energy Law & Business Advance Access*, August 5 2011).
5   In English law, this was established by *Heyman v Darwins* [1942] 1 All ER 337 and confirmed in *Fiona Trust & Holding Corporation v Yuri Privalov* [2007] EWCA Civ 20. It is also in Section 7 of the English Arbitration Act 1996. It is further recognised in Article 16 of the United Nations Commission on International Trade Law (UNCITRAL) Model Law. All of the major procedural rules recognise this principle – for example, see Article 6.9 of the ICC Rules; Article 23 of the London Court of International Arbitration (LCIA) Rules; Article 15.2 of the American Arbitration Association (AAA) Rules; Article 23 of the UNCITRAL Rules; and Article 21.2 of the Swiss Rules.
6   A notable exception is France, which has no formal requirements for arbitration agreements (Article 1507 of the French Code of Civil Procedure).

countries have ratified the New York Convention. Notable exceptions to the list of contracting states in the energy sector are Libya, Iraq and a large number of central and eastern Africa states.

The New York Convention is the bedrock of international arbitration. It obliges contracting states to recognise a written arbitration agreement, and therefore, at the request of one of the parties, to stop any proceedings that are brought in the courts in breach of a due process arbitration agreement. The New York Convention also obliges the national courts of contracting states to enforce awards that are made in other contracting states, unless:

- those courts deem the award to be against public policy;
- the subject matter of the dispute is not capable of settlement by arbitration in that state; or
- the award is invalid for one of the reasons set out in Article V.

3.2   Laws governing the arbitration

A defining characteristic of the international nature of arbitration is that parties may be subject to a possible four different governing laws to fit their circumstances and requirements.

First, they may choose a governing law for the substantive dispute. This could be either a national law or international general principles such as the UNIDROIT[7] Principles of International Commercial Contracts. The tribunal will then be obliged to refer to this law in making its award on the merits of the dispute. Parties are strongly encouraged to select a governing law. If they fail to do so, the arbitrators will select a governing law. For arbitrations with a London seat, this power is found in Section 46(3) of the Arbitration Act 1996, under which the tribunal is to apply the law determined by the choice of law rules which it considers applicable.

In practice, parties frequently agree to the substantive law of a 'neutral' state – that is, a state other than the states of incorporation of the contract parties.

In the energy sector, parties sometimes opt for the national laws of a host state qualified by a reference to consistency with general principles of law. Such compromise formulations may give limited comfort in terms of predictability of outcome. Arbitral tribunals have interpreted such clauses either from a perspective which entirely ignores the reference to the national law (as in the case of the two sole arbitrators in the Texaco[8] and BP[9] arbitrations brought against Libya following the cancellation of oil concessions), or by straining to ignore the reference to general principles and apply the national law without qualification.

Another well-known example of compromise between competing possible choices of governing law is represented by the Channel Tunnel construction contract, where the parties agreed to "the principles common to both English and French law, and in the absence of such common principles by such general principles

---

7   International Institute for the Unification of Private Law.
8   *Texaco Overseas Petroleum Company v The Government of the Libyan Arab Republic*, Award of January 19 1977.
9   *British Petroleum Company (Libya) Ltd wholly owned by British Petroleum Company Ltd (UK) v The Government of the Libyan Arab Republic*, award on the merits, October 10 1973.

of international trade law as have been applied by national and international tribunals".[10] The parties spent huge amounts arguing over what principles were common to English and French law.

Second, it is important that parties give careful consideration to the juridical seat of the arbitration, as this will dictate the law governing the arbitration proceedings (the *'lex arbitri'*). Major examples of national laws are the English Arbitration Act 1996, the US Federal Arbitration Act, the French Code of Civil Procedure (Articles 1504 to 1527), the German Code of Civil Procedure (Articles 1025 to 1066) and the Singapore International Arbitration Act. Most national laws are based on the United Nations Commission on International Trade Law (UNCITRAL) Model Law on International Commercial Arbitration, which is widely recognised as the common standard. If a national law departs significantly from the Model Law, parties should be wary of agreeing that country as the seat for arbitration.

The *lex arbitri* has significant implications for:

- the laws governing the definition and form of an arbitration agreement;
- the jurisdiction of a tribunal to hear a dispute;
- the identity of the relevant courts to which parties should apply for interim applications;
- the ability of the courts to supervise the arbitration (eg, to remove an arbitrator for misconduct);
- the right of the parties to appeal any award; and
- the nationality of the award for enforcement purposes.[11]

The *lex arbitri* also confirms which national laws will provide the procedural framework within which the arbitration should work, in conjunction with any institutional procedural rules that the parties adopt. For reasons of public policy, many national laws contain mandatory provisions out of which the parties cannot contract.[12]

Notwithstanding the importance of choosing a seat, if the parties choose one of the major institutional procedural rules (eg, the ICC Rules, the Singapore International Arbitration Centre (SIAC) Rules or American Arbitration Association (AAA) Rules) but fail to select a seat, the institutional court or tribunal will have the power to designate a seat and will, in most cases, choose a recognised and neutral place. In the case of the London Court of International Arbitration (LCIA), London will be designated as the seat unless the institutional court considers it appropriate to be elsewhere.[13]

With the comprehensive institutional procedural rules of the ICC, the SIAC, the AAA and the LCIA becoming increasingly authoritative and widespread, it may be questioned whether the *lex arbitri* is as significant as it might have been historically.

---

10   Clause 68, cited in *Channel Tunnel Group Ltd v Balfour Beatty Construction Ltd*, HL, [1993] AC 334.
11   See below for further discussion on the enforcement of arbitral awards.
12   For example, Schedule 1 of the English Arbitration Act 1996 sets out the mandatory provisions which relate to the courts' ability to remove arbitrators, the duties of the tribunal and the parties, the enforcement of arbitral awards and the parties' ability to challenge an award of the grounds of lack of jurisdiction or serious irregularity.
13   Article 16.1 of the LCIA Rules.

While this could be true for the procedural effects, the law of the arbitration proceedings still has considerable importance in the context of disputes which have a substantive law of a state whose courts have been unsupportive of arbitration. In that situation, it is essential that the seat is in an arbitration-friendly state.

Although parties may select a seat for arbitration, this does not mean that they must hold hearings at that location. It is not uncommon, for example, to have the seat of arbitration as London but, as a matter of convenience, to have some or all oral hearings in a different country. Many of the major institutional rules make it clear that the tribunal may decide to hold hearings at any venue that it deems appropriate, which may be different from the seat. Therefore, the parties should be aware that even though the arbitration is physically held in a particular country, this does not necessarily mean that the juridical seat is the same.

Finally, the parties must also have regard to the law of the country in which they want to enforce an award. Most commonly, this will be wherever the counterparty has most of its assets. The New York Convention obliges any signatory country to enforce an arbitral award where the seat of that arbitration is also a signatory country. However, the national courts that are requested to enforce an award may refuse to do so if the subject matter of the dispute is not capable of settlement by arbitration under the law of that country or if enforcement would be contrary to public policy of that country.[14]

3.3 Procedural rules

In addition to the national laws that govern the arbitration, the parties can elect to incorporate procedural rules which provide a framework in which the arbitration proceedings will be conducted. The use of institutional rules can add political or moral weight to awards so that if a court is asked to consider the procedural propriety of an award, it is less likely to set it aside. Institutional rules are also beneficial on a practical level, as they are designed to regulate the proceedings comprehensively from beginning to end and they contemplate contingencies that might arise, but which parties may have not anticipated themselves. Parties can also avoid the time and expense of drafting lengthy procedural rules from scratch and the fees and expenses of the arbitration are already defined, so no further negotiation is required.

There are now several established sets of institutional rules that parties might adopt. In particular, the ICC, LCIA and Stockholm Chamber of Commerce (SCC) Rules are regularly used by parties in Central Europe, while the SIAC Rules are commonly incorporated where the seat of arbitration is in Southeast Asia. Arbitrations in the United States usually adopt the AAA Rules and Chinese proceedings are likely to be conducted under the auspices of the Chinese International Economic and Trade Arbitration Commission. Alternatively, parties may not want to be restricted by the institutional rules and may elect to proceed on an *ad hoc* basis. In that situation, the parties should agree a set of procedural rules for the arbitration themselves and it is common to refer to the UNCITRAL Rules for guidance.

Choosing an institution is largely governed by parties' familiarity with particular

---

14   Article V(2) of the New York Convention.

rules or by opinion of the international acceptability or reputation of a given institution. According to the 2008 International Arbitration Study conducted by Queen Mary College, University of London, 45% of parties expressed a preference for the ICC as the institutional body, 16% chose the AAA and 11% selected the LCIA.[15]

The various institutional rules are largely similar and provide the framework for conducting an arbitration. Broadly, they set out how to start an arbitration, how the tribunal should be constituted, the obligations of the parties and the tribunal, the manner in which pleadings, witness statements and expert reports should be exchanged, the conduct of the hearing and the details of issuing awards.

However, differences do exist between the sets of rules. For example, the ICC Rules provide for an emergency arbitrator to be appointed before the constitution of the tribunal to hear any urgent applications for interim or conservatory measures. The emergency arbitrator does not then have to be a member of the tribunal that is appointed to decide the dispute. In contrast, the LCIA has a procedure for expedited tribunal formation. That tribunal remains in place to hear the dispute proper.

Another area where they differ is in relation to fees. The differences can be significant. For example, the LCIA calculates fees by reference to daily or hourly rates; the ICC and the AAA assess the arbitrators' fees by reference to the amount in dispute. In very high-value disputes this means that an ICC arbitration can cost the parties materially more than one conducted under the auspices of the LCIA.

3.4   Selection of arbitrators

In arbitration proceedings, the parties can choose whom they want to resolve the dispute. Normally, the parties will select either one or three arbitrators depending on the size and complexity of the dispute. If the parties are unable to agree on the identity of arbitrators, the major institutional rules provide that the institution itself will make the appointment.

To avoid reverting to the institutional rules position, or if no rules have been incorporated, the parties should set out in their arbitration agreement how they want to appoint the arbitrators. They are free to choose anyone they deem fit, or they may wish to restrict the choice to individuals with relevant expertise in the particular field. Individuals appointed to serve as arbitrators must be impartial. Certain institutional rules also stipulate that the arbitrator shall be independent of the parties. For example, the arbitration agreement might state that the parties should choose an arbitrator with at least 15 years' experience in the oil industry, or that the arbitrator must be a member of the Institute of Chartered Engineers.

If the parties agree to three arbitrators, each party can nominate one of the arbitrators, ensuring that at least one of the arbitrators is familiar with the national or legal culture of the country where the relevant party is based. However, the arbitrator is not an advocate of the appointing party in the deliberations of the arbitral tribunal. Appointing three arbitrators is often perceived as a 'safer' option as they are less likely to produce a maverick decision. When there are limited grounds

---

15   Queen Mary University of London School of Arbitration at www.arbitrationonline.org/research/ ArbitrationInstitStat/index.html.

for appeal, as is often the case in arbitration, this is an important consideration. Indeed, the institutional arbitration rules typically exclude any right of appeal against an arbitration award on its legal or factual merits.

The nomination of arbitrators is not always straightforward in energy disputes. If there are several parties to, for example, a joint operating agreement or a production sharing contract, then it is important to ensure that the arbitration agreement is drafted to allow the parties that comprise the claimant or the respondent to agree jointly the selection of the nominated arbitrator. For example, if Party A, Party B and Party C agree a joint operating agreement and an arbitrable dispute arises under that joint operating agreement such that Party A and Party B wish to make a claim against Party C, then Party A and Party B will have to agree on the nomination of the arbitrator to be appointed by the claimant. They cannot make separate nominations. The major institutional rules include provisions to account for this situation and provide that, in the absence of an agreement between the parties comprising the claimant or respondent, the institution itself will appoint all arbitrators.

3.5 Conduct of proceedings

The essence of arbitration is that the parties have significant influence over the conduct of proceedings. However, the institutional rules all provide for a similar format and it is common practice for the parties to follow those procedures, whether by incorporation of the rules themselves or by using the rules as a template to adapt according to the parties' particular requirements.

An arbitration is generally commenced by the claimant serving a request or notice for arbitration at the procedural institution (with the relevant filing fee) or, if no institution has been agreed, on the other party. The institutional rules set out the requirements for the contents of the request or notice for arbitration and include various formalities such as:

- the names and addresses of the parties;
- a description of the dispute;
- their nomination of arbitrator (in accordance with any requirements stipulated in the arbitration agreement);
- the relief sought; and
- the arbitration agreement itself.[16]

The request is not intended to be a comprehensive statement of case, but should be a summary of the claimant's position. It need not be accompanied by any witness statements or expert reports.

The respondent then typically has 30 days to respond, if it wishes, from the date that it receives the request or notice from the institution (if any) or the other party. The institutional rules also contain the formal requirements for the response and include the respondent's position on the claims put forward and its nomination of arbitrator (in accordance with any requirements stipulated in the arbitration

---

16 See Article 4 of the ICC Rules; Article 1 of the LCIA Rules; Article 2 of the AAA Rules; Article 2 of the SCC Rules and Article 3 of the UNCITRAL Rules.

agreement).[17] The respondent should also put forward any counterclaims that it wishes to raise in the response. As with the request, the response is not intended to be a comprehensive statement of case, but should be a summary of the respondent's position, and need not be accompanied by any witness statements or expert reports.

The claimant may then want to serve a reply to any counterclaims raised by the respondent. If so, some institutional rules stipulate that it shall do so within 30 days of receipt of the response.[18]

If the parties have agreed to have three arbitrators, and the two nominated by the parties are free and willing to act, then a third will be appointed in accordance with the procedure under the arbitration agreement. The institutional rules typically provide that the institute will appoint the third arbitrator, who will act as the chairman.[19] If the parties are unable to decide on their respective nominations, the institution (if incorporated into the arbitration agreement) will decide instead.[20]

If the parties have nominated the ICC to preside over the arbitration, the tribunal (once constituted) will seek to agree the terms of reference with the parties as soon as possible after it receives the parties' request, response and reply (if any). The terms of reference set out the details of the parties and their claims, the seat of arbitration and the details of the arbitrators. No new claims may be raised by either party once the terms of reference have been signed without the permission of the tribunal.[21]

Other institutional rules do not provide for an equivalent to terms of reference, but stipulate that the tribunal will draw up a procedural timetable in consultation with the parties, normally at a preliminary hearing.[22] At the preliminary hearing, the parties should consider how many rounds of submissions they wish to make and whether they wish to adopt a memorial-based system, whereby witness statements, expert reports and documentary evidence are all served with the statement of case; or would prefer an approach familiar to common law court systems of serving statements of case, providing disclosure of documents, serving witness statements and expert reports sequentially. It is also advisable to try to agree a date for a hearing well in advance, as the tribunal and the parties will find that the coordination of diaries can cause frustrating delays.

At the preliminary hearing, the parties may also wish, and commonly do, to agree to incorporate the International Bar Association (IBA) Rules on the Taking of Evidence in International Arbitration. These rules provide authoritative and trusted guidelines for the submission of statements of case, witness statements, expert reports and documentary evidence in international arbitration proceedings, and are regularly adopted throughout the world.

The claimant will typically submit its statement of case with all documents on which it relies (in accordance with the IBA Rules), including any witness statements

---

17   See Article 5 of the ICC Rules; Article 2 of the LCIA Rules; Article 3 of the AAA Rules; Article 5 of the SCC Rules and Article 19 of the UNCITRAL Rules.
18   See Article 5(6) of the ICC Rules and Article 3(2) of the AAA Rules.
19   See Article 8(4) of the ICC Rules; Article 5.6 of the LCIA Rules and Article 13(3) of the SCC Rules.
20   See Article 8(4) of the ICC Rules; Article 7.2 of the LCIA Rules; Article 6(3) of the AAA Rules and Article 13 of the SCC Rules.
21   See Article 23 of the ICC Rules.
22   See Article 16 of the AAA Rules and Article 23 of the SCC Rules.

and expert reports, by the date stipulated in the procedural timetable. This is also the procedure laid down by the ICC Rules of Arbitration.

The respondent will then submit its memorial with all documents on which it relies by the date stipulated in the procedural timetable.

A typical procedural timetable will provide that, following the first round of submissions, the parties will submit their requests to produce in relation to documents believed to be held by the other party. This is a contrast to disclosure in civil litigation and may be a shock to those more familiar with the US-style process of discovery. The IBA Rules set out a procedure for making requests to produce, and require the parties provide a sufficient description of the requested documents to identify them and a statement as to why those documents are relevant or material to the outcome of the case. If one party objects to a request, the tribunal rules on the disputed request.

One purpose of the IBA Rules is to prevent 'fishing expeditions' by either party. A criticism of the wide disclosure in common law litigation is that court procedures oblige parties to produce all documents that may be relevant to either side's case, and therefore vast quantities of documents may be provided, escalating the costs of the proceedings. The request to produce is intended to limit the number of documents that are exchanged to those that each party can identify as existing and that are likely to be directly relevant to the outcome of the case.

Following the exchange of documents, which can become somewhat protracted if the parties raise numerous objections requiring a ruling by the tribunal, the parties may agree to a second round of submissions. These should be limited to responding to points made in the first round, rather than a repetition of points already made.

Finally, the parties will attend an oral hearing on the dates agreed at the preliminary hearing. The extent of pre-hearing written pleadings is greater in arbitration practice than in many common law court systems. The oral hearing is the occasion for testing the evidence submitted by witnesses and considering the opinion evidence put forward by experts. During the hearing, the fact and expert witnesses are cross-examined. The hearing is conducted in private (unless agreed otherwise).

3.6 Enforcement

Arbitration awards are intended to be binding and the parties will carry out the decision made in an award without delay.[23] This is also an express term in the major institutional rules.[24]

In general, parties abide by awards without requiring recourse to the courts. A study by the School of International Arbitration at Queen Mary, University of London suggests that only 11% of arbitrations require enforcement proceedings and of those, only 20% encounter difficulties in enforcement.[25]

In theory, the enforcement of arbitration awards should be relatively

---

23   See Mustill & Boyd, *Commercial Arbitration* (Second Edition, Butterworths, 1989) p 47.
24   See Article 28(6) of the ICC Rules; Article 27(1) of the AAA Rules; Article 26.9 of the LCIA Rules; Article 40 of the SCC Rules and Article 32 of the UNCITRAL Rules.
25   Study by School of International Arbitration and Queen Mary, University of London (sponsored by PricewaterhouseCoopers LLP), entitled "International Arbitration: Corporate attitudes and practices 2008" pp 8 and 10, cited in *Redfern and Hunter on International Arbitration*, Redfern, Hunter et al (2009) at p 620.

straightforward. Under Article III of the New York Convention, the national courts of signatory countries are obliged to enforce any arbitral award issued in a fellow signatory country, unless those courts deem the award to be invalid for one of the following reasons under Article V:

- The parties were under some incapacity or the agreement was invalid under the law of the arbitration agreement or the seat;
- The party against which the award was made was not given proper notice of the appointment of the arbitrator or the arbitration proceedings;
- The award deals with a dispute that falls outside the scope of the arbitration agreement;
- The tribunal was not composed in accordance with the arbitration agreement; or
- The award is not binding or has been set aside by a competent authority at the seat of arbitration.

Additionally, the national courts of the country in which enforcement is sought may set aside the award if they consider that the subject matter of the dispute is not capable of settlement by arbitration under the law of the enforcing country or that enforcement would be against public policy.

Therefore, the New York Convention prevents the courts of the enforcing country from re-examining the merits of the case. Instead, those courts are restricted to examining the award for any procedural impropriety or contravention of public policy of the enforcing country. While this, in theory, promotes the enforcement of arbitral awards around the world, some national courts have invoked their right to set awards aside on the grounds of public policy by applying a very wide interpretation of public policy. This is true of the countries of South Asia, where courts have interfered with arbitration awards by finding that arbitrators have exceeded their jurisdiction in reaching a decision on the merits with which the enforcing court does not agree.[26]

However, parties should be aware that there is no treaty power to enforce an arbitral award if the assets of a losing party are based in a state that is not a signatory to the New York Convention. The winning party may have to bring a fresh claim in the courts of that state, potentially by way of enforcement of a debt using the award as evidence. This is not possible under some national laws.

3.7   Appeal

The parties' ability to appeal against an award is subject to the law of the seat of arbitration. Applications to set aside awards should be brought in the courts of the seat of the arbitration, unless a party is challenging the enforcement of an award, in which case the courts of the country in which enforcement is sought would have jurisdiction to hear any such challenge.

---

26   See the Indian cases of *Oil & Natural Gas Corporation, Ltd v Saw Pipes* (2003) 5 SCC 705 applied in *Venture Global Engineering v Satyam Computer Services Ltd*, Civil Appeal 309 (January 10 2008); the Philippines case of *Luzon Hydro Corp v Hon Rommel O Baybay & Transfield Philippines, Inc*; and the Indonesian case of *ED & F Man (Sugar) Ltd v Yani Haryanto*.

In England, there are only three grounds on which a party can appeal against an award. First, a party can challenge on the basis that the tribunal lacked jurisdiction to resolve the dispute.[27] However, a party may lose its right to challenge an award on this basis if it failed to make an objection at an early stage.

The second ground on which an award may be challenged in England is a serious irregularity.[28] However, the Arbitration Act 1996 sets out the limited circumstances in which a serious irregularity may have occurred and the test for satisfying one or more of these criteria is difficult to meet.[29] Section 68 states that a serious irregularity may have occurred if one or more the following is established:

- The tribunal failed to comply with Section 33 (general duty of tribunal);
- The tribunal exceeded its powers (otherwise than by exceeding its substantive jurisdiction, in which case an appeal may be brought under Section 67);
- The tribunal failed to conduct the proceedings in accordance with the procedure agreed by the parties;
- The tribunal failed to deal with all issues that were put to it;
- Any arbitral or other institution or person vested by the parties with powers in relation to the proceedings or the award exceeded its powers;
- There is uncertainty or ambiguity as to the effect of the award;
- The award has been obtained by fraud or the award (or the way in which it was procured) is contrary to public policy;
- There has been a failure to comply with the requirements as to the form of the award; or
- There is any irregularity in the conduct of the proceedings or in the award which is admitted by the tribunal or by any arbitral or other institution or person vested by the parties with powers in relation to the proceedings or the award.

The third ground of appeal is on a point of law arising out of the award.[30] However, the parties may agree to disapply this provision, and in fact many of the institutional rules do so.[31]

In the United States, awards can be challenged exclusively on the grounds set out in the Federal Arbitration Act or (if the seat is New York) the Civil Practice Laws and Rules. These grounds are that:

- the award was obtained by fraud, corruption or undue means;
- the arbitrators were biased;
- the unsuccessful party was deprived of a fair procedure; or
- the arbitrators acted beyond their powers or exercised their powers in such a way as to make the award unsafe.

Under most national laws, there is a notable absence of a right to appeal on the

---

27   Section 67 of the Arbitration Act 1996.
28   Section 68 of the Arbitration Act 1996.
29   See *Cameroon Airlines v Transnet Ltd* [2004] EWHC 1829 Comm for an example of an appeal that did succeed.
30   Section 69 of the Arbitration Act 1996.
31   For example, the ICC, the LCIA, the AAA and the SCC Rules all state that arbitral awards are final and binding.

merits of the case. Arbitration is intended to be a final and binding method of dispute resolution, and parties are therefore generally limited to appealing on procedural irregularities rather than opening up the merits in a national court.

This position is mirrored in the New York Convention so that although parties can resist enforcement, they can do so only on the basis of procedural irregularities or matters of public policy (as described above).

4. Prevalence of arbitration in the energy sector

There are obvious reasons for the popularity of arbitration in the energy sector. The sector is highly international. Further, contracts frequently involve parties from several jurisdictions, some of which are state or quasi-state entities.

4.1 Neutrality

In international contracts, there can be a perceived disadvantage in having a dispute referred to the 'home' court of a counterparty, particularly if the counterparty is a state entity. Arbitration permits the parties to refer their disputes to a neutral forum. In addition, the consensual nature of arbitration means that the parties can ensure that the composition of the tribunal, as well as the seat of the arbitration and the location of any hearings, is neutral.

This is particularly relevant to energy projects where state-owned companies are often the owners, operators or employers with foreign corporations acting as partners or contractors. In those circumstances, neither party may be happy with deferring control over the dispute to the courts of the other party's home nation.

4.2 Enforceability

Generally speaking, arbitration awards are easier to enforce than court judgments. The New York Convention provides an extensive enforcement regime for international arbitration awards. Most industrialised nations are signatories.[32] There is no real equivalent for the enforcement of court judgments.[33]

4.3 Flexibility

There is much greater scope for the parties to adapt procedures to the needs of a particular dispute in arbitration than in court. In arbitration, parties are generally free to agree a suitable procedure, hold hearings in a neutral country and appoint arbitrators who are of a different nationality from the parties. Arbitrators can also be empowered to decide a dispute under different substantive or procedural rules from the rules which a court is compelled to observe.

The flexibility that arbitration offers is particularly well suited to the energy sector. Projects are often carried out on tight timescales, and the arbitral proceedings can therefore be adapted to fit around the ongoing projects. Energy disputes also

---

32   See www.uncitral.org/uncitral/en/uncitral_texts/arbitration/NYConvention_status.html.
33   The Hague Convention on Choice of Court Agreements of 2005 is the litigation equivalent of the New York Convention. However, to date only Mexico has acceded to it. The United States and the European Union have signed it, but not yet ratified it. Two ratifications or accessions are required before it will enter into force, and it will be some time before it has the impact of the New York Convention.

tend to be highly technical and often require an expert in that field to understand and ultimately resolve the dispute. The flexibility of arbitration opens up the possibility of appointing an arbitrator to suit the requirements of a particular dispute rather than putting the parties at the mercy of the court's rota of judges and thereby risking having to explain technical points which an arbitrator of sufficient expertise would more easily understand.

4.4 Privacy/confidentiality

Court trials are open to the public, except in the most exceptional circumstances, and statements of case are publicly available (unless the court orders otherwise). Judgments are also published for anyone, including competitors, to see. In comparison, arbitration hearings are held in private and the documents produced and awards issued are generally confidential. Thus, commercial secrets and 'dirty linen' need not be exposed in public.

Where parties are choosing arbitration for privacy reasons, they would be well advised to ensure that an express confidentiality provision is included in the arbitration agreement or procedural order, as attitudes to confidentiality will vary in different jurisdictions.

4.5 Multiple parties and multiple agreements

Contracts relating to energy projects often have multiple parties or a suite of interlinking agreements that comprise the project agreement. Multi-party agreements or related agreements involving some, but not complete, duplication of parties present procedural challenges.

Typically, national court procedures permit the joinder of all relevant parties to a dispute so that all aspects can be resolved in one hearing. They also permit the consolidation of related actions – for example, where they all arise in respect of related contracts. There is no compulsory right of joinder or consolidation in arbitration, as an arbitral tribunal has jurisdiction only over those parties which have entered into the arbitration agreement. This means that where there are multiple parties and multiple agreements, there is a risk of parallel proceedings and inconsistent outcomes. Provision for joinder and consolidation in arbitration can be made, but requires careful consideration and drafting beforehand.

The recently amended ICC Rules include provisions that permit a tribunal to consolidate arbitrations if:

- the parties agree to the consolidation where the disputes arise from the same arbitration agreement; or
- the disputes arise under different arbitration agreements but between the same parties and in connection with the same legal relationship and the ICC Court deems the arbitration agreements to be compatible.[34]

The ICC Rules also permit the joinder of an additional party, although this is subject to a valid arbitration agreement existing between the party seeking joinder

---

34   Article 10 of the ICC Rules.

and the party sought to be joined. However, if such joinder is required after the appointment of any arbitrators, the consent of all parties is required.[35]

4.6 Speed and cost

Although it used to be said that arbitration was quicker than litigation, this has become less accurate with the increasing involvement of lawyers in arbitration, together with the difficulties in convening a three-person tribunal. The process has slowed to a similar pace to that of the courts. Overall, it is now difficult to make a generalised comparison between the speed of arbitration and litigation, as this will depend on many factors – for example:

- the availability of the members of the tribunal;
- the availability of the parties and their legal and expert advisers;
- the requirement of multiple interim applications;
- disputes over disclosure of documents; and
- disputes over jurisdictional issues.

If there is an appeal of a court judgment, arbitration will be significantly faster than litigation, given that there is little possibility of appealing an arbitration award (see above on finality of decision). The circumstances in which an arbitrator's award can be appealed in most jurisdictions – including England and Wales, the United States, China, Singapore, France and Switzerland – is now very limited indeed. In contrast, most court judgments around the world can be appealed relatively easily to a higher appellate court, involving more delay, cost and uncertainty.

Arbitration is often perceived as being cheaper than litigation, but this is now rarely the case. The fact that parties are not required to pay for the judge's time and the hire of the court, and the availability of procedures such as summary judgment, mean that court litigation can be cheaper. However, there is a substantial amount of front loading of costs in court proceedings, while flexible and more cost-efficient procedures can be agreed in arbitration. However, this is dependent on the parties cooperating.

4.7 Summary determination

A further limitation in international arbitration is that although in principle an arbitral tribunal can determine claims and defences summarily, in practice this power is rarely used. In contrast, court judges are happier to determine matters at an early stage – whether by way of preliminary issue or summary judgment. Therefore, if claims are likely to be straightforward and are indisputably due, court proceedings may be preferable.

4.8 Recalcitrant parties

Arbitral tribunals' coercive powers are much more limited than those of a court and, generally speaking, judges tend to be less tolerant of recalcitrant behaviour and more robust in imposing sanctions. As a result, there is more scope for a party to delay matters in arbitration.

---

35   Article 7 of the ICC Rules.

However, the major institutional rules and most national laws permit a tribunal to make an order of security of costs if it deems necessary.[36] Under some national laws, the tribunal may also dismiss a claim if a party refuses to comply with that order.[37] Under most national laws and institutional rules, the powers of the tribunal also extend to imposing interim measures and making orders for disclosure or orders requiring the attendance of witnesses at a hearing.[38] However, the effectiveness of such orders is somewhat untested.

If a party fails to adhere to an order made by the tribunal, the other party must rely on the national courts to enforce it. In England, the ultimate sanction that a tribunal can impose is to issue a peremptory order (under Section 41(5) of the Arbitration Act 1996); failure to comply with that order entitles the other party to make an application to the English courts for enforcement under Section 42 of the Arbitration Act. A party's failure to comply with a court order may result in that party being held in contempt of court and a criminal prosecution. The Arbitration Act also gives the courts power to make freezing orders over a party's assets[39] or orders to seize relevant evidence[40] or to secure the attendance of witnesses at a hearing.[41]

The courts in the United States have a similarly wide scope for enforcing tribunals' orders, including tribunals that sit outside the United States, but whose orders relate to evidence within the United States. The courts may subpoena witnesses, order depositions to be taken and order the production of documents.[42]

5. Conclusion

The neutrality and autonomy that arbitration offers make it an enticing option for parties in international energy disputes. The procedure under which the dispute will be heard can be adapted to suit the parties' requirements and the identity of the individuals to resolve the issues can be tailored to the technical intricacies that are inherent in energy disputes.

Arbitration is no longer an unknown quantity in the energy sector and is becoming – or is already – the default form of dispute resolution for many companies. The infrastructure around the world to deal efficiently and effectively with disputes by way of arbitration is firmly established.

In many ways, arbitration has become more than an alternative to litigation and is in fact the better option for parties in a dispute. While it invariably has its limitations – most notably the power of tribunals to deal with recalcitrant parties and the potentially high costs that arbitral proceedings involve – the overall benefits that arbitration brings to parties in confidential, complex and international disputes mean that it should be given consideration when agreeing dispute resolution procedures.

---

36 See Section 38(3) of the English Arbitration Act 1996; Article 28 of the ICC Rules; Article 25(2)of the LCIA Rules; Article 21(2) of the AAA Rules; Article 32(2) of the SCC Rules and Article 26(2) of the UNCITRAL Rules.
37 Section 41(6) of the English Arbitration Act 1996.
38 See Article 28 of the ICC Rules; Article 25 of the LCIA Rules.
39 Section 44(3) of the English Arbitration Act 1996.
40 Section 44(2)(c) of the English Arbitration Act 1996.
41 Section 43 of the English Arbitration Act 1996.
42 Section 7 of the Federal Arbitration Act and Section 7505 of the New York Civil Practice Laws and Rules.

Expert determination

James Farrell
Herbert Smith LLP

1. Introduction

Expert determination is widely used as a dispute resolution mechanism in energy-related contracts. Expert determination clauses can be found throughout the energy value chain, from upstream exploration and production agreements to wholesale power contracts. Many of the characteristics which make expert determination an attractive dispute resolution mechanism are particularly relevant to energy disputes.

The long-term nature of many energy agreements (eg, oil or gas sales or transportation agreements, long-term power purchase agreements, and many agreements relating to project financed assets) means that expert determination is often prescribed for appropriate disputes which arise during the currency of such agreements. It enables such disputes to be resolved without a more adversarial, and potentially public, process.

2. What is expert determination?

Expert determination is a dispute resolution mechanism wholly founded on the law of contract. Put simply, by using an expert determination clause in a contract, the parties have agreed to refer the resolution of a particular dispute to a third party (usually having specified technical or other expertise), and have agreed to accept his determination as final and binding. The clause will need to set out in sufficient detail how the particular dispute is to be formulated and the process and procedure by which the expert is to determine the dispute. The level of complexity of the procedure is up to the parties and in theory can involve several rounds of submissions and evidence and/or oral hearings before the expert. In practice, most expert determination procedures do not involve a hearing and provide for only limited exchanges of submissions. There are no statutes or civil procedural rules; the expert determination procedure (and its workability and success) is entirely dependent on the terms which the parties have agreed.

Whether the parties can enter into such an agreement, and whether it will be effective, will depend on the governing law of the contract. This chapter addresses the position from the perspective of English law. Under English law, parties can bind themselves to the determination of a third-party expert and, subject to various parameters which have developed in case law (particularly if issues of law are being determined), the courts will not interfere with that determination and will facilitate its enforcement.

The position in other jurisdictions varies considerably and it is essential when drafting international agreements that local law advice be taken as to the effectiveness of an expert determination clause and the enforceability of any determination. Perhaps unsurprisingly, many common law jurisdictions (eg, Canada, Australia and New Zealand) support procedures similar to English expert determination. In several European civil law jurisdictions there are mechanisms which bear similarities to English expert determination (eg, *schiedsgutachten* in Germany, *bindendadvies* in the Netherlands and *periziacontrattuale* in Italy). On the other hand, in a number of jurisdictions there appears to be no concept of expert determination (eg, China (excluding Hong Kong)), and an attempt to operate a binding dispute resolution mechanism outside the procedures of the local courts or an appropriate arbitral tribunal may fall foul of public policy and be of no legal effect.[1]

Expert determination, or its local equivalent, does feature in international energy contracts. In relation to oil and gas agreements, this is sometimes for historic reasons, where relatively standard form contracts which may have started out life in the North Sea have been exported and adapted in new international developments.

3. Advantages and disadvantages of expert determination for energy disputes

Expert determination enjoys a number of advantages as a dispute resolution mechanism when compared with litigation and many arbitration procedures. Some of these are particularly relevant in the energy sphere, where disputes arise in long-term agreements and are often technical in nature. There are also certain potential disadvantages.

3.1 Advantages

(a) Expertise

It is very common for only certain disputes arising under a contract to be carved out for reference to expert determination. These include disputes of a technical nature where the particular expertise of the expert makes expert determination a more efficient and effective mechanism than the residual litigation or arbitration provisions. A good example of this is the appointment of an inspector or independent surveyor to measure and assess the quantities and qualities of cargoes such as gasoil and LNG.

(b) Alternative dispute resolution

Expert determination is seen as a type of alternative dispute resolution (ADR). Although originally in England the term 'ADR' was used to refer to non-binding dispute resolution techniques (most importantly mediation), the broader US usage of the term is now more widespread. Expert determination in general is a less adversarial process than arbitration or litigation, and the usual absence of a hearing

---

1   *Expert determination*, fourth edition, by Kendall, Freedman and Farrell (Sweet and Maxwell, 2008) provides brief comparative guidance on the existence of dispute resolution processes similar to English expert determination in some 36 jurisdictions.

and protracted inter-party communications assists in making expert determination generally a less aggressive process. This is not to say that expert determinations cannot be combative; but what it does mean is that it is often a very suitable process to resolve disputes under an ongoing long-term contract or where there is a broader relationship between the parties in dispute, as is often the case in many energy disputes.

(c) Speed

In general, expert determination is a streamlined and speedy process. Often, expert determination clauses will set out a timetable for the determination, although in practice this may be extended by agreement. In appropriate instances the timetable will be very short – perhaps giving the expert 30 days from receipt of submissions to make a determination. In some energy disputes speed is important as the contract may still be in operation and the answer to the dispute is needed so as to enable the parties properly to continue the commercial relationship.

The ability to have a speedy expert determination process is usually a result of a simple procedure, without formal hearings and with limits on the number and scope of written submissions to the expert. The very fact that – particularly in expert determinations involving technical issues (eg, an oil or gas field equity determination dispute) – the expert is technically qualified will significantly reduce the amount of expert witness evidence or other explanatory technical materials that will have to be submitted to the expert (as compared with a lay arbitrator or judge).

(d) Cost

Many of the reasons which make expert determination a speedy process also make it a less expensive process than arbitration or litigation. As with all procedural issues in an expert determination, the question of who bears which costs needs to be set out in the contract. The parties will have to bear the costs of the expert (unlike those of a judge). The expert determination clause will often provide for such costs to be split between the parties. While the parties often bear their own legal costs, the contract may have provided for some variation on a 'loser pays' principle. Overall, given the generally less formal process and shorter timescales, expert determination is a relatively cheaper dispute resolution mechanism than the alternatives.

(e) Confidentiality

Expert determination is usually a confidential process and even if the original contract does not state this expressly, it is likely that the expert will be required to keep the subject matter of the determination confidential. As with the position in relation to arbitrations, this confidentiality will be lost in the event that there are related court applications. Confidentiality can be extremely important to those involved in a dispute, particularly in the context of long-term energy contracts and where the dispute concerns commercially sensitive information such as pricing.

(f) Power to draft contract terms

One of the advantages of expert determination is that the parties can require an expert to undertake a task which a court (and many arbitral tribunals) simply does not have jurisdiction to undertake. The most important example is the ability of experts, if the parties request it, to draft new provisions of a contract, or 'fill in the blanks'. This is commonly found in 'change in circumstances' clauses. Such clauses will usually prescribe that in the event of a relevant change in circumstances, the parties will endeavour to renegotiate certain terms of the contract; but that in the absence of such agreement the task of redrafting those terms will fall to an expert (having heard the parties' various proposals and submissions). This is not something which a court has any jurisdiction to do, even if the parties wished a judge to undertake the task. Similarly, unless an arbitrator has been given express powers to issue an award on this basis, drafting new terms will not be within the power of many arbitral tribunals. (Some institutional rules do expressly give arbitrators the power to 'fill in the blanks' – for example, the Electricity Arbitration Association Rules give arbitrators such a power in certain circumstances.) In 2001, when the New Electricity Trading Arrangements (NETA) were introduced in England and Wales, many 'change in circumstances' clauses were triggered in long-term power purchase agreements, resulting in a significant number of expert determinations where experts were being asked to redraft provisions so as to make the contracts NETA compliant.

3.2   Disadvantages

(a)   Enforcement

The determination of an expert is not of itself directly enforceable in the same way that a court judgment or an arbitral award might be enforceable. In the event that a losing party fails to comply with the terms of an expert's determination, the successful party will need to pursue a breach of contract claim under the relevant jurisdiction clause in the original agreement (this is likely to prescribe litigation or arbitration as the appropriate mechanism). The losing party is, in effect, being sued for a breach of its agreement that it would be bound by and comply with the determination of the expert. In international energy contracts, this also raises the question of whether an expert determination award would be enforceable under the relevant governing law and in the relevant jurisdiction; and as indicated above, considerable care will need to be taken at the drafting stage to ensure that the mechanism will work. That said, in long-term energy contracts when a dispute arises during the life of the agreement, enforcement may in practice not be so much of a problem. Some expert determination provisions provide that failure by a party to comply with an expert's determination will automatically be a default under the agreement (eg, in relation to a joint operating agreement for an oil or gas field). This could have potentially dire consequences for the party resisting enforcement, unless it was already in default.

(b)   Challenge

The determination of an expert can be open to challenge in certain circumstances; this is addressed in more detail below.

4. Key elements of an expert determination clause

As noted above, expert determination is based on the law of contract. There are no institutional arbitral rules or statute law to plug the gaps should an expert determination clause be deficient in failing to provide for one or more elements of the procedure. It is therefore critical that an expert determination clause fully permits the operation of the disputes process, from the appointment of an expert through to enforcement of a decision (by one party alone in the absence of any cooperation on the part of the other party). If the other party's agreement is required at any stage and it refuses to give it, there is a risk that the clause may not function (albeit that the uncooperative party may well be in breach of contract in not participating). Having drafted a clause, it is helpful to walk through the operation of the entire mechanism and at each stage to check that it is usable by one party without the other party's involvement.

The following are some of the key provisions of an expert determination clause, together with some of the pitfalls that need to be looked out for when drafting a clause.

4.1 Appointment of and identity of expert

Expert determination clauses almost always provide that the expert will be appointed by agreement between the parties, in addition to setting out the details of a default institutional appointing authority to be used in the absence of agreement. Usually, the clause will set out a timetable for the parties' appointment of an expert and/or reference to the institutional appointing body. Consistent with the theme that the clause must be operable by one party alone, the clause should provide that either party can instruct the appointing authority. It is important to ensure that the chosen appointing authority will actually appoint an expert; otherwise, the appointment cannot be made and the clause may be inoperable. It is equally important in long-term energy contracts to ensure that you have selected an appointing authority which will still be around towards the end of the life of the agreement (perhaps 15 or 20 years away). In a long-term contract it may be good practice to include a reference to 'X or any successor organisation' to cover the circumstances where an authority either changes name or status or merges with another body. For example, in 2003 the Institute of Petroleum (which functioned as an appointing authority) combined with the Institute of Energy to become the Energy Institute.

Many expert determination clauses also make some provision for the nature of the expertise required. For example, the Association of International Petroleum Negotiators (AIPN) Unitisation and Unit Operating Agreement 2006[2] provides that an expert to be appointed in relation to a field redetermination dispute should be "well-qualified, by technical training and experience, in geological and reservoir assessment, economic and subsurface evaluation". However, there is a balance to be struck between ensuring that a person is appointed with the right qualifications to determine the dispute properly and avoiding being so specific that you narrow the

---

2   The AIPN Unitisation and Unit Operating Agreement and other AIPN model contracts can be accessed by members or otherwise purchased at www.aipn.org.

pool of available potential experts to such an extent that it subsequently creates practical difficulties for the parties.

It is often sensible for the clause expressly to enable the expert to engage third-party professionals (these may include advisers with a particular technical expertise in a narrow specialist area or legal advisers). Such a provision not only enables the parties to clarify where the cost of such additional professional assistance falls, but may also avoid arguments that if the expert does seek third-party assistance, he is wrongfully delegating part of the determination which he should be undertaking.

4.2   Terms of reference

Once a dispute has arisen, the usual practice is for formal terms of reference to be drawn up and agreed between both parties and the expert. This then forms a tripartite contract setting out the procedures for the reference, the exact nature of the issues to be determined and practical matters such as the fees and the detailed terms of appointment of the expert. It is open to the parties to elaborate on or vary the procedures for the expert determination as compared with those set out in the original contract. Alternatively, if there is no need or desire to do so, or in the event that one party is refusing to cooperate with the expert determination process, there will be no tripartite terms of reference and the determination should be undertaken on the basis of the terms and procedures agreed in the original contract.

4.3   The issue

Given that expert determination clauses are almost always accompanied by another dispute resolution mechanism in a contract (whether litigation or arbitration), it is essential that the agreement makes clear which issues fall to be determined under which mechanism. While the precise wording of the particular issue for determination by an expert may well not be known until the dispute has arisen, the clause should at least make clear which types of issues are for expert determination and which are to be resolved under the residual dispute resolution clause.

4.4   The determination

The expert clause should provide that the expert is acting as an expert and not as an arbitrator, and that the decision will be final and binding. Many expert determination clauses also state that the determination should be final and binding 'save in the event of manifest error'. There has been a certain amount of case law on the meaning of manifest error, but at the least it will mean an error which is 'plain and obvious'.[3] Some expert determination clauses expressly state that the decision is final and binding unless challenged in an arbitration or the courts within a certain timeframe.

Care should be taken to ensure that the answer which the expert is being asked to produce in his determination actually provides the parties (or again, one party alone) with the desired outcome to resolve the dispute (whether that be the payment of money, a revision to an agreement or a specific action).

If the determination relates to the payment of money and it is desired that the

---

3   See also the analysis in *Veba Oil Supply & Trading GmbH v PetrotradeInc* [2002] 1 All ER 703.

expert be able to award interest, then this needs expressly to be agreed in the expert clause (perhaps with a provision for interest to be payable on late payment as well).

The clause should state whether the expert should give his reasons when making his determination. If the expert is not required to give his reasons, the determination itself can be very short, possibly even only a few numbers (in the case of a valuation or pricing dispute). The less detail contained in a determination, the harder it is to challenge it. However, sometimes the parties will consider that they wish to get some comfort from seeing how the expert got to the answer and will require reasons. In international energy contracts it may be worth considering requiring reasons to be given on the basis that enforcement outside the United Kingdom of a court judgment or arbitration award based on the expert determination might have an easier passage if the determination contains reasons rather than bare numbers.

Finally, some expert clauses provide that the expert should hand his determination down in draft to the parties so that they may correct any obvious errors. This has its advantages in avoiding some potential challenges to a determination, but the expert will need to be careful that this does not encourage a wholesale re-litigation of the issues by the losing party in an attempt to persuade the expert to change his mind.

5.   Jurisdictional issues and challenges

Some disputes involving expert determination will end up before the courts. This is usually for one of two main reasons: jurisdictional disputes and attempts to overturn the expert's decision. The fact that expert determination is commonly used in energy contracts is reflected in the high percentage of reported decisions in English case law on expert determination issues which concern energy contracts.

5.1   Jurisdiction disputes

Typically, a jurisdictional issue will arise at the outset of a dispute. It may also be possible for a party to reserve its position as to the jurisdiction of the expert to determine a particular issue and for the determination then to proceed, subject to that party's ability to raise jurisdictional issues in the courts subsequently (although this may be seen as an inefficient way of resolving the issue). In an oil field redetermination case the parties expressly agreed in the expert clause that no action or legal proceedings should be brought until the expert had undertaken all of the "key steps" in the redetermination process. When one party tried to get a declaration from the court halfway through the process, the court found that the self-imposed prohibition on bringing challenges until the end of the process was valid and stayed the proceedings until the expert had decided the issues.[4]

Jurisdictional challenges usually address questions concerning which issues the parties have agreed should be resolved by the expert and which should be remitted to the 'catch-all' dispute mechanism in the contract (litigation or arbitration). Often these questions are apparent only after a dispute has arisen when the breadth of the

---

4   *Amoco (UK) Exploration Co v Amerada Hess Limited* [1994] 1 Lloyds Report 330 in relation to an equity redetermination in the UK Continental Shelf Scott field.

matters in dispute means that the issues do not sit neatly within the particular areas carved out for resolution by the expert in the original agreement. Of course, the parties can agree after a dispute has arisen to redefine the expert's role and to broaden or narrow the range of disputes which fall within his remit. However, in the absence of agreement such jurisdictional disputes will end up before the court or arbitral tribunal.

One particular area for jurisdictional challenges involves the question of whether legal issues of contractual construction are to be determined by the expert. As with all jurisdictional issues, the question of whether the expert can determine the meaning of contractual terms will depend on the express wording of the parties' agreement in the expert's clause. However, often it is not clearly identified how questions of contractual construction are to be determined. Although in some cases the English courts have shown an inclination not to interfere, particularly if the contractual interpretation issues are closely bound up with the broader factual issues which the expert is determining, more recently there has appeared to be judicial reluctance to conclude that the parties intended non-legally qualified experts to determine legal issues.

5.2 Challenges to an expert's award

Disgruntled losing parties will always consider whether they can challenge or overturn an adverse decision from a tribunal and expert determination decisions are no exception. The losing party has, of course, agreed in the contract to be bound by the expert's determination; the main route for challenge, therefore, is that the determination which has been made by the expert was not arrived at in accordance with the agreed contract terms.

As would be expected, if there has been fraud on the part of the expert or collusion with one of the parties, then the determination will not be binding. In addition, if there has been partiality in the sense of actual bias by the expert, then the decision will be open to attack. Whether the expert needs to be 'independent' of the parties will depend on the terms of the agreement, and there may be grounds for challenge if the expert was required by the agreement to be independent, but was not in fact so.

The main ground for challenges developed in the case law in England and Wales over the last 20 years is that there has been a material departure by the expert from the instructions given to him. A distinction may need to be drawn between legal issues and non-legal issues which are before the expert for determination. In relation to non-legal questions, it is clear that the courts will not generally intervene in a matter which falls properly within an expert's jurisdiction, even if the expert appears to have come to the wrong answer. However, the expert will be open to challenge if he has not undertaken the task that he was required to do, such as answering the wrong question or not following the terms of the agreement which lay down how he is to conduct his determination. A number of relevant reported cases concern energy disputes, including a case where the inspector (acting as an expert) charged with

---

5   *Veba Oil Supply & Trading GmbH v Petratradelnc* [2002] 1 All ER 703 (CA)

testing a cargo of gasoil sold free on board Antwerp used the wrong ASTM testing methodology, with the result that the determination was not binding.[5]

In relation to legal questions, some expert clauses specifically give the expert jurisdiction to determine questions of construction. However, in a number of cases it has been held that except where limited issues of construction are closely tied up with the broader non-legal issues which the expert is determining, pure legal questions should be referred to the court (or arbitral tribunal). That is essentially a question of identifying the jurisdiction of the expert, but may give rise to a challenge after the determination award has been made on the basis that the expert has exceeded his mandate. It has been suggested more recently (although the point remains undecided) that even in cases where certain identified legal issues are within an expert's mandate, unless the parties have expressly or impliedly agreed that the expert's decision on such questions is not "open to review or treatment by the courts", the expert's resolution of the issues of law may be capable of challenge in the courts.[6]

6. Energy disputes which use expert determination

This section sets out, by way of illustration, some of the particular types of dispute in the energy sector where expert determination is used.

6.1 Power

Long-term electricity purchase agreements in the wholesale markets have for many years used expert determination for the resolution of certain disputes. These may include invoicing and pricing disputes, indexation issues and, importantly, change in circumstances clauses covering changes in law and changes to relevant industry documents. As mentioned above, expert determination provisions in change in circumstances clauses played an important role during the introduction of NETA in 2001. With the proposed introduction of long-term contracts for differences as a mechanism for the implementation of a feed-in-tariff for low-carbon generation under the UK Electricity Market Reform, and the possibility of changes to the structure of wholesale electricity markets in the United Kingdom and elsewhere, change in circumstances and law clauses will remain an important part of long-term power-related agreements.

Technical issues such as disputes arising from output metering equipment are also often referred to experts. In power purchase agreements for the supply of renewable energy, disputes which arise from changes to renewable benefits and embedded benefits, and how the risk and reward in relation to any such changes is to be apportioned between the parties, can be referred to an expert. Similarly, in tolling agreements experts have been appointed to resolve a range of disputes, including financial audits such as of a generator's fixed costs or outage losses, issues concerning the apportionment of transmission losses and engineering issues arising out of modifications to the generating station.

---

6 *BarclaysBank plc v Nylon Capital LLP* [2011] EWCA Civ 826; see in particular the *obiter dicta* of Lord Neuberger MR.

The nuclear power industry uses expert determination in long-term contracts in much the same way as other sectors of the energy industry. Expert determination clauses tend to be used for pricing and certain technical disputes, as well as 'change in circumstances/law' provisions, and these can be found in agreements including fuel supply and logistics contracts.

6.2 Coal

Contracts for the supply of coal, particularly on a long-term basis, sometimes use expert determination for a range of financial and technical disputes. Issues arising out of sampling and analysis (perhaps for sulphur content or other quality issues, or calorific value) and weighing are suitable for reference to an expert. Under a long-term take-or-pay coal contract, in the event of a shortfall in the offtake volumes, the producer will incur the expense of managing and maintaining the excess stocks until they are taken as make-up coal, and this cost may be passed on to the offtaker. A disagreement over the amount of these costs is a good example of a dispute which would be suitable for speedy and cheap resolution by an expert with knowledge of the industry.

6.3 Oil and gas

Expert determination is widely used as a dispute mechanism in oil and gas agreements. This is particularly the case in long-term agreements, but it is also used for technical issues such as quality assessment in oil and gas sales agreements.

(a) Unitisation and operating agreements

The long-term nature of unit operating agreements and the sometimes extremely technical geological issues involved in unitisation disputes mean that expert determination is commonly used. Issues such as changes to the unit area and redetermination of the tract participation of parties are often referred to experts for resolution. The unit operating agreement may contain detailed schedules setting out a variety of procedures for the redetermination, such as the expert guided proposal, where the parties conduct the redetermination exercise under the full-time guidance of an independent expert who resolves the disputes as and when they arise.[7] Other disputes which might be referred to an expert under a unit operating agreement include issues concerning a decommissioning work programme and budget, or disagreements between the parties as to the terms in which a non-unit facility should be tied into the unit facilities (in which case the expert could be instructed to 'fill in the blanks' and draft suitable terms in the absence of the parties' agreement). A number of reported cases have related to redetermination disputes. In *Shell v Enterprise*[8] an expert determination of an equity redetermination dispute in the Nelson field in the North Sea was held to be invalid because the expert had materially departed from his instructions in using the wrong computer mapping software package.

---

7   See, for example, the AIPN Model Form Unit Operating Agreement, which includes the expert guided proposal as one option.
8   *Shell UK Limited v Enterprise Oil plc* [1999] 2 Lloyds Rep 456.

(b)   *Joint operating agreements*

Joint operating agreements also make use of expert determination provisions. The Oil and Gas UK Joint Operating Agreement 2009, for example, has a suggested provision whereby a defaulting party's interest is to be valued by an expert in the event that the defaulting party and the remaining participants that are wishing to acquire its interest cannot agree the price.

(c)   *Oil and gas sales agreements*

Many sales agreements use expert determination for disputes as to quality, invoicing and payment disputes and, importantly, pricing disputes.

Long-term sales contracts often include provisions by which the contract price is calculated using a formula which is linked to published price indices. In the event that a published price to which the contract price is indexed ceases to be published or is changed significantly, expert determination is often provided to resolve any subsequent disputes if the parties cannot agree how to amend the price formula. Long-term contracts also often include price reopener clauses which allow a party to initiate a renegotiation of the price if a specified trigger event occurs. Such disputes are addressed in more detail elsewhere in this book. Again, expert determination can be used to resolve such disputes.

In long-term life of field gas or oil sales agreements, expert determination can be used for technical issues concerning the determination of economically recoverably reserves or, for example, disputes as to what the daily contract quantity should be as production declines towards the end of the life of the field.

(d)   *LNG and oil shipments*

Contracts for the shipment of LNG, gasoil or other hydrocarbons can provide for disputes as to quantity and quality to be resolved by an expert (sometimes referred to as an 'independent surveyor').

One reported decision[9] concerned the delivery of a cargo of ultra low sulphur auto diesel to Cardiff and whether the determinations as to quality and quantity issued by the independent inspector (acting as an expert) were valid.

7.   Conclusion

The technical nature of many disputes which arise in energy contracts and the fact that such agreements are often of a long-term nature mean that expert determination remains a valuable tool for those seeking to draft appropriate dispute resolution mechanisms in energy contracts. When used as a complement to litigation or arbitration, it can enable the effective resolution of issues in an efficient manner.

---

9   *Exxonmobil Sales and Supply Corporation v Texaco Limited* [2003] EWHC 1964.

Alternative dispute resolution

Georgia Quick
Deborah Tomkinson
Ashurst Australia

1.   **Alternative dispute resolution in the international energy sector**
      The international energy sector, together with the related construction industry, has
      been noted as forming "the largest portfolio of international commercial and state
      investment disputes in the world".[1] Given that energy projects generally involve a
      variety of stakeholders (both private and government), significant investment and
      programmes that span years, if not decades, it is unsurprising that they present
      unique challenges when it comes to dispute resolution, and that parties are
      increasingly seeking alternatives to more formal dispute resolution mechanisms such
      as litigation or arbitration.

      Energy sector participants commonly provide in their contracts for methods of
      dispute management that promote the continuation of amicable business
      relationships and enable the project to continue unimpeded and without delay
      through any dispute process.

      An earlier chapter introduced the concept of alternative dispute resolution (ADR)
      as a set of procedures that are particularly suited to the types of long-term contracts
      that are common in the energy industry. This chapter considers ADR procedures in
      greater detail, looking at the applicability and suitability of particular processes in the
      resolution of energy disputes.

2.   **What is ADR?**
      ADR is the label generally given to dispute resolution procedures that do not involve
      traditional court processes. While there is some debate as to which forms of dispute
      resolution fall within the ambit of ADR processes, commonly accepted examples
      include negotiation, mediation, early neutral evaluation and dispute review boards,
      as well as a number of others that are examined later in this chapter. There are
      differing views as to whether arbitration and expert determination can be considered
      to fall within the broader spectrum of ADR processes. Expert determination and
      arbitration are generally part of a more binding, rather than consensual, process.
      While ADR processes can be binding or non-binding, the ADR processes focused on
      in this chapter are generally non-binding. Further, arbitration is now increasingly
      considered to be a more formal dispute method, and references to ADR are often
      intended to exclude both litigation and arbitration. In any event, arbitration and

---

1   AT Martin, "Dispute resolution in the international energy sector: an overview", *Journal of World Energy
     Law and Business*, vol 4, no 4, 2011, p 332.

expert determination are considered in detail in other chapters and are therefore afforded only passing mention here.

ADR mechanisms are generally employed in one of the following three scenarios:

- as a part of an *ad hoc* process;
- pursuant to a contractual process; or
- as a result of a compulsory (court-ordered or legislated) process.

2.1 *Ad hoc* ADR

Regardless of their contractual arrangements, parties can agree, at any stage of a project or a dispute, that they would like to participate in some form of ADR in an effort to resolve issues between them without resort to more formal and potentially expensive methods. In some circumstances, the contract between the parties may provide expressly for *ad hoc* ADR (see Figure 1). In this regard, although provided for in the contract, the actual choice of process and participation in that process is entirely consensual.

Figure 1

An example of *ad hoc* ADR is contained in the CRINE/Logic 2003 General Conditions of Contract for Services (On and Offshore), a standard form contract for the UK offshore oil and gas industry which provides, in circumstances where negotiations fail to resolve a dispute, that "the parties may attempt to settle the dispute by a form of Alternative Dispute Resolution to be agreed between the parties" (Clause 30.2).

2.2 Contractual ADR

The principle of freedom of contract gives parties the right to agree to any method of dispute resolution that they consider appropriate in the circumstances. Courts will generally enforce contractual dispute resolution terms provided that it is not against public policy or contrary to applicable legislation to do so.

In comparison to consensual processes that are agreed to by the parties at the time when a dispute arises, contractual ADR mechanisms can often, by their nature (having been agreed at the outset of a project), be less flexible and may not be as well suited to the resolution of specific disputes as they arise in the course of the project. Nevertheless, their inclusion in a contractual dispute resolution mechanism can act as an impetus to early resolution and may assist in alleviating any potential concerns with regard to being the first party to propose an alternate method of resolving a dispute (and any related perception of weakness in doing so).

As noted elsewhere, ADR commonly forms a part of multi-tiered dispute resolution clauses in energy contracts. Different standard form contracts employ different ADR mechanisms for dispute resolution, although there are some common features. Three examples are provided in Figure 2.

In each of the cases set out in Figure 2, ADR constitutes a contractual dispute resolution mechanism, agreed by the parties as the best way in which to deal with disputes arising under the contract. Contractual ADR is to be contrasted with court-ordered ADR, an area that has seen significant growth in usage over recent years as courts have sought to improve their case management techniques.

Figure 2 – Table of ADR mechanisms in three different standard form contracts

Industry	Standard form contract	Structure of ADR mechanism
Oil and gas projects	Conditions of Contract for Engineering, Procurement and Construction Turnkey Projects (the Silver Book), published by the International Federation of Consulting Engineers (FIDIC).	• Disputes are referred to an *ad hoc* dispute adjudication board (which is expressly held not to be acting as arbitrator). • If either party is dissatisfied with the decision of the board, they may seek to settle the dispute amicably through negotiation. • If this step is unsuccessful, the matter is referred to international arbitration under the International Chamber of Commerce (ICC) rules.
Petroleum	Association of International Petroleum Negotiators Model Joint Operating Agreement 2012.	• Senior executive negotiations (optional provision). • Mediation (optional provision). • ICC pre-arbitral referee procedure (optional provision). • Arbitration. • Expert determination (optional provision for specified disputes).
Mining services	Model Mining Services Contract produced by the Australian Resources and Energy Law Association.	• Three initial levels of negotiations culminating in good-faith negotiations between the chief executive officers of both parties. • If negotiations fail, the dispute must be referred to mediation. • Once the agreed period for mediation expires, a party may refer the matter to expert determination (where the contract permits) or commence court proceedings.

2.3   Compulsory ADR

A focus on improving active case management techniques has seen an increased use of ADR mechanisms in pre-action requirements and as a part of court processes. This has been recognised both in legislative amendments to pre-action protocols in the

United Kingdom[2] and Australia,[3] and in the increased use of court-ordered ADR.

Pre-litigation requirements generally oblige parties to take genuine and reasonable steps to resolve the dispute by agreement (ie, before commencing proceedings) or to narrow the issues in dispute. The use of an appropriate form of ADR is encouraged. In Australia, once proceedings have commenced, some courts have the power to make an order, if it is deemed appropriate, referring the matter to ADR (usually mediation), with or without the consent of the parties.[4] In many jurisdictions ADR is a required step in particular types of dispute, such as labour or family-related matters. Recently, by way of example, Italy introduced mandatory mediation for finance disputes (including disputes concerning insurance, banking and financial contracts).[5]

The scope and application of compulsory ADR are jurisdiction specific and thus have not been considered in great detail. Parties should consider the potential application of such processes when agreeing to submit disputes to the jurisdiction of a particular court system.

3.   Common ADR mechanisms

The majority of ADR methods involve a third-party neutral. Negotiation is the obvious exception to this. The precise role of a neutral in the resolution process depends on the method chosen by the parties and any other agreement that has been reached between them with respect to the applicable procedure to be followed. Where a neutral is involved, he or she will be required, in all circumstances, to be impartial and independent of both parties in order to ensure party confidence in the process.

In contrast to court proceedings, parties seeking to resolve a dispute by way of ADR have the ability to select the most appropriate neutral to facilitate resolution of the particular dispute. It may be that the issues in dispute require a neutral with specific expertise, be it legal or technical. As the parties may find reaching an agreement as to the identity of the neutral difficult once a dispute arises, it is sensible to ensure that there is an agreed method set out in the contract by which the neutral can be appointed in the absence of agreement by the parties. Energy contracts commonly specify a particular professional institution to undertake the nomination of the neutral on behalf of the parties. Parties should take care in choosing a nominating institution and ensure that that institution will in fact undertake a nominating role. The inclusion in a contract of a body as a nominating authority that does not make appointments could render the relevant contractual clause inoperable.

---

2   In the United Kingdom, there are specific pre-action protocols for particular types of claim, including construction and engineering matters. The Civil Procedure Rules, Practice Direction: Pre-action Conduct (UK) applies to matters where no specific pre-action protocol is in place.

3   Pre-litigation requirements were introduced in the Federal Court of Australia in 2011 pursuant to the Civil Dispute Resolution Act 2011 (Cth). The introduction of similar requirements has been postponed in New South Wales. In Victoria, pre-litigation requirements introduced in 2010 were subsequently repealed in 2011.

4   For example, Section 26(1) of the Civil Procedure Act 2005 (NSW); Section 53A of the Federal Court of Australia Act 1976 (Cth).

5   Legislative Decree 28/2010 (Italy).

It is common practice, once the third-party neutral has been appointed, for the parties and the neutral to execute an agreement (usually in the form of a tripartite agreement) to govern the relationship between them. This agreement usually:

- identifies the boundaries of the neutral's role and responsibilities;
- defines the issues requiring resolution; and
- sets out the compensation payable by the parties for the services to be rendered by the appointed neutral.

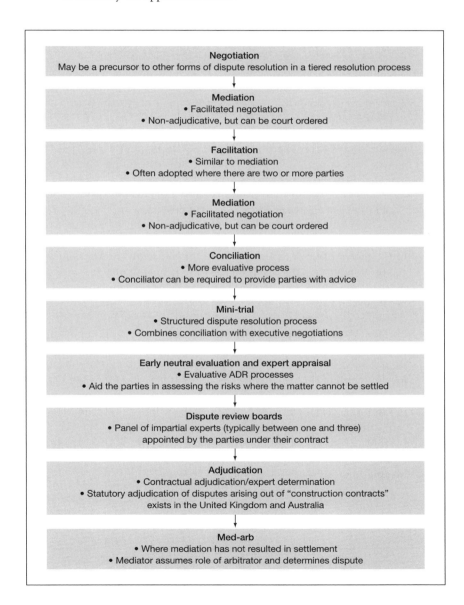

Negotiation
May be a precursor to other forms of dispute resolution in a tiered resolution process
↓
Mediation
• Facilitated negotiation
• Non-adjudicative, but can be court ordered
↓
Facilitation
• Similar to mediation
• Often adopted where there are two or more parties
↓
Mediation
• Facilitated negotiation
• Non-adjudicative, but can be court ordered
↓
Conciliation
• More evaluative process
• Conciliator can be required to provide parties with advice
↓
Mini-trial
• Structured dispute resolution process
• Combines conciliation with executive negotiations
↓
Early neutral evaluation and expert appraisal
• Evaluative ADR processes
• Aid the parties in assessing the risks where the matter cannot be settled
↓
Dispute review boards
• Panel of impartial experts (typically between one and three)
appointed by the parties under their contract
↓
Adjudication
• Contractual adjudication/expert determination
• Statutory adjudication of disputes arising out of "construction contracts"
exists in the United Kingdom and Australia
↓
Med-arb
• Where mediation has not resulted in settlement
• Mediator assumes role of arbitrator and determines dispute

The agreement will also often contain an agreed confidentiality regime to apply to the process.

Most of the ADR methods reviewed in this chapter are non-binding on the parties (sometimes referred to as facilitative, evaluative and advisory ADR processes). The role of the third-party neutral in these processes is to assist the parties towards finding a mutually acceptable resolution to the issues in dispute. The neutral has no power to impose a solution on the parties, though in some processes he or she may be given the power to provide a non-binding view which may be highly persuasive.

An illustration of a range of ADR methods is given on the previous page, from the least adjudicative/binding method (negotiation) to the most adjudicative/binding method (adjudication). The process of mediation-arbitration (med-arb), which is discussed further below as a follow-on from mediation, has been included as a slightly separate ADR process, which combines mediation with arbitration to resolve disputes.

In contrast, arbitration and expert determination (also referred to as contractual adjudication) are considered to be binding or determinative forms of ADR. Statutory adjudication, a method of ADR that is at first instance binding on the parties, is considered later in this chapter.

3.1 Facilitative, evaluative and advisory ADR processes

The advantage of non-binding ADR is that, ultimately, the solution reached is not imposed on the parties. Therefore, the parties are more likely to assume ownership of the process. In consequence, there is a significantly greater likelihood that the agreed solution will be implemented in practice. While the outcome of ADR processes generally represents a compromise between the parties, a mutually negotiated and agreed solution is less likely to result in either party perceiving that it was the 'loser' in the process.

More broadly, consensus-based processes are seen by some as a tool for societal preservation. For example, in China, there exists a general preference for processes such as mediation, based on the emphasis in Confucian philosophy on the need to preserve harmony in society which, in the context of disputes, means "compromise, yielding, and non-litigiousness".[6] Furthermore, despite challenges implicit in investor-state disputes in the oil and gas industry in Asia, mediation, for example, is increasingly preferred as a method to settle disputes.[7]

Some common examples of non-binding ADR processes are explored below.

3.2 Negotiation

(a) Key features and issues

Direct negotiation between the parties is most often used as a first step in an

---

6   AFM Maniruzzaman, "Resolving International Business and Energy Disputes in Asia – Traditions and Trends", *Transnational Dispute Management*, March 2011, p 6.
7   A Jennings, *Oil and Gas Exploration Contracts* (2002) Sweet & Maxwell, London, p 22.

escalating dispute resolution clause and is a common feature in energy contracts. It consists of the referral of disputes either to specified senior management representatives of each party as a single-step process (failing which the dispute is escalated to the next ADR process), or on through to higher levels of management if initial discussions fail to reach a resolution.

The utility of including a contractual requirement to negotiate can be questioned on the basis that it is a step that is likely to be taken, on a consensual basis, in any event. However, as noted elsewhere in this book, including negotiation as a prerequisite to more formal dispute resolution processes can act to circumvent any sensitivity that a party may have to proposing it as an option, due to concerns as to how that may reflect on the party's confidence in its case. In addition, there is an increasingly greater expectation on parties, reflected in the development of pre-action protocols and court processes, to attempt to resolve disputes before initiating proceedings. However, it should be kept in mind that including an obligation to undertake negotiation in a dispute resolution clause will result in some delay to the commencement of more formal dispute resolution steps.

The advantage of structured negotiation is that it takes the dispute out of the hands of those who have been intimately involved "at the coal face" and who, as a result, may have entrenched positions with regard to the issues in dispute. As such, the objective of negotiations undertaken at higher levels within the relevant organisations is to facilitate the separation of disputed issues from any emotion attached to them, in order to enable the parties to focus on their mutual interest in resolving the dispute and continuing their business relationship. In order to achieve this purpose, the obligation to negotiate should be a non-delegable one.

Negotiation ensures that the existence and content of a dispute remain private and is a relatively inexpensive form of dispute management in comparison with other ADR processes, with suitable levels of flexibility being provided for in a structured clause. However, in order to achieve a result, negotiation requires the full cooperation and commitment of both parties to the resolution of the dispute.

Negotiation is not in and of itself a binding form of dispute resolution, although it may result in the execution of a binding agreement to reflect the outcome of the party's discussions. In order to ensure that an agreement to negotiate is contractually binding, there must be no uncertainty as to when the negotiations should be taken to have failed – that is, the clause should provide a set timeframe for negotiations to occur and a clear indication of when the parties will have the right to pursue the next dispute resolution step.

(b) *Appropriate use of negotiation*
Negotiation should be kept in mind at all stages of a dispute. However, it is likely to be most effective either at the time when the issue first arises (before the parties have formed entrenched views on the matter, so making a commercial settlement potentially easier) or following a mediation or other structured ADR process, which provides the parties with an opportunity to understand better their respective positions (without having been put to the expense of court proceedings). Going through this process can often expose case strengths and weaknesses and provide

greater impetus for settlement. At this time it can also be beneficial, from a strategic perspective, to move the negotiations to senior personnel who have not been involved in the matter previously and who can view the relevant facts and positions dispassionately.

3.3   Mediation

(a)   *Key features and issues*

Mediation is considered to be the ADR "method of choice in the business community" (as an alternative to both litigation and arbitration).[8] It is an informal dispute resolution process in which an intermediary is appointed to assist the parties objectively in understanding and evaluating their positions, with the aim of reaching a negotiated settlement. In mediation, the focus is on the parties' interests and objectives, rather than on their strict legal entitlements.[9] Mediation affords parties a high level of control and flexibility of process, which can be adapted to suit the circumstances of the parties and the dispute.

Mediators each have their own approach and no mediation will be the same. In this regard, it is important to select the appropriate mediator for a particular matter. For example, a mediation may take place in a day or over the course of several weeks; it may involve joint and separate sessions, expert conclaves (where both parties' experts may meet with the mediator in the absence of the parties); and parties' legal representatives may be involved. Nevertheless, in general, mediation is a more consensual, less evaluative process than either facilitation or conciliation. The mediator is not usually required to express an opinion as to the issues in dispute; rather, the mediator aids the parties in reaching their own resolution. Although the parties control the process, in some circumstances they may wish the mediator to take on a greater evaluative role. Evaluative mediation – employing a mediator with specific technical expertise to make recommendations (which are not binding, but may provide guidance) – can be an appropriate technique in the context of energy project disputes.

Mediation is used extensively, on a domestic level, in many jurisdictions. It is employed less at an international level – principally as a result of the unregulated nature of the process, which consists, to a large extent, of *ad hoc* procedures that are not globally recognised.[10] In practice, there can be a cultural disconnect between parties to international contracts in their perception and understanding of mediation processes. Some authors have identified a clash between East and West – while Western societal norms are principally individualistic, Eastern societies tend to adopt a collectivist approach to life and society.[11] In practical terms, this may play

---

8   AT Martin, *op cit*, p 337.
9   See A Redfern and M Hunter, *Law and Practice of International Commercial Arbitration*, 4th edn, Sweet & Maxwell, London, 2004, p 37; R Fisher and W Ury, *Getting to Yes: Negotiating Agreement Without Giving In*, Penguin Books, New York, 1983, pp 41-44.
10   P Deane, W von Kumberg, M Leathes, D Masucci, M McIlwrath, L Mooyaart and B Whitney, *Making Mediation Mainstream: A User/Customer Perspective*, viewed February 2012 at http://imimediation.org/making-mediation-mainstream, p 2.
11   AFM Maniruzzaman, *op cit*, pp 5-6.

out in the status afforded to, and the use of, ADR at an international level. For example, consensus-based ADR is the preferred method of resolving disputes in many countries in the Middle and Far East and the Asia-Pacific region; and in China, mediation has been a primary method for dispute resolution for centuries, rather than an 'alternative' to litigation.[12] This is reflected in the incorporation of mediation and other forms of ADR in international contractual dispute resolution clauses in these jurisdictions. In addition, mediation does not share some of the other features of arbitration that make it so popular on an international level, including having in place applicable infrastructure to ensure enforceability of decisions on an international level. As progress is achieved in these areas, mediation is expected to grow at an international level. An example of recent movement in this direction was the approval by the European Parliament of the EU Directive on Certain Aspects of Mediation in Civil and Commercial Matters in 2008,[13] which was aimed at harmonising the framework for, and promoting the use of, ADR within the European Union.

A number of institutions provide model mediation clauses and guidance, including recommended rules, on mediation procedures, as well as administering mediations. Some well-known examples include:

- the Centre for Effective Dispute Resolution and the London Court of International Arbitration in the United Kingdom;
- the ICC in France;
- the International Centre for Dispute Resolution in the United States; and
- the Australian Commercial Dispute Centre (ACDC) and the Australian Centre for International Commercial Arbitration, both based in Sydney.

These institutions also offer support and administrative facilities for domestic and international mediation.

Any outcome achieved through mediation will not be binding unless and until the parties have recorded their agreement in an executed settlement document which can then be enforced if required.

(b)   *Appropriate use of mediation*

Mediation is a useful method of dispute management and resolution at any stage throughout the life of a dispute, whether incorporated in a stepped contractual dispute process or agreed to by the parties once a dispute arises. Generally conducted on a without prejudice or confidential basis (noting that privilege is not a recognised concept worldwide), mediation allows the parties to have a free and open dialogue on the issues. It should be considered as an option particularly in circumstances where the monetary value of a dispute does not justify the time and expense of more formal proceedings, or where the parties put a high value on the maintenance of

---

12   Legislative instruments providing for med-arb have been enacted in a significant number of jurisdictions across Asia. See further *ibid*, p 18.

13   European Parliament and Council, Directive 2008/52/EC of the European Parliament and of the Council of May 21 2008, viewed February 2012 at http://eur-lex.europa.eu/LexUriServ/LexUriServ.do? uri=OJ:L:2008:136:0003:0008:En:PDF.

their relationship. When dealing with a counterparty from an Asian or Middle Eastern background, it may also be a culturally sensitive consideration.

In general, mediation is used as a fairly early step in a multi-tiered dispute resolution clause. As such, mediation can often occur before the parties have fully explored and defined the issues in dispute. Similarly, in circumstances of court-ordered mediation, a reference to mediation is likely to occur at the beginning of the dispute resolution process. While mediation can be a useful resolution mechanism at this early stage (particularly in relation to less complex disputes), consideration should also be given to the use of mediation at the later stages of a dispute once the parties have a better understanding of their respective positions and the strengths and weaknesses of their case. This can be a strong impetus for settlement.

Mediation may not be suitable for very complex or technical disputes (often arising in the energy sector) which require both expert technical and legal analysis. While it is possible, as mentioned above, to have a mediator adopt an evaluative role, parties should consider at the outset whether this is likely to be required in order to ensure that they appoint a mediator with the right expertise. More complex matters may require greater involvement by the neutral and parties should consider whether an alternative process (eg, conciliation, expert determination or arbitration) is more appropriate in the circumstances.

3.4   Med-arb

(a)   Key features and issues
Med-arb is a process by which the parties agree that in circumstances where mediation proceedings have not resulted in settlement of the issues, the mediator is permitted to assume the role of arbitrator and determine the dispute. This has the advantage of certain procedural and time-related efficiencies, in that it removes any requirement to engage a separate arbitrator in circumstances where the mediation is unsuccessful.

This process can work the other way: parties to an arbitration may wish to suspend proceedings to allow for a mediation to take place in relation to all or only particular issues. In these circumstances, if the parties agree, the arbitrator can adopt the role of mediator (referred to as 'arb-med').

Med-arb and arb-med are employed extensively in China and across other parts of Asia – for example, they are contemplated in arbitration legislation in Hong Kong,[14] China,[15] Singapore,[16] Japan[17] and India,[18] and also in the procedural rules of some of the arbitration and mediation centres in these jurisdictions.[19] The process has also found some traction in consumer, labour and administrative tribunals in, for

---

14   Arbitration Ordinance (Hong Kong) cap 609, Sections 32 and 33.
15   Arbitration Law of the People's Republic of China (People's Republic of China) National People's Congress, Order 31, August 31 1994, Article 51.
16   International Arbitration Act (Singapore, cap 143A, 2002 rev ed), Section 17.
17   Arbitration Law (Japan) Law 138/2003, Section 38(4).
18   Arbitration and Conciliation Act 1996 (India), Section 30(1).
19   See, for example, Article 40 of the China International Economic and Trade Arbitration Commission Arbitration Rules and Rule 8 of the Japan Commercial Arbitration Association international Commercial Mediation Rules.

example, Australia[20] and Canada.[21] However, adoption of the process for the resolution of commercial disputes, including in the energy sector, in common law jurisdictions has been significantly less concerted. This is mainly due to concerns relating to potential bias on the part of the arbitrator who, acting as mediator, may have previously held private sessions with the parties and could be in possession of confidential information as a result.

The potential for issues of bias to arise in the context of med-arb or arb-med was highlighted in the recent case of *Gao Hai Yan v Keeneye Holdings Ltd*.[22] While an arbitration award rendered following a mediation process conducted by the arbitrator was ultimately upheld, certain mediation meetings were called into question and resulted in various rounds of appeal.

The uniform domestic arbitration legislation that is currently being implemented in Australian states[23] attempts to deal with the potential issue of apparent (and actual) bias by permitting an arbitrator to act as a mediator only in circumstances where provision has been made in the arbitration agreement or where the parties subsequently consent in writing. In addition, an arbitrator who has previously acted as a mediator is not permitted to conduct subsequent arbitration proceedings in relation to the same dispute unless all parties consent in writing, either when the mediation comes to a close or afterwards.

Further, the model legislation provides that the arbitrator (previously the mediator) is under an obligation to disclose to all other parties, before the arbitration proceedings commence, all confidential information that the arbitrator considers to be material and which was obtained from one party during mediation proceedings. These provisions are mirrored in the arbitration rules of the ACDC.

While legislative amendments of this nature assist with alleviating concerns of bias, there remains apprehension that parties to a med-arb or arb-med process may withhold important information from the mediator for fear that it be used against them in any arbitral proceedings. This has the unfortunate result of rendering the mediation process itself much less effective. It is also recognised that participation in these processes can provide unsuccessful parties with a potential opportunity to challenge any award on the basis of apprehension of bias or public policy grounds.

(b) *Appropriate use of med-arb*
For the reasons outlined above, the use of med-arb is likely to meet with some resistance by clients (and their lawyers) from common law backgrounds, who are more likely to prefer the engagement of a different arbitrator if a mediation is unsuccessful. Nevertheless, med-arb does provide a number of advantages to participants and may be considered appropriate in a complex dispute if mediation is unsuccessful.

---

20 See, for example, the Commercial Arbitration Act 2010 (NSW) Section 27D.
21 Arbitration Act, RSA 2000, Section 35.
22 [2011] HKCA 459.
23 Commercial Arbitration Act 2010 (NSW), Commercial Arbitration Act 2011 (Vic), Commercial Arbitration Act 2011 (SA). Tasmania and the Northern Territory have passed legislation which is yet to come into force. Western Australia currently has a Commercial Arbitration Bill before Parliament. Queensland introduced a Commercial Arbitration Bill in 2011; however, it lapsed on February 19 2012. The Australian Capital Territory has yet to introduce a bill.

3.5 Facilitation

(a) Key features and issues

The process of facilitation is in many ways fairly similar to mediation; however, it is characterised by greater flexibility and arguably allows for the facilitator to assume a broader role than is customary for a mediator. While a facilitator, like a mediator, must remain impartial, the level of facilitator intervention in the process may depend on the approach adopted by the particular neutral. Nonetheless, the roles of both facilitators and mediators remain limited to advising on or determining the process, rather than the content, of the discussion.

Some believe that a facilitator has a "much wider contributory role than that permitted to a mediator because of the different dynamics and procedures that apply" to a facilitation.[24] In this regard, facilitation frequently involves more than two parties (such that the requirements of a great number of stakeholders must be considered), and can be employed in a number of different circumstances to identify and define issues for resolution, at which point the facilitation may conclude, or alternatively continue further to explore options for reaching a solution.[25] Whereas the intended outcome of a mediation is most often the resolution of a dispute, the goals of a facilitation may be the resolution of specific problems or the need to accomplish certain tasks.[26] A facilitator's role can extend to setting a programme for fact finding and the holding of meetings, focusing the participants on agreed objectives and, where appropriate, making suggestions as to alternative ways to approach an issue.[27]

(b) Appropriate use of facilitation

Facilitation should be considered in more complex matters, where several stakeholders are involved and/or a number of steps need to be taken (with guidance provided as to those steps and a timetable for completion), in order for the parties to progress to resolution. It may be appropriate in circumstances where significant fact finding is required to be undertaken in order for the parties to fully appreciate their respective positions and be capable of reaching a settlement.

This form of ADR is less suitable for simple disputes that do not require the time input or more extensive intervention of the appointed neutral.

3.6 Conciliation

(a) Key features and issues

In contrast to mediation, conciliation is more often regarded as an evaluative process,[28] in that a conciliator is generally required to provide the parties with advice

---

24   R Charlton, *Dispute Resolution Guidebook*, Law Book Company Information Services, Pyrmont, 2000, p 265.
25   *Ibid*, p 263. See also Australian Commercial Disputes Centre, Definitions of ADR Processes, viewed February 2012 at www.acdcltd.com.au/what-is-adr/definitions-of-adr-processes.
26   Australian Commercial Disputes Centre, *op cit*.
27   R Charlton, *op cit*, pp 265-266.
28   T Sourdin, *Alternative Dispute Resolution* 3rd edn, Lawbook Co, Pyrmont, 2008, p 111.

as to potential options for resolution, their view on the issues in dispute and possible terms of settlement. It is not unusual for a conciliator to possess legal qualifications or have expertise that is relevant to the dispute between the parties.

The role of a conciliator has been described broadly to encompass, among other things, the identification of issues giving rise to disputation, the power to issue recommendations and directions, the assessment of the parties' genuine attempt at settlement and the facilitation of a mutually acceptable agreement.[29]

The process of conciliation is often considered to be less formal than the classical mediation model.[30] The process need not necessarily be governed by a particular set of rules; however, a number of international institutions offer comprehensive procedural rules to assist parties in managing a conciliation. Examples include:

- the United Nations Commission on International Trade (UNCITRAL) Conciliation Rules 1980;
- the UNCITRAL Model Law on International Commercial Conciliation 2002;
- the Institute of Civil Engineers Conciliation Procedure 1999;
- the ICC ADR Rules 2001 (which may be used for "whatever settlement technique" the parties consider appropriate); and
- the Institute of Arbitrators and Mediators Australia's Mediation and Conciliation Rules (the last of which are also applicable to mediation procedures).

There are discrepancies among the rules as to whether the decision of a conciliator will be binding on the parties (which is a relevant consideration when choosing a set of rules to adopt). For example, under the UNCITRAL Conciliation Rules, a conciliation is non-binding; in contrast, the ICE Conciliation Procedure provides that the conciliator's recommendation is binding on the parties, subject to an appeal to an arbitrator or adjudicator, which must be commenced within one month of the conciliation to avoid the recommendation being binding.

Significant inconsistencies between the definitions applied to conciliation across jurisdictions, as illustrated above, has led one critic to complain that "nobody is sure what it means".[31] Further, there are differing views as to whether conciliation is becoming an irrelevant or outdated form of ADR. However, another author alludes to a possible resurgence in interest.[32]

(b) *Appropriate use of conciliation*

Parties may choose to adopt conciliation in circumstances where it is considered that greater input from the neutral is required. In particular, it may be appropriate in circumstances where the parties consider that a non-binding view expressed by a qualified expert (either technical or legal) neutral would be beneficial in the settlement of the dispute.

---

29 David Bryson, "And the leopard shall lie down with the kid: a conciliation model for workplace disputes", *Australian Dispute Resolution Journal*, vol. 8, no 4, 1997, pp 245-246.
30 David Spencer, *Principles of Dispute Resolution*, Lawbook Co, Pyrmont, 2011, p 127.
31 Anthony Speaight QC, "Conciliation – the case against" (speech delivered at the International Conference of the Society Of Construction Law, London, October 7 2008, viewed February 2012 at www.myscl.org/publications_7_1_12.pdf.
32 AFM Maniruzzaman, *op cit*, p 10.

It is important, however, that the parties carefully consider the appointment of a conciliator and ensure that they are satisfied with the relevance and level of that person's expertise. Even in circumstances where any opinion or recommendations expressed by the conciliator are non-binding, it will be difficult for a party to resile from the expressed position in any ongoing conciliation or negotiations.

In circumstances where the parties are of the view that a binding outcome is preferable, consideration should also be given to other ADR methods that may be more suitable.

3.7   Mini-trial

(a)   Key features and issues

The mini-trial or 'information exchange' is a structured dispute resolution process which combines a form of conciliation with executive negotiations. The purpose of a mini-trial is to expose senior executives to the strengths and the flaws in their cases, such that they have an understanding of their likely position should the dispute escalate to litigation.

During a short hearing, the party's lawyers present a truncated version of their client's cases to senior representatives of both parties. A third-party neutral chairs the hearing and subsequently assists the party representatives in negotiations to resolve the dispute. The extent of the neutral's role in the process can differ depending on the agreement of the parties. In addition to facilitating the negotiations and encouraging resolution, the neutral may be required to advise on substantive legal issues or to provide the parties with a non-binding opinion as to the likely result should the case go to court. In this respect, the neutral's role is akin to that of a conciliator.

In the main, mini-trial clauses are brief and make reference to a particular procedure by which the parties agree to be bound[33] (Figure 3 shows an example of a model mini-trial clause). Although there is some variation between the specificity of requirements,[34] mini-trial procedures generally provide for the following:

- appointment of a neutral adviser or umpire by agreement;
- exchange of documents before the information exchange session, including:
  - written statements summarising the issues;
  - briefs and documents or other exhibits on which the parties intend to rely (and which are also provided to the neutral adviser); and
  - discovery between the parties (the scope of which may be prescribed by the relevant procedure), pursuant to which documents discovered may by agreement be used in subsequent litigation;
- exclusion of the rules of evidence (some rules of privilege may apply);
- neutral adviser's opinion to address issues of facts and law; and
- legal counsel to present the best case for their side at the settlement session.

---

33   For example, see the model mini-trial clauses drafted by the International Institute for Conflict Prevention and Resolution, the American Arbitration Association and the Oslo Chamber of Commerce.

34   For example, the Rules of the Arbitration and Dispute Resolution Institute of the Oslo Chamber of Commerce are comparatively brief and do not, for example, describe the nature of documents to be exchanged between parties.

Figure 3: American Arbitration Association model mini-trial clause
If a dispute arises out of or relates to this contract, or the breach thereof, the parties agree first to subject their dispute to a neutral advisor pursuant to the American Arbitration Association's MiniTrial Procedures administered by the American Arbitration Association before resorting to arbitration, litigation or some other dispute resolution procedure

Mini-trials are utilised primarily in the United States and Canada, and are not yet common in the energy sector.[35]

The most significant advantage of the mini-trial, compared to other forms of ADR, is the degree of preparation required, which becomes useful if a resolution is not reached.[36] Parties also retain a greater degree of involvement and control over the outcome than in more adjudicative processes, and the hearing affords both parties the opportunity to hear the other's position and to assess the relative strengths and weaknesses of their positions.

However, there are a number of perceived disadvantages of engaging in the mini-trial process.[37] First, the relatively high costs involved mean that expenditure has been wasted if the parties could have resolved the dispute through mediation. Furthermore, the process of preparation is similar to preparing for a trial, and is not focused on cooperation, which may further polarise the parties' positions. Finally, active participation by senior management is often required, which can be a time-consuming and wasteful use of management time in circumstances where progress is slow or commitment by the parties is lacking.

(b)   *Appropriate use of mini-trials*
Parties may wish to make use of the mini-trial process in circumstances where substantive legal issues are involved or extensive evidence is required to be presented, but they do not wish to undertake a more formal process such as arbitration or litigation. It may also be appropriate in circumstances where limited discovery would be of assistance to the parties in properly understanding their respective cases. As noted, this process exposes the parties' senior executives to the respective strengths and weaknesses of their cases, which can encourage settlement.

However, mini-trials are an expensive and time-consuming method of ADR and may not be appropriate in many cases where parties either do not require or do not wish to be put to the expense of extensive documentary evidence or discovery. It may be that a form of mediation or facilitation is sufficient to resolve the issues in dispute.

---

35   A Redfern and M Hunter, *op cit*, p 40.
36   Dispute Prevention and Resolution Services Department of Justice, *Dispute Resolution Reference Guide*, revised edn, 2006, Canada, viewed February 2012 at www.justice.gc.ca/eng/pi/dprs-sprd/ref/res/drrg-mrrc/05.html#iv.
37   Dispute Prevention and Resolution Services Department of Justice, *op cit*.

3.8   Early neutral evaluation and expert appraisal

(a)   Key features and issues

Early neutral evaluation and expert appraisal are both evaluative ADR processes. While they differ in application, both aid the parties in assessing the risks to which they may be exposed in circumstances where the matter cannot be settled.

Early neutral evaluation provides for the parties to present their cases, including evidence on which they rely, to a neutral dispute resolution practitioner in an attempt to resolve the dispute before further escalation of the issues. The neutral's role is to evaluate the respective strengths and weaknesses of the parties' positions and provide an initial non-binding assessment of the potential outcome should the matter become the subject of litigation. The neutral may then assist the parties in formulating a sensible approach to resolution.

Expert appraisal involves a primarily factual investigation by an expert with particular knowledge of the issues in dispute, following which the expert produces an opinion as to the likely position and advises the parties as to the manner by which a desirable outcome might be achieved.[38] It differs from neutral evaluation in that the opinion provided is usually focused on specified issues within the expertise of the practitioner, rather than the entirety of the dispute.[39] The process is similar to an expert determination; however, the opinion expressed by the expert is not binding on the parties.

(b)   Appropriate use of neutral evaluation or expert appraisal

The effectiveness of these processes depends heavily on thorough preparation by the parties before presenting their cases, so that the neutral or expert has the information required to ensure that any assessment of the likely outcome is meaningful and reflects the actual issues in dispute. As such, neutral evaluation and expert appraisal can be costly methods of ADR (eg, in comparison to mediation).

They may, however, prove useful in circumstances where the parties are deadlocked in relation to a particular issue or dispute. In that case, the provision of an evaluation of the merits from a highly regarded neutral practitioner or expert can be extremely persuasive and may provide a basis on which the parties can move towards resolution.

3.9   Dispute review boards

(a)   Features & issues to be aware of

Dispute review boards (DRBs), originally a US concept, consist of a panel of impartial experts (typically between one and three experts) appointed by the parties under their contract. The DRB operates from the time that the project commences, undertaking a dual dispute avoidance and dispute resolution role.[40] Depending on

---

38   National Alternative Dispute Resolution Advisory Council, *Dispute Resolution Terms*, viewed February 2012 at www.nadrac.gov.au/www/nadrac/nadrac.nsf/Page/What_is_ADRGlossary_of_ADR_Terms#EE.

39   R Charlton, *Dispute Resolution Guidebook*, LBC Information Services, 2000, p 348

40   P Loots and D Charrett, *Practical Guide to Engineering and Construction Contracts*, CCH Australia Ltd, Sydney, 2009, p 312.

the agreement reached between the DRB and the parties, the functions of the DRB can extend to making regular site visits, holding meetings (both before any dispute arises and in the event of a dispute), establishing procedures, conducting informal hearings and making recommendations for the settlement of disputes.[41] DRBs are employed, with some success, in the international construction industry, but have not yet been widely adopted in the energy sector. However, it has been suggested that they could be quite effective in the construction of large energy infrastructure projects.[42]

The advantages of the DRB mechanism lie in the technical expertise of board members, their 'on-the-ground' familiarity with the project and the speed at which the DRB can address any issues or disputes that arise. Recommendations made by a DRB are non-binding on the parties; however, organisations responsible for promotion of the process note that: "the DRB process is most effective if the contract language includes a provision for the admissibility of a DRB recommendation into any subsequent arbitration or legal proceeding."[43]

Given the DRB's expertise and ongoing involvement in the project, any recommendations it makes may be of significant evidential value in proceedings and may provide some assistance to the arbitral tribunal or the court in reaching a determination of the issues.

However, there are certain disadvantages to DRBs as a dispute avoidance tool. The retention of the expert panel, by way of retainer, over a considerable period is costly. In addition, over time, the panel's involvement in the project may also give rise to concerns relating to impartiality.

DRBs should be distinguished from dispute adjudication boards (DABs) that are, for example, employed in the FIDIC suite of contracts. In contrast to DRBs, DABs operate in a manner akin to an expert determination or adjudicative process, whereby the DAB makes decisions that are binding on the parties, at least until overturned by the final dispute resolution process provided for in the parties' contract.[44] For example, the ICC Dispute Board Rules distinguish between a recommendation made by a DRB, which parties may comply with voluntarily, but are not required to do so; and a decision made by a DAB, which is binding on the parties and with which parties must comply without delay.[45]

(b) Appropriate use of DRBs

As noted above, DRBs are most effectively used in long-term projects, where the cost of retaining the DRB is proportionate to the project value, as a dispute avoidance tool. They can be applied successfully to resolve technical disputes quickly and

41 D Jones, *Building and Construction Claims and Disputes*, Construction Publications Pty Ltd, Sydney, 1996, p 159.
42 Tim Martin, *op cit*, p 339.
43 The Dispute Resolution Board Foundation, viewed February 2012 at www.drb.org/concepts.htm; Dispute Resolution Board Australasia Inc viewed February 2012 at www.drba.com.au//index.php?option=com_content&task=view&id=6&Itemid=26.
44 P Loots and D Charrett, *op cit*, p 314.
45 See Dispute Board Rules Of The International Chamber Of Commerce, viewed February 2012 at www.iccwbo.org/court/dispute_boards/id4352/index.html#art4.

efficiently, which allows the project to continue unimpeded. DRBs are generally not appropriate for the resolution of disputes that involve significant legal issues or low-value projects.

3.10 Determinative ADR: adjudication

Expert determination or adjudication, one of the most prominent forms of ADR in the energy sector, is examined in another chapter. These processes involve the preparation of relatively brief submissions and a determination by a neutral third party. Statutory adjudication of disputes arising out of a 'construction contract', as defined in the relevant legislation, is in place in both Australia and the United Kingdom,[46] and is therefore of relevance to energy projects, which frequently involve a construction phase. However, certain construction contracts are excluded from the statutory regime (eg, contracts for drilling for or extracting oil or natural gas or extraction of minerals).[47]

The aim of Australia's security of payment legislation (and its UK equivalent) is to provide statutory rights of adjudication to contractors and subcontractors in relation to disputes relating to non-payment by principals. The policy rationale for the process is the transfer of payment risk up the chain and the alleviation of contractor cash-flow concerns.[48]

The relevant statutory processes are highly detailed and, in contrast to contractual adjudication or expert determination, are in no way flexible, in that prescribed timeframes and processes must be complied with. The nature and application of the legislation are outside the scope of this chapter. However, given the potential applicability to the construction phase of certain energy projects undertaken in these jurisdictions, brief mention has been made. Advice should be obtained if parties intend operating in these regions.

3.11 ADR clauses: enforceable or not?

There is some debate as to the enforceability of ADR processes as a part of contractual dispute resolution – that is, whether agreed ADR processes in a multi-tiered dispute resolution clause can be conditions precedent to the taking of the next step. The enforceability of an agreement to participate in ADR will depend on the terms of the contract in question. Courts will not enforce an agreement referring disputes to resolution by way of ADR if the terms of the agreement are insufficiently certain. The issue of whether an agreement to participate in ADR procedures is binding on the parties has arisen in the context of applications to stay proceedings on the basis that the condition precedent to commencing those proceedings had not been achieved.

---

46   See the Housing Grants, Construction and Regeneration Act 1996 (UK); the Building and Construction Industry Security of Payment Act 1999 (NSW); the Building and Construction Industry Security of Payment Act 2002 (Vic); the Building and Construction Industry Payments Act 2004 (Qld); the Building and Construction Industry Security of Payment Act 2009 (Tas); the Building and Construction Industry (Security of Payment) Act 2009 (ACT); and the Building and Construction Industry Security of Payment Act 2009 (SA)

47   See, for example, Section 105 of the Housing Grants, Construction and Regeneration Act 1996 (UK) and Section 5(2) of the Building and Construction Industry Security of Payment Act 1999 (NSW).

48   D Jones, *Commercial Arbitration in Australia*, Lawbook Co, Pyrmont, 2011, p 27.

In *Channel Tunnel Group Ltd v Balfour Beatty Construction Ltd*[49] the House of Lords granted a stay of proceedings that were brought, according to the court, in breach of an agreed method of resolving disputes. Lord Mustill considered that the parties, having negotiated a carefully drafted dispute resolution clause (which provided that, in the first instance, any dispute or difference arising would be referred to a panel of experts before arbitration), should be held to their bargain. The agreed ADR procedure should be followed, no matter whether the parties now found "their chosen method too slow to suit their purpose".[50]

In *Aiton Australia Pty Ltd v Transfield Pty Ltd*,[51] referring to an Australian Law Reform Commission review, the court noted that it considered the following to be applicable to all stages of a dispute resolution clause:[52] "The process established by the clause must be certain. There cannot be stages in the process where agreement is needed on some course of action before the process can proceed because if the parties cannot agree, the clause will amount to an agreement to agree and will not be enforceable due to this inherent uncertainty."

In this case, the court considered that the absence of a mechanism for apportioning the mediator's costs (mediation being only the first step in the dispute resolution clause) caused particular difficulties in this regard.

As previously mentioned, the courts may also refuse enforcement of an ADR provision in circumstances where it is found to be against public policy. A dispute resolution clause may be considered to be against public policy in circumstances where it is found to oust the jurisdiction of the court. This issue was considered, in the context of an expert determination clause, in *Baulderstone Hornibrook Engineering Pty Ltd v Kayah Holding Pty Ltd*.[53] However, the findings regarding ouster were the subject of subsequent criticism in *Straits Exploration (Australia) Pty Ltd v Murchison United NL*,[54] where the clause under consideration was ultimately distinguished from that in *Baulderstone*, in that it preserved and potentially widened the court's jurisdiction to review any expert determination.

In addition to the above, the inclusion in project contracts of a requirement to participate in ADR processes "in good faith" is quite common. The content of such an obligation is the topic of much debate; nevertheless, good faith as a concept is reflected in the legal norms of many countries, including in Europe, the Middle East and the United States. It has been the subject of recent judicial consideration in Australia. Previously, courts in Australia had refused to enforce such an obligation, given its inherent uncertainty;[55] more recent authority has been to the effect that a good-faith obligation is enforceable.[56] However, the remedy for the breach of such an obligation is unlikely to be more than procedural (ie, an order requiring the parties to attend a meeting) and therefore may be of little value.

---

49   [1993] AC 334.
50   *Ibid* [353].
51   (1999) 153 FLR 239.
52   *Ibid* [252].
53   (1997) 14 BCL 277.
54   [2005] WASCA 241.
55   See *Laing O'Rourke (BMC) Pty Ltd v Transport Infrastructure Development Corp* [2007] NSWSC 723.
56   See *United Group Rail Services Limited v Rail Corporation of New South Wales* [2009] NSWCA 177.

The above reinforces the need to ensure absolute clarity in the drafting of multi-tiered dispute resolution clauses in order to ensure both that the parties' intentions are properly reflected and that the clauses are enforceable.

4. Significance of ADR in the energy sector

Increasingly, trends in the energy and resources sector are shaping global economies. The scarcity of resources worldwide, combined with exponential growth in energy consumption, only highlights the importance of current energy projects. These projects are not conducted in a vacuum; they impact on a variety of different stakeholders, each with their own interests and agendas, and are frequently of significant political import. In consequence, disputes arising from such projects are many and varied in nature.

Given the complex and highly technical nature of most energy disputes, court proceedings can be lengthy, expensive and disruptive – not only to the progression of the project, but also to the underlying business relationships upon which the success of the project lies. In addition, court proceedings expose the parties to public scrutiny and can cause concerns with respect to the disclosure of confidential commercial information. In comparison to litigation in common law jurisdictions, ADR processes also avoid the risk of a potentially adverse precedent resulting from proceedings between parties.

As a result, ADR as a dispute management and resolution tool is a particularly crucial consideration for energy sector participants. Among the benefits that ADR can provide are increased privacy, greater control over the process and flexibility of procedure, and the ability to choose an ADR mechanism that is relevant to the particular circumstance and the issues in dispute. ADR also provides the parties with an opportunity to select a neutral with relevant energy sector expertise to guide the dispute resolution process. Further, the parties determine the scope of the neutral's role and the extent to which any recommendations or determinations of the neutral will be binding on the parties.

ADR provides participants with the opportunity to manage and resolve disputes before they escalate. This has significant time and cost implications, and can assist parties with the maintenance of critical business relationships without delay to project timelines.

Dispute resolution: an industry perspective

David Isenegger
Centrica Energy

1. Introduction

In the oil and gas industry, disputes are inevitable. The size and complexity of the projects involved, the political factors in play and the increasing technical complexity and risk mean that a lot can, and does, go wrong. In addition, cyclical product prices put contracts, projects and relationships under strain. In the upstream sector it is common for disputes to arise among joint venture partners, investors and their contractors. Disputes between energy companies and host states can arise in both the upstream and the downstream sectors.

Despite this proclivity for disputes, relatively few end up in formal litigation or arbitration, because dispute avoidance is often effective. The size of the investments, the long-term nature of the projects and the potential for good returns are all factors which militate in favour of settlement. In addition, the collaborative working environment means that it is vital for an energy company to maintain good relationships with other industry players and host states. Future business depends on being a reliable partner.

In-house counsel need to be prepared for disputes when they arise. The ability to manage a dispute to achieve a satisfactory result is key to protecting a company's investment. However, in an industry where disputes are commonplace (particularly the upstream oil and gas sector, where my experience lies), pursuing a dispute avoidance approach can be particularly challenging. A company's dispute resolution strategy and the way it structures its investment are essential in the effective management of disputes.

This chapter looks more closely at the approach that in-house counsel can take to position themselves to manage disputes, and the particular challenges faced in both the investor-investor context and the investor-state context.

2. The role of the transactional lawyer

Before going on to look at the role of in-house counsel in relation to disputes, it is instructive to consider how transactional lawyers can help to avoid them occurring in the first place.

Companies preparing and planning a project do not want to think about what will happen should it all go wrong: disputes, and in particular dispute resolution, are rarely a key consideration in transaction negotiations. That certainly holds true in a Western context. However, in an industry where disputes frequently materialise, it is essential that all those involved in planning oil and gas projects are aware of the problems that can arise and how to prepare for them. In-house counsel need to be confident that those involved in negotiating the transaction documents have a thorough understanding of, and an ability to evaluate carefully, the various contractual and other protections that are available and appropriate. This is particularly important when dealing with a state directly or through a national energy company (eg, a company will have little leverage for negotiating a satisfactory settlement where a badly drafted agreement provides for disputes to be referred to local courts). It is therefore an integral part of good risk management to ensure that the transactional lawyers appreciate the importance of a well-drafted dispute resolution clause.

In-house counsel should spend a lot of time early in a transaction on ensuring that the investment is structured to maximise the protection available. Various factors will need to be considered, including the size and nature of the project and the identity and location of the counterparty. Different contractual relationships raise their own particular challenges – dealing with other energy companies raises different issues from dealing with states and national oil companies.

3.   Investor versus investor disputes

Natural resources are accessed with increasing difficulty. To access oil and gas, energy companies now have to take on more difficult and complicated projects. For example, in March 2010 Shell started production from the Perdido platform in the Gulf of Mexico, the wells for which are 3,000 feet deeper than BP's Macondo well, which was designed to drill as deep as 30,000 feet[1] – and there are no plans to stop. It is thought that there may now be more rigs in the Gulf designed to drill in deep water than before the Macondo spill.[2] The remote location of some of this very complex machinery, in some of the world's most inhospitable environments, increases the operational risks.[3] Such complexity also has a human element: Shell's Pearls project in Qatar had a workforce of up to 40,000 people during construction.

Such large-scale endeavours and the technical, legal and political challenges they raise mean that even the major international energy companies rarely venture into them alone. Most projects must be undertaken by consortia of the larger international energy companies. In such large-scale projects, tensions and disputes invariably arise. Typically, investor-investor disputes arise:

- between holders of interests in oil and gas concessions, such as joint venture partners or those facilitating the buying and selling of such interests; and
- in relation to dealings between operators and service contractors, for services and equipment which enable the project to proceed.

3.1   Contractual protection: the joint operating agreement

The rise and fall of oil and gas prices and the difficult social, political, geological,

---

1   "BP Plans to Drill Deeper than Ever", www.upi.com, February 8 2012.
2   "Gulf of Mexico Deep Drilling Thrives 18 Months After BP Spill", *Huffington Post*, December 30 2011.
3   "Risk-Taking Rises as Oil Rigs in Gulf Drill Deeper", *New York Times*, August 29 2010.

geographical and technological issues faced by international energy companies have led to an increased use of model form contracts. Such standard form documents save considerable time in negotiations and avoid the 'battle of the contracts' which used to be a common feature of inter-investor dealings. They are also tried and tested, which brings with it considerable comfort.

The Association of International Petroleum Negotiators' (AIPN) Model International Joint Operating Agreement[4] is the model JOA often used in upstream projects. Other JOAs often used are those of the American Association of Petroleum Landmen (AAPL) and the Canadian Association of Petroleum Landmen (CAPL).

The primary purpose of the JOA is to set out the rights and liabilities of the joint venture partners, and in particular, the operator. All JOAs have certain aspects in common:

- the pooling of project assets;
- the conduct of joint operations;
- the apportionment of risks among the parties (and the operator); and
- the participation of the parties in the costs and revenues of the joint venture.

They may also deal with the operator's liabilities towards third parties – usually in the form of an 'exculpatory' clause, limiting or excluding such liability.

(a)   *Protection of the operator*
While model JOAs are intended to be flexible and contain alternate provisions so that they can be tailored to the particular circumstances, industry practice favours the incorporation of certain provisions above others as a matter of course. This is particularly true of provisions relating to operator liability. Of the optional provisions within Article 4 of the AIPN JOA, the provisions most commonly used provide either for no liability on the part of the operator or for liability only in the event of gross negligence or wilful misconduct – that is, actions or a failure to act which was intended to cause, or which was done in reckless disregard of, or wanton indifference to, harmful consequences to safety or property, which were known or should have been known by the operator.[5] It is also standard practice to require the gross negligence or wilful misconduct to take place at senior management level within the operator before the operator becomes liable for co-venturers.

Similar provisions are provided for in the AAPL and CAPL JOAs.[6] The Oil and Gas UK (OGUK) JOA (intended for use on the UK continental shelf) makes an allowance for acts or omissions which, while they could be deemed to be reckless, are done in good faith and are justifiable by reference to particular circumstances, such as the response to an emergency. This further reduces the chances of an operator committing an act of wilful misconduct. Even if an operator is found liable for wilful

---

4   The AIPN's most recent version, the 2012 Model International Joint Operating Agreement, was published on February 17 2012.
5   Article 4.6 of the AIPN's 2012 Model International Operating Agreement. These terms are not defined statutorily under English law – although examples of attempts have been made to set appropriate tests for wilful misconduct in English case law. The JOAs tend to define these terms themselves.
6   Section 5.2 of the AAPL JOA and Sections 4.01 4.02 of the CAPL JOA.

misconduct or gross negligence, liability is often capped, and it is not uncommon to exclude liability for consequential losses – as is the case under the OGUK model.[7]

Why such pared-back liability? The rationale is linked to the principle that operators should neither gain a profit nor suffer a loss as a result of accepting the role of operator, and that any loss is incurred on the same basis as the other non-operator joint venture partners, to the extent of their participating interest. If an operator faced increased liability, it would justify the making of a profit, which would result in raised costs for operations generally and, potentially, a more defensive and closed operating model. The economic justification for such limitation of liability is accordingly clear and well understood in the industry.

The protection of the operator is commonly reinforced by provisions providing for the parties to the joint venture to indemnify the operator, in the proportion of that party's investment interest, for losses incurred while acting as operator. Such outright protection is born from the need to ensure that the operator has suitable incentives to accept the mantle – otherwise, it may be difficult to encourage parties to accept the role of operator with its attendant risks, particularly in the biggest and most challenging projects, the budgets for which can run to billions of US dollars.

(b)   **The dispute resolution clause**

Regardless of the protections that may be afforded by the JOA, the terms of the dispute resolution procedure should never be neglected. The first point to make is that your dispute resolution strategy must be flexible. Each project is different, the parties you are dealing with will be different and a number of factors will dictate what contractual protection you need to put in place.

The preference within the industry for dispute avoidance means that it is common for energy companies to have tiered dispute resolution clauses in their contracts. Even if not followed to the letter, the fact that the clause provides for a process for negotiation encourages senior executives to discuss the problems in the hope of resolving the dispute before it escalates. However, while there is widespread support for discussions at a senior level, views as to the merits of mediation are mixed. Anecdotal evidence suggests that negotiated settlements have been used in certain cultures, particularly in Asian countries, long before mediation as we know it became a recognised alternative dispute resolution method. In the East, the cultural tendency is to settle disputes by way of a consensual approach – as opposed to the traditionally confrontational approach to dispute resolution taken in the West.[8] Others suggest that the slow take-up of mediation relates more to the fact that most oil and gas disputes are 'hard' technical or commercial disputes for which mediation is inappropriate. Also, and perhaps more tellingly, is the idea that this industry takes the view that it is made up of experienced commercial negotiators – whose response is to say, "Why do we need some unknown third party to help us?"[9]

7   This approach is optional in the AIPN JOA and the option is commonly used.
8   "The problems and challenges facing settlement of international energy disputes by ADR methods in Asia: the way forward", A Maniruzzaman, *International Energy Law & Taxation Review*, 2003.
9   "Dispute Resolution in the Oil and Gas Industry: an Oilman's Perspective", HR Dundas, OGEL; July 2004, Vol 2 issue 3.

Where tiered dispute resolution clauses are to be included, one word of caution: ensure that they provide for a clear process that sets out when each stage begins and ends. If such clauses are badly drafted, jurisdictional objections can be raised once the parties are in arbitration or litigation on the basis that the preliminary process has not been exhausted. Careful drafting avoids these issues. In particular, provisions which permit the parties to proceed to the next stage after a specified number of days are quite common and avoid the above problem.

Some energy companies are resorting to innovative methods of resolving their disputes: GE Oil and Gas refers disputes worth less than €50,000 to an online dispute resolution service, which provides for short pleadings, tight timeframes, closed settlement offers filed with an online administrator and online negotiations. If settlement is not achieved, the matter proceeds to a second stage, where an arbitrator assesses the papers and takes a decision online, without a hearing and before rendering a binding award.[10] The use of dispute boards or dispute panels is also increasing as an alternative to litigation and arbitration. These are set up to handle disputes that arise during the life of the project. Disputes are resolved in a quick and efficient manner which enables the parties to continue with their contractual obligations and with minimum disruption. Their use also ensures maintenance of relationships and minimal delay to project completion.

In deciding whether a dispute resolution clause should provide for arbitration or litigation, the approach will differ as between various companies and the size of their operations. Generally, given the global nature of the industry, arbitration is preferred. Model agreements such as the AIPN Model JOA make recourse to international arbitration under the rules of well-established institutions, or by reference to the United Nations Commission on International Trade Law (UNCITRAL) Rules, the preferred dispute resolution mechanism.[11]

(c)   Incentive to settle

As alluded to above, the nature of projects in the oil and gas sector, coupled with the environment in which they operate, means that parties often prefer to settle rather than fight disputes. The risk allocation provisions discussed above, and in particular the limitations on operator liability, mean that proceeding with a formal dispute will rarely be rewarding. Because the liability of the operator is scaled back, limiting liability to events of gross negligence or wilful misconduct of the operator's senior management, there is little scope for the other partners to take action – for example, in the event of negligence. Often, the only remedy available is to replace the operator and forfeit or buy out that party's interest in the joint venture.[12] Operator replacement is rare and forfeiture will not necessarily be a suitable 'disincentive' – for example, if the project is approaching the end of its useful life and decommissioning costs are in prospect.[13]

---

10   "GE Oil & Gas – Putting the A into ADR", Jamie Maples, *The Lawyer*, November 16 2011.
11   Indeed, Article 18 of the AIPN's 2012 Model International Operating Agreement does not suggest any option other than arbitration.
12   See, for example, Article 8 of the AIPN's 2012 Model International Operating Agreement.
13   "Fault-lines in the joint operating agreement: forfeiture", Peter Roberts, *International Energy Law Review*, 2008.

In addition, partners are aware that an operator's interests are aligned with those of the non-operating parties, and that it will suffer proportionately in any losses. This in itself is seen as an incentive to act appropriately in any given situation. The operator is also usually at least as technically competent as the non-operators – and in practice it can be difficult, on a relationship level, to criticise an operator's actions or claim negligence or lack of expertise.

Problems can arise in relation to operator liability if, for example, a governing law is chosen for the JOA which does not distinguish between 'negligence' and 'gross negligence', or which has an unusual approach to what constitutes wilful misconduct. Problems may also occur if operational arrangements change on the ground so that a non-operator starts to supply some or all of the services required by the JOA. Care is required to ensure that contract documentation keeps pace with operational change. Here the in-house legal department has an important role to play, by keeping indemnity wordings under review and ensuring that indemnities are extended to cover any non-operator supply of services.

The principal concern of investors in any investor-investor dispute is not necessarily to win. This is perhaps surprising to dispute resolution practitioners in private practice, but is based upon an entirely sound rationale. Ultimately, the interests of industry and its stakeholders are rarely best protected by fighting tooth and nail to the bitter end of any dispute. Often, an efficacious end to a dispute is the best way of protecting assets and stakeholders' long-term investments and, ultimately, the long-term viability of the business and business relationships.

The impact that pursuing a dispute to the bitter end can have on relationships is a further disincentive. In practice, the global relationships between multinational energy companies are so significant and interwoven that it becomes difficult to pursue a single discrete claim without affecting the global relationship. More important is the need to protect collaborative relationships with other joint venture partners and preserve the company's reputation as a reliable partner.

Finally, the time and cost involved in pursuing a claim in arbitration or litigation favour settlement.

Consequently, although tensions and disputes invariably arise, relatively few end up in formal litigation or arbitration; the structure of the industry is such that it drives settlement. However, this does not mean that the dispute resolution clause becomes redundant. As noted above, these provisions have an important part to play in ensuring that in-house counsel can negotiate a satisfactory solution and, should negotiations fail, in protecting the company's position by referring the dispute to an appropriate forum.

4. Investor versus state disputes

Globally, the oil and gas industry is one of the largest and most active, with international energy companies investing in the most challenging fiscal and political environments. The interaction between the energy companies and the states in which they invest is therefore key: it is the governments or national oil companies that grant the permits, licences and concessions that permit exploration. The risk inherent in that interaction is among the biggest facing the industry. Currently, the industry is experiencing a period of the most aggressive resource nationalism since the nationalisations and expropriations of the early 1970s.[14]

The inherent risks and costs of oil and gas exploration, together with the level of investment and technical expertise required to develop oil and gas fields, mean that many host states and national oil companies are not in a position to explore and exploit their reserves without private investment and expertise. Before their investment is made, energy companies enjoy their best bargaining position, with host states keen to encourage investment and offer attractive terms. However, once the energy companies have invested their capital and projects start to produce, the attitude of the host states often changes as they use their enhanced bargaining position to renegotiate the terms of their agreements at the expense of the energy companies. Regime change, political and environmental pressures, increasing scarcity of oil reserves and the surge in oil prices over the last decade are all factors contributing towards this increase in resource nationalism. Governments of host states are increasingly demanding an increased share of the returns. Tactics range from increasing taxation rates or royalty fees to negotiating more advantageous terms in the revenue sharing arrangements and, at the extreme end, expropriation. The potential for investor-state disputes has therefore increased significantly over the past decade.[15]

With this in mind, it is particularly important to have in place contractual and other available protection when dealing with states. Host states may well ignore the contract terms, but having adequate protection in place – and in particular the ability to threaten arbitration – provides an investor with leverage when renegotiating contract terms or defending its position. This requires proper planning early on in the project.

4.1 Investment treaty protection

With over 2,500 investment treaties in existence, in-house counsel will be looking to structure the investment so as to take advantage of the available bilateral or multilateral investment treaties, in particular the Energy Charter Treaty.[16] These offer broad, high-level guarantees of fair, equitable and non-discriminatory treatment and protection from major investment risks, particularly expropriation. They also offer

---

14 As illustrated by developments in South America (in particular Argentina, Venezuela and Ecuador) and in Bolivia, Russia and Kazakhstan.
15 As reflected by the number of investor-state disputes. According to International Centre for Settlement of Investment Disputes (ICSID) statistics published in 2012, 25% of all ICSID investor–state disputes are attributable to the oil, gas and mining sector (see http://icsid.worldbank.org/ICSID/ FrontServlet?request Type=ICSIDDocRH&actionVal=CaseLoadStatistics).
16 The importance of this is highlighted by ConocoPhillips' investment treaty claim against Venezuela. There is no bilateral investment treaty in place between the United States and Venezuela, but ConocoPhilllips structured its investment so that it was able to bring its claim under the Netherlands-Venezuela bilateral investment treaty via three subsidiaries incorporated in the Netherlands.
17 According to ICSID statistics, of the investor-state arbitrations concluded in 2011, 40% were settled or discontinued. A breakdown on industry division is not provided, but given that one-quarter of ICSID disputes are in the oil, gas and mining sector, it is reasonable to assume that several of those settlements were in the oil and gas sector (see http://icsid.worldbank.org/ICSID/FrontServlet?requestType= ICSIDDocRH&actionVal=CaseLoadStatistics). Anecdotal evidence also supports this. For example, Eni's agreement to invest in the Orinoco Belt was reportedly made two weeks after Eni had agreed to drop its claim that Venezuela had violated the Venezuela-Netherlands bilateral investment treaty ("Arbitration of Venezuelan Oil Contracts," Emily Witten, Texas Journal of Oil, Gas and Energy Law, September 12 2008).

attractive dispute resolution provisions, namely recourse to international arbitration. The threat of a bilateral investment treaty (BIT) action can be a valuable tool in dispute avoidance.[17] In addition to adding a layer of protection to contracts with host states, they will be particularly important when dealing with national oil companies, as often those contracts will not protect the investor against sovereign action. However, investment treaty arbitration is not a panacea. A BIT may improve an investor's bargaining position when a dispute arises. In practice, BITs, like other formal dispute resolution mechanisms, are usually employed following a country exit (the abandonment or sale of all investments in the host country).

4.2   Contractual protection

When negotiating with states posing increased political risk, there are three contractual provisions that in-house counsel should always try to negotiate: a stabilisation clause, a sovereign immunity clause and a properly drafted arbitration clause.

(a)   Stabilisation clauses

Stabilisation clauses are a contractual mechanism which assists in protecting an investment. They take various different forms, but generally protect an investor against a change in law which would detrimentally impact on its investment. So, for example, their effect could be to freeze the national legislation for the life of the investment or take the form of a guarantee from the government that any change of law would not disadvantage the investor. They used to be a common feature of investor-state contracts, but host states are increasingly resisting their inclusion. However, they should always be part of the negotiation, particularly if dealing with higher-risk countries.

(b)   Sovereign immunity clauses

It is also important, when contracting with a state or national oil company, to try to negotiate inclusion of a sovereign immunity clause. This has the effect of waiving the law of the host state with regard to its entitlement to claim sovereign immunity. The threat of arbitration will be a fairly empty one if ultimately the state can claim immunity against enforcement of the award. The waiver should extend to immunity for enforcement against state assets. In practice, there are few examples of awards being successfully enforced against states and significant hurdles exist to enforcement. However, securing a waiver puts an investor in a better position than if the state had the protection of immunity.

(c)   Dispute resolution provisions

It is becoming more difficult for investors to secure the level of investment protection or stabilisation provisions that was common in past decades. Increasingly, investors' last line of defence is strong, or at least workable, dispute resolution provisions in their investment contracts.[18]

---

18   The threat of arbitration was used by the UK BG Group and Italy's Eni to settle disputes the companies had with the Kazakhstan government ("Kazakhstan settles billion-dollar oil claims", *Global International Review*, December 16 2011).

States and national oil companies will often resist any suggestion that disputes be referred to the investor's home courts. The best protection for an investor is therefore arbitration in a neutral seat. However, states are increasingly pressing for their home courts and often the decision must be taken as to whether to take the risk or push for arbitration. In deciding how important a negotiating point this is, in-house counsel will need to consider:

- how transparent and reliable the local courts are. This involves considering how transparent the judicial process is, how competent and independent and free from political pressure the judiciary is, and the predictability and reliability of judicial decisions;
- how efficient the court process is. Look at the court's caseload and docket, whether the state runs a federal and state court system and, if so, where any disputes are likely to end up, as often they will have different timelines. If the appellate review process is extensive, a quick judgment could still involve years of appeals; and
- enforceability. Arbitration awards are generally perceived as being enforceable throughout the world as a result of the New York Convention. However, there are other enforcement regimes in place and it may well be that enforceability of a court judgment is not an issue.

As a general rule, energy companies that are investing in non-Organisation for Economic Cooperation and Development (OECD) countries will push for arbitration. However, securing agreement to arbitration is only half the battle – unless drafted properly (see below), an arbitration clause will provide little protection. In the current climate, investors will rarely succeed in negotiating an ideal arbitration clause. The key is to focus on and secure a structure that will work. The following guidance should be considered:

- It is essential to get the seat of the arbitration right. Transactional lawyers often do not understand the significance of the seat and, having secured the arbitration concession, can sometimes agree to a local seat. This can be as damaging as agreeing to the jurisdiction of the local courts, as the courts in non-OECD countries will often gratuitously interfere with proceedings. In addition, the state will be in a position to delay the arbitration process and it will be years before a result is achieved. More importantly, if that jurisdiction has not ratified the New York Convention, any award obtained will not be enforceable elsewhere. As a general rule, investors should try to secure a seat in a major financial centre where the local courts will respect arbitration and not interfere. If that cannot be achieved, at least ensure that the courts in the seat support arbitration and the jurisdiction has ratified the New York Convention.
- Ensure that a procedure is in place that cannot easily be frustrated. While the rules of the International Chamber of Commerce, the London Court of International Arbitration or UNCITRAL are preferred, if they cannot be agreed, at least make sure that the procedures proposed by the state are workable. Otherwise, you can find yourself in a protracted, expensive

procedure with scope for abuse on the part of the state.
- Ensure that the appointing authority exists and will appoint competent arbitrators. Once a dispute arises, the choice of arbitrator is key to achieving a satisfactory outcome.

(d) *Political risk insurance*
In practice, investors will look for more specific and detailed protection on the main political risks faced. Political risk insurance, and the extent required, will therefore need to be fully considered at a very early stage in the project. Political risk insurance operates like any other type of insurance, where the premium is calculated based on a variety of factors such as the value of the asset, the period of cover and the risk profile of the country where the investment is situated. In the oil and gas industry, it is common for the policy to last for many years and for premiums to be substantial. Risks covered include where:
- assets are expropriated and/or nationalised;
- assets are damaged as a result of political actions;
- licences that are fundamental to the project are cancelled without cause by the host government; or
- the ability to convert or transfer the local currency is restricted.

(e) *Incentive to settle*
Such a dispute-rich environment is particularly challenging for in-house counsel and, as with investor-investor disputes, the ability to avoid formal proceedings is equally important in relation to investor-state disputes.

Reputation: In the oil and gas industry, an energy company's reputation is of paramount importance. No one wants to have the reputation of being a difficult partner. An energy company that regularly resorts to arbitration would be viewed unfavourably by most host states.

Relationships: The second factor is the damage that a long, drawn-out investor-state arbitration does to the relationship between the energy company and the particular host state. As suggested above, full-blown investor-state arbitration follows or results in country exit. Host states have long memories: pursue a claim and it can take a generation before a company will be allowed back in. It is therefore only in extreme cases, where a company is prepared to sever all ties with that state or has other political objectives, that a company should pursue a dispute to arbitration.

Return on investment: More important is the return on the investment. Oil and gas exploration is difficult and high risk: the level of investment required for what is, in reality, a small chance of making a commercial discovery is significant. However, once that investment pays off, the returns are substantial. Most energy companies would rather accept revised terms than give up the revenue and the reserves.

Arbitration risk: Developments in Venezuela are a perfect case in point. In the 1990s the government encouraged the international energy companies to invest, offering generous terms. Investors included Exxon Mobil, ConocoPhillips, Chevron, Total, BP and Statoil. Taken together, they invested more than $16 billion in the Orinoco belt.[19] However, the regime changed in 1998 and within a couple of years, new legislation was enacted to increase royalty rates and tax rates were reinterpreted, with the international oil companies being told to pay back taxes or leave. Other measures were taken to increase government share in project revenues. Despite the heavy-handed tactics, the majority of the companies accepted the new contract terms. Only Exxon Mobil and ConocoPhillips decided to walk away from their investments. Since then, both have been embroiled in contractual and investment arbitration.

Even if your company proceeds to arbitration, it will not always offer a satisfactory outcome. Be prepared for a long, drawn-out process: the potential for delays is substantial, particularly in investment treaty arbitration, where there is a tendency to use preliminary issues as a delaying tactic. In addition, there is a sense in the industry that the tribunals are too deferential to states and spend too much time on international law arguments and jurisdiction issues – and not enough time on quantum. The damages claimed usually run to several billions, but actual recovery rates are low.[20] Once you secure an award, there is no guarantee that it can be enforced. In addition, the substantial legal costs involved mean that, even if successful, the company still takes a financial hit.

5.   Dispute resolution strategy once a dispute arises

If a dispute must be pursued, whether against a co-investor or a host state, the key concern of any in-house counsel will be to control the claim to the fullest extent possible. In-house counsel must ensure that the litigation, or more commonly arbitration, is run in the most efficient and cost-effective manner possible. Unfortunately, those cases that end up in formal litigation or arbitration tend to be high-value, complex disputes. By their nature, they will be expensive and time consuming. Although there will be many factors beyond in-house counsel's control, there are certain steps that in-house counsel can take to ensure that the process runs as smoothly and efficiently as possible.

A properly drafted dispute resolution clause will go a long way towards ensuring a smoother and more efficient process. As already mentioned, the choice of court – or arbitral seat – and a process that cannot be easily frustrated are crucial.

Selection of your external legal team is another factor that contributes to the efficient running of the dispute. It is becoming increasingly common for in-house counsel to require legal teams to pitch for the larger matters. Each matter will throw

19   "Arbitration of Venezuelan Oil Contracts", Emily Witten, *Texas Journal of Oil, Gas and Energy Law*, September 12 2008.

20   For example, after Venezuela's expropriation of its oil assets in 2007, Exxon Mobil Corp brought a claim before the International Chamber of Commerce. Exxon Mobil Corp was eventually awarded $908 million in compensation, less than 10% of the $10 billion it had sought (*Mobil Cerro Negro, Ltd v Petróleos de Venezuela SA* (Case 15415/JRF, December 11 2011)). In *RosInvestCo UK Ltd v Russian Federation* (SCC Arbitration V (079/2005)), the claimant brought a £230 million claim for unlawful expropriation by the Russian Federation of its investment in Yukos Oil. The Stockholm Chamber of Commerce tribunal upheld the claim, but awarded the claimant just $3.5 million.

up different requirements, but generally, in-house-counsel will be looking to see whether the team has the skills and resources necessary to handle the case, particularly the larger disputes where substantial manpower will be required. More importantly, is the legal team alive to the commercial issues in play and is their strategy in line with that of the company?

If the dispute is in national court litigation, there will be little that in-house counsel can do in terms of speeding up the process. Timetables are usually set by the courts. However, in arbitration, there is greater potential for efficiencies and delay. Consequently, once a dispute arises, the principal concern will be to ensure that the arbitration has the best possible chance of being resolved efficiently. Fundamental to that issue is the choice or choices of arbitrator. A good arbitrator, or a good chairman, can drive the arbitral process forward and materially reduce the duration and cost of an arbitration. Getting selection right is therefore key.

However, even with a robust tribunal, there is still potential for delay, particularly in investor-state arbitration, where states raise a myriad of preliminary and jurisdictional issues to block the arbitration process. In arbitrations with commercial parties, sensible agreement on the procedure is usually more easily achieved. It may also be possible to agree an expedited procedure, or at least a limited time in which the tribunal has to deliver its award (which can often add up to a year to the process).

Given the legal costs generated by these disputes, costs management and budgeting is another issue that in-house are particularly alive to, both internally and with external legal teams. Internally, it is common practice to keep records of in-house costs incurred, as these may be recoverable in part. External legal teams should also be required to prepare detailed budgets and provide regular detailed breakdowns of costs incurred. As with any project, good project management is crucial.

Managing large-scale energy disputes

Tim Reid
Joanna Wallis
Ashurst LLP

1. Introduction

Disputes in the energy sector are typically high value, involving multiple issues and multiple parties, often in politically sensitive jurisdictions. Invariably, they are also characterised by a need for extensive factual and expert evidence. All of these factors can combine to make effective dispute management a challenge.

The aim of this chapter is to provide practical advice for dispute management in both a litigation and an arbitration context. The authors begin with a case study which illustrates the extensive evidential considerations to which a typical dispute in the energy sector can give rise.

Against this background, this chapter addresses the following key areas:

- an initial case analysis to determine an overall case theory and strategy;
- management of the disclosure or document production process;
- some practice points for preparing factual and expert witness evidence;
- effective costs management; and
- strategies for settlement.

The suggestions set out in this chapter envisage the case preparation being conducted by lawyers. It is important that legal advice be sought in respect of certain activities, particularly in relation to the gathering of evidence.

Case study: *ExploreCo v the Government of Prospectavia*[1]

Facts

Prospectavia is a country undergoing a period of rapid political and economic change. Blocks 1 and 2 offshore Prospectavia have a high potential for the discovery of hydrocarbon deposits, but ground conditions make drilling difficult. Keen to attract foreign private investment and to acquire advanced technology for effective and profitable exploration of the deposits, the Prospectavian government engages a third party to market the blocks and oversee an extensive tendering process for prospective joint venture partners.

In the event, there is only one interested bidder for Blocks 1 and 2, ExploreCo. ExploreCo subsequently enters into a joint venture agreement with ProspectCo, a

---

[1] This case study is based on the facts of an actual International Chamber of Commerce (ICC) arbitration.

Prospectavian state entity, providing it with a full carry in the conduct of exploration activities in the area.

A few years into the joint venture agreement, ExploreCo has completed a number of difficult exploration wells and tension between it and the Prospectavian government is high. However, finally a commercial discovery of oil is made.

The government of Prospectavia subsequently pronounces that the terms of the joint venture agreement regarding returns on a commercial discovery are overly favourable to ExploreCo and inconsistent with new state tax laws. It declares that the joint venture activities should be suspended until the joint venture agreement is appropriately revised.

ExploreCo argues in correspondence that the joint venture agreement is still in existence and repeatedly requests that the government respect the terms. In response, however, the government takes the position that:

- the joint venture agreement is void or voidable because it was procured improperly in breach of state laws and fiduciary duties to the government of Prospectavia;
- the joint venture agreement should be terminated because of numerous breaches amounting to a repudiation by ExploreCo, including:
  - serious failures by ExploreCo in providing information to ProspectCo; and
  - imprudent drilling activities; or
- the joint venture agreement has been frustrated by a change in macroeconomic conditions.

ExploreCo decides that it has no option but to issue proceedings.

Making out ExploreCo's case
Very broadly, ExploreCo's case will involve the consideration and management of the following legal, evidential or procedural matters (many of which will need to be attended to in parallel).

Legal analysis
Legal argument and submissions will need to be developed to support ExploreCo's position, including that the joint venture agreement is not void. If ExploreCo is in breach, do these breaches amount to a repudiation of the joint venture agreement? Can a change in macroeconomic conditions constitute frustration of the contract? What legal remedies will ExploreCo seek?

Disclosure
Depending on whether the dispute is referred to arbitration or litigation, ExploreCo could potentially be required to search for, review and disclose a wide range of documents, including:

- documents relevant to the tender process and negotiation of the joint venture agreement (including communications with the Prospectavian government and the third party administering the tender, as well as its own internal documents and communications relating to the bid);

- documents and communications relevant to the adequacy of ExploreCo's reporting of information in the years since the inception of the joint venture agreement; and
- documents relevant to the allegations of imprudent drilling (eg, technical reports; minutes of technical committee meetings; communications with ProspectCo on the issues; internal communications).

Factual evidence

ExploreCo will need to proof, as potential witnesses:

- those individuals involved in the bidding process and negotiation of the joint venture agreement;
- those responsible for reporting and overall relations with ProspectCo; and
- technical staff who conducted the drilling operations.

Expert evidence

ExploreCo will need to adduce expert evidence to rebut Prospectavia's allegations that it conducted well activities imprudently. Depending on the nature of its alleged deficiencies, this could involve more than one expert. An independent expert on Prospectavian state tax law might also be needed and/or an economist to consider Prospectavia's arguments of frustration.

Assuming that ExploreCo seeks damages as an alternative remedy to specific performance of the JV Agreement, a further layer of complexity is added. In that case, ExploreCo will be required to demonstrate its losses. It will need to retain experts to opine on the likely volume of oil in the discovery well, the production scheme and costs which would need to be incurred to exploit the discovery, and also the net present value of the income stream expected over the life of the asset.

The above should illustrate why energy dispute management can be complex, and the more so when the procedural timetable is tight. Without a holistic, well-planned approach, ExploreCo risks compromising its legal or technical case and/or costs spiralling out of control.

The key message of this chapter is that, whether a claimant or defendant, effective dispute management is predicated on careful planning having been undertaken at an early stage. This involves identifying the central issues in the case so far as possible at the outset, as well as having an understanding of the key procedural milestones and what will be required to meet them. As should be evident from what follows, the foundations of dispute management lie in the case analysis.

2.   Conducting an initial case analysis

As a first step, it is imperative to conduct a robust case analysis and develop a case strategy as soon as possible after a dispute has crystallised, not least because the first procedural stage in any formal dispute will be submission of pleadings or written statements of case.[2] Clearly, it is important for a party to understand the relative strengths and weaknesses of its case as soon as possible. This also allows an informed assessment of the litigation risk and sets the parameters internally for any settlement discussions.

The various steps required for a developed case analysis are set out below.

2.1 Gather key case documents

Well before any formal disclosure search has been ordered by the court or document requests made, a more limited document review exercise should be undertaken in order to ascertain those documents which most strongly support a party's case, as well as those which could be most harmful. In international arbitration, the parties produce the documents on which they intend to rely at an early stage in any event. This will be either with their initial written statements or immediately after initial written statements have been exchanged.

In a litigation context, if key documentation is in the other side's possession or the other side alone has knowledge of key facts which cannot be obtained from other sources, this should be requested from the opponent as soon as possible.

In the context of litigation, all potentially relevant documents will need to be considered for the purposes of disclosure. Therefore, it is essential that no one within an organisation which is party to proceedings destroys any documents (even duplicate copies) which could be relevant, however unimportant in appearance and irrespective of whether their contents seem to be favourable or prejudicial to the party's case. This applies as much to handwritten scraps of paper as to formal documents.

All appropriate steps by parties should be taken to preserve documents in their possession relating to the dispute. This will involve suspending a party's normal document destruction policy with immediate effect and ensuring that members of the party's organisation are all fully briefed on the importance of preserving documents.[3]

2.2 Obtain an initial proof of evidence from witnesses

A party should identify potential witnesses and interview them as soon as possible. It is not necessary to obtain formal witness statements at this stage and it is likely that most of the individuals interviewed will not be called upon to give evidence in the proceedings. Rather, the intention of this process is to establish a 'warts and all' factual picture to inform the legal arguments.

---

2   This is assuming that any necessary pre-action steps have been followed in the context of a litigation in the English courts (eg, see the Civil Procedure Rules Practice Direction on Pre-action Conduct).

3   In England and Wales, there is no duty to preserve documents prior to the commencement of proceedings unless Practice Direction 31B (PD31B) applies. PD31B applies to all multi-track cases commenced after October 1 2010 and provides (at para 7):

> As soon as litigation is contemplated, the parties' legal representatives must notify their clients of the need to preserve disclosable documents. The documents to be preserved include Electronic Documents which would otherwise be deleted in accordance with a document retention policy or otherwise deleted in the ordinary course of business.

After the commencement of proceedings, the situation is radically different. From that point, solicitors owe a duty to the court, as officers of the court, to make sure, as far as possible, that no relevant documents have been omitted from the client's list of documents for disclosure (*Woods v Martins Bank Limited* [1959] 1 QB 55 (at 60)).

Also, as it is usually some time before a case is heard, potential witnesses may leave the organisation or memories might fade. Conducting early interviews allows a party to capture all potentially relevant information on file for future reference. It is useful to mark draft proofs of evidence 'privileged and in contemplation of litigation' in case there are any questions subsequently as to whether the documents are disclosable.

2.3   Obtain an initial opinion from an expert adviser

It is important to retain an expert adviser early (assuming that the dispute has any technical elements). This allows a party the benefit of an independent assessment of its technical case at the outset, and will also be helpful in analysing the merits of its opponent's case. A preliminary opinion from an expert can also provide a realistic picture of the value of the claim, which is especially important in the energy sector, where this can be uncertain.

Another advantage of not waiting until later in the proceedings to engage an expert is that the pool of quality experts for the specialism in question may be relatively small. An early approach to choosing an expert will prevent an opponent from retaining his services due to conflict (even if the original party does not ultimately choose formally to instruct the expert to give evidence in the proceedings).

2.4   Consider instructing counsel

Counsel's role is not just to prepare the pleadings and represent a party at trial. In addition to a party's external legal advisers, counsel offer a fresh pair of legal eyes on the dispute and can often provide the best advice as to how a court or tribunal might view the merits of a case. Counsel will work with general counsel and a party's expert adviser to identify the key issues in the case and the evidence which will be required in respect of those issues. Counsel can also be useful in assessing whether any form of early determination of the claim is possible – for example, summary judgment or a strike out of the claim.

Clearly, a balance must be achieved between minimising the risk of surprises further down the line which significantly affect the merits or trajectory of a party's case (as well as costs), against the danger of frontloading too much cost at an early stage, only for the dispute to settle shortly thereafter. Generally, however, a failure to invest adequate time and resources in building the foundations of a case will prove a false economy.[4]

2.5   Team management

Any large-scale dispute will invariably require several lawyers (whether internal or external) to conduct the case. It is important that all members of the team have a clearly defined role and understanding of their responsibilities. Often, for example,

---

4   Costs incurred by the successful party in preparing its case before proceedings are issued can be recoverable in litigation (see *Callery v Gray, Russell v Pal Pak Corrugated Limited* [2001] EWCA Civ 1117; *McGlinn v Waltham Contractors Limited* [2005] EWHC 1419) or arbitration (see Sections 59 to 68 of the Arbitration Act 1996).

lawyers will be assigned to certain factual or expert witnesses, or be primarily responsible for overseeing the disclosure process.

It is helpful for the team to meet regularly to ensure that everyone is aware of the status of the various work streams in the case (not least because they invariably impact upon one another), what actions will be required in the short and medium term, and who will be responsible for these. A clear understanding by team members of their responsibilities and effective communication will make management of the case much easier and minimise the risk of any matters being overlooked.

3. Managing the disclosure or document production process

The procedural matter which can often come upon a party all too quickly is disclosure, or document production. The case study above should demonstrate how extensive the search for documents can be – it is not difficult to imagine how ExploreCo's disclosure exercise could involve reviewing tens of thousands of documents.

For that reason, it is never too early for a party to plan its approach to disclosure. The time and resources required should not be underestimated, and it is essential to have a full and accurate understanding of the scope of its disclosure exercise before committing to a certain procedural timetable.

In international arbitration, the parties are generally not required to provide disclosure of all relevant documents in their possession, but only those on which they intend to rely to prove their case. Each party may then make requests for production of any additional documents that it considers should be disclosed. The disclosure process in the English courts, however, can be much more burdensome than document production in arbitration. For that reason, this section focuses on litigation and disclosure under the English Civil Procedure Rules, but many of the practical points can be equally applied to an arbitration context.

3.1 Identify the issues and potential custodians of documents

In most cases, 'standard disclosure' will be ordered by the court. Broadly, this requires parties to disclose all relevant documents which are helpful to its case and also those which are harmful to its case or helpful to its opponent's.

A party must ensure that it is in a position to target effectively the search for documents before embarking on the disclosure process. The case analysis should have provided a clear understanding of the issues in the case and hence the categories of documents falling within standard disclosure. Similarly, the initial witness interviews should also have identified those individuals who are likely to have in their possession documents which fall within the ambit of standard disclosure.

In any disclosure exercise, it is sensible to create a document which sets out the scope of the dispute and a list of the issues in dispute so that it is clear on what basis disclosure has been made.[5] This will be particularly important when disclosure must be revisited and initial decisions re-examined.

---

5   In the Commercial Court, the parties are in any event required to agree a list of issues setting out the key issues of both fact and law (see paragraph D6 of the Admiralty & Commercial Courts Guide, Ninth Edition 2011). The list of issues is intended to be used a case management tool as the case progresses to determine the scope of disclosure and of factual and expert evidence.

3.2   Electronic documents

Given how businesses operate today, it is likely that the vast majority of relevant documents will be held in electronic form. A party will therefore need to consider whether the case requires input from forensic experts. If a substantial amount of electronic data needs to be collected and a party's in-house IT capabilities are not equipped to manage the process, external consultants may be required to assist in harvesting the data.

3.3   Audit trail

Any disclosure exercise will invariably involve a number of different lawyers or paralegals making judgements as to the extent of the disclosure exercise, including the disclosure to be provided. It is essential that all decisions which concern the scope of the exercise or the documents that are, or are not, to be searched for and/or provided be recorded accurately and with sufficient detail so that:

- a consistent approach can be taken to disclosure (which is particularly important where a number of individuals are involved in reviewing documents for relevance and privilege);
- the list of documents can be completed – this is the procedural disclosure form and it requires detailed information as to the searches that both were and were not carried out during disclosure; and
- a robust defence can be mounted to any application to court by an opponent for specific disclosure.

Further, in a large and complex case, a party is advised to maintain a disclosure file or log containing the following documents:

- the list of issues against which disclosure has been made;
- a data map (a document showing where relevant documents might be held and by whom);
- the disclosure protocol that has been agreed for electronic documents (eg, search criteria, keyword searches, date ranges agreed); and
- a disclosure review document setting out an up-to-date position on where the party is in the search and review process.

Disclosure can become incredibly tactical and, if having to deal with any applications to the court, a party will be in a much better position if it has detailed records of the decisions that were taken and the searches made and can present those to the court.

3.4   Avoid creating new potentially harmful documents

Another important point of which to be aware in a litigation context is that the duty of disclosure is continuous.[6] As such, any new documents may also be required to be disclosed as part of the legal proceedings. Accordingly, a party should be careful that no compromising documents are created which are not covered by privilege and are

---

6   Civil Procedure Rule 31.11.

open to inspection. By way of example, a party should be careful when discussing the litigation with colleagues at board level or when recording discussions in minutes or internal memoranda. Board minutes should not contain expressions of opinion on any sensitive issues.

4. Factual witness evidence

4.1 Selecting factual witnesses

The role of a factual witness is to explain to the court or tribunal his first-hand knowledge of events. The case analysis should have identified all potential factual witnesses and the issues to which these witnesses will be required to speak.

Clearly, the number of witnesses that a case requires depends on the number and nature of issues in dispute and how the case is pleaded. It may be that a number of witnesses are needed each to give evidence on very specific issues, or that only one witness is required to give commentary on a wide range of facts and events. Generally speaking, it is advisable to keep the number of witnesses to a minimum – not only for costs and logistical reasons, but also because the performance of a witness under cross-examination can be uncertain. The more witnesses that a party calls to give evidence, the greater the risk of prejudice to its case.

It is important to remember that there is no property in a witness. In other words, there is nothing to stop one party from approaching and questioning a witness who may work or have worked for the other party. If one party thinks there is a chance that the other will want to interview a witness it is calling or interviewing, then it is advisable to ask the witness to agree to enter a confidentiality agreement, or at least to request that he treats the list of questions the party is putting to him as confidential. It is important not to share information with the witness as to the merits of the case or information about the overall strategy.

4.2 Keeping in contact with factual witnesses

The international nature of the energy industry can often present practical problems for factual witnesses. It is important to consider the availability of key witnesses before proposing directions for the procedural timetable. Similarly, as soon as the court or tribunal determines the timetable, notify all witnesses as soon as possible, ensuring that they will be available to prepare their statement, to assist counsel in trial preparation and, of course, for the hearing itself. A party should allow for slippage in the timetable or the possibility that a witness may be called earlier than anticipated. It is therefore sensible to ask that all witnesses give notification of any changes to their availability as soon as possible. It is surprising how easy it is to overlook these sorts of practical and logistical considerations.

4.3 Witness familiarisation

Giving evidence in legal proceedings can be a daunting prospect. Often, factual witnesses will have never been in a courtroom before. They may lack confidence or presentational skills. In that case, a party should consider whether some or all of its witnesses would benefit from witness familiarisation training shortly before trial.

Such training is provided by specialist organisations and aims to give witnesses an understanding of the practice and procedure of giving evidence. It will often entail mock cross-examination (based on case studies) which can improve their performance on the stand.

5. Expert evidence

Energy disputes can be won or lost on expert evidence. It is therefore essential that a party select the right expert witnesses and work with them effectively to ensure that their evidence is produced on time and is of the highest quality.

In international arbitration, most institutional rules contain provisions entitling the tribunal to appoint an expert to advise it on issues which arise in connection with the dispute.[7] In practice, however, most parties will also seek to adduce evidence from their own party-appointed expert reports in addition to any tribunal-appointed expert.

5.1 Finding an expert

Often, colleagues can give useful recommendations as to the eminent individuals in a required field. While it may be tempting for a party to engage an individual with whom it has worked closely before, any prior relationship that it has had with the expert will need to be disclosed and this may compromise the perceived independence of the expert.

A party's external legal advisers and counsel are also likely to have recommendations based on past experience of the individuals in question, which can often prove invaluable. Failing that, relevant energy industry bodies may keep a database or directory of members who offer expert witness services.

It is difficult to underestimate the importance of a good expert. Time spent in finding one is seldom wasted and it may be worth casting the net overseas. Experts must be both expert in their field and fluent in their written and oral submissions.

In a litigation context, once a court has given a party permission for a named expert in a particular field, it may not be able to change expert or, if it is, it is likely that the court will order that the first expert's report be disclosed.[8]

The considerations for selection include the following:

- Study the expert's CV closely. What makes the expert qualified to opine on the issues at hand? If necessary, check his credentials with the relevant professional body.
- Run internet searches on the proposed expert to ensure that nothing untoward is thrown up – an opponent will be looking for anything which may discredit the expert.
- Does the individual have experience of being an expert witness? Has he given evidence at a hearing and been cross-examined? Check any reported judgments in cases where he has been instructed for any judicial commentary on the quality of the expert evidence.

---

7   See, for example, Article 20(4) of the ICC Rules 1998; Article 25(4) of the ICC Rules 2012; or Article 21.1 of the London Court of International Arbitration Rules 1998.
8   *Beck v Ministry of Defence* [2003] WL 2149042.

- Read any articles he has written. How articulate is he? It is essential that the relevant expert can communicate technical arguments in a way that is accessible to a party's counsel and the judge or tribunal. Even if the expert is the most eminent in his field, it will usually be preferable to opt for an individual who is marginally less well known if he will make a more compelling witness.
- Meet with the proposed expert. How personable is he? How are his presentational skills? He must be able to work as part of a team and not be too pliant or dogmatic. Similarly, an expert who appears too partisan can lack credibility.
- Is he still working? If so, what percentage of his time can he devote to expert witness work? If he is no longer working, can his expertise still be considered sufficiently current?

As with factual witnesses, it is essential that a party ascertain the expert's availability for all of the periods he will be required in the proceedings.

5.2 Managing experts

A number of issues are typically encountered with respect to experts and their evidence, including:

- failure to meet deadlines;
- limited availability to assist when required;
- evidence which is full of technical jargon and lacks clarity;
- evidence which is not sufficiently detailed or analytical; and
- poor performance when giving oral testimony.[9]

These problems can often be addressed by careful selection of the expert at the outset and, crucially, by keeping in regular contact with the expert as the case progresses. While it is not appropriate for lawyers to attempt to persuade an expert to change the substance of his opinions, it is usual for legal teams to advise on the formulation of the expert's report – for example, by ensuring that all relevant issues have been addressed and that it is based on correct factual assumptions. Lawyers will typically also need to work closely with an expert to assist him in drafting his report in language which is accessible to a judge or tribunal, and to ensure that the expert remains focused on his instructions.

Witness familiarisation training can frequently be of assistance for expert witnesses as well as factual witnesses where they have limited experience of the process.

Other useful practice points relate to instructions given to experts during the course of the proceedings. If possible, a party or its legal advisers should ask the expert for an estimate of the time and cost involved before the expert does any work on instructions. Keep a note of all requests to the experts and preferably confirm them in writing, as this information may need to be disclosed.[10] Similarly, a party

---

9   For further information, see S Burn, *Successful Use of Expert Witnesses in Civil Disputes*, Shaw & Sons, 2005.

should ensure that an accurate record of all documents provided to the experts is kept, as this information may need to be disclosed.

5.3 Interdependent or interrelated expert evidence

In the case study, to make out ExploreCo's damages claim, it will need to adduce evidence of the likely volume of oil in the discovery well, its production costs and the commercial returns that it is likely to make over the life of the well. This is likely to require a number of experts in geoscience, production and facilities engineering, petroleum economics and accountancy.

Much of this expert evidence is interrelated, insofar as it will need to be based on the inputs or assumptions provided by the other experts. This is one of the particular challenges of these kinds of energy dispute and is why often, for the more generic expert disciplines, it is helpful from a dispute management perspective to engage an energy consultancy firm to provide and coordinate relevant experts from within its organisation. This allows a party to have one point of contact at the consultancy (who may or may not be instructed as an expert himself) who can:

- advise on the interdependencies and scope of the expert disciplines required by the issues and the party's instructions;
- suggest appropriate experts; and
- assist in coordinating the expert process.

6. Costs management

No one is interested in a pyrrhic victory. Managing a dispute should be approached in the same way as any energy project, with budget control and cost efficiency kept under constant review.

As to budget, a party should ensure that it obtains at the outset of the dispute an estimate of how much the proceedings are likely to cost, including the potential liability for its opponent's costs. This estimate should be broken down according to each stage of the proceedings. This costs profile will also inform the timing of any settlement negotiations (discussed further below).

A party's external legal advisers should have an effective costs monitoring and report system in place. A party should require them to match what was estimated with actual costs as the case progresses, in order to detect at the earliest possible stage when a budget is likely to overrun and take steps to prevent the overrun.

Cost efficiency should to some extent flow from effective planning at the case analysis stage. For example, a developed case analysis will have helped to identify the key issues and avoid wasting costs on developing points which later prove to be ancillary to the case. Similarly, the disclosure exercise is often one of the most costly stages in litigation. If a party searches without having identified the issues properly, this may result in the collection of a large amount of irrelevant material, the review of which will be extremely time consuming and costly. Clearly, keeping the expert

---

10   Instructions given to experts are not privileged from inspection. Further, Civil Procedure Rule 35.10(3) requires the expert to summarise his instructions in his report, both written and oral, on the basis of which the report is prepared.

and factual evidence limited strictly to that which is required to make out a party's case will also avoid wasting costs.

7.   Settlement

Settlement opportunities should be a key part of the overall case strategy and management. Although settlement is highly case specific, there are certain stages of proceedings where settlement is often considered – for example:

- just before or just after disclosure;
- after the exchange of expert reports; or
- before the payment of counsel's brief fees.

That said, opportunities for settlement, like costs, should always be at the forefront of parties' minds. A cost-benefit analysis of continuing to fight the case should be undertaken very early on and continually kept under review, with comparisons made against possible settlement outcomes.

For example, ExploreCo would be advised to engage in 'without prejudice' discussions with the Prospectavian government to determine the attractiveness of the government's proposed revisions to the joint venture agreement terms in light of the following considerations:

- the merits of ExploreCo's case;
- the value of its claim and taxation on any settlement payment;
- ExploreCo's estimated legal spend;
- the cost of its management time devoted to the proceedings; and
- the likelihood of being able to enforce effectively a judgment or award against the Prospectavian government.

Generally, if there is any prospect of settlement, this should be attended to sooner rather than later, when further legal costs will have been incurred. It can sometimes be the case that parties become more entrenched as the proceedings progress, limiting the opportunities for settlement.

8.   Conclusion

The key messages of this chapter are as follows:

- Careful planning at an early stage is crucial. Identify the central issues in the case, the key procedural milestones and what will be required to meet them.
- The disclosure process or document search should be attended to as early as possible and an accurate audit kept of all decisions and the approach taken.
- Factual witness evidence should be strictly limited to that which is required by the issues in dispute. Logistical and practical considerations such as witness availability should not be overlooked.
- Experts should be retained as early as possible and extreme care taken in their selection. Consider how the various expert disciplines might interrelate and how this will affect timelines and the work plan.
- Costs and settlement should be kept under constant review and are an integral part of any management strategy.

Lex petrolea in international law

Tim Martin
adrgovernanceinc

1. Introduction

The term *'lex petrolea'* entered the legal lexicon and the international oil and gas industry more than a quarter of a century ago. The term first emerged in a landmark international arbitration case in 1982, which concluded that the international petroleum industry in its disputes had "generated a customary rule valid for the oil industry – a *lex petrolea* that was in some sort a particular branch of a general universal *lex mercatoria*".[1] In a seminal 1998 article, the thesis was put forth that in the previous 25 years "an increasing number of international arbitral awards relating to the petroleum industry have been published [which] created the beginnings of a real *lex petrolea* that is instructive for the international petroleum industry".[2] A more recent article on the subject updated "all arbitral awards published since 1998 that relate to the international oil and gas exploration and production industry", while furthering the argument that "the published awards relating to the international exploration and production industry have created a *lex petrolea* or customary law comprising legal rules adapted to the industry's nature and specificities".[3] Those two articles primarily relied on a number of published awards from state investment disputes, along with a couple of commercial arbitration awards, to draw their conclusions on the meaning of *'lex petrolea'*.

This analysis supports the thesis that a *lex petrolea* has developed over the years, but widens the scope of inquiry to the full range of disputes encountered in the international petroleum sector. *Lex petrolea* primarily arises from international arbitration and court cases. However, it has also developed in a number of other forums, from governments' petroleum legislation and contracts to the industry's business practices, which are found in its model contracts.

Unlike the courts, the world of international arbitration is not bound by

---

1   *Government of the State of Kuwait v American Independent Oil Co* (AMINOIL), Award of May 24 1982, 21 International Legal Materials (ILM) at 976 (1982). Yearbook IX at 71 (1984). Note that in an article entitled *"L'Intervention de L'Etat en Matiere d'Hydrocarbures en France"* or "The Intervention of the State in the Hydrocarbons Sector in France", published by Professor Claude-Albert Colliard in the *Annals of the Faculty of Law and Economic Sciences of Aix-en-Provence* (Novelle Serie No 52, Annees 1960-1961), Colliard used the term *'petro-droit'* or 'petroleum law', indicating an emerging concept of *lex petrolea* in the international petroleum sector.
2   R Doak Bishop, "International Arbitration of Petroleum Disputes: The Development of a *Lex Petrolea*", XXIII YB Com Arb 1131 (1998).
3   Thomas C Childs, "Update on *Lex Petrolea*: The Continuing Development of Customary Law Relating to International Oil and Gas Exploration and Production", 4:3 J *World Energy Law & Business*, (September 2011), at 214.

precedent[4] – that is, decisions of arbitral tribunals are not binding on other tribunals. However, arbitrators make their decisions in context and not in a vacuum. Counsel use precedent in arguing their cases and arbitrators refer to precedent in writing their awards. The practical result is that precedent is relied on in international arbitration and a *lex petrolea* has developed accordingly.

The worlds of commerce and investment seek out consistency and predictability in making their decisions. So clarifying what *lex petrolea* means and how it is applied is helpful to both the world of international arbitration and the world of international oil and gas, which generates the largest percentage of disputes in both the investment state world[5] and international commercial disputes.[6] Arbitrators attempt to rely on credible sources in determining their arbitral awards. This analysis helps to explain where they can find such sources in deciding international oil and gas arbitration cases.

Lex petrolea is most often established from decisions arising from disputes within the international oil and gas sector, as this is where the contracts, legislation and treaties that affect the petroleum sector are tested and interpreted. Therefore, in order to determine the full extent of *lex petrolea*, the full range of disputes in the international oil and gas business must be considered.

2. Types of dispute

There are essentially four types or categories of dispute found in the international oil and gas sector.[7]

2.1 State versus state disputes

These are primarily boundary disputes concerning oil and gas fields that cross international borders, most of which are located in maritime waters. They involve governments, since only they can claim sovereign title and resolve boundaries with their neighbouring states. However, oil and gas companies sometimes get indirectly involved in these disputes when they are granted concessions that straddle disputed boundary lines.

2.2 Company versus state disputes

These are state investment disputes (sometimes called investor-state disputes). They occur when governments significantly change the terms of the original deal or nationalise (or 'expropriate') an investment. The investor (in this case an oil and gas company or a consortium of oil and gas companies) can base its claim on its

---

4   *Redfern & Hunter on International Arbitration*, Nigel Blackaby and Constantine Partasides (Oxford, 5th Edition, 2009) at paragraphs 1.113, 8.58, 9.195, and 9.212. Courts of first instance in some jurisdictions are not bound by decisions of higher or appellate courts.

5   See ICSID data on state investment disputes at http://icsid.worldbank.org/ICSID/ FrontServlet? requestType=ICSIDDocRH&actionVal=CaseLoadStatistics.

6   See ICC data on international commercial disputes at www.iccwbo.org/court/arbitration/ index.html?id=34704.

7   This categorisation was first used by the author in a primer on international dispute resolution written for the Independent Petroleum Association of America and the Association of International Petroleum Negotiators in 2011, which was subsequently published as: "Dispute Resolution in the International Energy Sector: an Overview", 4:4 *J World Energy Law & Business*, pp. 332-368 (December 2011).

investment contract (either a production sharing contract or risk service agreement) or an investment treaty, or possibly both. Most treaty claims are now made under bilateral investment treaties (BITs), and some under a multilateral treaty such as the Energy Charter. These are the disputes on which the two *lex petrolea* articles primarily based their analysis.

2.3 Company versus company disputes

These are international commercial disputes arising out of oil and gas contracts. There are two subcategories of dispute occurring between energy companies. The first is between holders of interests in oil and gas concessions such as joint venture participants or buyers and sellers of such interests or the production from such interests. They are found in agreements such as:

- confidentiality agreements;
- joint operating agreements (JOAs);
- unitisation agreements;
- farm-out agreements;
- area of mutual interest agreements;
- study and bid agreements; and
- sale and purchase agreements.

The second subcategory is disputes between operators and service contractors for providing services or equipment in the following kinds of agreement:

- drilling and well service agreements;
- seismic contracts;
- construction contracts;
- equipment and facilities contracts; and
- transportation and processing contracts.

They make up the majority of disputes in which oil and gas companies find themselves. Such disputes are primarily resolved in arbitration rather than in the courts in the international oil and gas business.

2.4 Individual versus company disputes

There are a number of situations where individuals initiate claims against oil and gas companies. The first is when an individual suffers a personal injury and begins a tort claim against a company. This is common in US jurisdictions, but increasingly happens in other countries. A second area of individual claims arises from human rights or environmental claims. These are sometimes filed in US courts using the Alien Tort Statute or in other jurisdictions using a variety of innovative legal mechanisms.[8] The third group of claims by individuals arises when promoters of oil and gas deals claim that they have an interest in a host government contract and the accompanying joint operating agreement as a result of a third-party tortious action

---

8   See Jonathan Drimmer, "Human Rights and the Extractive Industries: Litigation and Compliance Trends", 3:2 *J World Energy Law & Business* (July 2010) for more details on these claims worldwide.

or by way of agreement. The final group of claims concerns agents or consultants who demand payment under their agent agreements for winning a government contract for a company. There has been a series of arbitrations over the last 50 years where companies have refused to pay their agent based on corruption allegations after securing the host government contract.[9]

3.   Boundary disputes

"Because of the many undelimited maritime boundaries across the globe, international oil and gas exploration and production companies will often encounter boundary-related uncertainty as they enter new exploration areas."[10] As a result, boundary disputes between sovereign states form part of the body of *lex petrolea* that affects the world of international oil and gas. Boundary disputes clearly fall within the area of international public law. But it "is a somewhat esoteric activity and the number of true experts in the field is quite small".[11] That activity and that expertise often revolve around oil and gas operations.

Both land and maritime boundary disputes can involve control over natural resources, but the greatest number occur in the world's oceans and seas. The primary source of law for delimiting maritime boundaries is the United Nations Convention on the Law of the Sea (UNCLOS). Most of the world's states have ratified it and many of its provisions are now considered to be customary international law.

The primary forums for the binding resolution of international boundary disputes are:

- the International Court of Justice (ICJ) in The Hague, established under the Charter of the United Nations in 1945;
- the International Tribunal for the Law of the Sea (ITLOS) in Hamburg, established under UNCLOS in 1996; and
- *ad hoc* arbitration tribunals.

The ICJ has issued more than a dozen boundary awards and at the time of writing ITLOS has one boundary case pending. States involved in *ad hoc* arbitrations usually keep the results confidential. The awards from these cases interpret the customary international law around the delimitation of sovereign boundaries.

There is now sufficient jurisprudence in this area to provide some certainty around delimiting a boundary. However, both states and tribunals have sometimes been creative in establishing boundaries, so boundary delimitation is still as much an art as a science.[12]

There is an extensive body of boundaries literature. The most comprehensive study of international maritime boundaries and the relevant law is the American Society of International Law's *International Maritime Boundaries*.[13] An excellent

---

9   See Tim Martin, *International Arbitration and Corruption: An Evolving Standard*, 20th Annual Institute for Transnational Arbitration (June, 2009), available at www.timmartin.ca/qualifications/ publications.
10   Derek Smith and Martin Pratt, *How To Deal With Maritime Boundary Uncertainty In Oil And Gas Exploration And Production Areas*, 25 (AIPN, 2007), available at www.aipn.org.
11   *Id* at 31.
12   *Id* at 15.
13   *International Maritime Boundaries* Vols I-V, Martinus Nijhoff.

introduction to understanding how international boundaries are established and their impact on oil and gas companies is *How to Deal with Maritime Boundary Uncertainty in Oil and Gas Exploration and Production Areas*, published by the Association of International Petroleum Negotiators (AIPN).[14]

4. State investment disputes

Most of the published arbitration awards that have established a *lex petrolea* arise out of state investment disputes. Given their public nature and the rules of institutions such as the International Centre for Settlement and Investment Disputes (ICSID), those awards are usually published and made available in the public domain. These are the cases relied on by the two articles on *lex petrolea* by Doak Bishop and Tom Childs respectively. What is striking about those cases is that not only have they established a *lex petrolea*, but on a larger scale they have established the customary international law for dealings between states and private investors. This is because the oil and gas business has historically been one of the largest and most active global industries. The industry invests in very large, complex and capital-intensive projects with long lifespans. People, companies, governments and circumstances invariably change in such projects, and misunderstandings arise that often result in disputes. Hence the significant impact of *lex petrolea* on state investment disputes.

The impact of the early cases described in the first *lex petrolea* article has influenced the behaviour of both investors and governments in the post-1998 cases described in the second article. Most of the post-1998 awards arose from BIT claims. There were none prior to 1998. Only one award since 1998 deals with the nationalisation or expropriation of assets, whereas many of the pre-1998 awards are about this issue. Many of the post-1998 awards deal with claims relating to changes in the host state's fiscal regime (ie, creeping expropriation). In contrast, none of the pre-1998 awards addressed such claims.[15] Some of the highlights and observations on *lex petrolea* that flow from these state investment disputes follow.

4.1 Expropriation

States have the right to expropriate investments. However, in doing so, states must compensate the investor. It is only unlawful "if it is discriminatory, it is not motivated by the public interest of the expropriating country, it breaches stabilization clauses of the parties' contract, or if no compensation is paid, offered or other provision for it made. The modern effect of such illegality, however, is merely to permit an award of additional compensation".[16] The result under *lex petrolea* and customary international law is that once expropriation has been established, the only issue remaining is how to calculate properly the compensation to the investor.

4.2 Duress

The defence of duress is not effective in most creeping expropriation cases: "In the

---

14   Available at www.aipn.org.
15   Childs, *supra* note 3, at 215.
16   Bishop, *supra* note 2, at 1156 and 1158.

absence of a written record of reservations of rights, protests or a lack of consent, this claim is seldom given much credence."[17] Therefore, the best legal course for an investor that is suffering creeping expropriation is to establish a clear written trail of protests that it can point to in its arbitration with the state. Unfortunately, as a practical matter, this is often not a viable formula for working successfully on an ongoing basis with a government and its officials.

4.3 Force majeure

Force majeure clauses in an investment contract can be effective. Tribunals have held that *"force majeure* is a general principle of law that may be applied even if the contract is silent on the point".[18] However, these clauses cannot be taken for granted. Much will turn on the wording of the *force majeure* clause and the circumstances in which *force majeure* is invoked. Negotiators of host government contracts must therefore pay a lot of attention to what is included (or not included) in a *force majeure* clause.

4.4 Transfer of interest

Failure to obtain required government approvals on transfers of interest can result in termination of a host government contract. This risk can occur even when an oil company attempts to bifurcate the title and claim that no 'legal' title was transferred and thus prior government approval was not required.[19] This may be an acceptable practice in some domestic jurisdictions, but not in many international operations: "Even though bifurcation of title is regularly used in farmout agreements in North America where it is legally recognized and valid, that is not always the case in international farmout agreements in other parts of the world. If the HGC or hydrocarbon law does not recognize the bifurcation of title and requires prior government approval of a title transfer in the HGC to a third party, there is significant risk in not obtaining prior written government approval to a farmout agreement and the bifurcation and transfer of title."[20]

There are policy reasons around this risk. The control and development of natural resources are important to petroleum producing countries. One of the primary means that such countries control how their natural resources are developed is by approving which international oil companies (IOCs) are allowed to acquire an interest in their host government contracts. As a result, failure to obtain the prior authorisation of the designated ministry to the transfer of any interest in the host government contract may result in its termination and a potential state investment dispute with significant downside for the investor.

---

17   *Id* at 1164.
18   *Id* at 1168.
19   *Occidental Petroleum Corporation v Republic of Ecuador*, ICSID Case ARB/06/11, Decision on Provisional Measures, August 17 2007, paragraphs 9-24, 62-97.
20   Tim Martin, "Bifurcation of Title in International Oil and Gas Agreements", *A Liber Amicorum: Thomas Wälde*, 182 (J Werner & A Ali eds, Cameron May, 2009).

4.5   Remedies

(a)   Specific performance

Investors should not count on the remedy of specific performance in seeking to enforce their host government contracts. With one notable exception, international arbitration tribunals have consistently awarded damages rather than specific performance after determining that there has been an expropriation. That exception is *TOPCO v Libya*.[21] The sole arbitrator in that case "found that *restitutio in integrum* is an appropriate remedy under the Libyan Civil Code and Muslim law, and cited the *Chorzow Factory* case as applying the rule of *restitutio in integrum*".[22] Unfortunately for TOPCO, Colonel Gaddafi and his regime ignored the arbitrator's award that granted it specific performance and never did allow the company back into the country to perform its contract.

International tribunals have continued to take this approach as shown in recent cases. In *Al-Bahloul v Tajikistan* the tribunal denied the claimant's request that it order specific performance of Tajikistan's obligation under the Energy Charter Treaty's umbrella clause to issue exclusive exploration licences to the claimant because it would be materially impossible to implement a remedy of specific performance.[23] A tribunal denied Occidental Petroleum's request for provisional measures for specific performance of its contract, which Ecuador had terminated by declaring a '*caducidad*' on the grounds that Occidental had no right to specific performance under international law.[24] In another case, Argentine company Bridas Petroleum requested specific performance of its joint venture agreement with Turkmengeologia, a Turkmenian state company, but subsequently withdrew it.[25] The tribunal stated that it considered this a "wise" decision because it was unrealistic to assume either that Turkmengeologia would obey the tribunal's order of specific performance or that a national court having personal jurisdiction over it would enforce the order.

(b)   Damages

There are a number of approaches to calculate damages in any dispute, including asset-based, income-based and market-based approaches. Tribunals have considered and used many of them, such as net book value, discounted cash flow (DCF), going-concern value and liquidation value. Where more speculative assumptions are used in the calculations, tribunals become less comfortable with and unwilling to consider them. Tribunals are comfortable in awarding out-of-pocket costs and losses to investors. They are not so comfortable in awarding lost profits, even when the claimant cloaks them in creative ways.[26]

---

21   *Texaco Overseas Petroleum Co (TOPCO) v Government of the Libyan Arab Republic*, Award of January 19 1977, 17 ILM (1978) p 3, Yearbook IV (1979) p 177.
22   Bishop, *supra* note 2, at 1173.
23   *Mohammad Ammar Al-Bahloul v Republic of Tajikistan*, SCC Case No V (064/2008), Final Award, June 8 2010, paragraphs 35, 45-63.
24   Occidental *supra* note 20, at paragraphs 20-32, 75-94.
25   *Joint Venture Yashlar v Government of Turkmenistan*, ICC Arbitration Case No 9151, Interim Award, June 8 1999, paragraphs 538-40.
26   Bishop, *supra* note 2, at 1175 & 1176.

The DCF method is probably the most controversial valuation methodology. Investors rely on it in their preliminary investment decisions and their subsequent investment claims since they expect growth and profits in their investment. States often reject it because they consider the valuation method to be speculative and that any potential gains should stay with the ultimate owner of the resource (ie, the state). Some tribunals have accepted the DCF method of calculating value, "provided that the claimant could establish a likelihood of future lost profits with sufficient certainty".[27] Claims made on assets that are expropriated at the exploration stage where there is uncertain geology, questionable financing, no proven reserves, no production and no established revenue stream will have difficulty convincing a tribunal to apply the DCF methodology. Despite the uncertainty in the upstream petroleum sector, at least one tribunal has been willing to use a 'risk economics' methodology and awarded some value to an exploratory concession based on a dry well that provided information about the potential of the subsurface geology.[28]

5. Commercial disputes

The sources for determining the *lex petrolea* arising from commercial disputes in the international oil and gas business are different from those arising from state investment disputes. Most of the publicly available case law that interprets commercial oil and gas agreements comes from US (primarily Texas), Canadian (primarily Alberta) and English courts. Those cases deal with disputes arising from oil and gas operations in their own domestic jurisdictions. Oil and gas domestic operations and their agreements can vary significantly from the international industry's business practices and agreements, which are illustrated in the analysis provided below on JOAs and farm-out agreements. Therefore, domestic oil and gas case law often falls short in establishing a relevant *lex petrolea* for the international oil and gas business.

Disputes that arise from international oil and gas agreements are mostly decided by international arbitration tribunals, which reflect the dispute resolution forums chosen in those agreements.[29] Those decisions are usually not publicly available because of the confidentiality requirements under the applicable dispute resolution clauses. Since international commercial arbitration awards are invariably not publicly available and domestic oil and gas cases usually deal with very different kinds of operation and agreement, the best way of determining the *lex petrolea* of international oil and gas commercial agreements is by referencing the industry's business practices, which are captured in its model contracts.

---

27   Childs, *supra* note 3, at 253.
28   *Bettis Group Inc v Profco Resources Ltd*, AAA Case No 77-T-168-00228-98, Award, September 9 2000, at 13-14, available at LEXIS, 18-3 *Mealey's Int'l Arb Rep* 3 (2003).
29   The 2002 AIPN Model JOA drafting committee sent a list of questions to all AIPN members asking them how they used the existing JOA and what revisions would be most beneficial. The survey confirmed that few disputes arose under the 1995 model JOA, that international arbitration was the preferred forum and that English law was widely chosen (with Texas and New York law being chosen less often than was once thought). See Philip Weems and Michael Bolton, "Highlights of Key Revisions – 2002 AIPN Model Form International Operating Agreement" 6 *Int'l Energy L & Tax'n Rev* (2003) 169, 171. The result was that the 2002 AIPN Model JOA did not provide for litigation as a binding mechanism in its dispute resolution clause, but only international arbitration. This approach was continued in the 2012 AIPN Model JOA.

The international petroleum industry uses model contracts extensively in its transactions and operations.[30] They are developed and published by petroleum industry associations. Parties regularly use and accept model contracts in the negotiation and drafting of their agreements. Model contracts that are widely used contain clauses that reflect industry practice and commonly accepted terms.[31] Model contracts standardise the terms governing certain common types of agreement used in the petroleum business.[32] They are drafted to be flexible enough to allow the parties to pick and choose the alternatives and options that work best for them: "With the acceptance of a particular model contract, it becomes widely used as the industry standard. The result is that transactions are drafted and handled more consistently and it is easier for parties to understand how they have addressed key issues in their contracts. With increased consistency and understanding, parties inherently reduce potential grounds for dispute and, therefore, their litigation risk."[33]

5.1 Joint operating agreements

The most significant and long-term contract used among oil and gas companies in the upstream oil and gas business is the JOA. It sets out the fundamental and overarching relationships in a joint venture consortium, from the initial exploration to the ultimate production of hydrocarbons. A leading textbook on international petroleum transactions describes the primary purposes of an international JOA: "Each international JOA has two main functions. The first is to establish the basis for sharing rights and liabilities among the parties. In most cases, these will be shared in proportion to the interests of the participants in an operation. The second is to provide for the manner in which operations will be conducted by a designated operator subject to the supervision of an operating committee comprised of one representative from each party to the JOA."[34]

The evolution of JOAs in North America has been different from that in the international oil and gas business for a number of fundamental reasons: "The oil and gas operating agreement has evolved as an industry-wide document over several decades. The widespread need for it in United States onshore operations has resulted in the development of a relatively uniform agreement for domestic activities. However, as the complexity and size of the operation increases, as in the case of offshore and international exploration and production, modifications in standard terms of the onshore agreement become necessary. Domestic offshore and international JOAs are not only more detailed and significantly different from onshore counterparts but exhibit important variations from transaction to transaction."[35]

---

30   Tim Martin and J Jay Park, "Global Petroleum Industry Model Contracts Revisited: Higher, Faster, Stronger", 3:1 *J World Energy Law & Business* 6 (March 2010).
31   Tim Martin, "Model Contracts: a Survey of the Global Petroleum Industry", 22:3 *J Energy & Nat Resources* L284 (2004).
32   Martin and Park, *supra* note 30, at 4.
33   Martin, *supra* note 31, at 284.
34   Bruce M Kramer and Gary B Conine, *Joint Development and Operations in International Petroleum Transactions* 561 (2nd edn, Ernest E Smith *et al* eds, Rocky Mountain Mineral Law Foundation 2000).
35   Kramer and Conine, *supra* note 34, at 561-2.

Onshore domestic operations are relatively simple and straightforward. It is a less diverse and complicated operating environment. Operators usually conduct one operation at a time – for example, shooting seismic or drilling a well – by issuing an authority for expenditure that non-operators sign allowing the operator to carry out that particular operation without further ado. Parties delegate broad authority to an operator in onshore North American operations. The result is a relatively simple and uniform agreement for domestic activities.[36]

International projects are larger in scale and more technically difficult than most domestic operations, located in places where there may be very little infrastructure and lengthy logistical chains. Operators of international JOAs do not have broad discretion and do not make unilateral decisions on their own that bind non-operators. Instead, international JOAs provide for a management committee that exercises authority and control over operations. Management committees review and approve each item. The result is a more diverse and complex agreement.[37]

As a result, international oil and gas operations and their agreements are very different from agreements in domestic oil and gas operations.[38] Domestic US and Canadian onshore model JOAs[39] contain a limited number of elections, whereas the AIPN international model operating agreement[40] has many.

There is a limited number of published arbitration awards dealing with international JOAs or similar agreements. *ICC Case 11663*[41] involved three parties that had a shared management agreement (SMA) and participation agreement for a production sharing agreement. The SMA provided for the sharing of costs and expenses and required that if a party was in default for more than 60 days after receiving a default notice, it had to forfeit and assign its participating interest to the non-defaulting party on the request of that party. One of the parties consistently failed to pay its share of cash calls. The other two parties served it with a default notice and demanded that it assign its interest to them. The tribunal found that it was a "fundamental principle" of the SMA that each party must pay its share of cost and expenses under such an agreement and issued a declaration that the non-paying party had forfeited its participating interest in the project.[42] It found that this was consistent with standard practice in the oil and gas industry, as demonstrated by the AIPN model international JOA, which contained an alternative clause similar to what was in the SMA.

36   Andrew B Derman and James Barnes, *Inst on Oil and Gas Agreements, Autonomy versus Alliance: An Examination of the Management and Control Provisions of Joint Operating Agreements* (Rocky Mt Min L Fdn, 1996), §4.03 at 10.

37   Kramer and Conine, *supra* note 34, at 564.

38   Michael D Josephson, "How Far Does the CAPL Travel? A Comparative Overview of the CAPL Model Form Operating Procedure and the AIPN Model Form International Operating Agreement", (2003) 41(1) *Alta L Rev* 1, 3.

39   See the American Association of Petroleum Landmen (AAPL) (www.landman.org) for the Onshore JOA 610 and the Offshore JOAs (Shelf 710 and Deep 810), which are the standards for the US oil and gas industry, and the Canadian Association of Petroleum Landmen (CAPL) (www.landman.ca) for the CAPL Operating Procedure, which is the Canadian oil and gas standard.

40   See Model International Operating Agreement published by the AIPN at www.aipn.org, which is the standard used in the international oil and gas industry.

41   ICC Case 11663 of 2003, Final Award on Jurisdiction, in XXXII Y.B. COM ARB 60 (2007).

42   *Id* paragraphs 7-15.

In addition, the tribunal found that the management committee had the right to remove the operator and replace it with another party if it was in material breach of any of the parties' agreements. In this case, the non-paying party was also the operator and failed to provide a timely letter of credit to the ministry.[43] This case supports the ability of management committees to carry out their responsibilities under industry operating agreements. It also illustrates that tribunals are prepared to grant requests for specific performance (in this case, forfeiture and assignment of a JOA interest) in commercial disputes where damages are an inadequate remedy.[44] Based on this case, it can be concluded that a party that fails to pay its share of project costs and expenses can result in its default of a JOA and an obligation to forfeit and assign its participating interest to the other party(s) that pays the defaulting party's share.

5.2   Farm-out agreements

International oil companies will often raise capital for exploration work programmes by funding joint venturers through a farm-out. This helps them to spread both the risk and the cost associated with exploration. Farm-outs are usually structured in one of two ways with regard to when a farmor assigns a part of its interest to the farmee: "Farmout agreements traditionally have taken the form either of an agreement to convey or a conditional assignment. The essential difference in the two is the point in time when the farmee acquires an interest in the farmed out property. When the farmout is in the form of an agreement to convey, the farmee obtains its rights only if it performs the conditions made prerequisite by the contract. When the farmout is in the form of a conditional assignment, the farmee obtains an interest in the farmed out property when the agreement is made, subject to an obligation to reconvey or to automatic termination if the conditions subsequent are not performed."[45]

Traditionally, the term 'farm-out' is applied to a 'drill to earn' arrangement. What usually happens in the North American oil and gas industry is that the farmee in its own capacity undertakes either to shoot seismic or to drill a well or several wells (or both) on the farmor's oil and gas lease. Once the farmee completes that undertaking, it has earned its interest in that oil and gas lease. The farmee usually continues to operate that lease, rather than the farmor resuming its former operator role. These types of arrangement are relatively straightforward in North American operations, where the land registry systems are efficient and government approval is not required for the transfer of mineral rights. The international oil and gas industry also uses the term 'farm-out', but the mechanics of the transaction are handled differently. Quite often, the farmee agrees to provide the funds to the farmor so that the farmor can carry out the agreed-upon operations, while the farmee retains the ability to approve or not approve what the operator (ie, the farmor) does. This reflects the legal, political and operational challenges encountered in the international oil and gas business. Failure to take these differences into account can result in the kinds of dispute described in the *Occidental* case referenced above.

---

43   *Id* paragraphs 48-56.
44   *Id* paragraphs 69-72.
45   John S Lowe, *Analyzing Oil and Gas Farmout Agreements*, 41 Sw LJ 759, 796 (1987).

5.3   *Lex petrolea* in international oil and gas commercial disputes

Only a few jurisdictions (most of which are listed above) have a developed and sophisticated oil and gas jurisprudence. Most jurisdictions in which international oil and gas operations are conducted have little or no such jurisprudence. As shown in the above examples of JOAs and farm-out agreements, the agreements used in the international oil and gas business are quite different from those used in the domestic oil and gas business. This makes any reference to domestic oil and gas cases (even from well-developed oil and gas law jurisdictions) quite limited in understanding how international commercial oil and gas agreements work and what they mean. International commercial arbitration awards are also often little help in establishing a *lex petrolea*, given the scarcity of such published awards. Therefore, the determination of the *lex petrolea* of international oil and gas agreements and the disputes arising therefrom is primarily found in the industry's business practices, which are recorded in the model contracts and the guidance notes, commentary and research arising from such models. The manner in which the industry develops its model contracts is the most thorough, documented and peer-reviewed process for international oil and gas agreements and thus the most credible source of *lex petrolea* for such agreements.[46]

There is a series of steps (as appropriate) that arbitrators can take in determining the correct interpretation of international commercial oil and gas agreements being disputed and the *lex petrolea*. Similar to any contractual dispute, arbitrators must first look to the contract itself and what it has to say. However, the disputing parties usually have different interpretations of the same language because of some ambiguity, unexpected event or unique circumstance, which often leaves this initial inquiry short in definitive conclusions.

Arbitrators can then consider the choice of law in the contract and its general principles of contract interpretation. The common law usually requires that the contract be honoured as written and that adjudicators keep their inquiry within the "four corners of the contract", even if there is an unfair result. The civil law is generally concerned that the contract is fair to all parties and is performed in good faith. *Sharia* law, similar to the common law, uses precedent and strictly interprets contracts as written. But, as required by the Koran, *Sharia* prohibits practices such as *ribat* (interest/usury) and *gharar* (speculation on uncertainty). While common law, civil law and *Sharia* law jurisdictions share many similarities within their respective systems, due to the possibility of varying solutions to the same issue found in different countries, one must consider the specific governing law in an oil and gas contract to determine whether there are any relevant precedents or principles.

Arbitrators should next look at the facts of each particular case, which is where many of these cases are determined. Consideration must be given to relevant case law, keeping in mind the limitations of domestic oil and gas case law and the dearth of published international commercial arbitration awards. Arbitrators should then turn to industry practice to confirm how these agreements are used and interpreted. The primary source of determining such business practices in the oil and gas industry

---

46   Martin, *supra* note 31, at 284.

is its model contracts. The model contracts developed and published by the AIPN are the main source for confirming business practices in the international oil and gas business.

6.   Individual and non-governmental organisation disputes

A body of *lex petrolea* has developed over the past two decades where individuals and groups, including non-governmental organisations and plaintiff lawyers who represent them, have pursued international oil and gas companies in US and other courts around the world on charges of human rights and environmental violations. One of the largest and most spectacular cases is the *Lago Agrio* case against Chevron. This long-running case has been fought in multiple forums, including international arbitration tribunals and US, European and Ecuadorian courts. It arose from the operations of Texaco (which was acquired by Chevron in 2001) in the Lago Agrio area of the Oriente region of Ecuador between 1964 and 1990. The plaintiffs, who are native Indians, allege that Texaco dumped toxins into the water supply that resulted in the destruction of the local rainforest and physical harm to the indigenous people. In February 2011 a judge in Sucumbios Province, Ecuador, delivered a judgment of \$18.2 billion against Chevron. The native Indians are represented by a group of US plaintiff lawyers who are financed by publicly traded investment funds.[47] There have been subsequent legal actions by Chevron in the US and European courts against the lead plaintiffs' lawyers alleging fraud, intimidation of judges, fabricated evidence and criminal collusion. At the time of writing, the case is still unresolved, even though Chevron has recently been successful on several claims dating back to 1991 in a United Nations Commission on International Trade Law dispute administered by the Permanent Court of Arbitration in The Hague.[48]

The majority of human rights cases have been brought in the United States under the Alien Tort Statute. However, there is an increasing trend of such cases being brought in other domestic courts around the world, such as Ecuador, Colombia and Australia; and before international bodies, such as the committees responsible for the following UN conventions:

- the Torture Convention;
- the Optional Protocol to the International Covenant on Civil and Political Rights; and
- the Convention on the Elimination of All Forms of Discrimination against Women.

Other tribunals responsible for regional conventions are getting involved in similar human rights charges, such as:

- the Convention for the Protection of Human Rights and Fundamental Freedoms, enforced by the European Court of Human Rights;

---

47   Roger Parloff, "Have You Got a Piece of this Lawsuit? The Bitter Environmental Suit Against Chevron in Ecuador Opens a Window on a Troubling New Business: Speculating in Court Cases", 163:8 *Fortune* (June 13 2011) 69.

48   www.chevron.com/chevron/pressreleases/article/08312011_chevronawarded96millioninarbitration claimagainstthegovernmentofecuador.news.

- the American Convention on Human Rights, enforced by the Inter-American Commission; and
- the African Charter on Human and Peoples' Rights, enforced by the African Commission.[49]

Oil and gas companies will likely see a continuing increase in these cases in multiple forums. They therefore need to be aware of developments in this particular area of *lex petrolea* in order to manage their risks properly.

7.   Conclusion

Lex petrolea covers a wide area of international law, given the size and significance of the industry. It can be viewed either as the application of international law to the petroleum sector or as a specific legal regime that has evolved to meet the particular needs of the international oil and gas sector – or as both.

The growing development of *lex petrolea* in areas such as boundary disputes, human rights and environmental claims is more akin to the former – that is, the application of international law to the petroleum sector; whereas the areas of international commercial disputes and state investment disputes are more the latter – that is, a customary law of the international petroleum sector that has been adapted to the industry's nature and specificities. No matter what the view adopted, *lex petrolea* has clearly affected a great deal of international public and private law as we know it today. It is also a law that directly impacts on oil and gas disputes around the world and, subsequently, on how companies and governments conduct their oil and gas operations.

---

49   Drimmer, *supra* note 8, at 133.

Contract pricing disputes

Ted Greeno
Caroline Kehoe
Herbert Smith LLP

---

1. Introduction

Contract pricing disputes in the energy industries typically arise in the context of long-term contracts under which an initial price agreed by the parties must be adjusted over the life of the contract to reflect changes in the underlying market price or prices for the product. Where there is a readily ascertainable market index against which such an initial price can be tracked, problems rarely arise, unless that index itself is discontinued or for some reason ceases to be relevant due to structural changes in the relevant market. However, as market indices for the price of gas or LNG in many end-user markets have not traditionally been available, it has been necessary for price formulae under gas and LNG supply contracts to resort to tracking the prices of other competing fuels on the assumption that fluctuations in these prices will themselves reflect the market price for gas, albeit in an imperfect way. In seeking to anticipate events, and also to balance the interests of buyer and seller following negotiation, such formulae are inevitably complex and prone to controversy as to how they were intended to work when the assumptions on which they were based (which may not have been shared) change over time.

1.1 The gas and LNG markets

Historically, producers have sold gas under long-term sale and purchase agreements (SPAs) either for the lifetime of the field or for a fixed period of up to 20 years. The price formulae used to determine the price over this period applied a multiplier to an initial fixed price with a view to escalating the price over time in line with changes in a weighted average of published prices of an agreed selection of other fuels over the contract year and often also annual inflation. In the United Kingdom, such fuels typically included one or more of electricity, fuel oil, gas oil and sometimes coal. In other parts of the world, notably continental Europe, prices were escalated by reference to crude oil prices, usually Brent. The reason for indexing against other fuels was that there was little or no gas to gas competition in end-user markets, which were dominated by state-owned utilities. In the absence of market competition, there was no published 'market price' for gas against which the sale price of the gas to be supplied could be indexed.

As a result of the liberalisation of key gas markets in Europe and the development of an international trading market in LNG, the position has now changed significantly. Markets are now interconnected, although pricing can be significantly different in end-user markets depending on whether there is an active trading and spot market and whether the particular market where the gas is sold is still a relatively isolated market.

We are now in a period of significant price volatility. Since the global economic downturn in 2008, benchmark oil prices have remained significantly higher than they were when many SPAs were entered into. However, gas prices in end-user markets have fallen as a result of reduced demand, as well as increased supply from new sources, including unconventional gas, and the development of spot markets in which gas trades significantly below long-term prices. The consequence is that prices linked to oil based prices under many long-term SPAs have not tracked market prices for gas in end-user markets.

1.2 Long-term SPAs and pricing formulae

Long-term take-or-pay agreements which require the buyer to take delivery of a minimum quantity, or pay in any event, continue to be the standard in the industry. As their pricing provisions endure for the life of the contract, it is essential that they accommodate the competing interests of buyer and seller for them to remain viable in the long term. The seller will generally have to make a significant capital investment and will therefore seek a secure and guaranteed income stream from sales to underwrite the cost and provide an acceptable return on investment. Over and above that, the seller will also want a price which reflects an increase in the value of the gas in the market and so maximises that return. The buyer, on the other hand, commits to taking or paying for defined volumes of the gas and so will be concerned to ensure that it will be able to sell it, or convert it into power, at a price which will give it the maximum possible profit margin and avoid a loss.

Although these are the traditional motivations of buyers and sellers, there is an obvious tension between the two and buyer and seller will negotiate hard for a formula which they believe will favour their long-term interests.

Most long-term energy supply contracts also contain provisions to allow the parties to reset or renegotiate the contract price either at regular intervals or on the occurrence of a particular event or circumstance. These take two forms: indexation and price reopener clauses.

Indexation clauses are designed to adjust the contract price annually by the automatic application of the price formula. As noted above, such formulae operate to apply a multiplier to an initial price by reference to a basket of alternative fuel indices, or crude oil, and possibly inflation. The multiplier is calculated as a fraction in which the denominator represents the alternative fuel prices at an initial point in time and the numerator reflects alternative fuel prices over a recent review period. The multiplier therefore represents the relative increase in the price of the alternative fuels since the base period. The calculation is therefore as follows:

$$\text{Contract price} = \text{Initial fixed price} \times \frac{\text{Value of alternative fuel(s) in the review period*}}{\text{Value of alternative fuel(s) in the base period*}}$$

An inflation index may also be applicable

Some pricing provisions adopt two formulae so as to limit the upward or downward effect of price movements. These are known as 'top-stop' or 'bottom-stop' formulae. Alternatively, LNG contracts which escalate the gas price against movements in crude oil often provide for a maximum and minimum oil price to be used. This type of formula, often described as an 'S-curve', breaks the linear relationship between the contract price and a nominated fuel price into three separate relationships so that, effectively, three different formulae apply depending on the level of that particular fuel price. For example, different formulae might apply when the crude oil price is below $x per barrel, when it is between $x and $y per barrel and when it is above $z per barrel. The price will decrease more slowly below $y per barrel and increase more slowly above $z per barrel (the 'inflexion points' or 'pivot points' in the price formula). S-curves are attractive to a buyer because the price rises more slowly above the upper pivot point, which helps to maintain the buyer's onsale margin when the nominated fuel price is high. Equally, they are attractive to a seller because the slower decrease in the price below the lower pivot point will provide comfort to the seller that its revenues will be maintained and it will be able to meet its debts and operating costs even when the nominated fuel price is low.

Potential disputes will arise if changes are made to some element of an index used in the formula or if it ceases to exist, and these clauses will generally include provisions specifying how and on what basis the parties should seek to agree either to amend or replace the index or, in default of agreement, to refer to the issue to expert determination or arbitration. The wording of such provisions can vary widely and, of course, their meaning and effect can also vary depending on their proper construction.

Price reopener clauses oblige the parties to review price when circumstances change (the 'trigger event') and set parameters for that review. They are often drafted in general and open terms which give little guidance as to what changes constitute a trigger event, how value is to be measured or how the price formula should be revised to reflect changes. This lack of particularity is often intentional so as to allow, as far as possible, for future unforeseen or unpredictable events and address any situation which may arise over the life of the contract. The corollary, however, is that they are often open to interpretation when unforeseen events do arise, leading to disputes as to their meaning and to the relevance or application of underlying market and other factual data.

The financial implications of the outcome of a pricing dispute are usually significant.

Complex price reopener disputes are now more frequent and an increasing number are being taken to arbitration. Typical areas of dispute and uncertainty (which we deal with further below) tend to fall into four categories, concerning:

- whether the trigger event has arisen (or is necessary);
- the definition of the 'comparator' or relevant market and the analysis of the relevant change;
- the methodology for revising the price; and
- the scope of the revisions which the expert or arbitral tribunal can make.

2. Forms of dispute resolution

It is highly unusual for the parties to choose to resolve disputes by litigation in the national courts. Such disputes are by their nature multinational and frequently involve nationally strategic issues which are more suitable for determination either by arbitration or by expert determination. However, there may be scope in some cases for at least the issue of whether a trigger event has occurred to be referred to the courts if the clause is drafted (often inadvertently) in such a way as not to confer jurisdiction on the expert or arbitrator to decide this threshold issue.

2.1 Expert determination

Expert determination is a flexible, confidential dispute resolution procedure that is binding by agreement. It can be highly effective where, at the contracting stage, the parties anticipate a specific type of technical dispute arising in which the expertise of the decision maker is considered to be a critical part of the dispute resolution process. It is also a less adversarial form of dispute resolution and therefore appropriate for a long-term contract where the parties will have an ongoing commercial relationship. It was therefore common to refer indexation disputes to expert determination.

Given the very specific reason why the parties have chosen to refer the dispute to an expert, such expert determination clauses may require the expert to have specific technical or industry experience in the particular subject matter of the dispute. This will normally make agreement on the identity of the expert easier, as it avoids a divergence of opinion between the parties at the time the dispute arises as to the particular expertise required.

Expert determination is occasionally undertaken on a non-binding basis. However, this carries with it a real risk of polarising the positions of the disputing parties, wasting time and costs if either or both parties choose not to be bound by the determination. A further disadvantage is that the primary issue in dispute is often the interpretation of the clause and, if the expert is technically rather than legally qualified, the outcome will be less predictable.

The appointment of the expert, his terms of reference and powers will be governed by agreement between the disputing parties. Many expert determination clauses in long-term contracts do not contain detailed provisions as to the process and usually the parties will draw up separate agreements after the dispute has arisen to appoint the expert (the terms of engagement) and then to set out the agreed procedure in the terms of reference.

2.2 Arbitration

It is rare for price review disputes to be referred to expert determination. Such disputes tend to be under SPAs between parties from different countries, so giving rise to enforcement issues, and where expert determination is not an established method of dispute resolution. Arbitration is also a more formal and regulated method and better suited to resolving legal rather than purely technical issues.

Arbitration offers neutrality and autonomy to the parties in their choice of procedure (institutional or *ad hoc*), of place (so as to ensure a jurisdiction favourable to arbitration) and of arbitrators (to ensure that they have the right qualifications and background). It also provides the comfort of enabling the parties to select a country which is a party to the New York Convention in order to ensure that the award can be enforced.

Although desirable, arbitrators will not necessarily have specialised knowledge of the relevant gas or LNG markets or of pricing mechanisms and practice in the industry. One frequent complaint made in relation to price review arbitrations is that arbitrators who do not have the relevant technical expertise will avoid a decision which makes any substantial change to the price and will often find what they perceive to be a 'middle ground' which may be unsupported by any clear commercial or economic rationale and which is out of line with industry practice. The constitution of the arbitral tribunal is therefore an important consideration. The appointment of a tribunal of three arbitrators as opposed to a sole arbitrator allows the parties to nominate an arbitrator with relevant expertise in the light of the issues in dispute and to balance the parties' nominations and their expertise with a suitably qualified chairman.

We deal with some of the strategies for managing the risks in price indexation or price review disputes below.

3.   Key components of price review clauses

Price review clauses can be structured in numerous ways, but they usually comprise the following elements:

- a 'trigger' event;
- the methodology for determining the price adjustment;
- a process for negotiation; and
- the scope of the price review.

Traditionally, although not always, contracts also provide for a staged approach. First, the trigger event must be established to entitle either party to seek a revision of the contract price. The right to commence a review will ordinarily be conditional on service of a notice which must be compliant with the provisions of the SPA. These generally require a notice to be served specifying, first, the trigger event which it relies upon and, second, the proposed revised price formula and the evidence to support it. There will then be a period of negotiation which, if unsuccessful, will be followed by the determination of an expert or arbitral tribunal. If it is established that a trigger event has taken place, the clause will provide for the price to be revised to reflect the change and the effect that change has had on the value of the gas sold under the contract.

3.1   Trigger event

Price review clauses typically provide for a review to take place automatically at a specified time or at regular intervals during the life of the contract. For example, they may occur on the third anniversary of the commencement date of deliveries under the SPA and on each three-year anniversary thereafter. The advantage of this is certainty, although the specified interval needs to be sufficiently long so as to avoid too frequent reviews which would destabilise the contract price.

Even with frequent reviews, however, the parties may be prevented from adjusting the contract price when the underlying economics would otherwise warrant doing so. In order to accommodate this possibility, clauses may therefore also provide for a 'special' review to take place on the occurrence of a particular change in circumstances. It is also common to limit each party's right to initiate a 'special' price review to a specified number over the course of the contract.

Triggers can be drafted by reference to the occurrence of one or more objective events, such as a fall in a party's rate of return or, most commonly, by reference to benchmark crude price indices, using a formula or ratio so that a change in index will give a right to change the price. Often this is specified as a magnitude of change. However, while the change is in theory easily quantifiable, in practice the operation of these clauses is often sufficiently complicated to generate disagreement. For example, the formula may inadvertently refer to elements which are themselves too vague or unspecific, such as taking 'fuel price data...covering all the competing fuels...in the immediate region'. In some cases, an attempt to achieve certainty may therefore be counterproductive and a cause of greater uncertainty. Objective triggers also need to be considered in the context of the long-term duration of the contract to allow for short-term fluctuations without triggering frequent reviews. That, too, can be difficult to define and can be a source of dispute when considering whether the trigger has been satisfied and also when applying the methodology for adjusting the price.

The level of change required to trigger a price review is often defined in terms which are open to subjective interpretation, such as a 'significant', 'material' or 'substantial' change in circumstances. A relevant change in circumstance may similarly be loosely defined in terms such as a substantial change in 'economic circumstances', 'market circumstances' or the 'energy market of the buyer (or seller)'. Usually, a causal link must be shown. In other words, it will be necessary for the party invoking the trigger to show that the change is affecting the value of the gas or LNG sold under the SPA:

- in comparison with its value and/or with the value of competing fuels in the relevant market; and
- by reference to an earlier, prescribed date.

Needless to say, buyers and sellers usually have very different views on what comprises the 'market' (be it wholesale, industrial or residential), and the relevant market and any market-based test should ideally be defined quite specifically.

Some clauses will specify that the change must also be anticipated to have 'lasting effect' or will exclude 'short-lived changes', in order to avoid triggering a review in response to a short-term fluctuation. Again, however, it can be difficult to define what is short lived and what is lasting in the abstract. Where state-owned entities are involved or a party has market dominance for some other reason, the clause may also stipulate that the market change must not have been induced by the requesting party.

While loosely defined terms allow for a certain degree of flexibility, such terms are inevitably open to interpretation and accordingly provide fertile ground for disputes, such as those concerning the following questions:

- Is there a clear trigger for a price reopener?
- What constitutes a sufficient change in a market?
- What is the relevant market? For example, is the change referable to the end-user market of the buyer's country and, if so, which market sector or sectors? Alternatively, is the clause directed to the market price of imports? Or both?
- What is the effect of the relevant changes in the market on the value of the product sold and purchased under the SPA and what is the causal link between the two?
- What is meant by 'market value'? Is it the same as market price?
- Does the party requesting the price review have any control over the alleged material change in the relevant market?
- Is the change only a short-lived market fluctuation or can it be anticipated to have lasting effect?
- To what extent does the trigger test remain relevant once it is determined that a review has been validly triggered? Is the tribunal required to refer back to the trigger event in deciding how to revise the price formula?

Not all clauses provide for an objective trigger event; rather, the trigger may be subjective and based only on a belief that trigger event has occurred. However, such a belief or opinion could be either objective or subjective, depending on the wording of the clause.

Esso Exploration & Production UK Ltd v Electricity Supply Board [2004] EWCH (Comm) 723 is an example of a case where not applying the right trigger also invalidated the notice under the price review clause.

ESB claimed that Esso's price review notice was invalid because Esso had applied the wrong comparator and therefore no dispute had arisen of a kind contemplated by the contract which could be referred to arbitration. Both parties proceeded on the assumption that service of a valid price review notice was necessary for the arbitrators to have jurisdiction and the court agreed.

The contract was for the sale and purchase of certain quantities of natural gas each year for 15 years. In addition to automatic review and adjustment on a six-monthly basis, the parties were allowed to give four price review notices in relation to the energy charge throughout the life of the contract, at carefully defined intervals. Notice could not be given by the seller (Esso) unless "it is reasonably satisfied in good faith that the Energy Charge…is at the time of giving such Price Review Notice eighty five per cent (85%) or less than the Comparator."

The energy charge contained two elements, one of which was a fixed amount expressed in pence per kilowatt hour, whose initial value the parties had fixed by agreement at a level that reasonably reflected the market price obtainable at the date of the agreement for the sale of reasonably similar quantities of gas:

- over a reasonably similar period;
- on reasonably similar terms and conditions;
- between parties of reasonably similar commercial and financial standing; and
- for use in a reasonably similar type of power station in the United Kingdom or Ireland.

The comparator was defined as "The market price...at the date of the relevant....Notice for natural gas being supplied on the basis described above" – that is, on the basis of the sale of reasonably similar quantities and so on. The party giving notice was obliged to specify in the notice itself the value of the energy charge it was requesting and to provide the other party with a reasonably detailed explanation of how that figure was reached, together with all reasonably available published and non-confidential information to support its position.

The court held that the expression 'reasonably satisfied' meant "satisfied on reasonable grounds", which imported an element of objectivity and provided a degree of protection to the other party by ensuring that there was a proper basis for putting the machinery of the price review clause into motion.

As to the meaning of the comparator, there was a real practical issue to address because there was no active market for the long-term sale of gas on terms comparable to those of the Esso/ESB contract. Much evidence was submitted as to the practical impossibility of obtaining any reliable information about prices under comparable long-term contracts, not least given the usual confidentiality provisions contained in such contracts. In the absence of such information, Esso argued that prices for short-term supplies should be used. However, the court decided that the natural meaning of the words used showed that the parties intended the comparator to represent prices as prescribed in the contract and not a notional market price for short-term supplies.

The court therefore held that since Esso's notice had been based on the notional market price for short-term deliveries, it could not have had reasonable grounds for being satisfied that the energy charge had diverged to the extent required by the contract to trigger a price review. The notice was therefore held to be invalid and there was no dispute capable of being referred to arbitration. Perhaps surprisingly, the first instance judgment was not appealed.

3.2   Methodology for determining price adjustment

Drafting clear benchmarks and parameters for the calculation of a price revision is crucial, but difficult. On the one hand, it is desirable to avoid disputes; but on the other hand, it is debatable whether the clause can provide adequately for all uncertainties which could affect the economics of the contract for both parties. Some contracts provide broadly for the formulae to be revised in such a way as to restore the relationship between the contract price and the market price which had been agreed at the outset; or for the relevant index to be changed so as to restore its validity as a comparator over time. However, all contracts are different and many are silent as to the method of assessment of the price adjustment. In such cases there is no guidance either for the parties or for the expert or arbitrators appointed to determine the revised price. There is accordingly considerable scope for different methodologies to be adopted. General guidelines such as 'fair', 'equitable' or 'appropriate' are too vague to give any certainty as to the likely outcome, although they do allow the flexibility to achieve the stated intentions of the parties in maintaining a mutually beneficial long-term relationship.

One key question often forgotten at the drafting stage is the date on which any price revision should take effect. This could be for the period of the change, from the date of the change in benchmark, from the date that the price review clause was invoked or from the date that the parties or the tribunal reach a determination. And related to that, at what point in time are the relevant changes in value or market circumstances to be considered? Can the expert or tribunal take account only of circumstances which existed at the review date or the trigger notice (if different); or can regard be had to subsequent events and, if so, is there any cut-off date before the issue of the decision? This issue is well illustrated by *Superior v British Gas* [1982] 1 Lloyd's Law Reports 262, which is also instructive on the operation of a subjective trigger mechanism.

The sales agreement in that case provided for a periodic price review in every third contract year, at the request of either party, based on a formula for adjusting prices by reference to variations in certain index figures, with the object of offsetting the effects of inflation on capital and operating costs and/or maintaining a reasonable competitive position in relation to the major competitive fuels. There was also provision for a review in the event of "any substantial change in the economic circumstances relating to this Agreement and either party feels that such change is causing it to suffer substantial economic hardship". The parties were required to meet to consider what adjustment in either the prices or the price revision mechanism, if any, was justified in the circumstances "in fairness to the parties to offset or alleviate the said hardship caused by such change". The matter was to be resolved by a panel of three experts, if the parties could not reach agreement, and any revised prices or changes to the mechanism were to take effect six months after the request for review.

The primary dispute between the parties, which the Court of Appeal ultimately decided, related to the phrase 'substantial economic hardship' and the words at the end of the clause, 'the said hardship'. The court decided that 'substantial' economic hardship meant something more than difficulties arising from ordinary day-to-day economic variations, must have a real impact rather than merely transient effect and must be something weighty or serious.

The parties also disagreed as to the principles on which the adjustment should be calculated, and the court then had to decide on the duty of the experts to determine what adjustments to prices should be made to offset or alleviate the hardship – whether it was the substantial element of the hardship only or the whole of the substantial hardship, and over what period. Its decision that the experts could both fix a price to remove substantial hardship for the future and compensate for past hardship illustrates the wide discretion which can be given to an expert and also the scope of potential argument arising from the general terms in which these provisions were drafted.

3.3   Process for negotiation

A negotiated resolution avoids a potentially negative adversarial process where there is an ongoing long-term relationship to preserve and also removes the uncertainty inherent in any dispute resolution process. It can help the process and encourage full engagement for the clause to provide some structure for the negotiation. For example, stipulating the time period within which negotiations should be commenced, a fixed period for the negotiations and requirements for the exchange of information helps to ensure a meaningful dialogue. The stipulated period for negotiation before either party can refer the matter for determination is therefore generally quite generous, to allow the maximum opportunity for the parties to reach agreement, and it is not unusual for the parties to agree to extend such a period. In doing so, however, it should be remembered that supervening events, including further market changes during the period of the negotiation, may have to be taken into account if the matter is referred for a decision.

3.4 Scope of the price review

The clause should stipulate the elements of the price review mechanism which are subject to review. The review could be of all indices in the formula as a whole and/or the method of calculation used in the contract price formula, or it could be confined to a specific element of the mechanism or a specific index.

It may not be possible to anticipate all of the factors which might affect the relevant market and hence the price under a long-term contract, but at least some of them should be identifiable and specified at the outset in order to provide some framework for the scope of the price review. The consequence of not doing so is potentially to lose control to the expert or arbitrators and to have an unexpected outcome that is completely out of line with either the expectations of the parties or normal industry practice. Such an outcome arose in *Gas Natural Aprovisionamientos, SDG, SA v Atlantic LNG Company of Trinidad and Tobago*, the first arbitration dispute to enter the public domain in the US District Court for the Southern District in New York.

In that case, the terms of the SPA did not set a limit on how the price revision should be operated. The price review clause required only that there should be "a fair and equitable revision" of the contract price. The tribunal was accordingly held to have acted within its powers in deciding to impose a dual pricing formula which sought to maintain a reasonable level of profitability for Gas Natural in the changed market conditions, but which neither of the parties had sought.

4. Managing the risks in price indexation or price review disputes

Issues in price review arbitrations are becoming more complex as a result of changes in gas markets and, where relevant due to gas consumption for power generation, power markets. Whereas previously arbitrators were dealing with relatively self-contained aspects of a largely agreed revision, now they are deciding issues which, because they can have a financially significant impact over a significant period of time, are increasingly fractious. Every step of the review process is therefore open to close inspection and it is vital to ensure not only that every point is considered and properly implemented, but also that the risks of adopting a particular position are properly understood. Both the terms of the price review clause and the way that a review is handled can have a significant impact of the outcome. We explain some of the key issues below.

4.1 Notice provisions and invoking a price review

Both objective and subjective triggers can easily lead to disputes as to whether the trigger has been reached. They can also be an important commercial tool and can be used to bring commercial pressure to bear – the more general the clause, the more scope to apply pressure.

The party invoking the review would be well advised to consider the construction of the trigger clause very carefully and to carry out a thorough review of all relevant economic evidence before invoking the trigger. The upfront costs of doing so could be considerable, but those costs will not be wasted if a negotiation and/or arbitration goes ahead. It is also worth bearing in mind that a spurious application for review will also have cost consequences. As the Esso case demonstrates, it is important to understand whether a price review notice is merely a mechanism enabling one party to commence the review process or whether it requires a rather more diligent and objective consideration of the relevant triggering factors.

4.2   Strategies for renegotiation

Having a consistent and cohesive argument from the outset increases the likelihood of being able to negotiate a revision to the price. Parties should therefore conduct extensive market and economic analysis before serving, or responding to, a trigger notice. If more than one event or change in circumstances is to be relied upon, care should be taken to ensure that there is no inconsistency between them or, if there is, that there is a logical explanation as to why they can both be invoked.

Nor should a party have regard only to the present review or short-term considerations. Positions adopted as to the meaning of the pricing provisions or the relevance of particular markets or market sectors at one review will be difficult to resile from at a review later in the lifetime of the agreement. For example, a seller that contends that the import market value is the relevant comparator in one review will lack credibility if it contends in a later review that the end-user market value is the relevant comparator, and may even be estopped from doing so.

If the scope of the arbitrator's powers and the range of possible outcomes have not been limited in the drafting of the SPA, it is possible to structure a price review arbitration so as to ensure a more predictable – and desirable – result as intended by the parties. One way of achieving this is to agree a split process:

- an initial hearing to determine whether a trigger event has occurred and whether there is any basis for revising the price; and
- if so, a further hearing to determine the appropriate revision.

The parties will have the opportunity to flush out any issues concerning the interpretation of the trigger event. A negotiated settlement as to how the price should be revised is then more likely, based on the tribunal's findings as to whether there has been a trigger event and what those changes are. And if there is no settlement, the parties can limit the evidence that they submit to those material changes accepted and identified by the tribunal in its preliminary award. This, of course, will not be workable in all cases, depending on the relationship – if any – between the trigger event and the basis of the price revision.

4.3   Procedural matters

(a)   *The expert*

While the expert determination clause will provide for the expert to decide a dispute concerning the contract price or the price formula, the terms of reference should contain a precise definition of the issue which the expert is to decide, since that will define the expert's jurisdiction. These can simply repeat the formulation in the expert determination clause or go further and clarify or refine it.

Similarly, while the expert clause may contain some requirements as to the procedure to be followed, it is open to the parties to agree different or additional steps. Although an expert is, by definition, retained for his own expertise, it is usual expressly to permit the expert to pursue independent investigations and, if he deems it appropriate, to instruct technical or legal experts. However, it is advisable to retain some control over the expert for this purpose, so that the parties have some say in whom the expert consults and how such a third party is instructed.

Again, the procedure for delivery of the expert's decision will often be dealt with in the expert determination clause, but in any event should be included in the terms of reference. The expert is not required to give reasons for his determination, unless the parties specifically stipulate that reasons should be given.

Other matters to consider include whether the expert should be required to provide the parties with a draft decision in advance of the final determination. The purpose of this will usually be to provide the parties with an opportunity to point out any fundamental errors before the determination becomes final and not to make any further submissions. However, it should be made clear that this is not an opportunity for the disappointed party substantially to reargue its case. In addition, care should be taken if the expert is to be given a date by which to make his determination. While this helps to ensure a timely determination, it can be difficult to predict, at the time of drafting, how much time is sensibly required to ensure that the expert has an adequate opportunity to obtain the information necessary to reach a proper – and correct – determination. There is thus a risk that the expert will cease to be empowered to deliver a binding decision if the deadline has passed, unless it is made clear that this will not be the consequence.

(b)   *The arbitral tribunal*

As discussed above, the constitution of the tribunal and the qualities of the arbitrators can be key. An arbitrator's qualifications should therefore be thoroughly vetted before nomination in light of the issues in dispute. It is also important to bear in mind cultural issues where an international contract is involved. Having an arbitrator from a common law background on the tribunal will often provide comfort that a party's interests will be properly understood and adequately represented on the tribunal.

An arbitration will tend to be a more formal process than an expert determination and the rules governing its procedure will to some extent be prescribed by the law of the place where the arbitration is to be held, as well as any institutional or other rules which the parties have agreed should apply.

As noted above, there is a risk that a tribunal which is legally qualified to decide issues as to the meaning of the pricing provisions will feel less confident when dealing with technical, economic and market issues in order to decide how a formula should be revised. Moreover, if the tribunal has been given very wide powers to revise a formula, such as occurred in the *Gas Natural* case, an unexpected outcome can follow.

One option which can prevent a tribunal from arriving at a result which is not expected or undesirable for either party is to agree to a 'pendulum' arbitration (also known as 'baseball' or 'final offer' arbitration), where the tribunal is allowed only to adopt one or other of the parties' solutions and cannot reach its own independent solution. Another advantage of this process is that it encourages the parties to adopt less extreme positions so as to avoid the risk of the tribunal choosing the other's more reasonable solution. The result is that the differences between the parties are likely to be narrower at the end of the negotiation period, making a negotiated settlement more likely. There is no reason why such a pendulum process cannot be agreed even after the price review notice has been served.

4.4 Scope of expert/tribunal's mandate

Understanding the scope of the expert or tribunal's mandate is essential to understanding the potential outcomes and therefore potential risks or rewards in a price review.

In *Contact Energy Ltd v The Attorney General* [2005] UKPC 13, the clause referring indexation disputes to an expert was relatively narrowly drafted so that the expert had jurisdiction to determine only disputes as to the appropriate replacement index, and not disputes as to the mechanism for implementation of the new index, which was why the matter came before the courts.

In *Esso* the court decided that the jurisdiction of the arbitrators was limited to determining the amount of the comparator, so they did not have jurisdiction to determine the real question in issue, which was the construction of the clause and the nature of the comparator. In fact, had the arbitrators been required to determine the amount, it is questionable whether they would have been able to do so, given the difficulty in obtaining any reliable information about prices under comparable contracts. Similar wording undoubtedly exists or existed in other long-term gas sales contracts entered into around the same time in the late 1990s.

5. Conclusion

Increasing volatility in the energy markets due to widening fluctuations in demand and supply, as well as the internationalisation and deregulation of markets, will continue to put pressure on prices agreed under long-term contracts for both buyers and sellers. Against this background, there is a natural increasing willingness of parties to invoke price review provisions in order to preserve value, and pursuing the issue into arbitration or expert determination is becoming more common and so more commercially palatable.

Pricing provisions are necessarily drafted in broad terms to allow for reviews to compensate for unexpected future events which change the economic balance of an agreement beyond that which the parties may have agreed (or thought they had agreed) was acceptable. As a result, they are often open to widely differing interpretations – as are the market data and dynamics which such provisions are intended to reflect. Disputes will therefore inevitably arise under such clauses. In view of the complexity of the interplay between the legal, economic and statistical issues thrown up by these disputes, and the fact that positions taken by a party will be difficult to resile from later in the life of the contract, great care should be taken to understand all of their implications before putting them forward in a formal process.

Joint venture disputes

Elie Kleiman
Freshfields Bruckhaus Deringer LLP

1.   Introduction

Joint venture disputes in the energy sector meet several requirements for drama: high stakes, powerful players, fierce competition, economic volatility, long-term contractual arrangements and political and economic instability. These are just a few of the most obvious factors that often converge in a single dispute. The same reasons for which joint ventures are seen as a highly effective medium for the sharing of risks, resources, know-how and technology also explain why joint venture arrangements can result in complex and protracted disputes. Within the energy sector, the oil industry has the longest history as both an investment destination and a theatre of contention. As one scholar has observed:

> *Historically, oil has been the subject of the most important international agreements and disputes. Many of the legal doctrines applicable to transnational private arrangements have been developed in response to the arrangements by which oil has been extracted and sold… Moreover, no other commodity, either historically or currently, can match the importance of petroleum to the world's political and economic order.*[1]

Few businesses are as capital intensive and adventurous as the oil business. Oil companies and, more recently, gas companies regularly invest vast sums of money in hydrocarbon exploration and exploitation activities in places with minimal infrastructure, underdeveloped legal systems and unstable political environments. While history has shown that 'farming the frontier' can be very profitable, it can also be fraught with risk and technical difficulty. In addition, the petroleum industry is characterised by a diversity of participants with varying degrees of risk aversion, financial strength and expertise. These considerations increasingly motivate oil and gas companies to enter into various kinds of joint ventures as ways of sharing risk, pooling capital and maximising the technical expertise available for the project. The joint venture is therefore probably the most important contracting model for the modern international oil and gas industry.

As is often the case in commercial law, the law follows the market. Although many legal systems now recognise the term 'joint venture', sometimes as a branch of the law of partnership, the origins of joint ventures lie in commercial practice and custom. Accordingly, while the term 'joint venture' may be defined in different ways in different places,[2] among its commercial users it means any contractual

---

1   EE Smith et al (eds), *International Petroleum Transactions*, (2000) pp ii-iii, cited in T Martin, "Model Contracts: A Survey of the Global Petroleum Industry", (2004) 22(3) *JENRL* 281.

arrangement in which two or more legally distinct parties cooperate with a common goal – that goal being, at broadest, the realisation of profit.[3]

In the oil and gas industry, joint ventures take various contractual forms, each of which is subject to theoretically infinite permutations consistent with freedom of contract. Joint ventures require a legal instrument to establish the rights and obligations of the parties among themselves and a framework for the commercial and technical conduct of the relevant operations. This chapter focuses on four main 'upstream' joint venture agreements:

- participation and bidding agreements;
- 'farm-out' agreements;
- joint operating agreements; and
- unitisation agreements.

Each of these is the subject of a growing number of 'model forms' developed by professional associations and industry bodies.

Concentrating on the oil and gas industry within the energy sector, the purpose of this chapter is to identify the types of disputes and related procedural issues that most commonly arise in the upstream joint venture context. To that end, this chapter commences with a brief overview of these four main classes of upstream joint venture agreements, using the leading model contracts as working examples. The focus then shifts to dispute resolution and, more specifically, international arbitration. The point is made that while certain procedural issues are arguably endemic to upstream joint venture disputes, the adjudicatory risk that they present can be managed with proper contract drafting, diligent contract administration and specialist advice.

2. Upstream joint venture models

Today, most upstream joint ventures are based, either closely or loosely, on some form of model contract or precedent. Most sophisticated parties in the global petroleum industry use a relatively narrow range of model contracts in their relations with other companies. Although model contracts cannot claim to address every contingency and often contain certain compromises intended to satisfy the general preferences of the various parties involved, the perceived and actual advantages of model contracts are well known. These include:

---

2   Practically speaking, in the oil and gas industry, a joint venture can be described as follows: "The mineral and petroleum joint venture is an association of persons (natural or corporate) to engage in a common undertaking to generate a product to be shared among the participants. Management of the undertaking is divided: specified activities are to be performed by a designated person (the operator or manager) as agent for the participants; the power to determine certain matters is vested in a committee (the operating or management committee) upon which participants are represented and entitled to vote in accordance with their interests in the venture; and other matters are decided at the outset by the participants as terms of the association. The relationship among participants is both contractual and proprietary: the terms of the association are fixed by agreement and property employed in the undertaking is held by the participants as tenants in common." M Crommelin, "The Mining and Petroleum Joint Venture in Australia" (1986) 4 *J Energy Nat Resources and Environmental L*, p 65-66.

3   Indeed, the term 'joint venture' was developed as a business concept rather than a legal one. As such, scholars were for some time divided over the legal definition of a 'joint venture' and its legality in reference to other legal vehicles. See Talal Al-Emadi's discussion of the development of the concept in "Joint Venture Contracts (JVCs) among Current Negotiated Petroleum Contracts: A Literature Review of JVCs Development, Concept and Elements", (2010) 1 *Geo J Int L* 1.

- reduced transaction costs (eg, shorter negotiating time, reduced involvement of external counsel);
- increased certainty of rules and predictability of outcomes; and
- general improvement of counterparty relationships.[4]

To academic eyes, the increased acceptance and use of model contracts can be seen as evidence of the continuing development of the *lex petrolea*, the emergence of which has been the subject of significant academic and arbitral discourse,[5] including other chapters of this book.

The first model contracts in the oil and gas industry grew out of the drafting practices and demands of dominant players which could use their negotiating power to impose their preferred terms on counterparties.[6] However, in more recent years industry associations, rather than dominant players, have driven the proliferation of model contracts covering a wide range of upstream and midstream activities. These organisations include the Association of International Petroleum Negotiators (AIPN), where model contracts are used as examples in this chapter.[7]

Upstream – meaning the exploration, development and production phase of the petroleum business – the main AIPN agreements are:

- the Study and Bid Group Agreement 2006 (SBGA);[8]

---

4   Timothy Martin highlighted the tangible benefits of these contracts, arguing: "A well drafted model contract allows the parties quickly and easily to agree on 80 percent of the contract, which is commonly referred to as 'boilerplate', that is usually non-controversial and repetitive from one contract to another. The parties can then focus their attention on the 20 percent of the contract that adds value or where there are significant differences of opinion. Model contracts increase the speed of transactions. They often cut transaction times in half and sometimes as much as 90 percent." Further, he argues that although no empirical studies exist on the question, "much anecdotal evidence suggests that, at least for the international industry, contract negotiations for many large projects have been reduced from two years to six months with accompanying overhead costs for negotiating and signing contracts slashed from US$2 million to US$0.5 million. These kinds of cost and time savings are repeated hundreds, if not thousands of times throughout the international energy industry on an annual basis. Aside from direct cost savings in drafting agreements, there are many broader benefits that model contracts provide to the industry including avoiding significant project delays, reallocating corporate resources to high-value business opportunities and building strong partner relationships through abbreviated negotiation sessions as opposed to lengthy and repetitive ones." See T Martin, "Model Contracts: A Survey of the Global Petroleum Industry", (2004) 22(3) *JENRL* 4.

5   See R Doak Bishop's seminal article entitled "International Arbitration of Petroleum Disputes: The Development of a *Lex Petrolea*", (1998) 23 *YCA* 1131. In his article, Bishop examines the range of rules established through a survey of all reported international arbitral awards relating to the petroleum industry at the time of publication. Thomas Childs recently updated Bishop's article, summarising and classifying the key substantive rulings in all awards published since 1998 relating to the international exploration and production industry. See his "Update on *Lex Petrolea*: The Continuing Development of Customary Law Relating to International Oil and Gas Exploration and Production", (2011) 4(3) *Journal of World Energy Law and Business* 214.

6   An often-cited example is the British National Oil Corporation, which during the 1960s and 1970s successfully established its joint operating agreement as the standard for North Sea operations.

7   Other leading industry bodies include the American Petroleum Institute, the Canadian Association of Petroleum Landmen, the United Kingdom Offshore Operators Association and the Australian Petroleum Production and Exploration Association.

8   The SBGA is of great interest when groups or consortia will be used to conduct exploration, development and production activities. The AIPN SBGA designates the party that will serve as operator for negotiating a contract with the host state and provides details on how the evaluation process will be conducted. In addition, the model agreement sets out the proportionate interests that the participants will have, the application procedure and what should take place in the event of a default of a party in paying in full any amount due. Finally, the AIPN SBGA provides for exclusivity in that each party is required to refrain from submitting any bid or application covering any part of the study area either alone, with or through an affiliate or any third parties.

- the Farm-out Agreement 2004 (FOA);[9]
- the Joint International Operating Agreement 2002 (JOA); and
- the Unitisation and Unit Operating Agreement 2006 (UOA).[10]

Each of these joint venture agreements creates a complex scheme of rights and obligations, any one of which could be the subject of a dispute and consequent need for adjudication. This chapter does not examine the substantive provisions of these agreements, but instead focuses on their dispute resolution clauses, using them as a canvas on which to paint a picture of joint venture dispute resolution generally. In the finer strokes, the options available under the dispute resolution clauses of the AIPN suite of model contracts are used to illustrate certain recurring procedural themes.

For the uninitiated, the JOA is probably the most common form of joint venture agreement in the oil and gas industry. Indeed, on one view it is a "necessary extension" of a joint venture agreement.[11] The AIPN is best known for its model JOA, at the core of which is an arrangement whereby a single party designated as the 'operator' is given responsibility for exploration and development under the supervision of an operating committee.[12] The operator can be a co-venturer, an unaffiliated third party or a company established by the co-venturers to carry out specific operations. The JOA establishes a democracy at the operating committee level, where all co-venturers have an active say (usually in the form of voting rights proportionate to their participating interest) in the management of the joint venture. Under most JOAs, the participants collectively own the equipment, facilities and hydrocarbon production that flow from the permits held.[13] Another common feature of JOAs is joint and several liability.

Over the years, JOA drafting practice has responded to certain commercial and regulatory trends. For example, in the 2002 revision of the previous 1995 version of the AIPN JOA, the revision committee adopted the incorporation of a health, safety and environment (HSE) provision in the model form.[14] As this chapter observes,

---

9   The FOA is an agreement by a party that owns drilling rights – the farmor – to assign all or a portion of those rights to another party – the farmee – in return for drilling and testing on the property. Under the AIPN FOA, the farmor can explore alternative means of financing exploration activities. Whereas years ago the FOA was conducted orally, today the AIPN FOA includes provisions concerning the assignment of interest and the conditions precedent to assignment, such as governmental approval or an optional environmental assessment at the sole cost of the farmee.

10 The UOA provides a model unit agreement for companies that have interests in an oil or gas reserve which stretches into different tracts operated by different interest holders. The evolving trend is increasingly towards unitisation in situations where common petroleum reservoirs straddle the boundary between ownership interests of two or more parties. The AIPN UOA provides for the creation and effect of the unit, tract participations and unit interests, a unit operator and a unit operating committee, as well as provisions on decommissioning.

11 T Al-Emadi, "Joint Venture Contracts (JVCs) among Current Negotiated Petroleum Contracts: A Literature Review of JVCs Development, Concept and Elements", (2010) 1 *Geo J Int L* 18.

12 The operating committee is comprised of representatives from all the parties to the JOA.

13 For example, the JOA between Tullow Ghana Limited, Sabre Oil and Gas Limited and Kosmos Energy Ghana HC established the respective rights and obligations of the parties with respect to operations in the Deepwater Tano contract area, offshore Ghana. Tullow, the operator, enjoyed a 55.5% share of participating interests, Sabre 4.5% and Kosmos 40%. A provision of the JOA nonetheless recognised the rights of the Ghana National Petroleum Corporation (GNPC) and the government of the Republic of Ghana, pursuant to which GNPC has a 10% participating interest in all petroleum operations under the contract and a right to acquire an additional 5% participating interest.

another drafting trend is the preference for arbitration as the method for the resolution of disputes.

In procedural terms, the main thing that the four AIPN model contracts have in common is that they provide for international arbitration as the method for resolving disputes, either alone or as a 'longstop' to other dispute resolution procedures such as senior executive negotiation,[15] mediation[16] or expert determination.[17] For example, the arbitration clause of the AIPN FOA reads as follows:

Except as may be otherwise agreed in the JOA, any and all claims, demands, causes of action, disputes, controversies and other matters in question arising out of or relating to this Agreement, including any question regarding its breach, existence, validity or termination, which the Parties do not resolve amicably *within a period of ____ days, shall be resolved by* three arbitrators *in accordance with the Arbitration Rules of the _____. Each Party shall appoint one arbitrator within thirty (30) days of the filing of the arbitration, and the two arbitrators so appointed shall select the presiding arbitrator within thirty (30) days after the latter of the two arbitrators have been appointed. If a Party fails to appoint its Party-appointed arbitrator or if the two Party-appointed arbitrators cannot reach an agreement on the presiding arbitrator within the applicable time period, then the _____ shall appoint the remainder of the three arbitrators not yet appointed.* The place of arbitration *shall be _____. The proceedings shall be in the _____ language. The resulting arbitral award shall be* final and binding, *and judgment upon such award may be entered in any court having jurisdiction thereof. A dispute shall be deemed to have arisen when either Party notifies the other Party in writing to that effect. Any monetary award issued by the arbitrator shall be payable in _____. It is expressly agreed that the arbitrator shall have no authority to award special, indirect, consequential, exemplary or punitive damages.*[18] *(emphasis added)*

The broad, largely standard language of the AIPN FOA arbitration clause can be supplemented by the use of a number of optional clauses. These options cover issues such as waiver of the right to appeal on a point of law[19] and the power of the arbitrator

---

14 See Article 4.12 of the AIPN JOA, which reads: "With the goal of achieving safe and reliable operations in compliance with applicable HSE laws, rules and regulations (including avoiding significant and unintended impact on the safety or health of people, on property or on the environment), Operator shall in the conduct of Joint Operations: (1) establish and implement an HSE plan in a manner consistent with standards and procedures generally followed in the international petroleum industry under similar circumstances; (2) design and operate Joint Property consistent with the HSE plan; and (3) conform with locally applicable HSE laws, rules and regulations and other HSE-related statutory requirements that may apply." However, the model contract provides for varying degrees of control and oversight of the implementation and scope of HSE plans and procedures.

15 See, for example, Article 18, Option (B) of the AIPN JOA 2002 and Article 20.2, Option (B) of the AIPN UOA 2006.

16 See, for example, Article 18, Option (C) of the AIPN JOA 2002 and Article 20.2, Option (C) of the AIPN UOA 2006.

17 For example, Article 18 of the AIPN JOA 2002 contains an "Optional Provision 18.3" which provides for expert determination in the following terms: "For any decision referred to an expert under Articles [8.4, 12.2 or 12.3], the Parties hereby agree that such decision shall be conducted expeditiously by an expert selected unanimously by the parties to the Dispute. The expert is not an arbitrator of the Dispute and shall not be deemed to be acting in an arbitral capacity."

18 AIPN FOA 2004, Article 11.2.

19 AIPN FOA 2004, Article 11.2, Option A.

to grant equitable forms of relief (including specific performance and interim measures of protection).[20] The other AIPN model contracts take a similar approach. Even more detailed optional clauses are contained in the AIPN JOA, covering:

- the form and content of the notice of dispute;[21]
- negotiation[22] and mediation[23] (as optional preconditions to arbitration);
- the rules of the arbitration;[24]
- the number of arbitrators[25] and the method for their appointment;[26]
- consolidation;[27]
- seat;[28]
- language;[29]
- entry of judgment;[30] and
- notice.[31]

Although these options are sometimes overlooked as fine-print or seen as matters too specific for the eleventh hour in which dispute resolution clauses are often negotiated, they cover important issues.

3. Typical disputes

It should come as no surprise that disputes are common in upstream oil and gas joint ventures. Leaving aside the multitude of economic, physical (especially geological and environmental) and political inputs that may cause a dispute to arise in an international oil and gas project, one of the reasons why disputes are common in upstream joint ventures is that the joint venturers are often direct competitors.[32]

---

20   AIPN FOA 2004, Article 11.2, Option B: "The Parties acknowledge that remedies at law may be inadequate to protect against breach of this Agreement. The arbitrators may therefore award both monetary and equitable relief, including injunctive relief and specific performance. A Party may apply to any competent judicial authority for interim or conservatory relief. The application for such measures or for the enforcement of such measures ordered by the arbitrator shall not be deemed an infringement or waiver of the agreement to arbitrate and shall not affect the powers of the arbitrator."

21   AIPN JOA 2002, Article 18.2, Option (A); and AIPN UOA, Article 20.2, Option (A). Establishing clear requirements for the form and content of a notice for dispute can be very helpful, as it can avoid the situation where one party issues a notice of dispute and the responding party denies that the notice of dispute is valid – for example, because it does not disclose the existence of a dispute or is deficient in some other formal sense.

22   AIPN JOA 2002, Article 18.2, Option (B); AIPN UOA 2006, Article 20.2, Option (B).

23   AIPN JOA 2002, Article 18.2, Option (C); AIPN UOA 2006, Article 20.2, Option (C).

24   AIPN JOA 2002, Article 18.2, Option (D)(1); AIPN SBGA 2006, Article 20.4.4; AIPN FOA 2004, Article 11.2 ; and AIPN UOA 2006, Article 20.2, Option (D)(1).

25   AIPN JOA 2002, Article 18.2, Option (D)(2); AIPN FOA 2004, Article 11.2; AIPN SBGA 2006, Article 20.3, Alternative 1A or 2B; and AIPN UOA 2006, Article 20.2 Option (D)(2).

26   AIPN JOA 2002, Article 18.2, Option (D)(3); AIPN FOA 2004, Article 11.2; AIPN SBGA 2006, Article 20.3, Alternative 1A or 2B; and AIPN UOA 2006, Article 20.2, Option (D)(3).

27   AIPN JOA 2002, Article 18.2, Option (D)(4); and AIPN UOA 2006, Article 20.2, Option (D)(4).

28   AIPN JOA 2002, Article 18.2, Option (D)(5); AIPN FOA 2004, Article 11.2; AIPN SBGA 2006, Article 20.4.1; and AIPN UOA 2006, Article 20.2, Option (D)(5).

29   AIPN JOA 2002, Article 18.2, Option (D)(6); AIPN SBGA 2006, Article 20.4.2; AIPN FOA 2004, Article 11.2; and AIPN UOA 2006, Article 20.2, Option (D)(6).

30   AIPN JOA 2002, Article 18.2, Option (D)(7); AIPN SBGA 2006, Article 20.9; AIPN FOA 2004, Article 11.2; and AIPN UOA 2006, Article 20.2, Option (D)(7).

31   AIPN JOA 2002, Article 18.2, Option (D)(8); and AIPN UOA 2006, Article 20.2, Option (D)(8).

32   This is, in some ways, a distinguishing characteristic of the international oil and gas industry. As Timothy Martin and Jay Park QC observed, "[i]t is difficult to imagine Coke and Pepsi negotiating a joint venture, but international oil companies do so frequently." See T Martin, JJ Park, "Global Petroleum Industry Model Contracts Revisited: Higher, Faster, Stronger", (2010) 3(1) *JWELB* 4.

Joint venture disputes also frequently arise because one of the parties becomes dissatisfied with the original risk allocation model. When one participant is sold to or merges with a third party, the dynamic of the joint venture can be radically altered. The same thing can happen where one participant is a national oil company and there is a change of government. Upon a review of published arbitral awards and anecdotal evidence, it is apparent that the most common disputes in upstream oil and gas joint ventures are as follows:

- Deadlocks – a deadlock will occur at the operating committee level in relation to an item of expenditure proposed by the operator, such as an authority for expenditure to carry out drilling or seismic works which are not obviously within the scope of the minimum works obligations attached to the permits held by the joint venture.[33] In this situation, the arguments will usually focus on the voting rights of the parties (which may have changed due to acquisitions, assignments and farm-outs) and whether the authorised expenditure is justified (ie, the scope of the minimum works obligations and the commercial and technical merits of the proposed exploration activities).

- Default and dilution – one party will fail to answer a cash call issued by the operator, and the non-defaulting parties will move to dilute the defaulting party's participating interest in accordance with the default and forfeiture provisions of the agreement. In this situation, the arguments will usually focus on the validity of the unanswered cash call (and its preceding authority for expenditure), whether the expenditure that is the subject of the unanswered cash call is justified, whether the operator has complied with the accounting standards required by the JOA, whether proper notice of default was issued by the operator, whether the cure period has expired and other legal questions attached to the enforceability of the dilution provisions of the agreement[34] (eg, 'penalty' arguments).

- Loss of permits – the operator fails to perform its duties,[35] the joint venture loses its good standing with the regulator and the permits revert back to the host state. In this situation, there may be administrative proceedings brought by the operator on behalf of the joint venture against the regulator (and

---

33 In a case brought before the US District Court for the District of North Dakota, plaintiff Magnum Hunter Resources Corporation, filed an *ex parte* motion for a temporary restraining order arguing that the defendant, Eagle Operating Incorporated, should be enjoined and restrained from performing any primary or secondary recovery operations on oil and gas properties jointly owned by the parties, as two of the proposed wells included in the authority for expenditure were not identified in a mutually agreed-upon business plan. The court granted the motion, holding that the business plan's absence posed a significant risk to the performance of the oil and gas properties. See *Magnum Hunter Resources Corporation v Eagle Operating Inc* (NW Nd 2010).

34 In the final award on jurisdiction in ICC Case 11663 of 2003 (A Jan van den Berg (ed), (2007) 32 YCA 60), this was the exact scenario: Company C concluded a shared management agreement with companies A and B in the framework of crude oil production in Yemen. Article 8.7(a) of the shared management agreement provided that if a defaulting party remained in default for more than 60 days after receipt of a default notice, it would be obliged upon request of a non-defaulting party to forfeit and assign its participating interest to that party. A dispute arose between the parties when C allegedly breached its obligations under the shared management agreement by failing to deliver letters of credit and to make timely payments of cash calls. Before the tribunal, C argued that the provision was "draconian", amounting to a penalty, and as such was not applicable under English law. However, the tribunal dismissed C's arguments and granted the claimants' request for specific performance, ordering C to assign its participating interests to A and B and resign as operator.

possibly claims for expropriation under applicable investment treaties), and secondary damages claims by the joint venturers against the operator for negligent breach of its contractual duty to maintain the permits in good standing.

- Farm-out disputes – the farmee either fails to make good on its obligations under the FOA[36] (in which case the farmor will typically dispute the farmee's entitlements), or the farmee completes its obligations and 'earns in' to the joint venture, but without its works having yielded any benefit to the joint venture. In this situation, any number of substantive issues can arise, including questions as to the validity of the FOA (eg, assignment and joint venture approvals for the farm-out), factual inquiries as to whether the farmee completed the works allocated to it under the FOA, arguments concerning the operating committee composition and the voting rights of the farmee, and the rights of the farmee to any hydrocarbons discovered or extracted.

- HSE breaches – the operator is prosecuted under the HSE regulations of the host state and seeks to rely on the indemnities given to it by the other parties under the joint venture agreement. The other parties deny liability to indemnify the operator, arguing that the violation that is the subject of the complaint was due to the gross negligence of the operator. In this situation, the legal arguments will usually focus on the interpretation and construction of the operator's indemnities and the fact-intense question of whether the operator was grossly negligent (which will be a matter of expert evidence on 'good oilfield practice').

---

35   The question of operator negligence is illustrated by *Joint Venture Yashlar v Government of Turkmenistan* (ICC Case 9151/FMS/KGA), interim award, June 8 1999. In this case, the claimants were Bridas and the joint venture controlled by Bridas. The respondent was the Turkmenian Ministry of Oil and Gas Industry and Mineral Resources. The respondent advanced several grounds for termination of the joint venture, one of which was the argument of an entitlement to repudiate the joint venture agreement on account of alleged breaches by Bridas with respect to operations in the field. The respondent claimed that there were numerous and persistent repudiatory breaches as well as violations of fiduciary duties towards the respondent committed by Bridas during the drilling of two exploratory wells. Expert testimony was of prime importance, but after careful consideration of the evidence, the tribunal disagreed with the respondent.

36   In *RSM Production Corporation v Grenada* (ICSID Case ARB/05/14) Award, March 13 2009), RSM, the claimant, entered into a written agreement with Grenada. The agreement recorded a contractual arrangement whereby RSM intended to apply for an exploration licence from Grenada for oil and gas over a designated area in the waters off the islands of Grenada. In the event of commercial discovery, RSM intended to apply for one or more development licences granted by Grenada. When RSM applied to Grenada for an exploration licence under the agreement, Grenada refused to grant the licence, terminating the agreement. Grenada advanced the counterclaim of unlawful misrepresentation as a ground for rescinding the agreement under Grenadian law. Grenada argued that RSM's intentions from the outset were materially different from those expressed to Grenada, which was led to believe that RSM was willing and able to carry out the exploration and development to be envisaged in the agreement, but that in reality RSM planned to lock up Grenada's territory until the agreement could be farmed out to other companies that would do all of the work, pay all of the costs and take all of the risks, thereby 'carrying' RSM's interest. RSM denied the existence of any misrepresentation, stating that FOAs are standard business practice in the international oil industry. However, Grenada contended that RSM never intended to assume any financial risk or to carry out any of its obligations under the agreement. The tribunal sided with RSM, asserting that there was no unlawful misrepresentation on their part relating to farm-outs which could justify rescission of the agreement.

This is by no means an exhaustive list of the disputes that can arise in an upstream oil and gas joint venture. Many other issues can lead to disputes in this context, including representations as to prospectivity, the fiduciary duties of operators, tax liability, hardship and *force majeure* events, insolvency and winding up of a party. But for the purposes of this chapter, these five typical disputes will be used to illustrate the procedural problems that are commonly encountered at the arbitration stage.

4. Causes of procedural problems

As has been observed, joint ventures are a common form of commercial undertaking in the oil and gas industry, typically involving at least one sophisticated actor, extensive pre-contractual negotiations, protracted commercial and operational planning phases, and specialist advisers. This backdrop raises the question of why procedural problems are so often encountered when joint venture disputes are taken to arbitration.

4.1 Number of parties

The first reason is numbers. Although joint ventures are often born as agreements between two parties, such as two international oil companies or an international oil company and a national oil company, they often expand by way of farm-outs and acquisitions to become multi-party, multi-contract undertakings. Additionally, a new local entity may be forced into the joint venture by virtue of the mandatory requirements of the investment code of the state in which the permits are located.

When a dispute erupts in a multi-party joint venture context, the following procedural questions will commonly arise:

- Which parties have the right to appoint arbitrators?
- Can the parent companies of the joint venturers be joined?
- If separate arbitrations must be commenced, can they be consolidated?

If the joint venture has expanded from a bipartite form into a multi-party undertaking, the dispute resolution clause in the original agreement might well be silent on these points. In such a situation, it will largely be a question of what the arbitration rules chosen by the parties dictate, and what the law of the seat permits the arbitrators to do.

4.2 Party characteristics

The issue of party characteristics is closely related to the issue of numbers. The fact is that some actors have particular strengths and peculiar weaknesses. To use the cash call example, junior explorers are often cash poor, but skill rich. As such, once they have farmed-in, they are more likely than their senior partners (eg, international or national oil companies) to become distressed if project costs suddenly increase. Indeed, cost increases that might go virtually unnoticed by an international oil company may be enough to sink a junior explorer. If a farmee becomes insolvent, one procedural consequence may be that the other parties to the joint venture may be unable to commence arbitration to enforce dilution of the insolvent farmee's participating interest. The same problem can arise with local entities, where the appointment of a liquidator may affect the standing of these parties to arbitrate and be arbitrated against.

Complications can also arise when local entities are introduced to the joint venture and their conduct is regulated by mandatory laws which may not be consistent with the terms of the joint venture agreement. The reconciliation of the laws governing these actors with the law governing the joint venture generally is no simple exercise, and can (if not properly conducted by the arbitrators) jeopardise the enforceability of an award made in relation to them. Similar issues can also arise where the joint venture is established through the incorporation of a local joint venture company.

At the other end of the scale, international oil companies tend to avail of complex corporate structures by using local subsidiaries, holding companies and even other joint ventures as vehicles for counterparty interactions. Performance of the contract is often shared among the 'outer' members of the corporate group, with the 'centre' supplying command, capital and expertise. Similarly, when disputes arise in joint ventures that involve national oil companies, they are often complicated by politico-strategic factors. For example, when a national oil company is involved, the existence of a dispute may implicate the host state. If a claim is made against a national oil company, the claimants may wish to join the host state on the basis of international law principles of attribution and state responsibility, or even bring the claim directly against the host state under an investment treaty.[37] The published awards – of which there have been dozens in the last decade – show that these types of claim raise complex questions of jurisdiction and admissibility. Alternatively, the claim for attribution may be made at the enforcement stage, when the successful joint venturers engage in 'hot oil litigation' in an attempt to attach the assets of the national oil company (or the host state) in other countries.

4.3   Subject matter

The second reason why arbitration of oil and gas joint venture disputes is often afflicted by procedural problems is subject matter. Oil and gas projects are high-risk ventures involving large-scale capital commitments over long periods. When disputes arise, the parties often want more than money. For this reason, when arbitrations occur in this context, claimants regularly seek orders of specific performance and declaratory relief, rather than damages, as a means of 'getting what they bargained for'. To return to the dilution example, the non-defaulting parties might seek a declaration that the defaulting party is in default, and that they are

---

37   The procedural options open to the claimant investor will vary depending on the investment treaty in question. When drafting the arbitration clause, if the host government is a party to the agreement in question and the Washington Convention, it must be determined whether the Rules of Procedure for Arbitration of the International Centre for Settlement of Investment Disputes (ICSID) would be appropriate and, if so, whether an alternative arbitral institution should also be selected for disputes for which ICSID may lack jurisdiction. In choosing an institution, account should be taken of various issues, including the historic forum preferences of the state respondent (eg, eastern European states display a preference for the Stockholm Chamber of Commerce), the possibility of intervention by third parties (either as proper parties or by way of *amicus* briefs) and whether any aspects of the claim might make it susceptible to set aside proceedings at the seat (or annulment in the ICSID system).

entitled to dilute its participating interest in accordance with the dilution provisions of the JOA. It may also be necessary for the non-defaulting parties to seek an order of specific performance that compels the defaulting party to transfer its registered interests in the relevant permits to the non-defaulting parties.

The occurrence of a default can raise difficult legal issues, as a participant's failure to answer a cash call may place the operation in jeopardy and require the other participants to make up the difference on short notice. Devices used to deal with default include:

- forfeiture;
- 'withering clauses';
- abatement or dilution of the defaulting party's interests;
- liens; and
- loss or suspension of rights to production, rights of purchase and claims for debt (including charges over the defaulting party's participating interest and other assets).[38]

Not all legal systems recognise the enforceability of these types of arrangement or the powers of arbitrators to grant the types of relief necessary to carry them into effect. Unless the parties have chosen appropriate bodies of substantive and procedural law to govern their contract and any arbitral proceedings that may occur under it, their prayers for relief may be denied.

Similarly, it will often be of the utmost importance that the parties continue to perform their obligations while the arbitration takes place. In the deadlock example, if the parties cannot agree on the expenditure proposed, the progress of the project may be obstructed and the good standing of the permits may ultimately be jeopardised (eg, by failure to maintain the minimum works timetable agreed with the regulator). In this situation, interim measures of protection may be required, for example to compel continuing performance of minimum works obligations pending final determination of the dispute as to voting rights. In the dilution example, the defaulting party may need interim measures of protection to prevent the non-defaulting parties from diluting its participating interest. However, like specific

---

38   See JG Adlam, "Joint Venture Operating Agreements", (1989) *Petroleum Conference Proceedings*, New Zealand, p 450. See also C Gallagher, "Default Provisions in JOAs: What are the consequences when a party cannot meet their cash calls?", Unpublished Research Paper, Univ of Dundee, Centre for Energy, Petroleum and Mineral Law and Policy; N Etteh, "Default Provisions under a JOA and Relief Against Forfeiture", Unpublished Research Paper, Univ of Dundee, Centre for Energy, Petroleum and Mineral Law and Policy; and N Etteh, "Joint Operating Agreements: Which Issues are Likely to be the most sensitive to the parties and how can a good contract design limit the damage from such disputes?", Unpublished Research Paper, Univ of Dundee, Centre for Energy, Petroleum and Mineral Law and Policy. In addition, when revising the 2002 AIPN Model JOA the revision committee took note that in Australia, precedent exists supporting the view that an Australian court could arrive at the conclusion, depending on the given circumstances, that requiring a party to forfeit the whole of its participating interest is a penalty which cannot be enforced. Despite the fact that such provisions are enforceable under English law, in various US states and in continental Europe, the revision committee prudently chose to include in Article 8.4 of the model contract an alternative which allows negotiators to avoid forfeiture enforceability questions altogether. The revision committee also rejected the withering interest approach as an alternative, whereby the defaulting party's interest would gradually be reduced to the amount in default. For an analysis of the AIPN revision process on this important question of default, see P Weems and M Bolton, "Highlights from Key Revisions – 2002 AIPN Model Form International Operating Agreement" (http://www.kslaw.com/library/pdf/2002_JOA.pdf).

performance and declaratory relief, the availability of arbitrator-ordered interim measures of protection will depend on the arbitration agreement and the *lex arbitri*.[39]

Subject matter can also raise questions of arbitrability. For example, where the liability of the joint venture under the public laws of the host state is at issue (eg, in the HSE example), it may be impossible to resolve questions of secondary (ie, joint venture-level) liability without impinging on the exclusive jurisdiction of the courts of the host state. Similarly, dilution disputes can also raise questions of arbitrability insofar as they may ultimately go to the 'public status question' of which party holds a registered interest in a given exploration permit.

Another common source of arbitrability arguments is corruption. The principal assets of an oil and gas joint venture are the exploration and production permits that it holds. Obtaining and maintaining these permits requires a direct and constant interface with representatives of the host state. Over the lengthy duration of an oil and gas project, these host state representatives may invite or require the investors to make payments in cash or kind to 'keep the ink flowing'. If a dispute arises, these dealings may undermine the enforceability of the joint venture agreement. While under the laws of many leading seats an allegation of corruption will not void the arbitration agreement, such an allegation makes good stock for non-arbitrability (and related admissibility) arguments. The application of 'long-arm' statutes such as the US Foreign Corrupt Practices Act[40] can also play a part in this context.

International relations may also trigger arbitrability and admissibility arguments. The recent experiences of certain oil and gas companies in Libya and Syria illustrate how UN and EU trade sanctions – the effects of which may be framed in terms of hardship or *force majeure* – can implicate the authorities and prerogatives of international arbitrators. Given that, under the Convention on the Recognition and Enforcement of Foreign Arbitral Awards 1958 (New York Convention) system, non-arbitrability is a ground for refusing to enforce the award,[41] great care needs to be taken to ensure that these issues do not 'infect' the award. The best way to manage the risk of non-arbitrability is to select an advanced, 'arbitration-friendly' seat for the tribunal. However, due to the multiplicity of laws that can govern arbitrability, even with the selection of an advanced seat, the risk of non-arbitrability findings in enforcement courts may remain. Ultimately, the appointment of experienced arbitrators is the best insurance that the parties can take out.

5. Procedural problem solving

The best way to solve procedural problems is to anticipate them. The long-term nature of an oil and gas joint venture is such that the eventual occurrence of a dispute should, as a matter of prudence, be assumed. The officers and staff tasked with the day-to-day management and operations of the joint venture must be

---

39 Most arbitration rules now expressly address the issue of interim measures of protection. For example, see Article 26 of the United Nations Commission on International Trade Law (UNCITRAL) Rules; Article 28 of the 2012 International Chamber of Commerce (ICC) Rules; Article 34(a) of the American Arbitration Association (AAA) Commercial Rules; Article 25(1) of the London Court of International Arbitration (LCIA) Rules; and Article 183 of the Swiss Private International Law Act.
40 15 USC Sec 78dd-1, *et seq.*
41 New York Convention on the Recognition and Enforcement of Foreign Arbitral Awards, Article V(2)(a).

trained so that they develop a 'dispute resolution-oriented culture'. It must be understood that the occurrence of dispute is not a failure *per se* – what constitutes a failure is the inability to anticipate a possible dispute and be ready to deal with it efficiently when it arises.[42]

Arbitration is a highly specialised discipline, and anticipating when and how arbitration will occur requires specific expert input. The need for the assistance of experienced arbitration practitioners is heightened by the fact that the law and practice of international arbitration is in a phase of rapid, user-driven development. Oil and gas companies are among the biggest users of arbitration, and so many of the areas in which the jurisprudence is developing fastest are directly relevant to oil and gas joint venture dispute resolution. These areas include:

- the ways in which the jurisdiction of the arbitral tribunal can be extended to non-signatories; and
- the powers of arbitrators to grant interim measures of protection and non-monetary relief, such as orders of specific performance and declarations.

With the selection of the right governing law and arbitration rules and the proper drafting of the arbitration clause, it is possible to obtain the benefit of these developments and avoid many of the procedural problems that are experienced when oil and gas joint venture disputes go to arbitration.

5.1 Multiple parties and joinder of non-signatories

In relation to multi-party arbitration, the choice of seat is crucial. If the joint venture will (or may) involve more than two parties, care should be taken to select an appropriate seat for the tribunal. Even within the group of leading seats, some are better developed than others when it comes to multi-party arbitration. Understanding the tolerances of each seat is a fine point. For example, it is often said that French law has recognised the so-called 'group of companies doctrine' as a basis for exercising jurisdiction over non-signatories.[43] There is some exaggeration in this, in particular because there is no such equivalent doctrine in French company law. What is known as 'group of companies doctrine' in international arbitration could be more precisely defined as a presumption of consent to arbitration; in other words, where companies share a number of common factors – including corporate branding, ultimate shareholders and senior management – and where a non-signatory company within that group had some form of involvement in the circumstances of a given dispute, this non-signatory company can be presumed to have accepted to be bound by the arbitration clause entered into by one or several of the other group companies. This doctrine has its origins in International Chamber of

---

42   In this regard, oil and gas companies would do well to observe the contract management practices of large construction companies, where compliance with correspondence and record-keeping protocols often lead to significant time and cost savings in document production and witness preparation required for arbitration.

43   *Dow Chemical v Isover Saint Gobain*, ICC Case 4131 (1982), September 23 1982, 9 YB Com Arb 136 (1984); see Yves Derains's comment in (1983) *JDI* 899. The award was confirmed by the Paris Court of Appeal in *Dow Chemical v Isover Saint Gobain* (October 21 1983, Rev Arb 1984, p 98). See also WW Park, "Non-Signatories and International Contracts: an Arbitrator's Dilemma", (2008) 2 Disp Res Int 84.

Commerce (ICC) jurisprudence and has been accepted by a number of arbitral tribunals[44] and national courts[45] in recent years. In other jurisdictions, such as England,[46] the courts have displayed a preference for contractual and equitable theories (eg, agency and estoppel) as bases for 'joining' non-signatories.[47] The ability to invoke equitable estoppel as a basis for exercising jurisdiction over non-signatories is also recognised in ICC jurisprudence.[48] When the choice of seat is made for a dispute resolution clause in a multi-party contract, care must be taken to avoid jurisdictions where the courts are hostile to these principles, or where narrow notions of privity prevail in the arbitral context.

The choice of seat does not overcome all of the problems that can be associated with the exercise of jurisdiction over non-signatories. This is because once the arbitral tribunal finds that it does have jurisdiction over a non-signatory, that non-signatory will be entitled to the full set of procedural rights enjoyed by the other parties, including the right to appoint an arbitrator. As the *Dutco* case[49] illustrates, denying a party the right to participate in the formation of the tribunal will be a ground for setting aside or refusing to enforce the award. In practice, two main approaches can be taken to mitigate the '*Dutco* risk':

- Where the parties have a preference for a three-member tribunal, the parties should use arbitration rules (eg, the 2012 ICC Rules[50]) which provide that in circumstances where there are three or more parties and the parties cannot 'form sides' for the purposes of appointment, all three arbitrators will be appointed by an agreed appointing authority; or
- The parties can simply agree to a sole arbitrator who, in the event that there are three or more parties and no agreement can be reached, will be appointed by an agreed appointing authority.[51]

---

44   See, for example, ICC Case 5721; ICC Case 6519; ICC Case 8910; and ICC Case 11405.
45   See Supreme Court of Singapore, *Aloe Vera of America Inc v Asianic Food Pte Ltd* (2007) YCA 489; Swiss *Tribunal federal*, ASA (1996) Bulletin 14; and in Australia see *Altain Khuder LLC v IMC Mining Inc* [2011] VSC 1.
46   See, for example, *Petersen Farms, Inc v C&M Farming Ltd* [2004] 1 Lloyd's Rep 603, where the English court rejected the existence of the 'Group of Companies Doctrine' in English law.
47   *International Paper Company v Schwabedisen Maschinen & Anlagen GmbH*, 206 F3d 411 (Fourth Circuit, 2000). In French law, estoppel is known as "*le principe de l'interdiction de se contredire au detriment d'autrui*". As opposed to English law, in French law the notion of estoppel is intimately linked to that of good faith. On this nuance, see P Pinsolle, "*Distinction entre le principe de l'estoppel et le principe de bonne foi dans le droit du commerce international*", (1998) *JDI* 905. See also E Kleiman, "Stop! *Définition nécessaire de l'estoppel, entre faveur à l'arbitrage et droit d'accès au juge*", *JCP* 2010, 303.
48   MW Buhler and TH Webster, *Handbook of ICC Arbitration* (2005), 100. For example, estoppel by 'direct benefit' was accepted as a basis for exercising jurisdiction over non-signatories in ICC Case 2375 of 1975 and ICC Case 5730 of 1998.
49   Cass, Civ 1, *Siemens AG v Dutco Construction Company*, January 7 1992. The case began as an ICC arbitration commenced by Dutco against BKMI and Siemens. The three parties were members of a consortium formed to construct a cement plant in Oman. When a dispute arose, it became evident that the contract did not indicate how the arbitrators were to be appointed, and yet the two respondents were unrelated corporations with differing interests and failed to agree on the appointment of an arbitrator. The two respondents in *Dutco* were indeed independent and had potentially conflicting interests in the arbitration. As Eric Schwartz notes, the claimant had separate and distinct causes of action against each of them. See EA Schwarz, "Multiparty Arbitration and the ICC in the Wake of *Dutco*", (1993) 110 *J Int Arb* 5. See also R Ugarte, T Bevilaqua, "Ensuring Party Equality in the Process of Designating Arbitrators in Multiparty Arbitration: An Update on the Governing Provisions", (2010) 27(1) *J Int Arb* 9.
50   See Article 12(8) of the 2012 ICC Rules.
51   See Article 12(8) of the 2012 ICC Rules; Article 7(2) of the UNCITRAL Rules; and Article 8.1 of the 1998 LCIA Rules.

Taking either approach will minimise the *'Dutco* risk' and go a long way to ensuring that if a non-signatory is brought into the proceedings, that party is not denied its fundamental procedural rights. Experience suggests that the optimal combination of law and rules is, for this purpose, French procedural law and the 2012 ICC Rules. An alternative combination would be English procedural law and the London Court of International Arbitration (LCIA) Rules.[52]

If the joint venture comprises multiple contracts from the outset, such as an SBGA and a JOA,[53] the parties must ensure that the dispute resolution provisions of each contract are identical, and that either the law of the seat or the chosen arbitration rules (or ideally both) allow for consolidation of related disputes. Again, some seats are ahead of others in this regard. For example, Australia has enacted a 'Model Law Plus' consolidation provision in its international arbitration statute,[54] making it a suitable seat for multi-contract arbitration. If the chosen arbitration rules do not allow for consolidation and the law of the preferred seat is also silent, the tribunal can be empowered to consolidate by express stipulation in the dispute resolution clause. Returning to the AIPN model contracts, this can be achieved by selection of Article 18.2, Option (D)(4) of the AIPN JOA 2002.[55]

5.2 Sovereign immunities
Regarding party characteristics, as has previously been observed, the involvement of national oil companies can raise problems of sovereign immunity. Given the commercial nature of joint venture agreements in the oil and gas sector, the 2002 AIPN model JOA added a waiver of sovereign immunity clause to Article 18.4. The purpose of this waiver is to prevent a government-owned party from claiming sovereign immunity in relation to dispute resolution proceedings or, more broadly, any action brought to enforce any decision or settlement, award or judgment against it. To use the example of a joint venture in which a national oil company will participate, the commercial parties would be well advised to seek an express waiver of sovereign immunity from both jurisdiction and execution.

5.3 Fast-track arbitration
For certain parties, time is of the essence. This is especially true of operators and junior farmees. A common complaint of oil and gas companies is that, in disputes that are essentially only about the payment of joint venture costs, arbitration takes too long. If it takes two years to get an award, the cash flow of the joint venture (and the parties to it) may be damaged, potentially beyond repair. One way of solving this

---

52   See D Mildon, "Unique Issues in Oil and Gas Disputes", (2006) 3(5) *TDM* 1. In response to the *Dutco* decision, the ICC, AAA and LCIA have recently adopted rules that allow the institutions to appoint all arbitrators when there are more than two parties to an arbitration and either all claimants or all respondents are unable to agree on the joint appointment of an arbitrator for their side. See ICC Rules Article 12(8); AAA International Rules Article 6(5); and LCIA Rules Article 8.1.
53   In 2002 the AIPN JOA revision committee rightfully decided to address the possibility of multi-party arbitration. In the event of a lack of agreement, the model JOA currently provides that the arbitral institution must appoint either the arbitrators not already appointed or all three arbitrators. The second alternative thus addresses the *Dutco* dilemma.
54   See International Arbitration Act 1974 (Cth), Section 24.
55   See also Article 20.2, Option (D)(4) of the AIPN UOA 2006.

problem is by agreeing to use a special procedure for disputes in relation to authority for expenditure and cash calls, such as 'baseball' arbitration.

In a baseball arbitration (also referred to as 'pendulum' arbitration), the proceedings are tightly programmed and the parties must put forward their best offer. The arbitrator's mandate is then usually limited to accepting the offer of one party or the other, a model which is seen as ensuring that both parties make the most reasonable offer possible. An example of this baseball model can be found in the AAA Rules.[56] Naturally, this form of arbitration is inappropriate for complex disputes. Accordingly, if the parties wish to include a baseball option, the arbitration agreement must be carefully drafted to ensure that the circumstances in which baseball arbitration can be used are clearly defined. Specialist assistance is essential in this regard.

Another way to resolve this issue is to effectively combine a 'classic' institutional arbitration clause (eg, an ICC or LCIA model clause) with a bespoke fast-track procedure. Some institutional rules are better suited than others to this kind of tailoring. For example, the ICC allows the parties to shorten the various time limits set out in the rules.[57] However, for this to be effective, one needs to set reasonable and realistic time limits, define milestones for each step in the proceedings (including the issuance of the award), and allow for some flexibility where this is necessary to ensure compliance with principles of due process.[58]

5.4   Subject-matter issues

While subject matter-driven problems are more difficult to account for, they can, to some extent, still be managed in advance through the selection of an appropriate seat and the inclusion of specific empowering language in the arbitration clause. To use the common example of remedies, because certain types of joint venture dispute may require the availability of specific performance and declaratory relief in order to be resolved, it is essential that these remedies be available to arbitrators under the procedural law that governs the arbitration. It is not enough that the arbitration agreement states that the arbitrators can grant these types of relief, as the procedural law of the arbitration may contain mandatory prohibitions that invalidate these aspects of the *compromis*.

In many countries, the arbitration law recognises a presumption (sometimes referred to as 'seat theory' or '*approche territorialiste*') that by selecting a certain seat for the tribunal, the parties intended that the law of that jurisdiction would be the procedural law of the arbitration.[59] While there is a view that specific performance

---

56   See the Rules for Expedited Procedures of the American Arbitration Association.

57   See Article 32(1) of the 2010 ICC Rules and Article 38(1) of the 2012 ICC Rules.

58   The ICC Rules are well developed in this respect. They provide that the court, on its own initiative, may extend any time limit which has been modified by the parties if it decides that it is necessary to do so in order for the arbitral tribunal and the court to fulfil their responsibilities in accordance with the rules. See Article 32(2) of the 2010 ICC Rules and Article 38(2) of the 2012 ICC Rules.

59   'Seat theory' is not accepted everywhere. For example, French international arbitration law refuses to consider that the mere fact that the seat of arbitration proceedings is in France subjects the arbitration to the French legal order. This approach is known as 'delocalisation' and can be distinguished from the *approche territorialiste* that prevails in certain other jurisdictions. For this proposition, see P Mayer, "*L'obligation de concentrer la matière s'impose-t-elle dans l'arbitrage international*", [2011] *Cahiers de l'Arbitrage*, p 418 ; E Gaillard and J Savage, *Fouchard, Gaillard, Goldman on International Commercial Arbitration* (first edition, 1999), p 635; and D Hascher, [2005] *Répertoire de droit international*, para 113.

and declaratory relief are general principles of law[60] or even part of the emerging procedural *lex mercatoria*, the safer view is that the availability of these remedies is a jurisdiction-specific question. Accordingly, parties to upstream joint venture agreements should check whether these remedies can be granted by arbitrators before the choice of seat is finally made. England is an example of a jurisdiction where the arbitration law expressly empowers arbitrators to grant specific performance and declaratory relief.[61] French law also recognises the power of arbitrators to grant specific performance[62] and to order a pecuniary sanction – generally a lump sum payable for each day of delay (known as an *'astreinte'*) – in addition to a principal order, in the event that the debtor does not comply with the principal order within the timeframe set by the judge.[63] The selection of these seats is therefore advisable for parties entering into FOAs and JOAs in which the obligation to contribute to joint venture expenses is backed up by default and dilution rules.

6. Conclusion

This chapter has described the main reasons why upstream oil and gas joint ventures are prone to disputes and why the arbitration of such joint venture disputes can lead to certain procedural problems. Proper drafting of the arbitration clause, including express reference to the remedies that are essential to preserve the intended risk allocation and essence of the bargain, can help parties to avoid many of the procedural problems that are too often experienced when joint venture disputes arise.

The fastest route to safety is through the use of the options offered in many model joint venture contracts, such as those of the AIPN suite. But for some matters, bespoke drafting is required. Examples include fast-track procedures and waivers of sovereign immunity. For these elements, a balance must be struck between simplicity and efficacy, the key being to avoid creating problems in the process of anticipating them. After all, the experiences of many parties illustrate that it is certainly possible to be 'too clever' when drafting an arbitration clause.

The dispute resolution 'wish list' of any international oil and gas joint venture participant should be an advanced, arbitration-friendly seat (where the courts do not unnecessarily interfere), modern institutional rules and a tribunal with powers that are clearly defined and which allow for the bargain struck to be enforced. Paying due attention to these elements of the arbitration clause will ensure that, to the fullest

---

60   See, for example, ME Schneider, "Non-Monetary Relief in International Arbitration: Principles and Arbitration Practice", (2011) in ME Schneider and J Knoll (eds), *ASA Performance as a Remedy* 6, where the author comments: "More thorough examinations of the subject have shown that specific performance is so widely available in legal systems that it can be considered a general principle of law."
61   See English Arbitration Act 1996, Section 48(3) of which allows for declaratory relief, and Section 48(5)(b) of which permits arbitrators to grant specific performance.
62   See Paris Court of Appeal, May 19 1998, *Torno SPA v Kagumai Gumi Co Ltd* [1999] Rev Arb 601, where the court refused to set aside an award on the ground that the arbitrators had ordered specific performance of an obligation to transfer a company's shares; see also Paris CA, April 7 1994, *Lechevalier v Société Croisière Loisir et Communications Internationale*, [1999] Rev Arb 61; Cass Civ 1, March 25 2009, [2009] Bull Civ I 63; E Loquin, "*Arbitrage, Compétence arbitrale*", JurisClasseur Procédure civile (2009), para 11.
63   See New Article 1468 of the Code of Civil Procedure, which provides that the arbitral tribunal has the power to order any interim measure and to subject its performance to penalties.

extent possible, joint venture participants enjoy all of the unassailable advantages of arbitration, including neutrality, speed and enforceability under the New York Convention.

The views expressed in this chapter are solely those of the author. The author expresses his gratitude to Sam Luttrell, an associate in the international arbitration group of Freshfields Bruckhaus Deringer, for his invaluable help.

EPC claims and construction disputes

Jeremy Farr
Simon Hems
Charles Lockwood
Ince & Co LLP

1. Introduction

No matter what the type of project or where it features in the supply chain, a project will not get off the ground and return a profit without putting the hardware in place. However, it is not the users of that hardware who possess the necessary expertise to do so. As with construction in any industrial sector, specialist contractors are employed to undertake the required design, fabrication, erection and installation work; and whatever the scale of the project, more often than not the work is tendered out by the operators to main contractors on an engineering, procurement and construction (EPC) basis. The purpose of so doing is effectively to hand over completely the responsibility and risk associated with some of the most technically complex construction projects anywhere in the world involving offshore units, pipelines, refineries and other facilities necessary for the production, processing and transportation of oil and gas, often in a hostile environment with poor local infrastructure, security concerns and long supply chains.

'EPC' refers to the scope of the contractor's work. When an employer contracts with a contractor on an EPC basis, the contractor will be responsible for the design of the facility and the procurement of all necessary materials and equipment, as well as the actual construction phase. It is usually up to the contractor to decide whether to undertake the entire work itself, but it is not unusual for it to subcontract various elements to more specialist contractors.

There are many variations of this type of contract, including EPIC (which brings installation and commissioning into the scope) and EPCM (which adds management).

This chapter discusses key aspects of EPC contracts which typically give rise to disputes, the nature of the claims and how they are addressed, available remedies and the handling of evidence created during the life of an EPC project.

2. Key aspects of EPC contracts giving rise to disputes

2.1 Schedules/programmes

(a) Failure to meet delivery date and other milestones

Importance of scheduling: The contract will provide for deliverables on one or more dates, but it is not unusual for EPC projects to overrun. The contract will usually require a schedule to be prepared by the contractor (and submitted to the employer), setting out how the project will be completed by the completion date (and how milestone dates will be achieved). The schedule should identify all of the activities required to achieve completion, the duration of each activity, sequencing, links and overlap. Such a schedule is an important tool for both parties, but it will only be as good as the logic used by the programmer.

The contractor should update the schedule regularly and the contract will require it to report actual progress against budgeted progress, usually monthly. However, in the authors' experience, the relationship that such reports bear to reality is variable. A poor correlation is typically due to one or a combination of several factors: use of inadequate software, insufficient level of detail, inaccurate reporting, wishful thinking and deliberate manipulation of the data. The Society of Construction Law (SCL) Delay and Disruption Protocol 2002 provides useful guidance on project planning and delay analysis. However, while the SCL protocol has been referred to by the English courts in some cases, it does not have the force of law and the terms of the particular contract will prevail.[1]

Accurate scheduling will assist with the performance of the contract, particularly with time and resource management. It is also an invaluable tool for establishing and quantifying time overruns. Inaccurate scheduling leads to disputes and complicates their resolution.

Addressing delay: There are three broad categories of delay:
- delay caused by a contractor risk event;
- delay caused by an employer risk event; or
- delay caused by something which is out of the parties' control (eg, *force majeure*).

The latter two may be classed together in the contract as 'permissible delay'.

While the English courts have considered delay on many occasions and there is established precedent in relation to many of the common issues, the court will generally decide cases on their facts and in light of the terms of the particular contract.

In the case of a contractor risk event, the contractor is entirely responsible for meeting the completion date and any contractual milestone dates, save to the extent that it can demonstrate an entitlement to an extension of time. That will require the operation of an employer risk event or some other form of permissible delay.

When the contractor is responsible for delay which adversely affects the completion date or a contractual milestone date, the rights that arise in favour of the employer will depend on the terms of the contract. These terms typically include:
- a right to claim general damages at common law;
- a right to liquidated damages provided under the contract;

---

1   See, for example, *Balfour Beatty v London Borough of Lambeth* [2002] BLR 288; *Mirant Asia-Pacific Construction (Hong Kong) Ltd v Ove Arup Partners International Ltd* [2008] Bus LR D1, [2007] EWHC 918; *Great Eastern Hotel Company Ltd v John Laing Construction Ltd* 99 ConLR 45, [2005] EWHC 181; *Adyard Abu Dhabi v SD Marine Services* [2011] BLR 384, 136 ConLR 190, [2011] EWHC 848.

- a right to terminate the contract; and
- a right to rescind the contract and to claim a refund of the instalments paid.

If the employer can prove at any stage of the project that it is impossible for the contractor to meet the delivery date or any contractual milestones, the employer may have a claim in respect of an anticipatory breach and, in some cases, may be entitled to terminate the contract. However, such a claim is rarely without its risks, since it is usually possible for the contractor to accelerate the work to some extent, particularly where the project is in its early stages. If the employer purports to terminate wrongly, it may itself be held in repudiatory breach.

The primary grounds for an employer risk event are:

- a failure to provide essential employer deliverables on time or at all, or which are compliant with requirements of the specifications; and
- variations or changes to the work scope instructed by the employer.

It is quite normal, particularly in the energy industry, for the employer to be responsible for certain packages, usually specialist high-value equipment with a long lead time. The employer will contract separately with the third-party supplier and the EPC contractor's responsibility might be no more than to install such equipment. The relationship between the employer, its EPC contractor and its equipment contractor will usually be documented in a separate agreement dealing with the interface between the two contractors. If the equipment is delivered late, there may be consequences with regard to the ability of the EPC contractor to meet the completion date or some other contractual milestone, or there may be additional costs caused by the need to reschedule work or accelerate work, or simply because of prolongation if the completion date is not met. The EPC contract would be expected to provide that such time and cost would be caused by an employer risk event. If the contract does not state this expressly, then the contractor will seek an extension of time and damages on the basis of the employer's breach of contract in failing to provide the deliverables within the time specified in the contract. If no time is specified, the employer will be deemed to be entitled to a reasonable time taking all relevant factors into account.[2]

Usually, the contract will specify the time within which a variation order request must be submitted. This gives certainty to the employer so that it can be confident that it will not be faced with multiple claims for additional compensation at the end of the project. It also means that any time impact on the completion date can be assessed contemporaneously and steps taken to revise the schedule as necessary. Even if the delay is caused by an employer risk event, the contractor is still under a duty to mitigate any delay to the extent it is able.[3] Care should be taken by the contractor to ensure that variation order requests are submitted within the

---

2   *Multiplex Constructions (UK) Ltd v Honeywell Control Systems* [2007] BLR 195, 111 ConLR 78, [2007] EWHC 447 (TCC); *Trollope & Colls Ltd v North West Metropolitan Regional Hospital Board* [1973] 2 All ER 260, [1973] 1 WLR 601.
3   *British Westinghouse v Underground Railways Co* [1912] AC 673, [1911-13] All ER Rep 63; *Andros Springs (Owners) v Owners of World Beauty, The World Beauty* [1968] 3 All ER 158, [1970] P 144.

prescribed time limit; failure by the contractor to do so may amount to a waiver of its rights of recourse against the employer. Even assuming that a variation order request is submitted on time, if the contractual procedure – particularly requirements to address cost and schedule impact – is not followed to the letter, the contractor may still lose out. Simply reserving the contractor's rights in relation to either a cost or time impact is unlikely to be effective if the contract does not allow for that.

By definition, variation order requests originate from the contractor and are commonly refused on grounds that the work was always required by the contract scope of work or was necessary to repair or replace defective or improper workmanship. If such disputed variation order requests are simply left unresolved, schedule issues are also left unaddressed. This becomes an acute problem where a contractor considers that it is entitled and works to an extended completion or milestone deadline which is not recorded in the contract.

If the delay is caused by events outside the control of both parties and is sufficiently serious, it may be dealt with by way of *force majeure*. However, English law does not have a common law remedy of *force majeure*, so its availability will depend on the existence and form of a *force majeure* clause. 'Boilerplate' *force majeure* clauses are unlikely to be suitable for an EPC project, as there will be a number of potential blockages to progress consequent from the nature and location of the work from which the contractor (which is likely to be the one most affected) will wish to be protected. An example is where river transportation of sections of the work from the contractor's premises to another location for completion, installation or hook-up is required, but there are drought or tidal issues affecting that transportation. There may also be circumstances where the contractor is protected for certain defaults of its subcontractors – notably, where the subcontractor is performing the work in a politically difficult environment. However, the agreement of a broad *force majeure* clause must be approached with caution, as the usual consequence of a defined period of *force majeure* delay will be a right of termination.

Typical disputes in relation to *force majeure* clauses concern the applicability of a defined event to the actual facts, proof of a *force majeure* event to the required standard set out in the clause and timeliness of notices.

For completeness, frustration should also be mentioned. It is sometimes alleged that a contract has been frustrated. If the facts giving rise to the alleged frustration are in fact a *force majeure* event for which the contract provides a remedy, there can be no frustration. In any event, frustration is extremely difficult to establish and the argument which is sometimes raised – that an event has occurred which would make it extremely expensive to continue with the contract – does not give rise to a frustration.[4]

(b) *Establishing claims in respect of delay and disruption*

Delay and disruption claims are common under EPC contracts. In order to substantiate a claimed entitlement to an extension of time arising from an employer risk event or some other form of permissible delay, the contractor must prove actual

---

4   *Ocean Tramp Tankers Corporation v V/O Sovfracht "The Eugenia"* [1964] 2 QB 226, [1964] 1 All ER 161.

delay to the critical path which affects the completion of the project or part of it. Not every employer risk event gives rise to an entitlement to an extension of time. 'Disruption' means a disturbance, hindrance or interruption of a contractor's normal work progress, resulting in lower efficiency or lower productivity than would otherwise be achieved, but which does not necessarily result in delay.[5]

In the simple case, the claim for an extension of time or disruption costs will arise from an agreed increase to the scope of work and the parties will agree the time and costs consequences in a variation order before the work has commenced. In that case there will be a prospective assessment of the consequences. Frequently, however, that prospective assessment is not agreed, the variation procedure is not followed or the claim arises from an alleged breach by the employer, and the contractor nonetheless proceeds with the work. By the time that the contractor comes to present (or re-present) its claim, the initial assessment of the additional time or costs will have developed, perhaps because the impact of the relevant event is now known, enabling the effects to be assessed retrospectively.

Concurrent delay: The contractor's entitlement to an extension of time where two or more delaying events occur at the same time – one an employer risk event and the other not – is an area of some controversy. In *Adyard* Justice Hamblen reviewed the authorities and concluded that there is concurrence only if both events in fact cause delay to the progress of the works and the delaying effect of the two events is felt at the same time.[6] In those circumstances, if there are two concurrent causes of delay, one of which is an employer risk event and the other is not, the contractor is entitled to an extension of time for the period of delay caused by the employer risk event notwithstanding the concurrent effect of the other.[7]

Delay analysis: The appropriate analysis to be used in any given case will depend on the terms of the contract and the availability of supporting information – any assessment of delay will likely need to be supported by documentary evidence, including programmes if these were produced and evidence from an expert in the programming of construction projects.

A number of techniques have been developed. These are described in the SCL protocol and short descriptions are given below.[8] The availability of any particular method will depend on the amount of information available. Some of the methods identified below are simplistic and the assessments of schedule impact are accordingly less reliable:

- Time impact (windows) – this method can be applied either prospectively or retrospectively. It takes the as-planned programme at the time of the event and adds sub-networks of events that have occurred (or are anticipated to occur) in

---

5   Definition based on Appendix A of the SCL protocol.
6   *Adyard Abu Dhabi v SD Marine Services* [2011] BLR 384, 136 ConLR 190, [2011] EWHC 848.
7   *Henry Boot Construction (UK) Ltd v Malmaison Hotel* (Manchester) Ltd (1999) 70 ConLR 32. See also *Royal Brompton Hospital NHS Trust v Hammond* (No 7) (2001) 76 Con LR 148, [2001] EWCA Civ 206; and for further reading, John Marin QC, "Concurrent Delay" (2002) 18 *Const LJ* No 6 436.
8   The SCL Protocol provides useful guidance on analysis of delay and disruption. However, it does not have the force of law and the terms of the particular contract will always prevail.

order to calculate their effect on that programme. This method therefore takes account of any changes to the programme or delay that has occurred up to the time of the event, and can take account of concurrence and any resequencing, mitigating action or acceleration. Since continuous progress data may not be available, derivations of this method (eg, 'windows analysis') are often used. Windows analysis uses progress data at the intervals it is available (assuming that it has been updated periodically rather than continuously) and looks at events which affect progress in a specific time period (or window). The as-planned programme can then be updated at the end of each window. The SCL protocol states that time impact is the most thorough method of analysis and the best technique for determining an extension of time, and recommends that it be used wherever circumstances permit, whether prospectively or retrospectively. However, it is essential that accurate programmes have been prepared and updated regularly during the project.

- Collapsed as-built – this method of analysis, which is also known as 'as-built but for', is conducted by removing from an as-built programme activities or a series of activities which relate to an identified delaying event (or events) to show what the completion date or other key dates would have been 'but for' the occurrence of the delaying event(s). This method is highly subjective. It addresses only the identified delaying events and relies on the retrospective creation of as-built logic for activities and creation of sub-networks to reflect the effects of a delaying event. These sub-networks are then removed from the as-built programme in a chosen sequence. This method will not identify concurrency of delays or the effects of mitigation, resequencing or acceleration.

- Impacted as-planned – impacted as-planned analysis (or as-planned impacted and impacted plan analysis) is a prospective method of analysis in which an identified delaying event is imposed into the original as-planned programme, which is then recalculated to establish a revised completion date. This can be repeated where there are multiple delaying events in order to establish a revised completion date based on multiple impacts. The difference between the original completion date and the revised completion date is the period of delay attributable to the delaying event(s). Again, this method is simplistic and takes account of neither the actual progress (or any existing delay) up to the time when the delaying event occurred nor any change to resourcing, logic or durations in the programme. While this method of analysis is useful where no as-built records exist (since as-built data is not required), it will produce accurate results only where the original as-planned programme is a close reflection of the as-built sequence of work. Further, this method is unlikely to identify a delaying event and assumes that the identified events are causative of delay.

- As-planned versus as-built – this method compares the duration of an as-planned activity with the as-built duration of that activity once it is known (ie, on a retrospective basis). Both planned and as-built programmes are required in order to carry out this analysis, which demonstrates the importance of preparing accurate programmes which are regularly updated as the as-built status of a project progresses and any changes are made to the planned activities. While this method is in principle considered to be the best way of ascertaining the causes of any delay to completion, it is simplistic and cannot identify concurrency of delays or the effects of mitigation, resequencing or acceleration.

(c)   *Liquidated damages and time of the essence provisions*
This is relevant where the contractor is delayed, but is not entitled to an extension of time. Liquidated damages are the most commonly used contractual remedy for delay in energy construction contracts, and provide that if the contractor fails to complete the works within a specified time or by a specified date, a liquidated sum (ie, fixed and agreed when the contract is entered into) will be payable by the contractor for the period up to the date on which the works are finally completed.

Liquidated damages are advantageous to the employer as there is no need to prove the actual amount of loss that has been suffered as a result of the contractor's delays. Such calculations can be extremely complex, time consuming and expensive for the employer to perform. Similarly, the contractor will be aware from the outset of what its liabilities will be if it causes delay to the works and factor such risk into the tender price. Liquidated damages are usually calculated with reference to the contract price, payable on a daily or weekly basis from the project completion date set out in the contract until a maximum amount or period of time has been reached. Often, a contractor's liability for liquidated damages will be subject to an overall cap, often expressed as a percentage of the contract price.

An express provision in any contract which states that time is of the essence enables the party relying on the clause to terminate the agreement and, if appropriate, claim damages if the other party fails to perform by or within the contractually specified timeframe. Difficulties arise where there are both liquidated damages and time of the essence provisions. The question concerns whether there is a fundamental conflict between liquidated damages clauses and an express time is of the essence provision.

A liquidated damages clause will conflict with time of the essence provisions only if it is intended that liquidated damages be the sole remedy for late performance. Liquidated damages provisions and express termination provisions may well override a boilerplate clause declaring time to be of the essence, as they provide evidence as to the intention of the parties and their chosen regime in respect of damages for delay. If delay in completion continues beyond the maximum amount or period specified for liquidated damages, the employer may nevertheless then be entitled to terminate the contract, except where it was intended that liquidated damages be the sole remedy for late performance.

2.2   Warranties

(a)   *Standard of work*
The contractor is likely to have an express obligation under an EPC contract to construct the required structure or facility in compliance with detailed specifications,

often expressed with an accompanying warranty to perform the work to a specified standard. Conditions may also be implied under the Supply of Goods and Services Act 1982 to the effect that the structure or facility provided will correspond with the description, which is likely to include the specifications, and be fit for the specified purpose.

Such implied terms will be subject to the terms of the contract and it is not uncommon for parties to exclude them from an EPC contract. Where they are not so excluded, a failure to have those requirements in mind can catch out the unwary contractor. The consequences of a breach will depend on how the contract or, failing that, the law treats the breach in the context of the subject facts. As a minimum, the employer will have a claim for damages, but it may also be that it is entitled to refuse delivery or even terminate the contract.

Whether work is defective is a prime source of argument. There is often a fine line between work that is defective due to the way in which it has been executed, the impact of defective materials supplied by the employer or a third party and inherent defects in the design of the facility that is being constructed. It may appear to be obvious where responsibility lies in each case, but careful consideration of the complete facts will always be required. For example, might it be the case that there was a defect in design by the contractor due to reasonable reliance on information contained in the employer's specifications, such as inaccurate – but at the time unverifiable – details of the specification of crude oil to be delivered into first-phase processing facilities? Equally, what if defects in materials supplied by the employer arose out of erroneous design parameters supplied by the contractor? Further, were pertinent issues raised by one party, but not addressed satisfactorily by the other? A clearly written and comprehensive scope of work is essential for any EPC project. Shortcomings in that regard will often compound disputes arising out of allegations about the extent to which a contractor has failed to meet its warranties regarding compliance with the scope of work and standard of performance.

Under the contract, the employer will usually retain the right to make regular inspections throughout the life of the project and will usually have employer representatives on site during the construction works, either permanently or on an 'as needed' basis, to monitor the quality of the work and raise any concerns with the contractor at an early stage. Notification of defective work will be provided by way of non-conformance reports or similar, and will detail the problems identified, along with the necessary remedial work that is required. Punch lists should be generated by the parties to identify work that remains on the 'to do' list.

In relation to defective work, it is common for the employer to reserve its right under the contract to reject any part of the work that does not comply with the contract specifications. If such defective work is identified, the employer may request that the contractor promptly remedy the work; if the contractor subsequently fails to do so within a specified or reasonable time, the employer may, subject to the terms of the contract, suspend or terminate the work. Any costs associated with remedying defective work will be for the contractor's account, including any costs incurred by the employer in utilising a third party to complete the outstanding or defective work scope. A fertile area for disputes arises where the parties differ over whether work set out in a non-conformance report was in fact to remedy defective work or was additional work entitling the contractor to a variation (and possibly also a crucial time extension).

(b) Defects warranty period

Under most EPC contracts, the contractor agrees to provide the employer with an extended warranty to cover defects in the facility constructed which are discovered after completion. Such a warranty is likely to be limited to a specific period after delivery, installation or start-up, after which the rights under the contract in respect of any defects may be extinguished.

Claims under such warranties are not uncommon and, where a defect is present in the facility constructed, the employer is likely to be entitled to have the defect made good or the defective part replaced by the contractor. The employer is often given the additional right to undertake the necessary repair or rectification itself should the contractor fail to do so within a specified time, and to obtain reimbursement by the contractor for the costs incurred in doing so. Where only the contractor can remedy the particular defect (eg, because only it has the necessary tools, expertise or rights to do so), the employer may need to seek an order for specific performance to enforce its claim under the warranty. Needless to say, similar disputes to those possible during the construction phase arise in relation to claimed defects. However, by this time the battleground has generally shifted from a matter of defect versus variation to defect versus mal-operation.

2.3 Liabilities and indemnities

(a) Knock-for-knock

Liability for the contract works will fall to the contractor during the project. Other liabilities will be dictated by the terms of the contract and in relation to each party's property and personnel (and those of third parties). Particularly in offshore construction contracts, liability for property and personnel is usually dealt with by way of reciprocal – or 'knock-for-knock' – indemnity provisions.

A knock-for-knock clause essentially provides that each party will retain responsibility for and indemnify the other in respect of damage sustained to, or loss of, its own personnel or property irrespective of fault, negligence or breach of duty. Such clauses are enforceable provided that clear words are used to ensure that the clause applies to the cause of the loss intended to be covered, most notably negligence.[9]

While it may seem commercially imprudent for a contractor to accept the risk of loss or damage to its own personnel or property irrespective of fault, it provides a clear and certain framework of liability, which can then be insured, and is intended to save both time and costs by removing the need to submit to the lengthy process of establishing fault. Clearly, this decreases the likelihood of the parties ending up in litigation.

---

9   See, for example, *Canada Steamship Lines v R* [1952] AC 192, [1952] 1 All ER 305; EE *Caledonia v Orbit Valve* [1994] 2 Lloyd's Rep 239.

Knock-for-knock provisions are applied very strictly by the courts. In *The A Turtle*[10] the English court reiterated that a knock-for-knock provision is a commercial allocation of risk and should be enforced except in the extreme case of a radical breach, such as a total failure to perform (as opposed to mere negligent performance of the contractual obligations).

It is common for the parties to exclude wilful misconduct, and sometimes gross negligence,[11] from the knock-for-knock regime.

Regardless of any limitations on the application of a knock-for-knock regime, the parties should satisfy themselves that adequate insurance is in place to back up the various indemnities provided. It is preferable for the parties to be included as additional assureds under each other's policies and for provision to be made for the insurers to waive rights of subrogation. It is also common for any applicable limitations of liability to be extended to the amount of cover available, in order that the maximum available recovery can be made from the applicable policy.

(b)   Third-party liabilities

With regard to the position in relation to third-party liabilities, under the contract it is usual for each party to indemnify the other and hold it harmless from any third-party claims in respect of personal injury or property damage sustained as a result of that party's negligence or breach of duty.

(c)   Consequential losses

An EPC contract will often provide a mutual exclusion of liability of each party for consequential or indirect losses of its counterparty. The effectiveness of the exclusion will depend on how well the clause is drafted. Under English common law, a party is entitled to recover losses which flow naturally from the breach and losses which were in the contemplation of the parties when they entered into the contract as the probable result of a breach.[12] The second of these 'limbs' has become regarded as descriptive of indirect or consequential losses. Problems arise where claims are made in respect of loss of profit, production, revenue and contract. There is a misconception, perpetuated in many EPC and other contracts in current use, that such losses fall within the second limb of *Hadley v Baxendale*, such that a mere exclusion of indirect or consequential loss will suffice. However, such losses could just as easily be direct losses recoverable under the first limb. Such disputes can be avoided by making express reference to such types of loss and excluding liability for them, whether direct or indirect.[13]

---

10   *Turtle Offshore SA v Superior Trading Inc (The A Turtle)* [2009] 1 Lloyd's Rep 177, [2009] 2 All ER (Comm) 624.

11   Except in regard to certain aspects of criminal law, English law does not recognise degrees of negligence. However, its common use in international contracts has led the English courts to recognise it should be accorded a meaning. See the *obiter* comments of Justice Mance in *The Hellespont Ardent* [1997] 2 Lloyd's Rep 547; *Camarata Property Inc v Credit Suisse Securities (Europe) Ltd* [2011] BCLC 54, [2011] EWHC 479; *Winnetka Trading Corporation v Julius Baer International Ltd* [2011] EWHC 2030.

12   *Hadley v Baxendale* (1854) 9 Ex 341, (1854) 156 ER 145, [1843-60] All ER Rep 461, (1854) 23 LJ Ex 179.

13   See also, for example, *Millar's Machinery Company Limited v David Way and Son* [1935] 40 Com Cas 204, *Croudace Construction Ltd v Cawoods Concrete Products Ltd* [1978] 2 Lloyd's Rep 55, 8 BLR 20; *BHP Petroleum Limited v British Steel plc* [2000] 2 All ER (Comm) 133, 74 ConLR 63.

2.4 Suspension and termination

Energy-related EPC contracts tend to be complex, long-running and often performed in regions which give rise to difficult socio-political and environmental issues. Therefore, an EPC contract will typically incorporate a suspension and termination regime.

(a) *Suspension*

It is unusual (but not unknown) for a contractor to be able to negotiate a right of suspension, although it might wish to have one in order to address non-payments. The employer will often have such a right which is exercisable for its convenience or for breach on the part of the contractor. A right of suspension might relate to all or part of the contract works.

(b) *Termination*

The contractor does not usually have a contractual right of termination, save in respect of the employer entering into an arrangement with its creditors or insolvency (although persistent and prolonged failure to pay sums due might well give rise to a repudiatory breach at common law, which the contractor could accept and terminate the contract).

The employer will usually have a right to terminate for its own convenience or for breach of contract by the contractor, or if the contractor enters into an arrangement with its creditors or insolvency. Where the employer terminates for its own convenience, the contract should contain a mechanism for the contractor to be paid, not only in respect of works completed, but also in respect of contract works not yet performed.

(c) *Notice of default and the consequences of termination for default*

Termination is a draconian remedy and is a right to be exercised cautiously by the employer. Wrongful termination will be a repudiatory breach by the employer, entitling the contractor to accept the repudiatory breach as itself terminating the contract, and/or to claim damages. It is therefore in the interests of both the employer and the contractor that there be provision for a notice to cure before crystallisation of the right to terminate, and it is usual to find such a notice requirement in EPC contracts. This usually allows the contractor a limited period of time from the date on which the notice of default is served in which to remedy, or commence steps to remedy, the default. If the contractor fails to take the required actions within this time period, the employer is usually entitled to terminate all or part of the remaining works under the contract.

The precise actions that the contractor must take if it is to avoid termination will depend on the terms of the clause. It is not uncommon to find that the default must be remedied within a short period to the sole satisfaction of the employer. Sometimes this obligation is qualified – for example, by stipulating that the contractor will commence within a specified period and thereafter continuously proceed with actions to remedy the default to the reasonable satisfaction of the employer.

In addition to arguments over whether there has been a default as a matter of fact, disputes arise where the right to terminate under the contractual provisions is not expressed as an exclusive remedy and the employer purports to terminate with immediate effect by accepting an alleged repudiatory breach at common law.

2.5   Guarantees and performance bonds

Guarantees are used in relation to EPC contracts to manage the risk of a liability remaining unsatisfied. The guarantee may be issued by an acceptable bank, but commonly it is a parent company guarantee. This usually takes the form of a performance guarantee procured by the contractor from its parent company in favour of the employer to guarantee the contractor's performance under the contract. The scope of any guarantee will always be subject to the wording used and the required wording is often found as an annex to the contract. Under a parent company guarantee, the employer is likely to have a right of action against the guarantor in respect of any default by the contractor and is likely to be entitled to recover from the guarantor any loss suffered as a result by way of damages at large or, where they are provided for under the contract, liquidated damages. Recovery of damages may be subject to the same restrictions (eg, exclusions and limitations) as apply under the EPC contract.

Parent company guarantees are commonly provided in the form of a 'see to it' guarantee such that the guarantor is obliged to rectify any default by the contractor. It may be that the parent company guarantee requires the employer to prove that the contractor has defaulted and that it has suffered loss in the amount claimed. Alternatively, the parent company guarantee may be provided in the form of an 'on-demand' guarantee, which may be called on by the employer without having to prove the default and damages. Much will depend on the strength of the parties' negotiating positions.

There is considerable scope for disputes to arise in relation to whether a parent company guarantee extends to cover a contractor's obligations arising out of variations to the scope of work to be performed. If the contractor's obligations are altered without the guarantor's consent, the guarantor may not be bound. However, this issue will not arise where the guarantor has agreed in the parent company guarantee to be bound by variations to the scope of work, or where the alteration is trivial, unsubstantial or will not conceivably cause prejudice to the guarantor.[14]

The employer may additionally, or alternatively, require the contractor to procure a refund guarantee, which will most commonly be provided by a bank of good standing. Again, the scope of such an instrument will be determined by the wording used, but generally will address the return of payments made to the contractor as the project progresses in circumstances where, for example, the contractor has become insolvent, leading to the employer rescinding the contract. Guarantees are sometimes also provided by employers, generally in order to guarantee payment, and in such case the guarantor may be a bank or a parent company. Alternatively, the employer may be obliged to arrange a letter of credit to cover payment. Such steps are, of course, intended to minimise the risk that the

---

14   *Holme v Brunskill* (1877) 3 QBD 495.

employer cannot pay for the goods and services provided to it, and the need for such measures to be taken will depend on the credit risk of the employer.

3. Dispute resolution: pre-legal proceedings

3.1 Security and liens

Once litigation is in contemplation, a key consideration for a contractor will be whether it is possible to obtain security in respect of its claim. While the project is ongoing and the contractor has care, custody and control of the facility under construction, the contractor has significant leverage in any discussion with the employer. Because of this, the employer may insist on the inclusion of a clause in the contract which prevents the contractor from exercising a lien over the facility or any of the materials provided during the construction process. Such a clause may provide for the contractor to indemnify the employer against any claims associated with an illegitimately asserted lien.

3.2 Alternative dispute resolution

In an attempt to avoid formal litigation or arbitration, the parties to EPC contracts often include a tiered dispute resolution clause, which requires the parties to complete various steps before the commencement of legal proceedings. These usually consist of commercial negotiation involving individuals with increasing levels of responsibility within the parties' organisations or mediation of the dispute. Such provisions may also include adjudication, expert determination or similar alternative dispute resolution procedures.

3.3 Preservation of evidence

Assuming that the claims are not resolved amicably, one of the main considerations in terms of taking a claim forward successfully is the preservation of evidence. The nature of EPC projects means that many of the workforce, even those in senior and management positions, may be employed on contracts for the duration of the project. As soon as the project is over, the contractor's key witnesses may scatter across the globe and start work on other projects for other contractors. This can lead to problems obtaining clear details regarding events during the project.

Associated with the loss or unavailability of witnesses is the potential loss of documentary evidence. Ideally, all documents should be gathered and stored centrally as the project progresses. Failing that, it is important that all documents be copied from personal laptops or smartphones, or physically handed over, after completion but before the individuals' employment contracts come to an end. In circumstances where, for example, employees may be working from a personal laptop, it is all too easy for key documents to go missing. Indeed, it is not unheard of for individuals to be all too aware of just how damaging some documents might be to a case. There is every reason for the legal team (whether in-house or external) to get involved early to capture all available evidence. This is not just to be able to form a view on the merits of a dispute from the outset, but also to avoid the possibility of members of the project team destroying or otherwise suppressing documents which they do not think would be 'helpful'.

As to documents held on site during the construction phase, these will generally be documents passing between the parties in relation to various project issues and possibly disputes. Although a significant quantity of such documents will be sent in electronic format, and thus should be preserved that way, many hard-copy documents must also be carefully preserved. The example of a project team which simply put all of its documents into archive boxes and stacked them in a container in the yard is hardly a paradigm: as a consequence of having them stored in this way over a long period, in outside temperatures ranging from 40 degrees Celsius to -30 degrees Celsius, a wealth of crucial information became totally unusable.

4. Dispute resolution: legal proceedings

The contract should specify the proper law applicable to the contract and the jurisdiction for disputes. If the parties have specified arbitration, the English courts (and commonly many other courts) will enforce that choice. If the contract contains a jurisdiction clause, the dispute should generally be referred to the court of the specified country.[15] If the parties have specified the English courts, the court will accept jurisdiction even if neither the parties nor the subject matter of the contract has a connection with England. If the contract is silent as to jurisdiction, the dispute should be referred to the court having jurisdiction pursuant to the relevant conflict of laws rules. It will always be open to the parties to agree to use a particular form of dispute resolution at any stage, although this may prove difficult if the parties are unable to settle their differences amicably.

Once a dispute is underway, care should be exercised to ensure that any continuing obligations under the contract are satisfied. However, where one party has purported to terminate the contract, the parties will need to consider whether it is consistent with their respective positions to continue performing the contract, and difficult issues can arise here as to repudiatory breach and waiver of rights.

The following sections describe the typical types of claim that arise under EPC contracts by reference to the remedies that are commonly available and the evidence that will generally be required.

4.1 Remedies

(a) Damages

Subject to the terms of the contract, general damages may be available to either party at common law for breach of any term of the contract by the other party. Such damages will generally be assessed on the normal contractual basis – that is, what is necessary to put the innocent party in the position in which it would have been had the contract been properly performed. As with all commercial contracts, the availability of such damages will be subject to the requirement at common law to mitigate, the common law rules of remoteness and the terms of the contract.

---

15 Where a jurisdiction clause states that a particular court has exclusive jurisdiction, disputes should be referred only to that court. However, where jurisdiction is non-exclusive, references may be made to other courts in particular circumstances.

Claims by an employer for damages often arise in relation to delays in the construction process by the contractor (subject to provision made for liquidated damages), non-compliance with specifications or pursuant to warranties. From a contractor's perspective, claims for damages may arise on account of the employer's failure to pay or due to an employer risk event (eg, a variation), which may entitle the contractor to additional costs for both the variation works and any prolongation of the works.

When assessing an entitlement to damages, account should be taken of any contractual limitation and/or exclusion clauses.

As noted above, liquidated damages provisions are widely used in EPC contracts. However, a liquidated damages scheme will generally be enforceable only where the level of liquidated damages is deemed to be a genuine pre-estimate at the time the contract was entered into of the loss that would be suffered as a result of a breach of the particular obligation. If this is not the case, it may be that the liquidated damages specified are held to be unenforceable on the basis they amount to a penalty for breach.[16] EPC contracts will often specify that liquidated damages are the exclusive remedy for the particular breaches to which they apply. However, the claimant may still be entitled to other, non-financial remedies such as termination – perhaps pursuant to an express right of termination following a specified period of delay or where time is stated to be of the essence and the delivery date is not met – or an injunction to prevent breach.[17]

Exclusion and limitation of liability are subject to statutory restrictions under English law, primarily under the Unfair Contract Terms Act 1977. This statute does not apply to a significant portion of international supply contracts,[18] but where it does, liability for death or personal injury resulting from negligence cannot be excluded or limited. Further, where one party is dealing on the other's written standard terms of business, liability for other losses can be excluded or limited only insofar as the exclusion/limitation satisfies the requirement of reasonableness.[19]

(b)   Time

As explained above, where delay has been caused to the works under an EPC contract, the contractor may be entitled to additional time if the delay has been caused by the employer or by another event outside the contractor's control. Most EPC contracts will provide the contractor with an express right to an extension of time in such instances and a procedure whereby such an extension must be claimed. If the contract makes no provision for extensions of time, it is possible that time could be set 'at large' where delay is caused by the employer's actions. Under the

---

16   However, see *Azimut-Benetti Spa (Benetti Division) v Healy* [2011] 1 Lloyd's Rep 473, 132 ConLR 113, [2010] EWHC 2234 (Comm), where the court held that certain clauses may not fall into either the genuine pre-estimate of damages or penalty category, but nevertheless may be commercially justifiable.

17   Although a claimant cannot have both an injunction and liquidated damages in respect of a single breach. See, for example, *Sainter v Ferguson* (1849) 1 Mac & G 286, (1849) 47 ER 1460, (1849) 19 LJ Ch 170, 1 H&Tw 383, (1849) 7 CB 716, 18 LJCP 217.

18   Section 26 of the Unfair Contract Terms Act.

19   For details as to the test of reasonableness, see Section 24 and Schedule 2 of the Unfair Contract Terms Act.

prevention principle, an employer cannot hold a contractor to a specified completion date if the employer has, by an act or omission, prevented the contractor from completing by that date. Where such prevention occurs and the contractor has no express right to an extension of time under the contract for such an event, time will become 'at large' and the obligation to complete by the specified date will be replaced by an implied obligation to complete within a reasonable time.[20] In such case any claim for liquidated damages will generally be invalid and the employer will be required to prove any damages it has suffered as a result of any breach by the contractor.[21]

Should an employer refuse the contractor an extension of time, the contractor's legal remedy is to seek a declaration of its entitlement to an extension.

Further, notwithstanding an employer's refusal of an extension of time and any counterclaim for liquidated damages due to the delay, an employer may seek to take delivery of the equipment once the works have been completed or, if the equipment is already on the employer's site, may seek to use it. In such circumstances, subject to the merits of the contractor's claim for an extension of time, and issues as to whether it would be adequately compensated in damages for such removal or use of the equipment by the employer, the contractor may be able to obtain an injunction preventing the employer from removing or using the facility pending the determination of its claim for an extension of time. Alternatively, the contractor may have a lien over the facility – although, as noted above, parties to EPC contracts often agree to waive such rights. If such a lien exists, the contractor will be entitled to retain possession of the equipment until it is paid in full for the works and such a right may also be enforced by way of an injunction. There are also circumstances in which the contractor may have a right of arrest over an offshore unit/vessel in order to secure its claim in respect of that unit/vessel. Detailed discussion of such circumstances falls outside the scope of this chapter.

(c)   *Termination*

Where either party has breached a term of the contract and that term is, on its proper construction, deemed to be a condition (or an innominate term and the breach is sufficiently serious to give rise to a right of termination), the innocent party may treat that breach as repudiatory and terminate the contract (as well as claiming damages). As already noted, EPC contracts commonly provide express rights of termination on the occurrence of particular events, such as the insolvency of the other party or for breach by the contractor. Where any right of termination is exercised, this will generally cause the contract, at least in part,[22] to come to an end and, if it is exercised before delivery, the employer will have no obligation to accept delivery of the equipment. To the extent that disputes arise out of a purported

---

20   See, for example, *Multiplex Constructions (UK) Ltd v Honeywell Control Systems Ltd* (No 2) [2007] BLR 195. 111 ConLR 78, [2007] EWHC 447 (TCC); and more recently, in relation to two shipbuilding contracts, *Adyard Abu Dhabi v SD Marine Services* [2011] BLR 384, 136 ConLR 190, [2011] EWHC 848.

21   See, for example, *Holme v Guppy* (1838) 3 M&W 387, (1838) 150 ER 1195; *Dodd v Churton* [1897] 1 QB 562, 66 LJQB 477; and *Wells v Army and Navy Co-op Society* (1902) 86 LT 764.

22   Particular parts of the contract, such as an arbitration clause, may survive.

termination, it may be appropriate to claim a declaration that the right to terminate had accrued and was validly exercised.

4.2   Evidence

The steps in and the conduct of a formal dispute will be determined by the forum chosen by the parties. The issues discussed below will be common to most disputes.

(a)   *Documents*

Where a dispute is to be resolved in the English High Court,[23] the parties will generally be required to disclose all documents (including electronic versions of all correspondence, handwritten notes, plans and photos) in their control on which they wish to rely, which adversely affect their case or which support or adversely affect another party's case.[24] If the dispute is to be resolved via arbitration, the parties will also have a duty of disclosure, although the scope of this duty may differ significantly from the duty that applies in the English court. At least under English law, in the absence of an agreement between the parties, it will be for the tribunal to determine the scope.[25] However, the extent of disclosure is specified in some arbitration rules commonly used in relation to EPC contracts and which the parties may agree to apply. Such rules include the International Bar Association rules,[26] which apply a restricted duty on the parties to disclose only those documents on which they rely, subject to the opposition parties' right to request the production of any particular documentation that is relevant and material to the outcome of the case.[27] This can offer potentially significant cost savings in complex disputes, which are often document heavy, not least because of the increasing use of email and the duration of many EPC projects. Since contemporaneous documentary evidence is often the most persuasive form of evidence in EPC contract disputes, and in English proceedings any form of document is potentially admissible, a party would be well served to preserve all documentation produced throughout a project (as discussed above).

(b)   *Witnesses*

First-hand evidence of key witnesses who have an intimate knowledge of the project is often decisive when issues arise as to who did (or did not do) something. If there is a dispute over the scope of clarifications to the design information, the individuals who analysed the drawings and entered into correspondence addressing the clarifications will be best placed to give evidence as to whether the clarifications changed the scope of work. If there is a dispute as to defects in employer-supplied items, which caused delay, the individuals who inspected the items or attempted to fit them will be best placed to speak to the status of such items.

---

23   The expertise available in both the Technology and Construction Court and the Commercial Court provides a very competent forum for the resolution of EPC disputes.
24   Civil Procedure Rule 31.6.
25   Section 34(2)(d) of the Arbitration Act 1996.
26   International Bar Association Rules on the Taking of Evidence in International Arbitration (2010).
27   Article 3 of the International Bar Association Rules.

Those individuals who were involved in the project (from project managers to welders) will also play a significant role in the investigation of the factual circumstances surrounding the issues in dispute. This investigation is essential to assess the merits of a party's position and is an ongoing process, preferably starting well in advance of any formal dispute and continuing through the life of a dispute as further information becomes available, via disclosure and the exchange of factual and expert evidence.

Indeed, the individuals who were intimately involved in the project will be able to assist with steps in the litigation process – for example, identifying categories of document not disclosed by an opponent or identifying documents which speak against statements made in witness evidence.

It is therefore essential that key witnesses be spoken to at the earliest opportunity and close contact with them be maintained throughout the life of a dispute. Best practice is to obtain a preliminary signed statement from key witnesses as early as possible, not least to counter against any change of mind as matters progress – project managers or engineers employed on term contracts can have a habit of turning up in the employment of an opponent once a project has concluded. If it is possible to obtain a signed statement from individuals involved in the project on behalf of an opponent, this will counter against the effect of any contrary evidence produced at a later date.

The availability of a key witness is another issue which requires close management. A party cannot compel an individual who has left its employment or who is residing outside the jurisdiction where proceedings are taking place to give evidence. If the unavailability of evidence from key witnesses will have an adverse impact on a party's position, steps should be taken to address this.

While witnesses can be key to success in fact-heavy disputes, there is also potential for them to be the downfall of a good case. First, becoming involved as a witness in a formal dispute can be a daunting experience. Lay witnesses usually have no previous experience of the litigation process and little understanding of their role in that process. It is essential to explain in full detail how the litigation process operates, the role of a witness of fact and what is involved in giving evidence. It may be beneficial to provide witness familiarisation training to prepare a witness for the difficult task of giving evidence in an adversarial environment.

Second, it is often the case that an individual has a (real or perceived) personal interest in defending the actions which they took during the course of a project. If this is the case, there is a risk that a witness may give inaccurate or incomplete evidence. This needs to be managed by strict cross-referencing to contemporaneous documents and inquisitive interviewing.

(c)   *Experts*

Experts will often be instructed by the parties at the stage when a dispute is first contemplated in order to provide an independent assessment of technical issues that have arisen and assist in an evaluation of the merits of a dispute. Such experts should generally be instructed on the parties' behalfs by the lawyers advising them in order that their instructions, and the experts' opinions, are protected by legal privilege. It is not uncommon to discover that an expert who a party wishes to retain in legal proceedings was previously involved during the life of the project, acting on instruction from that party rather than from its lawyers. While using the expert before dispute resolution proceedings is often a useful step to take, to do so directly is unlikely to attract privilege in the work product and may well lead to unpleasant (but unavoidable) requests for disclosure later on.

In addition to these roles, of course, experts are often required to perform the role of an expert witness. Expert witnesses are commonly instructed by each party, or a single joint expert may be appointed by the judge or tribunal; but in either case their primary duty is to provide objective assistance to the court or tribunal on matters within their expertise, despite being instructed and paid by the parties. In line with this overriding duty, the opinions provided by expert witnesses must be independent and uninfluenced by the pressures of litigation. Experts should not assume the role of an advocate for their instructing party. Any perception of bias will greatly increase the risk of their evidence being ignored.

The types of expert commonly employed in relation to disputes over EPC contracts include programming experts, who generally opine on issues of delay and disruption and may be required to conduct delay analyses and to opine on which method of analysis is appropriate in the particular case. Technical experts may also be required to opine on engineering or quality-related issues – for example, in relation to alleged variations or defects. Where the quantum of damages is in issue, quantity surveying or accounting experts may be required to provide opinions on issues such as reasonable cost of repair or loss of profits, and market experts may be required to provide valuations or evidence related to financial conditions.

In order that the opinion of an expert be as persuasive as possible, not only should the expert be independent, but care should be taken by the instructing party to ensure that he or she is sufficiently well qualified to provide authoritative opinions on the relevant matters within his or her expertise. An expert's credibility will quickly be stripped away if it is demonstrated in cross-examination that the expert has little or no experience of the particular issues. There are a number of instances of 'experts' being exposed in this way in disputes under EPC contracts and their evidence being rejected.

Expert witnesses will typically be required to provide written evidence of their opinions in the form of an expert report (and often supplemental reports), and will generally be called on to give oral evidence at trial and to be subjected to cross-examination by the opposing party. Different courts have different approaches, but the English Technology and Construction Court will generally require the experts to meet and produce a joint report identifying the areas on which they agree and disagree, and then to exchange reports limited to the matters on which they disagree. The High Court will generally require the experts to meet after a first exchange of reports. Whatever the precise procedure, the emphasis is on the experts having a dialogue and seeking to agree as much as they can before trial in order to limit the issues on which they are required to provide oral evidence and which the court or tribunal are required to determine.

In this regard, although it is not uncommon for an expert to utilise assistants in the preparation of a report (eg, to perform testing or analyse data), there is no substitute for the expert who will sign the report and give oral evidence being on top of the issues at all times. For example, in a dispute concerning allegations of defective workmanship in welds in onshore condensate processing facilities, the expert relied on an assistant's analysis of test results and gave preliminary views on it without actually having considered the pleadings. When the expert finally did get to grips with the issues and the evidence, only two weeks before finalising the report for service in arbitration, the result was a complete change in position, as a consequence of which the party's entire case collapsed. Neither, of course, can an expert consult with an assistant while being cross-examined.

It was once the case that experts were immune from prosecution due to errors or negligence in their performance as an expert. That is no longer the case[28] and it remains to be seen what impact this will have on future matters. It is imperative to preserve the objectiveness of expert evidence and to avoid the risk of concerns about being sued being allowed to cloud evidence. It may be the case that the pool of experts – particularly individuals not attached to larger, corporate organisations – who are prepared to accept instructions reduces. Possibly a more likely development will be the increased use of limits of liability in the formal retainers agreed between lawyers and experts.

One final point to note in the context of experts is the increasing practice of 'hot-tubbing', where all experts on a particular subject give their oral evidence concurrently, primarily answering questions from the judge or tribunal and the parties' counsel raising anything else afterwards. This has the potential to generate a useful discussion between the experts from which it readily becomes clear what the answer to any particular issue should be. However, it is an approach which equally runs the risk that a less robust expert will find his voice drowned out by his counterparts, which could in turn lead to a party's case being presented less forcefully than if its expert were the only voice speaking in a traditional procedure for evidence.

The authors would like to thank Anna MacDonald and Robin Acworth for their assistance in the preparation of this chapter.

---

28   *Jones v Kaney* [2011] 2AC 398, [2011] 2 All ER 671, 135 ConLR 1, [2011] 4 LRC 757, 119 BMLR 167, [2011] UKSC 13.

Decommissioning disputes

Ben Holland
CMS Cameron McKenna LLP

1. Introduction

This chapter addresses disputes arising from the decommissioning of offshore oil and gas installations in the United Kingdom. 'Decommissioning' means the abandonment and making safe of offshore oil and gas installations. It is the process of assessing options for the removal and safe disposal of installations at the end of their working life, including planning – and obtaining government approval for – the selected option, and its eventual implementation. This is normally achieved by the removal or partial removal of the installation.

At present, there are approximately 470 offshore oil and gas installations in the UK continental shelf. These are located in the northern, central and southern North Sea, as well as in the waters west of Shetland and the Irish Sea. In addition, there is a network of at least 10,000 kilometres of pipelines linking shore facilities with oil platforms, gas platforms and a large number of subsea structures.[1] The UK decommissioning regime covers both offshore oil and gas installations and submarine oil and gas pipelines. Unless referred to separately, these are referred to together below as 'structures'.

The decommissioning regime in force in the United Kingdom is largely untested by the courts. Since 1999, when the decommissioning regime established by the Petroleum Act 1998 came into force, no disputes have appeared in the law reports. Few in the industry are misled by this lack of reported case law. It is widely acknowledged that future disputes are very likely. This is due to uncertainty as to how government agencies will construe the scope of duties imposed under the regime. It is also due to the fact that the extent and allocation of decommissioning obligations between participants will increasingly affect the ongoing economic viability of mature fields. Establishing who pays for decommissioning, and how much should be earmarked for this, will become a factor in determining whether to decommission earlier in the life of the field, instead of waiting until further reserves have been exhausted.

The Petroleum Act 1998, as amended by the Energy Act 2008, regulates decommissioning on the UK continental shelf. In addition, the United Kingdom has international obligations under the 1992 Convention for the Protection of the Marine Environment of the North East Atlantic (OSPAR) and the 1982 UN Convention on the Law of the Seas (UNCLOS). Under these and other international

---

1   Oil & Gas UK 2011 Economic Report, p 7.

treaty obligations, the government remains liable for decommissioning. The responsibility for ensuring that the Petroleum Act 1998's requirements are met currently lies with the Department for Energy and Climate Change (DECC).[2]

As might be expected, the decommissioning rules and requirements are complex. Details are referred to below only where necessary to consider disputes that might arise under them. The default position under international law is that any installations or pipelines that are disused shall be removed in their entirety and brought back to land to be reused, recycled or disposed of, although the possibility of obtaining a derogation exists under OSPAR to keep parts of the structures in place, depending on the installation.[3]

2. Disputes as to which parties may be liable for decommissioning

Participants in the UK continental shelf will want to know which of them are liable (or potentially liable) for decommissioning, and to what extent they may challenge such liability. Under the Petroleum Act 1998, the appropriate secretary of state may, by written notice (commonly referred to as a 'Section 29 notice'),[4] require the submission of a costed decommissioning programme for an offshore installation or pipeline. Activities covered by the Petroleum Act 1998 include the exploitation of mineral resources, gas storage and carbon dioxide storage[5] and most other circumstances for which a structure will exist. In practice, the secretary serves Section 29 notices early in the life of a field, when the operator and any co-venturers are submitting a development plan to the secretary for approval.

The current decommissioning regime is engineered to ensure that the UK taxpayer will not bear the costs of removing disused structures from the UK continental shelf. To some degree, this conflicts with the secretary's policy of maximising recovery by attracting investment in the UK continental shelf from a diverse range of companies, including new entrants. One feature of the Petroleum Act 1998 relevant to disputes is that all holders of a Section 29 notice in relation to a structure are jointly and severally liable to carry out the approved programme. This means that any one person served with a Section 29 notice could potentially be liable for the entire decommissioning costs. A second relevant feature is that the secretary has the power to serve a Section 29 notice on a wide range of parties connected to each individual offshore installation under Section 30(1) of the Petroleum Act 1998, or each individual offshore pipeline under Section 30(2). Many of these are contentious in some respects.

The relevant parties are as follows:

- Operators – "the person having the management of the installation or of its main structure" (Section 30(1)(a)). This wording indicates that only one person can manage the installation. The DECC has indicated that it does not

2   The DECC has published comprehensive guidance notes on the decommissioning regime, available on its website at www.og.decc.gov.uk/regulation/guidance/decomm_guide_v6.pdf.
3   These are considered below.
4   Section 29 of the Petroleum Act 1998.
5   Section 30 of the Energy Act 2008 extends the decommissioning regime in the Petroleum Act 1998 to gas storage.

intend to serve Section 29 notices on contractors which may have day-to-day management of an installation, as facilities contractors will have no role in strategic decisions regarding the operation of an installation. Rather, the DECC's interpretation "is that the Operator approved by the Secretary of State under the Petroleum Act licence would be the manager".[6] Where an installation is tied back to a host installation, the host operator will not normally be regarded as the manager of the tieback installation. Matters may be different where the host operator has a role in strategic decisions and takes benefit from the tieback's production, rather than lesser benefits such as tariff income.[7]

- Licence holders and those with similar rights – "a person who has the right to exploit or explore mineral resources in any area, or to unload, store or recover gas" (Section 30(1)(b)). This would generally refer to the licensees under the relevant licence, so long as they derive any financial or other benefit from the activity of exploiting or exploring mineral resources at the installation. The DECC has indicated that 'benefit' will be interpreted as "the substantive equivalent of an ownership or equity interest in the field and installation e.g. by receiving production or payments, royalties or bonuses in lieu of production" and not lesser benefits.[8] The term 'right to exploit or explore mineral resources' is broader than a 'holder of a licence', which could readily have been substituted. Given the purpose of the Petroleum Act 1998, it is considered that the secretary would have grounds to argue that it would catch a party with a contractual right to a share of production that was not a licensee. This might catch parties to illustrative agreements or possibly overriding royalty agreements which are not licensees, but have a beneficial interest in the field; although it could be argued that the latter have no right to exploit mineral resources, but merely a right to the proceeds of such exploitation.

- Former licence holders that have transferred without consent – "a person… who… (i) transferred the right… to another person, and (ii) has not obtained a consent required" (Section 30(1)(ba)). Unapproved transfers of licence interests that go uncontested by the secretary are nevertheless effective. This provision was introduced by the Energy Act 2008 to clarify that licensees who transfer an interest to another party without prior approval of the secretary may still be served with a Section 29 notice at any point until such consent is retrospectively obtained.

- Parties to joint operating agreements (JOAs) and similar agreements – "a person outside paragraphs (a) and (b) who is a party to a joint operating agreement or similar agreement relating to rights by virtue of which a person

---

6   DECC, Decommissioning of Offshore Oil and Gas Installations and Pipelines under the Petroleum Act 1998, Guidance Notes (Version 6, March 2011), para 3.15.

7   DECC, Decommissioning of Offshore Oil and Gas Installations and Pipelines under the Petroleum Act 1998, Guidance Notes (Version 6, March 2011), para 3.16.

8   DECC, Decommissioning of Offshore Oil and Gas Installations and Pipelines under the Petroleum Act 1998, Guidance Notes (Version 6, March 2011), para 3.23.

is within paragraph (b)" (Section 30(1)(c)). This category catches all parties to a JOA, so long as they derive any financial or other benefit from the activity of exploiting or exploring mineral resources at the installation. The DECC has indicated that 'benefit' will be interpreted as entitlement to part of the production from the installation and not lesser benefits. This category also catches parties which have contractual rights under agreements that are "similar to" a JOA where such contractual rights "relate to" the rights set out in Section 30(1)(b) of the Petroleum Act 1998, namely rights "to exploit or explore mineral resources in any area, or to unload, store or recover gas". Despite rather imprecise drafting, this operates to ensure that parties which have no right to exploit or explore mineral resources, but have a right to the proceeds of these activities, may still be served with a Section 29 notice. This may include parties to illustrative agreements that are not licensees. Similarly, beneficial interest holders under unitisation and unit operating agreements, and royalty owners which are not licensees but have become parties to a JOA to obtain production information without confidentiality restrictions, are likely to be caught.

- Platform owners – "a person... who owns any interest in the installation otherwise than as security for a loan" (Section 30(1)(d)). This provision might include, for example, the owner of a floating production storage and offtake system (FPSO) or a drilling rig being used as a production platform, but which otherwise had no beneficial interest in the field. It is contentious for the following reasons:
    - There is no requirement for them to have derived any financial or other benefit from the activity of exploiting or exploring mineral resources at the installation, and any benefit that they did derive may have been minimal in proportion to the decommissioning liabilities;
    - The Energy Act 2008 removed a restriction that this category of participant could be served only where the secretary is not satisfied that adequate arrangements (including financial) have been made by other Section 29 notice holders;[9]
    - As the use of FPSOs grows, disputes under this provision can be expected because the ownership of FPSOs may change during the field life and this provision may allow liability to be imposed on a potentially large number of participants, which need not have derived any financial or other benefit from the activity of exploiting or exploring mineral resources at the installation to be caught;[10] and

6   DECC, Decommissioning of Offshore Oil and Gas Installations and Pipelines under the Petroleum Act 1998, Guidance Notes (Version 6, March 2011), para 3.15.
7   DECC, Decommissioning of Offshore Oil and Gas Installations and Pipelines under the Petroleum Act 1998, Guidance Notes (Version 6, March 2011), para 3.16.
8   DECC, Decommissioning of Offshore Oil and Gas Installations and Pipelines under the Petroleum Act 1998, Guidance Notes (Version 6, March 2011), para 3.23.
9   Sections 31(1) and 34(3) of the Petroleum Act 1998, each as amended by Schedule 5 to the Energy Act 2008.
10   This intent is made clear in DECC, Decommissioning of Offshore Oil and Gas Installations and Pipelines under the Petroleum Act 1998, Guidance Notes (Version 6, March 2011), para 3.26.

- The exception in this provision relates only to security for a loan and it would appear that this section could catch a bank following enforcement of its security, as it would no longer have an interest "as security for a loan", but would assume ownership itself.

  The extension of liability by the secretary under this broad provision will need to be exercised having regard to public law principles to avoid potential judicial review (as discussed below).

- Designated owners/capacity users of pipelines – "a person designated as the owner of a pipeline" (Section 30(2)(a)). Section 27(1A) of the Petroleum Act 1998 sets out the process of designating any person in whom the pipeline is vested and any person that has the right to use capacity in the pipeline where that right is for a period of one year or more and is capable of being assigned or disposed of. This can be more than one person. Parties having ownership or capacity reservation or usage rights over the pipeline, if they have been so designated, fall within this category.

- Other pipeline owners – "a person... who owns any interest in the whole or substantially the whole of the pipeline, otherwise than as security for a loan" (Section 30(2)(b)). This is similar in effect to Section 30(1)(d) above, but applies to pipelines. In its guidance, the DECC suggests that in most cases, Section 29 notices be issued only to the designated owners of a pipeline.[11] However, the power does extend to catch co-owners of the pipeline that have not been 'designated' under Section 27 of the Petroleum Act 1998 and there is no requirement that this person have derived any financial or other benefit from the activity at the pipeline.

- Parent and sister corporate bodies – "a body corporate which is... associated with a body corporate within any of those paragraphs" (Sections 30(1)(e) and 30(2)(c)). This provision has the effect of piercing the corporate veil so that parent and sister bodies corporate of any body corporate falling within any of the categories above may themselves be served with a Section 29 notice. The use of 'body corporate' covers limited liability partnerships. While it may be legitimate for the government to seek to prevent the creation of a special purpose vehicle for an individual field which is allowed to become insolvent after reaping all benefits from the licence, the scope and uncertainty of the provision have been criticised. Section 30(8A) contains a broad definition of 'control', which includes instances where a body corporate "possesses or is entitled to acquire ... (a) one half or more of the issued share capital" of another body corporate. This could catch any party, possibly a bank, with an option to acquire half or more of the shares in a body corporate falling within Sections 30(1)(a) to (d) or Sections 30(2)(a) and (b). This is wider than the scope of Section 30(1)(d), which is limited to circumstances where security rights have been exercised. This provision is a reserve power and a Section 29

11 DECC, Decommissioning of Offshore Oil and Gas Installations and Pipelines under the Petroleum Act 1998, Guidance Notes (Version 6, March 2011), para 3.6. This also states that parent and sister bodies corporate of the owner may be served where concerns exist, but is silent as to whether this would be additional to service on those falling under Section 30(2)(b).

notice can be served under this category only where the secretary is not satisfied that adequate arrangements (including financial) have been made by other Section 29 notice holders, which serves to encourage these steps to be taken.[12] The extension of liability by the secretary under this broad provision will need to be exercised having regard to public law principles to avoid potential judicial review (as discussed below).

- Participants in adjacent licence blocks – under the UK licensing regime, a licence may cover a number of sub-areas, which may or may not coincide with the different blocks covered by the licence. Over time, the ownership of interests in these sub-areas may develop so that different sets of co-venturers are active in different sub-areas. All co-venturers will generally remain as licensees across all sub-areas.[13] Because all licensees are *prima facie* entitled to exploit petroleum resources across the whole licence area (subject only to contractual arrangements between themselves), licensees in one sub-area appear liable to be served with Section 29 notices in relation to installations serving another sub-area. The Energy Act 2008[14] amended the Petroleum Act 1998 so that the secretary may not serve a Section 29 notice on a licensee or party to a JOA in respect of an installation where it has derived no financial or other benefit from the activity of exploiting or exploring mineral resources at the installation. The DECC has also indicated that 'benefit' will relate to the production from the installation, and not lesser benefits which may accrue to adjacent sub-areas which have infrastructure connections to the installation (eg, tariff income, export route or fuel gas supply).[15] Under the current DECC guidance, if the installation served only one sub-area within a licence and not another, only those parties to the first sub-area would be served, although a concern exists that the DECC guidance might be changed.
- Participants in tiebacks – where an installation is tied back to a host installation, the secretary must determine whether it is to be treated as an installation separate from the host installation. Although a tieback depends on the host installation to transport (and sometimes process) production, this does not mean that it will automatically form part of the host installation.[16] Under current DECC guidance, this will depend on factors including whether it is exploiting a different field or is on a different licence to the host. Where it is separate, only persons benefiting from production from the field for which the tieback was built will be served with Section 29 notices. Where it is not, there will be no liability separate to that of the host installation, although there is concern that the DECC guidance might be changed.

---

12   Sections 31(1) and 34(3) of the Petroleum Act 1998; see also DECC, Decommissioning of Offshore Oil and Gas Installations and Pipelines under the Petroleum Act 1998, Guidance Notes (Version 6, March 2011), Annex F, para 22.
13   Unless, rarely, sub-licences have been granted.
14   Section 72(7) of the Energy Act 2008, which amends Section 31 of the Petroleum Act 1998.
15   DECC, Decommissioning of Offshore Oil and Gas Installations and Pipelines under the Petroleum Act 1998, Guidance Notes (Version 6, March 2011), para 3.23.
16   DECC, Decommissioning of Offshore Oil and Gas Installations and Pipelines under the Petroleum Act 1998, Guidance Notes (Version 6, March 2011), paras 3.17-3.21.

- Former participants in any of the categories above – where it appears to the secretary that a party that has been served with a Section 29 notice has failed or may fail to discharge its liability, including where the secretary has become responsible for carrying out the programme, the secretary has broad power to make additional parties liable to carry out decommissioning. Section 34 of the Petroleum Act 1998 allows the secretary to impose liability on any party which could have received a Section 29 notice at any time since the first Section 29 notice was issued in respect of the structure. The extension of liability by the secretary under this broad provision will need to be exercised having regard to public law principles to avoid potential judicial review (as discussed below).

- Parent and sister corporate bodies of former participants in any of the categories above – due to the interaction of the secretary's powers under Sections 30(1)(e), 30(2)(c) and 34 of the Petroleum Act 1998, potential liability may attach to parent and sister bodies corporate of any body corporate that may have fallen into any of the categories above (including licensees, operators, owners or JOA parties) at any point since the first Section 29 notice was issued in respect of the structure. Parent and sister bodies corporate could be made responsible for carrying out the entirety of the programme and the associated costs, even though their affiliate may have ceased all connection with the structure and even though the parent or sister had no connection to the structure at all. Given the frequency of transfers of interest in the UK continental shelf, many bodies corporate may fall within this category over time. The extension of liability by the secretary under this broad provision will need to be exercised having regard to public law principles to avoid potential judicial review (as discussed below.)

3.   Disputes relating to incorrectly served Section 29 notices

Despite these wide statutory powers, the DECC guidance suggests that it expects the obligation to decommission to fall primarily on licensees. This section therefore considers the grounds and processes by which a licensee may challenge the service of a Section 29 notice. It also considers how other participants that fall within the secretary's wide powers (eg, FPSO owners, banks following enforcement of security and parent and sister bodies corporate that have never themselves been associated with the structure) may judicially challenge the service of a Section 29 notice.

The secretary is required to give prior notice to any person on which he intends to serve a Section 29 notice. That party will be given the opportunity to make written representations as to whether the Section 29 notice should be served on it.[17] The DECC guidance suggests that if a party believes it has been incorrectly served with a Section 29 notice, it should contact the DECC Offshore Decommissioning Unit to establish the grounds on which the secretary's decision to serve a Section 29 notice was based.[18]

---

17   Section 31(4) of the Petroleum Act 1998.
18   DECC, Decommissioning of Offshore Oil and Gas Installations and Pipelines under the Petroleum Act 1998, Guidance Notes (Version 6, March 2011), para 3.14.

If the secretary fails to provide the opportunity for written representations before serving a Section 29 notice, or if there is disagreement as to whether the person served falls within the category of persons that can be served with a Section 29 notice, there is a statutory appeal process under Section 42 of the Petroleum Act 1998. This allows the aggrieved party to make an application to court to rule on the validity of the secretary's decision.

Section 42(1) states: "If any person is aggrieved by any of the acts of the Secretary of State mentioned in subsection (2) and desires to question its validity on the ground that it was not within the powers of the Secretary of State or that the relevant procedural requirements had not been complied with, he may within 42 days of the day on which the act was done make an application to the court under this section."

Section 42(2), referred to in Section 42(1) above, lists the following key decisions to be taken by the secretary in relation to decommissioning:

- deciding to serve a Section 29 notice;
- approving or rejecting a programme under Section 32;
- making a determination under Section 34 (to impose liability on former participants);
- withdrawing approval for a programme at the request of one or more of the persons that submitted it under Section 35; and
- requiring a party to take steps (including providing security) under Section 38(4).

Under Section 42, the court has the power to quash the secretary's decision.[19] A challenge must be made within 42 days of the date on which the act was carried out (eg, the date on which the decision was given).[20] This is a firm deadline and imposes a tight timeframe to submit a statutory challenge. No extension is permitted.

Section 42(4) purports to exclude any legal challenge to the secretary's decisions in relation to the matters listed in Section 42(2), other than as permitted under the Section 42 statutory appeals process. Although Section 42 expressly allows for challenges "on the ground that it was not within the powers of the Secretary of State" (in other words, an *ultra vires* use of discretion) and on the ground "that the relevant procedural requirements had not been complied with", a far wider range of potential legal challenges exist in public law. Decisions applying the wrong legal test, taking into account a factor that ought not have been taken into account, taking into account an irrelevant consideration (including acting unreasonably or disproportionately) or not taking into account a legitimate expectation without good reason would all still be decisions made "within the power" of the secretary under the Petroleum Act 1998. Section 42 does not expressly cover challenges of this nature. In relation to such challenges, it might be thought to act as an 'ouster clause'.

On their face, such challenges are seemingly not subject to review under the Section 42 statutory appeal process, and any legal challenge to the secretary's decisions in relation to the matters listed in Section 42(2) on such grounds would be

19   Section 42(3) of the Petroleum Act 1998.
20   Section 42(1) of the Petroleum Act 1998.

excluded. Despite the words "except as provided by this section, the validity of the acts of the Secretary of State shall not be questioned in any legal proceedings whatsoever", the better view is that the court's jurisdiction to review the decision on such grounds is not ousted. Where a decision maker breaks the rules of natural justice, applies the wrong legal test or takes into account a factor that it had no right to take into account or an irrelevant consideration (including acting unreasonably or disproportionately), the determination is a nullity.[21] Where an ouster clause operates to exclude the courts' jurisdiction to review that determination, a determination that is a nullity is not subject to the scope of the ouster clause and therefore the courts have jurisdiction to review the decision.[22]

In the author's view, where the acts of the secretary of state mentioned in Section 42(2) are to be challenged by a party on grounds wider than those set out in Section 42(1), all available grounds for challenge should be argued under the Section 42 statutory appeal process, and not through the general judicial review process. In England, judicial review requires permission before bringing an action.[23] Parties should use judicial review only as a last resort.[24] The principle that no other statutory remedy be available is equally applicable in Scotland.[25] Permission for judicial review proceedings may be declined where the claimant has followed the Section 42 statutory appeal process but, planning to bring a later judicial review if unsuccessful under the Section 42 statutory appeal process, did not seek to persuade the court that the secretary's decision should be quashed using all potential arguments available to it.

The effect of Section 42(4), therefore, is not to oust the court's jurisdiction over the secretary's decisions in relation to the matters listed in Section 42(2), but to require challenges to such decisions to be made through the Section 42 statutory appeal process, including the 42-day time limit, and not through the judicial review process. There would appear to be no scope to use the general judicial review process to challenge any category of decision under the Petroleum Act 1998 that is reviewable by the court under the Section 42 statutory appeal process if no challenge has been made in time.[26] The judicial review process appears to be appropriate only to challenge any category of decision under the Petroleum Act 1998 that is not reviewable by the court under the Section 42 statutory appeal process. For instance, it will need to be determined by the courts whether the Section 42 statutory appeal process, which relates to decisions concerning "the giving of" a Section 29 notice,

---

21   In English law at least, *Anisminic Ltd v Foreign Compensation Commission* [1969] 1 All ER 208 HL; see also Woolf, Jowell and Le Sueur, *De Smith's Judicial Review* (2007, 6th Ed) paras 4-029 and 4-049. Industry commentators also agree with this analysis – see, for example, Daintith, Willoughby and Hill, *United Kingdom Oil & Gas Law* (May 2010, 3rd Ed) para 3-903.

22   *O'Reilly v Mackman* [1982] 2 AC 237 at 278, per Lord Diplock. This established the principle that any excess of powers ought to be subject to restraint by the court in order to increase legal certainty.

23   Civil Procedure Rules, Part 54.4.

24   Pre-action Protocol for Judicial Review, para 3.1; *R v Chief Constable of Merseyside Police Ex p Calveley* [1986] QB 424.

25   The procedure in Scotland is governed by Chapter 58 of the Rules of the Court of Session (RCS 1994).

26   In English law at least, and likely also in Scottish law; see Woolf, Jowell and Le Sueur, *De Smith's Judicial Review* (2007, 6th Ed) para 4-024: "Once the period in which a statutory remedy is available has expired, the circumstances in which a decision or order protected by a preclusive clause has been successfully challenged in proceedings other than specific statutory one are extremely limited, if they exist at all."

would apply to a challenge to the secretary's decision to withdraw a Section 29 notice before the submission of the programme (considered below).

If a participant is served with a Section 29 notice, but the secretary decides not to serve a Section 29 notice on an eligible co-participant, the aggrieved participant could challenge service on itself should there be grounds to do so – for example, that the decision was made unreasonably or disproportionately. It would not appear to be possible to challenge the decision not to serve on the co-participant, as this would likely not amount to a decision at all. In such circumstances, the aggrieved party could alternatively await approval by the secretary of the programme and apply to have decommissioning liability extended to the co-participant, if necessary to do so, under Section 34(1)(b), in relation to which any decision by the secretary can be challenged under the Section 42 statutory appeal process.

Arguments that may be raised in order to challenge service of a Section 29 notice and issues as to jurisdiction are considered in relation to challenges under Section 34 (considered below). This is because parties may decide not to challenge the service of (or failure to serve) a Section 29 notice until decommissioning liabilities crystallise under Section 34 (also considered below).

4.   Disputes relating to withdrawal of Section 29 notices

Section 29 notices can be withdrawn at any time before submission of the programme.[27] The DECC expects that the Section 29 notice holders will be called to provide the programme towards the end of the life of the field and the structure, which will likely be a considerable period after the initial Section 29 notices were served.[28] Therefore, this section considers the grounds and processes by which a challenge to a decision regarding the withdrawal of a Section 29 notice may be made. The withdrawal of a Section 29 notice does not necessarily divest a party of any potential liability for decommissioning, which may still arise under powers combined within Sections 34, 36 and 37 of the Petroleum Act 1998 (considered below).

Where an interest in an installation or pipeline is transferred, the vendor will often request withdrawal of its Section 29 notice. The secretary has the power to do so under Section 31(5). The DECC guidance clarifies its policy on the exercise of its discretion to withdraw.[29] The DECC will calculate the risk of withdrawal by calculating the relative net worth of the incoming participant.[30] Essentially, it will analyse the assets of the incoming licensee and its corporate group to determine whether they are adequate to meet the decommissioning liabilities, but it will also consider other issues such as the strength of other licensees, their other decommissioning commitments in the UK continental shelf and the likelihood of

27   Section 31(5) of the Petroleum Act 1998.
28   As a guide, this period will be around three years before cession of operations, or five years if a derogation is to be sought: DECC, Decommissioning of Offshore Oil and Gas Installations and Pipelines under the Petroleum Act 1998, Guidance Notes (Version 6, March 2011), paras 3.8 and 5.8.
29   DECC, Decommissioning of Offshore Oil and Gas Installations and Pipelines under the Petroleum Act 1998, Guidance Notes (Version 6, March 2011), Annex F, paras 8-26.
30   DECC, Decommissioning of Offshore Oil and Gas Installations and Pipelines under the Petroleum Act 1998, Guidance Notes (Version 6, March 2011), Annex F, para 13. Net worth is calculated using the formula: shareholder funds/equity minus intangibles.

their remaining on the licence. If the calculation suggests that the release of the Section 29 notice poses a medium or high risk to the taxpayer, the DECC will consider whether the incoming participant has a UK parent or sister body corporate with sufficient assets in the United Kingdom to cover its decommissioning costs when required. The DECC is unlikely to withdraw a Section 29 notice from a vendor where the sale results in a sole licensee with 100% ownership (where there are two or more remaining licensees, the DECC will take comfort from the fact that they will police each other's decommissioning due to a concern of joint and several liability).[31] The DECC will also consider whether any security has been put in place. Other holders of Section 29 notices in relation to the relevant installation or pipeline are given a chance to comment on any proposed withdrawal.

The DECC guidance states that it aims to withdraw as many Section 29 notices as possible in light of the level of risk, but states that any guidance provided is indicative and reserves the discretionary nature of the secretary's powers. It would appear that a party wishing to challenge a decision not to withdraw a Section 29 notice may not use the Section 42 statutory appeal process, which relates to decisions concerning "the giving of" a Section 29 notice. A decision (or refusal) to withdraw a Section 29 notice before submission of the programme is not listed as one of the decisions within the scope of the Section 42 statutory appeal process. The purported ouster of the courts' jurisdiction to review the secretary's actions applies only to matters listed in Section 42(2).

It follows that a party wishing to challenge a decision not to withdraw a Section 29 notice may have grounds to make an application for judicial review. Arguments that may be raised to challenge a decision on the withdrawal of a Section 29 notice and issues as to jurisdiction are set out in relation to challenges under Section 34 (considered below).

5.   Disputes relating to the decommissioning programme

Towards the end of the life of the field and the structure, which will likely be a considerable period after the initial Section 29 notices were served, the Section 29 notice holders will be called to provide the programme. This section therefore considers the grounds and processes by which a challenge to a decision about the approval, rejection or withdrawal of approval for the programme may be made.

The Petroleum Act 1998 requires the submission of a single programme in relation to the installation, irrespective of how many parties received a Section 29 notice relating to it. If the programme can be agreed between the relevant Section 29 notice holders, it is submitted to the secretary for approval. The programme must have an overall cost estimate on a year-by-year expenditure basis, and provide the sensitivities and assumptions on which this is made.

Under Section 32, the secretary may approve the programme (with or without conditions) or reject it, giving reasons. If the secretary rejects the proposed programme, or no programme is submitted due to internal disagreements or

---

31   DECC, Decommissioning of Offshore Oil and Gas Installations and Pipelines under the Petroleum Act 1998, Guidance Notes (Version 6, March 2011), Annex G, para 5.

otherwise, the secretary may prepare a programme at the cost of the parties.[32] Wide consultations are now undertaken in advance with non-governmental organisations (NGOs) and interested parties before the programme is submitted. This maximises the prospects of approval.[33] After the programme has been approved by the secretary, it is the duty of the parties that submitted it to see that it is carried out and that any conditions to which the approval is subject are complied with.

The programme will need to anticipate any future alternative uses and this will need to be agreed with the secretary. Following approval of the programme, new exploration techniques, newly located neighbouring reserves and alternative uses of reservoirs may lead to the review (and re-review) of past assumptions. The secretary can amend the programme or any conditions attached to it, either on his own initiative or at the request of those submitting it.[34] Although the secretary may take into account any identified opportunities for further development of reserves, vessel availability and coordination of activity with neighbouring fields, the DECC suggests that a "robust case" in support of deferment will need to be demonstrated.[35] Approval of the programme can also be withdrawn by the secretary at the request of one or more parties that submitted it.[36] In each case, the secretary is required to give prior notice to affected parties, which will be given an opportunity to make written representations.[37] Due to the wide consultation commonly undertaken before submission and approval of a programme, it may be unlikely that any change is required.

The following all fall within the scope of the Section 42 statutory appeal process set out above:

- a decision or refusal to approve a programme or to impose conditions under Section 32 of the Petroleum Act 1998;
- a decision or refusal to amend a programme under Section 34 of the Petroleum Act 1998; and
- a decision or refusal to withdraw the programme after its submission under Section 35 of the Petroleum Act 1998.

Arguments that may be raised in order to challenge any such decision and issues as to jurisdiction are set out in relation to challenges under Section 34 of the Petroleum Act 1998 (considered below). The 42-day time limit applies to all challenges.

6. Disputes relating to the secretary's power to require security

Participants in the UK continental shelf will want to know which of them are liable, or potentially liable, to put aside security for decommissioning, and to what extent they may challenge such liability. If the secretary is not satisfied that a group of

---

32   Section 33 of the Petroleum Act 1998.
33   The impact of intervention by NGOs is considered further below.
34   Section 34(1)(a) of the Petroleum Act 1998.
35   DECC, Decommissioning of Offshore Oil and Gas Installations and Pipelines under the Petroleum Act 1998, Guidance Notes (Version 6, March 2011), para 5.18.
36   Section 35(1) of the Petroleum Act 1998.
37   Sections 34(4)-(5) and 35(2) of the Petroleum Act 1998.

Section 29 notice holders will be capable of discharging their decommissioning duties, he can require that any party that has been served with a Section 29 notice put security in place under Section 38(4) of the Petroleum Act 1998.[38] The DECC guidance sees this is a measure of last resort if other mitigation measures (eg, serving a Section 29 notice on a parent or sister body corporate) cannot be used effectively to reduce the risk to the taxpayer.[39] The secretary may require the licensees of a new field development to provide security if he considers that it poses a high risk to the taxpayer. This addresses the risk that the field fails to produce as expected, resulting in an inability to meet project finance payments, as happened in the case of the Ardmore field. The situation will be reassessed approximately six months after the commencement of production, and receipts from production may make additional security unnecessary until closer to the time of cessation of production.[40]

Challenges to any decision of the secretary under Section 38(4) fall within the Section 42 statutory appeal process, considered above. Arguments that may be raised in order to challenge any such decision and issues as to jurisdiction are set out in relation to challenges under Section 34 of the Petroleum Act 1998 (considered below). The 42-day time limit will apply to any challenge.

7.   Disputes relating to liability imposed for decommissioning costs

Despite the availability of redress, it is noteworthy that no party has successfully sought to challenge the service or withdrawal of a Section 29 notice through review by the courts. As well as a desire within the industry not to damage relations with the secretary, this is likely due to the fact that the failure to serve or the withdrawal of a Section 29 notice pursuant to Section 31(5) of the Petroleum Act 1998 does not necessarily divest a party of any potential liability for decommissioning. The DECC guidance provides that "a company may, in certain circumstances and following the approval of a programme, be placed under a duty to carry out that programme even though it has previously been released from a notice under section 31(5)".[41] This section therefore considers the grounds and processes by which a challenge to the imposition of liability for decommissioning costs can be made.

Section 36 of the Petroleum Act 1998 imposes a duty on all persons that submitted the programme to ensure that it is carried out. Use of the words 'each of the persons' suggests joint and several liability. Section 37 grants certain powers to the secretary to require any of those persons that submitted the programme to carry it out or take remedial action.[42] Failure to comply with this notice will permit the secretary to carry out the remedial work himself and recover any expenditure incurred in doing so, plus interest, presumably through a civil claim; it may also

---

38   DECC, Decommissioning of Offshore Oil and Gas Installations and Pipelines under the Petroleum Act 1998, Guidance Notes (Version 6, March 2011), Annex G, para 6.
39   DECC, Decommissioning of Offshore Oil and Gas Installations and Pipelines under the Petroleum Act 1998, Guidance Notes (Version 6, March 2011), Annex F, para 23.
40   DECC, Decommissioning of Offshore Oil and Gas Installations and Pipelines under the Petroleum Act 1998, Guidance Notes (Version 6, March 2011), Annex F, paras 28 and 29.
41   DECC, Decommissioning of Offshore Oil and Gas Installations and Pipelines under the Petroleum Act 1998, Guidance Notes (Version 6, March 2011), para 3.11.
42   Section 37(1) of the Petroleum Act 1998.

constitute a criminal offence.[43] Therefore, liabilities arising pursuant to Sections 36 and 37 can apply only to those Section 29 notice holders that submitted the programme. However, as set out above, the secretary may use Section 34 to make additional parties liable for decommissioning. The secretary can extend such liability to parties within Sections 30(1)(e) and 30(2)(c) (associated bodies corporate) and persons within Section 30(2)(b) (non-registered owners of interests in a pipeline) only where it appears to the secretary that another party already under a duty has failed or may fail to discharge its liability, including where the secretary has become responsible for carrying out the programme. In addition, parties within Sections 30(1)(b) and (c) (licensees and JOA participants) served with Section 29 notices before the entry into force of the Energy Act 2008 can now be made liable under Section 34 of the Petroleum Act 1998 only if they derive any financial or other benefit from the activity of exploiting or exploring mineral resources at the installation.[44]

To date, the secretary has not invoked this wide-ranging power, which is seen as a last resort. The preferred strategy has been first to ensure that adequate security is available.[45] Should Sections 34, 36 and 37 of the Petroleum Act 1998 be used, the Petroleum Act 1998 is silent as to how they may be applied and what order or hierarchy may apply to those which the secretary may target. In all respects, the secretary's power will be required to be exercised in accordance with due process, and in a proportionate manner consistent with public law principles; if not, it may be liable to challenge. The Section 42 statutory appeal process is applicable to a determination by the secretary under Section 34. Each challenge will turn on its facts. However, the following grounds for challenge may apply.

7.1 General principles for review

A detailed account of the grounds for judicial review that are most likely to become engaged in the context of energy disputes is set out in another chapter. The basic function of the court is to guard the rights of the individual against the abuse of official power. The courts will not normally impede a public body in determining the public interest. The courts are unwilling to interfere with the balancing act performed by public bodies in assessing between competing public interests. In the context of decommissioning, these aims will include:

- compliance with international treaties;
- ensuring a low-cost burden to participants in the UK continental shelf, many of which are smaller companies investing in mature fields; and
- ensuring that the taxpayer is not exposed to the risk of default.

It can be expected that courts will strive to allow the secretary a reasonable discretion before quashing a decision.

In England, judicial review applications must be submitted promptly, and in any

43 Sections 37(2) and 37(3) of the Petroleum Act 1998.
44 Previously, Section 29 notices could be served on such participants notwithstanding a lack of financial or other benefit.
45 DECC, Decommissioning of Offshore Oil and Gas Installations and Pipelines under the Petroleum Act 1998, Guidance Notes (Version 6, March 2011), Annex F, para 23.

event within three months of the decision. In Scotland, there is no formal time limit within which judicial review proceedings must be started, but the process is designed to give a speedy solution and a delay may give rise to defences.[46] It is therefore essential that any party seeking to challenge the secretary's decision make an early assessment of the potential claim and act as soon as possible and within the prescribed deadlines.

7.2 Jurisdiction of the courts

Section 42(6) of the Petroleum Act 1998 provides that challenges to the court under the Section 42 statutory appeal process will be to the High Court in relation to England and Wales, the Court of Session in relation to Scotland and the High Court in relation to Northern Ireland. It will be essential to mount any challenge, either under the Section 42 statutory appeal process or under the general judicial review process, in the correct jurisdiction in order to avoid jurisdictional objections. The allocation of jurisdiction between the courts of England and Wales and Scotland will depend largely on the location of the structure to be decommissioned. Other factors may include the location where decommissioning is being organised by the operator and from which office the secretary's officials are making decisions.[47] Procedural restrictions in Scotland limit the class of parties that may bring a judicial review to parties with title and interest to sue – in other words, parties normally need to demonstrate a more strict direct personal interest to raise judicial review proceedings in Scotland than in England and Wales. This is of particular importance in relation to potential challenges made by NGOs, as considered below.

7.3 Grounds for challenge by the courts

Grounds for judicial review are set out in detail in another chapter. In summary, grounds for review can exist where the decision taken was:
- illegal (eg, it took into account irrelevant matters, failed to take into account relevant matters or contained a mistake of fact);
- procedurally unfair; or
- irrational (eg, so unreasonable that no reasonable authority could ever have come to it – known as '*Wednesbury* unreasonableness').

Although not a separate ground for judicial review, as a general principle of EU law, proportionality will continue to influence the decisions of the English courts in cases involving the interpretation of domestic law made under EU legislation, and is viewed as a component of unreasonableness.

The merits of any challenge are highly fact specific. Each case must be assessed on its merits. In the absence of any case law, what follows is an illustrative, non-exhaustive list of certain potential circumstances where, depending on the facts, it may be unreasonable for the secretary to impose Section 34 liability:
- Failure to follow the DECC guidance – where the DECC guidance can be

---

46   *Atherton v Strathclyde Regional Council* 1995 SLT 557.
47   *R v Secretary of State for Scotland, ex parte Greenpeace Limited* (Popplewell J), May 24 1995 (unreported). This case related to the Brent Spar.

shown to give rise to a legitimate expectation and this is departed from without good cause. Although the DECC guidance cannot be relied on to fetter the exercise of a discretion conferred to the secretary by the Petroleum Act 1998, and although the secretary may revise the DECC guidance,[48] this does not mean that the secretary can amend the DECC guidance in advance of a decision contrary to a legitimate expectation in order to avoid the court's scrutiny of such decision. Due to the timescales between service of Section 29 notices and implementation of the programme, participants should have regard to changes to a policy on which they have previously relied, as well as proposed and eventual revisions to the DECC guidance. The consequences of a failure by the secretary to meet such legitimate expectation could vary greatly, depending on the nature of the expectation and the factual matrix surrounding the secretary's decision.

- No fair or reasonable distribution – where the secretary imposes Section 34 liability on one party (or its parent) that no longer holds an interest in the field, without seeking to spread such liability among other persons that may be liable under Section 34, in particular if they are in comparable circumstances. It seems likely that a fair and reasonable distribution of the liabilities in discussion with the companies concerned would be appropriate – for example, a distribution related to the revenues earned by the various companies during their involvement in the field.[49] It also seems likely that members of a class of participant (eg, those that drew benefit from the installation) would, in the absence of other factors, be treated in a similar way, and that a hierarchy would be applied to liability such that participants in this class would, in the absence of other factors, be treated differently from participants in a different class (eg, those that drew no benefit from the installation).
- New installations – where a Section 29 notice holder is held liable for new installations on a field after the assignment of its interest, as opposed to where a Section 29 notice holder is held to be liable for any new equipment added to an installation for which it held the existing Section 29 notice.[50]
- Exploration licences – where a party that leaves a licence before any development took place is made liable for installations developed after its departure.
- Discrimination based on seat of incorporation or convenience – where the secretary imposed liability based on convenience – for example, focusing on one or more participants with 'deep pockets' in the jurisdiction, particularly if other participants were of similar economic standing and had enjoyed comparable benefit from the field, but were not asked to contribute.
- Sister bodies corporate – where liability is imposed on an autonomous and

---

48 DECC guidance notes were first issued in August 2000. They "provide a framework and are not intended to be prescriptive. They will be reviewed regularly and updated as necessary". In March 2011 they were already in their sixth version.
49 Suggested in DECC, Decommissioning of Offshore Oil and Gas Installations and Pipelines under the Petroleum Act 1998, Guidance Notes (Version 6, March 2011), para 3.11.
50 DECC, Decommissioning of Offshore Oil and Gas Installations and Pipelines under the Petroleum Act 1998, Guidance Notes (Version 6, March 2011), para 3.13.

separately owned sister body corporate, which received no benefit from its affiliate and had no connection to any exploration of the relevant field, this may be a disproportionate exercise of discretion, although imposing liability on a parent body corporate may be proportionate. The scheme of the Petroleum Act 1998 suggests that the financial position of parent bodies corporate be considered by the secretary in making decisions about the affiliate. For example, when considering whether to withdraw Section 29 notices, the secretary will analyse the assets of the incoming licensee and its corporate group to determine whether they are adequate to meet the decommissioning liabilities, considering the other decommissioning commitments of the corporate group in the UK continental shelf.[51] As the corporate veil is assumed to be pierced when making decisions to withdraw Section 29 notices from a participant, this suggests that it may be fair and appropriate for the secretary to pierce the corporate veil when also making decisions to impose decommissioning liability. On the other hand, if a parent or sister body corporate had operated as a single economic entity with its affiliate, received benefit from it, had a connection with production from the licence or acquired a controlling interest in the affiliate at a time when it had already been served with a Section 29 notice, it may well be seen to be proportionate for decommissioning liability to attach to it.

While, as mentioned above, Section 42(4) of the Petroleum Act 1998 purports to exclude any legal challenge to determinations by the secretary under Section 34, other than as permitted under the Section 42 statutory appeal process, for the reasons above the author considers it unlikely that the court, in any challenge made under Section 42, would accept that it had no jurisdiction in relation to a potential challenge under the general public law.

7.4   The Human Rights Act 1998

An alternative challenge may exist under the Human Rights Act 1998. Under the Human Rights Act, it is unlawful for a public authority to act in a way which is incompatible with a right provided under the Convention for the Protection of Human Rights and Fundamental Freedoms 1950.[52] One such right is that every natural or legal person is guaranteed certain rights in relation to property – specifically, that no one shall be deprived of his or her possessions except in the public interest and subject to the conditions provided for by the general principles of international law.[53] In the event that the court finds the public authority's decision to have been unlawful, it has the right to award a just and appropriate remedy.[54] The Human Rights Act applies to corporate bodies, although the general rule is that

---

51   DECC, Decommissioning of Offshore Oil and Gas Installations and Pipelines under the Petroleum Act 1998, Guidance Notes (Version 6, March 2011), Annex F, paras 13-16.
52   Human Rights Act 1998, Section 6(1).
53   Schedule 1, Part II, Article 1 of the Human Rights Act 1998.
54   Section 8(1) of the Human Rights Act 1998. However, damages are available only in situations as prescribed in Sections 8(2) to 8(4).

shareholders have no claim based on damage to a corporate body.

The act provides that an interference with, or control over the use of, property by the government can be justified only if it:

- satisfies the requirement of legal certainty;
- serves a legitimate aim in the public or general interest; and
- is proportionate to that aim.

Proportionality will require a proper and fair balance to be struck between the demands of the taxpayer and the protection of the individual's fundamental rights, and will be breached where the individual has to bear "an individual and excessive burden".[55] Given this test, and although this remains to be determined by the courts, there would appear to be little added by the Human Rights Act to general public law principles. Under the Convention for the Protection of Human Rights and Fundamental Freedoms, governments have "a wide margin of appreciation" to conduct social policy and judicial interference will follow only if a decision is "manifestly without reasonable foundation".[56]

While, as mentioned above, Section 42(4) of the Petroleum Act 1998 purports to exclude any legal challenge to determinations by the secretary under Section 34 of the Petroleum Act 1998, other than as permitted under the Section 42 statutory appeal process, for the reasons above the author considers it unlikely that the court, in any challenge made under Section 42, would accept that it had no jurisdiction in relation to a potential challenge under the Human Rights Act if good grounds for such challenge were otherwise capable of being made out.

7.5 Contribution claims

Section 36 of the Petroleum Act 1998 imposes a duty on all persons that submitted the programme to ensure that it is carried out. It may be that one party with sufficient means incurs costs in compliance with this provision and must then seek a contribution. This may be permitted under the terms of the JOA. However, many parties, such as former Section 29 notice holders, may not be in a contractual relationship with the paying party. If so, contribution may be claimed under the Civil Liability (Contribution) Act 1978 from "each of the persons" that shared this joint and several liability. The statutory limitation period for bringing such claim is two years after the date on which the right to a contribution accrues.[57]

8. Disputes relating to security under decommissioning security agreements

8.1 Decommissioning security agreements

Given that co-licensees will be jointly and severally liable for any decommissioning costs, the industry has reacted to the decommissioning regime by the development of decommissioning security agreements (DSAs). Under such DSAs, each participant

---

55 *Sporrong and Lonnroth v Sweden* (1983) 5 EHRR 35, ECtHR at 69, 73; *AGOSI v United Kingdom* (1987) 9 EHRR 1 ECtHR at 52.
56 *James v United Kingdom* (1986) 8 EHRR 35, ECtHR at 46.
57 Section 10 of the Limitation Act 1980.

in a JOA will agree to pay cash or other types of security into a trust, held until the end of the decommissioning process. The share of decommissioning costs will usually – although not always – correspond to a participant's shareholding under the JOA. DSAs provide counterparties with a greater degree of security in the event of default. If a party to the DSA falls into financial difficulty, its security is called on and the funds are held in a trust until the decommissioning is completed. The DECC recognises that "the over-riding aim of a DSA is to ensure that guaranteed funds (which may include future revenues in appropriate cases) will be available to cover the decommissioning costs at all times".[58] DSAs assist in extending the producing life of fields on the UK continental shelf by facilitating, so far as possible, the transfer of mature fields from established companies to smaller participants with fewer assets, by assisting avoiding duplication of security. Oil & Gas UK has produced a template DSA, together with guidance notes, to capture industry practice.[59] The Oil & Gas UK standard form JOA suggests that the JOA parties enter a DSA before submitting a development plan for the field. Security is usually given by letter of credit or in any other form agreed between the parties to the DSA.

Where an interest in an installation or pipeline is sold, the vendor will often request withdrawal of the Section 29 notice. If the vendor is not released, it will be concerned about its continuing joint and several liability to carry out decommissioning and is likely to require security from the purchaser. Even if the vendor is released, security is still routinely required from the purchaser, as the vendor could still be exposed as a former Section 29 notice holder as one of the more likely participants to be caught under Section 34 of the Petroleum Act 1998. Upon an application for withdrawal, the secretary will consider whether any security has been put in place, and is unlikely to require security under Section 38(4) of the Petroleum Act 1998 if an acceptable DSA is in place in respect of the field.[60] Challenges to the decision of the secretary relating to the withdrawal of a Section 29 notice are set out above.

8.2 Parties to a DSA

The primary parties to the DSA will be each of the co-venturers under the JOA – the 'first-tier participants' – each of which provides security. If the secretary is concerned that a group of Section 29 notice holders will be incapable of discharging their decommissioning duties, the secretary may also be a party to the DSA to ensure that the DSA cannot be amended without his written consent and to empower him to take action in the event of default.[61] A provision in the template DSA allows for any additional current and former Section 29 notice holders, even if not co-venturers under the JOA, which are at risk of being caught under Section 34, to be identified as 'second-tier participants'. Vendors join this category upon transfer of their

---

58 DECC, Decommissioning of Offshore Oil and Gas Installations and Pipelines under the Petroleum Act 1998, Guidance Notes (Version 6, March 2011), Annex G, para 2.
59 Both developed with support from CMS Cameron McKenna LLP for the Brownfields Work Group on DSAs. References are to the March 2009 version, available at www.oilandgasuk.co.uk.
60 DECC, Decommissioning of Offshore Oil and Gas Installations and Pipelines under the Petroleum Act 1998, Guidance Notes (Version 6, March 2011), Annex F, para 24.

interest.[62] This enables a wider category of person to benefit from the security by being able to enforce the terms of the DSA, but without obligation to provide security. This serves to reduce the vendor's need for any additional security from the purchaser. It also gives the second-tier participants the right to consent to changes to the DSA, obtain confidential information on the decommissioning process and invoke reference to an expert in the event of certain disputes, as detailed below. Under the template DSA, other former owners which have no Section 29 notice – but are at risk of being caught under Section 34 may become 'third-tier participants'. Vendors that have had their Section 29 notice withdrawn and others that could have been, but were not prepared to be, a second-tier participant may opt to be included in this category. Third-tier participants are not parties to the DSA and do not provide security, but can, by agreement, benefit under the Contracts (Rights of Third Parties) Act 1999 from the security by being able to enforce the terms of the DSA if caught under Section 34 of the Petroleum Act 1998.[63]

8.3   Disputes over the calculation of net cost and net value

One area already giving rise to significant disputes is the calculation of the amount of security that ought to be placed in trust. The template DSA requires that every year, each party to the JOA pay an amount equal to that party's share of the net cost (multiplied by a risk factor) less its share of the net value, less the amount of any security that it may already have provided. Both net cost and net value are assessed on a net present value basis. Where the net present value of the net cost exceeds the net present value of the net value, security is required to cover the difference. As production continues, the amount of security increases so that it fully funds decommissioning at cessation of production. Disputes arising from default in payment under the DSA are considered shortly. More critical, for present purposes, are disputes about what 'net cost' and 'net value' should be taken to mean, and disputes arising from the calculation itself.

(a)   Net cost

Net cost represents the best estimated cost of performing all decommissioning activities at the time at which they can be best estimated to need to be performed. A significant scope exists for disputes over this calculation. There are many different forms of installation, constructed individually to deal with individual field characteristics. Each installation will therefore require an individually tailored, and untested, method of decommissioning. A core assumption inputted into the calculation of net cost is the expected date of decommissioning. This date may significantly impact on the cost estimation. Despite ageing infrastructure, finding alternative uses for some structures (particularly pipelines) through tiebacks and brownfield developments made possible by high oil prices and new technology such

---

61   DECC, Decommissioning of Offshore Oil and Gas Installations and Pipelines under the Petroleum Act 1998, Guidance Notes (Version 6, March 2011), Annex G, para 3.
62   Oil & Gas UK Industry Model Form Decommissioning Security Agreement (March 2009), paras 2.3 and 2.4.
63   Oil & Gas UK Industry Model Form Decommissioning Security Agreement (March 2009), para 13.2.

as enhanced oil recovery may postpone the date of decommissioning.[64] This, in turn, will reduce the net cost, which will be discounted back (through the net present value calculation), with the effect that the amount of security required will be less the later the decommissioning is assumed to take place. It will also likely postpone the trigger date for provision of security.

This issue may give rise to a challenge from second-tier participants concerned that unrealistic assumptions are being made on alternative uses or other factors impacting on the estimated date for decommissioning, leading to inadequate security. Optional language under the template DSA governs:

- whether second-tier participants have a right to approve the operator's proposals or merely comment on them;
- whether only estimates approved by the joint operating committee are to be used to calculate net cost;
- whether the operator's best estimates, acting as a reasonable and prudent operator, are adequate; and
- other alternatives.[65]

If challenged, any unresolved dispute is resolved by the expert (considered below).

Following approval of the programme, new exploration techniques, newly located neighbouring reserves and alternative uses of reservoirs may lead to the review (and re-review) of past assumptions. The question arises of whether the operator can take into account a potential deferment (before this has been approved by the secretary) and submit a net cost estimate based on a decommissioning date that is different from that in the programme. Oil & Gas UK suggests that such an approach would require agreement in individual cases.[66] Presumably, this is agreement by the parties to the DSA, as such agreement is unlikely to be given by the secretary until a formal application has been made under Section 34(1)(a) of the Petroleum Act 1998. If so, any party to the DSA challenging the operator's net cost estimate on the grounds that it assumes a decommissioning date different from that in the programme can do so by reference to the expert.

Further scope exists for disputes over whether net costs should be based on a 'left in place' basis for installations capable of attaining a derogation.[67] Adopting this approach would reduce net cost. The DECC guidance suggests that it is likely to require the decommissioning costs for large concrete structures to be estimated on this basis.[68] However, derogations may become less common due to advances in technology, and if this approach changes net cost may increase significantly.[69]

Net cost estimates will usually be prepared on a P50 basis and use the risk factor in the security calculation to provide a degree of caution against possible price rises.[70]

---

64   Oil & Gas UK estimates that 50% of UK continental shelf decommissioning activity will be complete by 2022; previously, this date had been 2018, showing that decommissioning is now estimated to take place later: Oil & Gas UK *2011 Economic Report*, p 18.

65   Oil & Gas UK Industry Model Form Decommissioning Security Agreement (March 2009), Appendix 5, paras 6.10 and 6.11.

66   Oil & Gas UK Decommissioning Security Agreement Guidance Notes (March 2009), p 10.

The risk factor reflects uncertainties about the net cost estimate. These uncertainties should reduce with time as the operator obtains a better understanding of these costs, and optional language in the DSA allows the contingency to be reduced in a stepped process. Normally, net costs are calculated on a pre-tax basis, due to uncertainty as to whether tax relief will be available at the time that decommissioning is conducted. A consultation was announced in the 2012 Budget to introduce a mechanism by which current rates of tax relief will be contractually 'locked in' by the UK government through contracts for difference. If introduced, this would remove the uncertainty as to the existence and level of tax relief. Upon execution of such agreements in the future, the net cost calculation may likely take tax relief into account.

(b) Net value

Net value will be based on production receipts from the field, normally on a post-tax basis (including royalties, corporation tax/supplemental charge, petroleum revenue tax; such deductions for tax being made in order to be conservative), but taking into account any tax relief or grants given or expected to be given other than those relating to the costs of decommissioning. Optional language under the template DSA governs:

- whether only estimates approved by the joint operating committee are to be used to calculate net value;
- whether the operator's best estimates, acting as a reasonable and prudent operator, are adequate; and
- other alternatives.[71]

Without clear drafting, significant scope exists for disputes on these assumptions. Fluctuating oil prices will have a significant impact on net value. Regular recalculations may lead to periodic changes in net value as oil and gas prices rise and fall. Assumptions as to future oil and gas prices should be clearly stated in the DSA.[72] Published indices for oil and gas prices will need to be agreed. Any gas price indexation formula contained in any existing gas sales contract should be used when calculating future gas revenue.[73]

Many fields also receive significant revenues from tariff and other receipts from

---

67   A limited number of installations may be eligible for derogation from the prohibition on the dumping, or leaving wholly or partly in place, of offshore installations. Parties may apply for derogation for the 'footings' of large steel jackets weighing more than 10,000 tonnes and concrete installations because of the difficulty in removing these structures. Derogation will be granted only if there are significant reasons why it is a preferable means of disposal than reuse, recycling or disposal on land.

68   DECC, Decommissioning of Offshore Oil and Gas Installations and Pipelines under the Petroleum Act 1998, Guidance Notes (Version 6, March 2011), Annex F, para 14. The threshold criteria for attaining a derogation may tighten as new technology makes more feasible the removal of large installations, although concerns about the carbon budget of extensive decommissioning operations may alternatively lead to more derogations being granted.

69   Oil & Gas UK Decommissioning Security Agreement Guidance Notes (March 2009), p 38. The threshold criteria for attaining a derogation may change as new technology makes the removal of large installations more feasible.

70   Oil & Gas UK Decommissioning Security Agreement Guidance Notes (March 2009), p 39.

71   Oil & Gas UK Industry Model Form Decommissioning Security Agreement (March 2009), Appendix 5, para 6.10. See also Oil & Gas UK Decommissioning Security Agreement Guidance Notes (March 2009), p 39.

third parties, such as tiebacks. As these form revenue from the field, in the absence of express provision in the DSA to the contrary, as a matter of common sense they should be included. A dispute may emerge as to the degree of certainty required that these receipts will accrue. At one extreme, these receipts should be taken into account only in situations where send-or-pay arrangements ensure that such tariff income is secured. At the other, such tariff income can be taken into account even though no agreement has been concluded, or where such agreement has been concluded but is of only limited duration, as long as there is no other route to export for the tieback. The template DSA contains options to address these alternatives.[74] Where no such language is selected, it would seem most likely that in a dispute, the expert would include such receipts only where satisfied based on prevailing accounting practices. Revenue may also arise from the sale of field property. Components sold in the normal course of business before decommissioning can be included in the calculation by inclusion of language in the template DSA. Net value will be affected by the introduction in 2013 of Phase III of the EU Emissions Trading Scheme, which will significantly increase the costs of operating mature assets with declining production.

8.4 Expert determination under DSAs

Under the template DSA, the cost estimation set out above forms an important part of the operator's decommissioning schedule and budget (the 'proposed plan'), which will also set out the operator's estimated dates for cessation of production and commencement and completion of decommissioning. The operator will submit the proposed plan for approval by the parties to the JOA. Disputes may be referred to determination by the expert if:

- the proposed plan performed by the operator is challenged;
- the operator fails to produce the proposed plan or perform the cost estimation; or
- the operator's determination that decommissioning has been completed is challenged.[75]

The expert is also engaged when the cost estimation performed by the operator needs to be independently reviewed, even where no dispute exists between the parties to the DSA.[76] To address this last issue, the template DSA provides options that allow for a review of the net cost and net value calculations by an expert at regular intervals; or alternatively to have less frequent reviews initially followed by annual reviews later in the field life.[77] A provision that a review is triggered if the operator

72 Oil & Gas UK Decommissioning Security Agreement Guidance Notes (March 2009), p 39.
73 Oil & Gas UK Decommissioning Security Agreement Guidance Notes (March 2009), p 39. However, see below in relations to concerns as to confidentiality.
74 Oil & Gas UK Decommissioning Security Agreement Guidance Notes (March 2009), p 10.
75 Oil & Gas UK Industry Model Form Decommissioning Security Agreement (March 2009), paras 3.3, 3.6 and 8.8.
76 As a result of the DECC guidance, this is currently at least every three years. DECC, Decommissioning of Offshore Oil and Gas Installations and Pipelines under the Petroleum Act 1998, Guidance Notes (Version 6, March 2011), Annex G, para 19.

believes that there has been a change in net cost or net value over an agreed tolerance may also be included.

Under the template DSA, unanimity of all parties to the DSA is required on the proposed plan. Challenges by parties to the DSA to the operator's proposals can be made by reference to the expert.[78] The template DSA also contains optional language allowing reference to the expert to be made by second-tier participants (or the secretary) which, depending on the language, may have rights to approve the cost estimation.[79] As second-tier participants will have no percentage interest in the field, no weighted voting will be possible, and so the template DSA assumes a 'one party, one vote' system, with silence being deemed as approval. Unanimity is similarly required for approval of the operator's determination that decommissioning has been completed.

(a) Appointment of the expert

For challenges to the proposed plan, the template DSA has an initial requirement for negotiations over a 90-day period from the date of submission of the proposed plan by the operator.[80] For challenges to the operator's determination that decommissioning has been completed, similar negotiations are required over a 30-day period from the date of submission of the operator's determination.[81] Following this, a reference to the expert can be made. For challenges to the proposed plan (but not for other challenges), the template DSA limits the right to refer the matter to the expert to "any Objecting Party" (the party objecting to the proposed plan). This might present difficulties for the operator, which would not appear to have the right to refer the matter to the expert should the objecting party fail to do so. Nor, in the absence of either unanimity or determination by the expert, can the proposed plan become approved. It may be necessary to apply to the court for an order that the objecting party refer the matter to the expert or, in default, be deemed to have done so.[82] Conversely, under the template DSA only the operator, not the other parties to the DSA, can submit the cost estimation for independent periodic review. However, if the operator fails promptly to comply upon notice to do so, any other party to the DSA may itself refer the cost calculation to the expert.[83]

The template DSA contains options for appointment of the expert – either:

- the expert shall be selected by unanimous vote of the parties to the DSA; or
- each party to the DSA shall nominate three candidates who are ready, willing and able to act, to be scored by all parties to the DSA in order of preference.

---

77   Oil & Gas UK Industry Model Form Decommissioning Security Agreement (March 2009), para 3.4.
78   Oil & Gas UK Industry Model Form Decommissioning Security Agreement (March 2009), para 3.1.
79   Oil & Gas UK Industry Model Form Decommissioning Security Agreement (March 2009), para 3.2. The ability to challenge gives the vendor a significant degree of control over security under the DSA and so discourages secondary security from being demanded.
80   Oil & Gas UK Industry Model Form Decommissioning Security Agreement (March 2009), para 3.3.
81   Oil & Gas UK Industry Model Form Decommissioning Security Agreement (March 2009), para 8.8.
82   Where parties refuse to cooperate in an expert determination, in many circumstances a term may be implied that they should do so – see *Cream Holdings Limited v Davenport* [2011] EWCA Civ 1287, Patten LJ.
83   Oil & Gas UK Industry Model Form Decommissioning Security Agreement (March 2009), para 3.6.

The expert need not be an individual person; a firm or company can be appointed. The expert may not have "any financial or personal interest in the result". This restriction is very wide and does not allow for nominal shareholdings or for the expert to have financial connections to the parties. Coupled with the absence of immunity from suit, this may deter acceptance of the appointment.[84] Many candidates with experience of decommissioning likely work for the main offshore contractors and may have connections to some of the parties in dispute. The parties in dispute might wish to widen the field of candidates by agreement that any interests of the expert be disclosed to the parties and any objections made or waived by the parties before the expert accepts instructions. The expert must be qualified or experienced in the discipline appropriate to the nature of the dispute.[85] If agreement on the selection of the expert is not possible within 10 business days, the template DSA allows any party to the DSA to apply to the president of the Energy Institute to appoint the expert. The Energy Institute is a reliable and effective appointing authority.

(b) *Scope of expert's power*
Expert determinations – despite being capable of quickly and effectively resolving technical disputes through the appointment of a specialist expert in the relevant area – do not, without specific provisions to the contrary, require:
- adherence to rules of natural justice (eg, the right to a hearing);
- the expert to come to decisions within (rather than outside) the range suggested by the conflicting parties; or
- the expert to be independent of the parties.[86]

Decisions of experts are binding even in the presence of fraud or manifest error, unless agreed otherwise or unless the expert sets about answering the wrong question.[87] This introduces a degree of uncertainty to the process. The template DSA seeks to limit this by requiring that a party challenging the proposed plan or the operator's determination of completion of decommissioning express a stated written objection.[88] In any challenge to the proposed plan (but not the operator's determination of completion of decommissioning), the expert must consider and determine this area of concern. He or she cannot step beyond the scope of this challenge in order to re-determine other elements. Limiting the expert in such a way also seeks to limit the cost of the expert process. In practice, parties may seek to raise additional statements of objections at a later stage in proceedings. Judicious use of

---

84 Immunity of suit is often seen as desirable to prevent an expert being unfairly pressured by either party through threats of claims in negligence upon an adverse determination. However, given that there is no requirement in the template DSA for a reasoned determination, it may be impossible to tell whether a negligent error has been made.
85 Although note the comments below about consideration of a legally qualified expert.
86 Although independence from the parties is addressed at Oil & Gas UK Industry Model Form Decommissioning Security Agreement (March 2009), para 10.3.
87 Although appeal for fraud or manifest error is addressed at Oil & Gas UK Industry Model Form Decommissioning Security Agreement (March 2009), para 10.8.
88 Oil & Gas UK Industry Model Form Decommissioning Security Agreement (March 2009), paras 3.3 and 8.8.

the expert's power to control the procedure of the determination will be necessary in deciding whether supplemental statements of objections are permissible and within what timeframe.

The template DSA suggests that the parties to the DSA agree carefully defined 'assumptions' which the operator must apply in drawing up the proposed plan and which the expert must also follow when determining challenges to the proposed plan and when subjecting the cost estimation to independent periodic review.[89] These may be contentious and will be subject to individual negotiation between the parties to the DSA. In addition to the assumptions, it is common practice in expert determinations for an expert and all those appointing him to sign terms of reference further specifying his obligations and remuneration. Offshore contractors acting as experts may, following their normal practices, seek agreement of complex work schedules governing likely work which may cause significant delay if unanimity is required.

(c)   *Procedural matters for determination by expert*

Under the template DSA, a very speedy determination is envisaged. This is because it is desirable for any reference to the expert to be completed in time to allow security to be replaced before existing security expires. Otherwise, interim invoices may need to be raised. The expert shall notify the operator of his preliminary decision within 30 business days of acceptance of his appointment and the parties shall then be given 10 business days to make representations. The expert shall, having taken account of such representations, reach a final decision within 30 days of notification of the preliminary decision to the operator.

However, there is potential for many references to an expert to have a very broad scope. The timings envisaged may not be feasible, especially for large or multi-installation assets, or for the review of the first cost estimation for the installation. The expert may need assistance from specialist disciplines, such as reservoir engineering, offshore engineering, process engineering, drilling, sub-sea contractors, heavy-lift/barge contractors and disposal/refurbishment contractors. The template DSA allows the expert to obtain technical and legal advice and, if the dispute engages multiple specialisms, it seems likely that this may need to be exercised in many cases.[90] If multiple expert disciplines are engaged, the expert may be relying on and assessing the views of several others rather than relying on his own qualifications and experience. These views would all need to have been commissioned by the expert (normally with the approval of the parties in dispute) and provided to and considered by the expert before the preliminary decision can be released, with a delay in any element preventing further progress. It may also be hard for the parties to have confidence that the expert – even with this technical assistance – can manage all technical and procedural aspects, especially if any party is seeking to prolong the process, for example by seeking to refer the expert to an increasing number of 'relevant' documents. In the construction industry, a trend towards the

---

89   Oil & Gas UK Industry Model Form Decommissioning Security Agreement (March 2009), Appendix 5.
90   Oil & Gas UK Industry Model Form Decommissioning Security Agreement (March 2009), para 10.5.5.

appointment of legally qualified adjudicators rather than those with engineering qualifications has evolved in certain disputes. Therefore, there may be cause to consider appointment of a legally trained expert possessing relevant UK continental shelf decommissioning experience, who can request technical assistance from relevant disciplines, as an alternative approach. In complex multiple disciplinary cases this might assist good governance of the procedure. Quantity surveyors with similar experience may otherwise be considered. In relation to documents, a significant hurdle to be overcome in practice is the task of supporting the operator's assumptions with corroborative material, much of which will be confidential. Revealing information about, for example, gas sales prices and day rates to other industry participants might also infringe competition law. Unlike in arbitration, it is not fatal to the integrity of an expert determination for the parties in dispute to agree to provide documents to the expert without copies to other parties; however, this may not be an ideal solution in many cases.

The determination can be valid even if only a simple value, or date as appropriate, is determined, unless a reasoned determination has been agreed to be given. If the expert determines that greater security be paid than estimated by the operator, that additional security must be paid. Options exist in the template DSA for payment of the expert's fees and expenses, depending on the nature of the dispute being referred, with the starting point that challenges to the proposed plan and the operator's determination of completion of decommissioning will be paid by the challenging party. Options also exist in relation to the recovery of parties' own legal and other costs, which will be the subject of individual negotiation.

8.5   Default under DSAs

Failure to provide security or otherwise to comply with the terms of the DSA normally allows the defaulting party's security to be realised. Default will often occur hand in hand with insolvency, as with the administration of one of the owners of the Ardmore field before decommissioning. Default under the template DSA triggers a cross-default under the JOA. This will normally allow the other parties to the JOA to require forfeiture of the defaulting party's participating interest under the licence, assuming this interest themselves *pro rata*, together with a share of the decommissioning obligations. Any amounts paid in by the defaulting party are called by the trustee and divided proportionately among those that have taken over the defaulting party's liabilities.[91] It may be unwise to allow disputes about the amount of security due to be paid under the DSA to proceed slowly. The longer the length of the dispute, the greater the other participants' exposure will be on insolvency, as delay will hold up the payment of any additional security that the expert may eventually determine to be necessary. After forfeiture, the remaining parties to the JOA are likely to continue to produce from the field to gain revenues, bearing between themselves any shortfall in decommissioning costs due to the default. Where only one licensee remains and is in default, any security paid under

---

91   Oil & Gas UK Industry Model Form Decommissioning Security Agreement (March 2009), paras 7.3 and 7.4.

the DSA will be standing for the benefit of the second-tier participants (and possibly the secretary). There will be no JOA under which to trigger a cross-default. The second-tier participants would have no redress in the event of a default. Therefore, the template DSA provides optional language that no net value is included in the cost calculation above in this circumstance, to ensure adequate security.[92]

Where the operator defaults, the normal redress under the template DSA will be to trigger a cross-default under the JOA, removing the operator. In the interim period before a new operator is confirmed, the non-defaulting parties to the DSA may act by unanimity.[93] If all parties to the DSA are in default, the second-tier participants may act by unanimity instead. If no second-tier participants are able and willing to act, under the template DSA a third-tier participant may ask the secretary to endorse it to act instead.[94] The DSA will be novated to this party, which in the meantime can enforce rights under the DSA under the Contracts (Rights of Third Parties) Act 1999.

It is conceivable that decommissioning obligations may fall to the secretary in the event that all the other parties to the DSA default, and so the secretary may need to draw on security arranged by the parties. If so, the secretary may require that he be made a party to the DSA, in which case he will:

- impose minimum requirements for the content of the DSA;
- be unwilling to accept PCGs as a form of security; and
- have minimum requirements for the rating of financial institutions providing letters of credit.[95]

Alternatively, the template DSA permits the secretary to benefit from the DSA even if not a party, under the Contracts (Rights of Third Parties) Act, in which case these minimum requirements need not be met.[96]

Disputes may arise as to the date after which no further security is required. The template DSA suggests that security be provided for 12 months after the submission of the close-out report to the secretary, in case further work is requested, with a further 12-month extension possible.[97]

Except where disputes are referred to the expert, jurisdiction over disputes under the template DSA is vested in the courts of England and Wales. Action to enforce rights under the DSA on default in all circumstances above will therefore be brought before the courts rather than a potentially more speedy expert determination.

9. Disputes arising from NGO challenges to decommissioning proposals

The 1995 Greenpeace campaign against the planned decommissioning of the Brent Spar, a floating storage and offloading column operated by Shell, is the most publicised dispute involving decommissioning liabilities in the UK continental shelf.

---

92   Oil & Gas UK Industry Model Form Decommissioning Security Agreement (March 2009), para 5.1.
93   Oil & Gas UK Industry Model Form Decommissioning Security Agreement (March 2009), para 7.5.
94   Oil & Gas UK Industry Model Form Decommissioning Security Agreement (March 2009), para 7.6.
95   DECC, Decommissioning of Offshore Oil and Gas Installations and Pipelines under the Petroleum Act 1998, Guidance Notes (Version 6, March 2011), Annex G, paras 7-14.
96   Oil & Gas UK Industry Model Form Decommissioning Security Agreement (March 2009), para 13.2.1. The secretary can also recover costs incurred decommissioning under para 8.6.
97   Oil & Gas UK Industry Model Form Decommissioning Security Agreement (March 2009), paras 5.4.

This section considers the possibility of challenges to an agreed programme by NGOs and similar groups. It also considers the consequences of these challenges for participants that fall within the secretary's wide decommissioning powers.

The Greenpeace campaign centred on opposition to the programme approved by the secretary in late 1994. Greenpeace claimed that the environmental impact of the approved deep-sea method would be greater than stated. This led to the boarding of the Brent Spar by Greenpeace, a consumer boycott, violence against Shell service stations in Germany and opposition to deep-sea disposal by the governments of Germany, Denmark, Netherlands and Sweden. Throughout the campaign, both Shell and the secretary maintained that the deep-sea disposal envisaged by the programme remained the best practicable environmental option. Alleged discrepancies relied on by Greenpeace were still being investigated by the secretary when a decision was taken by Shell to cancel the proposed deep-sea disposal and to dispose on land, at around three times the cost. Despite retaining the support of the secretary and acting in accordance with its legal obligations, Shell had lost the increasingly relevant public relations battle.

The Brent Spar dispute occurred before the entry into force of the Petroleum Act 1998. To minimise the prospect of similar challenges, the secretary has adopted the practice of recommending that NGOs be widely consulted before any programme is approved,[98] allowing NGOs greater access to information about the proposed programme. The DECC publishes all programmes under consideration and approved programmes on its website.[99] NGOs can challenge decisions of the secretary to approve (or reject) a programme under the Section 42 statutory appeals process. For any legal challenge, the allocation of jurisdiction between the courts of England and Wales and Scotland must be determined. This was a feature of the Greenpeace challenge: the English courts declined jurisdiction on the basis that factors suggested that Scotland was the appropriate forum.[100] The Scottish courts were also considered likely to decline jurisdiction, due to procedural restrictions limiting the class of parties that may bring a judicial review in Scotland to parties with title and interest to sue. This resulted in no legal challenge advancing.

The right for NGOs or similar groups to advance a challenge by way of judicial review in Scotland is very limited. EU Directive 2003/35/EC seeks to provide a more transparent and open system for environmental decision making and to provide procedural rights for individuals.[101] The directive requires access to environmental justice, including the right to challenge environmental decisions. On April 6 2011 the European Commission announced that it was taking the United Kingdom to the European Court of Justice over the high cost of challenges to decisions on the environment which, it is argued, prevents NGOs and individuals in the United

98   DECC, Decommissioning of Offshore Oil and Gas Installations and Pipelines under the Petroleum Act 1998, Guidance Notes (Version 6, March 2011), Annex G, para 6.24.
99   See www.og.decc.gov.uk/upstream/decommissioning/programmes/index.htm.
100   R v Secretary of State for Scotland, ex parte Greenpeace Limited (Popplewell J), May 24 1995 (unreported). Relevant factors considered when determining jurisdiction are considered above.
101   EU Directive 2003/35/EC adopted the Aarhus Convention on Access to Information, Public Participation in Decision Making and Access to Justice in Environmental Matters 1998, which was ratified in the United Kingdom in 2005. The directive requires implementation by the UK and Scottish governments.

Kingdom from bringing environmental claims. There is wider concern that the judicial review procedure in Scotland does not meet the directive's requirements that the procedure be fair, equitable, timely and not prohibitively expensive.

Once a party wishing to bring a challenge has identified the jurisdiction in which it is appropriate to begin proceedings, under the Section 42 statutory appeal process a challenge must be brought within 42 days of approval (or rejection). No extension is permitted by the Petroleum Act 1998. In practice, this may prove to be a significant restriction. In a change of general practice since the Brent Spar case, under the Petroleum Act 1998 the secretary will now typically approve a programme years before decommissioning is due to commence, so NGOs will need to challenge any decision when the programme is approved, not when it begins to be put into effect. NGOs making a challenge at the time that decommissioning activities commence will be out of time. There would appear to be no scope for NGOs to use the general judicial review process to challenge the approval of a programme at the time of commencement of decommissioning activities if the NGO declined to raise a challenge under the Section 42 statutory appeal process within the permitted timeframe.[102]

Regardless of whether a legal challenge is presented, NGOs can exert considerable commercial pressure on an operator, as witnessed by Shell during the Brent Spar campaign. If, due to commercial pressure, an operator decides to depart from the approved programme at or before the time of commencement of decommissioning activities, it will need to propose an alteration to the programme to the secretary under Section 34(1)(a) of the Petroleum Act 1998, or will remain obliged under Section 36 of the Petroleum Act 1998 to ensure that the programme is carried out as agreed. An application for an alteration requires the persons submitting the programme to act together.[103] Other parties to the JOA concerned by the operator's reaction to commercial pressure may decline to agree to an application to alter the programme if such alteration results in increased financial exposure. If the operator has adequate voting power under the JOA, such concerns may be outvoted, as the Oil & Gas UK standard form JOA states that all participants will be bound by such decisions.[104] Otherwise, the operator may need to make a case that the alteration is necessary to operate in a proper and workman-like manner in accordance with good oilfield practice, and in compliance with best practice standards in respect of health and safety and of the environment.[105] If the parties to the JOA vote in favour of changing the programme and the secretary agrees to amend the programme, any additional cost will be allocated as agreed by the parties to the JOA. If the parties to the JOA vote against the operator, no application to alter the programme can be made to the secretary and the operator's only options may be to offer to fund the additional cost itself in order to secure co-venturer support or to threaten to resign

---

102   See Woolf, Jowell and Le Sueur, *De Smith's Judicial Review* (2007, 6th Ed) para 4-024.
103   Clause 13.3 of the Oil & Gas UK template JOA also requires the approval of the joint operating committee before the decommissioning programme and budget can be amended and so would require the support of the parties to the JOA.
104   Oil & Gas UK standard form JOA, Clause 9.8.4.
105   Oil & Gas UK template JOA, Clauses 6.2.2(a) and 9.1(a).

as operator – it is unlikely that other co-venturers would wish to step in due to negative publicity.

10. Disputes with contractors during the decommissioning process

This section considers the implementation of the approved programme and disputes arising from decommissioning activities – in particular, the scope for disputes with contractors. The first task in implementing the programme is to create or formalise a contractual framework for carrying out the project. The operator may choose to outsource the project management to a project management company or manage the work itself. In addition, a single or multiple contractors might be employed. In either case, the decommissioning of a structure is likely to involve multiple parties, not all of whose interests will be aligned. The DECC guidance promotes the decommissioning phase as "an ideal opportunity for companies to share decommissioning expertise" – partly, it seems, on the basis that "the competitive pressures are less [at the decommissioning phase] than at the development or production phase", and that "Oil & Gas UK, the Pilot Scheme and The Early Decommissioning Synergy Group (TEDS) all promote co-operation".[106] However, unlike the development and production phases, decommissioning is a zero-sum activity, and in the absence of the potential future upsides at the development and production phases, parties may be less amenable to settling disputes amicably.

As set out above, a programme will typically be approved three to five years in advance of cessation of production. A programme might also provide for phased implementation or, in certain circumstances and with the prior agreement of the secretary, delayed implementation.[107] Despite this, the programme must include an overall cost estimate on a year-by-year basis, and provide any sensitivities and assumptions on which it is made. This cost estimate will be subject to the same uncertainties as any tender or estimate for a similarly complex construction or engineering project. The three main categories of potential dispute are:

- Cost of variation/scope of work – the risk of disputes concerning scope of work is most likely to arise between the operator and contractors. Such disputes may involve claims that the descriptions of work in the tender documentation or subsequent contracts were ambiguous or later needed to be revised in circumstances where unexpected additional work arose. The Housing Grants, Construction and Regeneration Act 1996, which provides parties to certain types of construction contract with a statutory right to refer disputes to adjudication, does not apply to contracts for the "demolition of plant or machinery, or... steelwork for the purposes of supporting or providing access to plant or machinery, on a site where the primary activity is... the production, transmission, processing or bulk storage [of] oil [or] gas".[108] Disputes between the operator and the contractor in relation to

106 DECC, Decommissioning of Offshore Oil and Gas Installations and Pipelines under the Petroleum Act 1998, Guidance Notes (Version 6, March 2011), para 17.1
107 DECC, Decommissioning of Offshore Oil and Gas Installations and Pipelines under the Petroleum Act 1998, Guidance Notes (Version 6, March 2011), para 5.19.

decommissioning work could therefore prove lengthy and costly to resolve, in the absence of contractual mechanisms that provide a speedy alternative. The same may also apply to disputes between contractors and sub-contractors.

- Project management – disputes concerning the management of the project are most likely to arise between the operator and the other participants which are liable for decommissioning costs. The operator of a structure in the decommissioning phase could also be the operator of several other structures which are yet to be decommissioned. The operator would have a commercial interest in maintaining good working relationships with individual contractors on a medium to long-term basis. This will not necessarily be the case for all other participants, some of which may have an interest only in the decommissioning of the structure. This could mean that project management decisions made in the best commercial interests of the operator may not be in the best interests of other participants. As noted above, since there is no potential future upside to the decommissioning phase, a difference of opinion between the operator and other participants regarding project management decisions that may impact the overall cost of decommissioning may lead to disputes.
- Subcontractor disputes – the risk of disputes arising between the contractor and various subcontractors is high. The most common disputes can arise out of delay caused by contractors or subcontractors, disputes as to scope of work and instances where there is a cash-flow squeeze imposed by the contractor or subcontractors.

11.   Disputes relating to decommissioning legacies

The Petroleum Act 1998 allows the secretary discretion to allow the deferral of decommissioning activities once a structure is no longer in use. Deferment may become particularly common in future years for pipelines, as they have the potential for reuse in connection with future hydrocarbon developments (and other uses such as carbon dioxide storage). The Petroleum Act 1998 also allows the secretary the discretion to allow certain installations, or part of them, to remain in place, under the derogation regime permitted by OSPAR Decision 98/3.[109] Derogations have already been granted in relation to certain structures – for example, on the Frigg, NW Hutton and Ekofisk fields. Any residual liability for installations left in place following decommissioning remains in perpetuity with the owners, not with the wider class of parties potentially liable for decommissioning. In other words, the owners of a structure at the time of its decommissioning will remain the owners of any residues, even if the licence has been relinquished. Ownership will normally be established by the last JOA, in the proportions stated. If, due to restructurings, insolvency or dissolution, certain of these companies cease to exist, their liabilities will pass *pro rata* to other co-owners.

108   Housing Grants, Construction and Regeneration Act 1996, Section 105(2)(c)(ii).
109   This governs UK practice, although the resolution itself has no force in law in England and Wales (or Scotland). It does not apply to pipelines.

Any claims for compensation by third parties for damage caused by residues following decommissioning will be governed by general law in tort (or delict in Scotland).[110] Negligence will need to be established. This may be difficult, given that the secretary will have approved the installation remaining in place, a minimum water clearance of 55 metres is required and extensive rules exist regarding marking for shipping purposes. Nevertheless, the UK Fisheries Offshore Oil & Gas Legacy Trust Fund Limited has been established by Oil & Gas UK to register seabed hazards and to act as a residual compensation fund in the event of insolvency of owners found to be negligent. Government liability is unlikely in all cases where the OSPAR Convention and UNCLOS have been followed by the secretary through appropriate decommissioning steps and proper marking of residues, except for where the secretary has taken ownership of structures, which he will do for decommissioned wellheads[111] – although here the risk of damage to other ocean users is negligible. More significant is likely to be any exposure to environmental claims as any remaining structures degrade over time. Despite the economic uncertainty of this perpetual liability, it is unlikely that owners will make provision in the programme for the full decommissioning of the installation regardless of any derogation, as alternative decommissioning methods may not be possible or would have costs which would outweigh any residual risk.

12. Disputes relating to health and safety and the environment

Given the nature of the task of decommissioning and the environment in which it is undertaken, companies operating on the UK continental shelf will be concerned with potential disputes arising out of injury or fatalities. In addition, companies must comply with a large body of environmental legislation when carrying out the decommissioning process. Failure to comply with such legislation may give rise to claims from government agencies responsible for ensuring compliance or third parties affected by any breach. While both are significant areas of potential dispute, these two areas are outside the scope of this chapter.

The author would like to thank Judith Aldersey-Williams, partner, CMS Cameron McKenna LLP in Aberdeen for her assistance with the production of this chapter. Assistance was also received from Roni Pacht, Amy Smart and Natasha Broumpton of CMS Cameron McKenna LLP.

---

110 DECC, Decommissioning of Offshore Oil and Gas Installations and Pipelines under the Petroleum Act 1998, Guidance Notes (Version 6, March 2011), paras 16.1-16.5.
111 Petroleum Licensing (Production) (Seaward Areas) Regulations 2008, Schedule 1, Model Clauses for Seaward Area Production Licences, para 19(14).

Judicial review in England and Wales

Helen Clark
Mark Clarke
Tom Cummins
Ashurst LLP

1.   Introduction

The power of the state permeates the energy industry. Licences and approvals are required for the exploitation of hydrocarbon reserves, permission must be sought for the construction and installation of infrastructure, and the viability of projects may depend upon subsidies and the transient support of governments. Even in a market in which substantial deregulation has taken place, energy companies are subject to constant regulatory oversight. An unfavourable decision or a change of government policy may have serious financial consequences.

Companies active in the energy industry require assurance that public bodies will exercise their powers legally, fairly, rationally and reasonably. If they consider that this has not happened, they may seek means of redress. They may wish to have decisions reconsidered or actions reversed, in the hope that a more favourable outcome will result.

This chapter considers the means by which companies operating in England and Wales may do this by judicial review. Although the chapter approaches the subject from the perspective of a private sector energy company, explaining the claims which such company may have and the remedies which it may be awarded, it is intended as an overview of the topic which may interest any reader. Indeed, energy companies may often find themselves not directly involved in judicial review claims, but in the position of third parties awaiting the outcome of claims by individuals or pressure groups against public authorities.

The chapter approaches the dense and unique law of judicial review by means of a series of questions, of the type which the general counsel of an energy company might be asked by his colleagues upon receipt of an adverse decision:

- What is judicial review?
- Why is judicial review relevant to the energy sector?
- What remedies are available in judicial review?
- In what circumstances can a claimant bring a claim for judicial review?
- What is the role of third parties in judicial review?
- When must a judicial review claim be brought?

The chapter explores the statutory basis for judicial review – the Senior Courts Act 1981 – and the wealth of case law which has developed as judicial review increases in popularity and significance, not least in the energy sector.

2. What is judicial review?

Judicial review is the process whereby the courts ensure that public law functions are exercised lawfully. It should be distinguished from a right of appeal against a decision which may be available to a party under specific legislation. Judicial review is a mechanism which has general application. It enables a party which has been affected by a decision or action with a public law element to apply to court, requesting that the court consider the lawfulness of such decision or action.

Judicial review is an important element of public administrative law. In the words of one judge, writing in 1899, "I know of no duty of the Court which it is more important to observe, and no power of the Court which it is more important to enforce, than its power of keeping public bodies within their rights."[1]

Judicial review is not concerned with questioning the merits of decisions. Those exercising public law functions are afforded a wide degree of discretion by the courts. It is only where such functions are exercised improperly that judicial review may have a role to play.

This chapter is confined to judicial review in England and Wales. Although judicial review is available in Scotland and Northern Ireland, the procedure is significantly different and beyond the scope of this chapter.

3. Why is judicial review relevant to the energy sector?

The number of judicial review claims in England and Wales has increased markedly in recent decades. In 1974 there were 160 applications for permission to seek judicial review in England and Wales. In 2010 there were 10,600 applications for permission to apply for judicial review, up from just over 9,000 claims in 2009, just over 7,000 claims in 2008 and over 6,000 claims in 2007. These claims frequently do not involve commercial parties. Rather, they arise from asylum or immigration matters.

However, so-called 'commercial' judicial review has also seen a marked increase. This is particularly evident in the energy sector. Claims which had arisen recently at the time of writing included:

- Total's and ConocoPhilips's 2011 judicial review of the Marine Management Organisation's rejection of their application to take ownership of the oil terminal at the Port of Immingham. The companies claimed that the efficient supply of oil to their nearby refineries at Killingholme was threatened by a plan from Associated British Ports to take back control of the terminal and run operations itself;[2]
- the judicial review brought by a number of solar companies in 2011 against the Department of Energy and Climate Change's (DECC) decision to commence a fast-track review of subsidies for renewable electricity generation known as 'feed-in tariffs';[3] and

---

1   *Roberts v Gwyrfai District Council* [1899] 2 Ch 608.
2   http://www.yorkshirepost.co.uk/news/at-a-glance/main-section/oil_giants_begin_high_court_bid_to_seize_control_of_humber_port_1_3846516.
3   http://www.guardian.co.uk/environment/2011/apr/19/solar-legal-action-feed-in-tariffs.
4   http://www.greenpeace.org.uk/media/press-releases/greenpeace-takes-government-court-over-nuclear-power-expansion-20110826.

- Greenpeace's 2011 claim for review of DECC's decision to progress plans for new nuclear power stations despite the consequences of the Japanese nuclear disaster at Fukushima.[4]

These claims illustrate certain characteristics of commercial judicial review in the energy sector.

First, it may provide an opportunity for parties to seek the intervention of the courts where an element of public law exists in what might otherwise appear to be a private law dispute (the Total/ConocoPhilips claim).

Second, judicial review may be a means of seeking redress against decisions arising from the reallocation of public funds (the solar companies claim). This may become increasingly prevalent in the light of ongoing economic malaise in the United Kingdom.

Third, decisions regarding the use of energy arouse controversy and debate. Claims by pressure groups (frequently Greenpeace) and other interested parties are a feature of judicial review in the energy sector. These may take the form of individual homeowners protesting against the decision to site wind farms close to their property or well-resourced pressure groups seeking to provoke debate about future sources of the United Kingdom's energy mix.

4. What remedies are available?

Parties considering judicial review will wish to know, at the outset, what remedies may be granted by the court. If the outcome sought by a potential claimant is unlikely to be available or to be granted, there may be little point in commencing a judicial review claim.

If a judicial review claim is successful, the principal remedies granted by the court are:

- a mandatory order (requiring the body under review to do something);
- a prohibitory order (restraining or preventing the body from doing something); or
- a quashing order (setting aside the decision of the body).[5]

It is also possible for the court to grant declarations or injunctions where they are "just and convenient" in all the circumstances.[6]

The remedies in judicial review are discretionary. A claimant may be able to show that a decision maker has acted unlawfully, but may be denied the relief sought. So, for example, where detriment would be caused to third parties, the court might decline to set aside a decision or remit it for reconsideration.

A claimant will often apply for a quashing order, setting aside a previous decision, and a mandatory order requiring that the body reconsider its decision. Where the court makes a quashing order, it is empowered either to remit the decision for reconsideration by the decision maker or to substitute its own decision for the decision of the decision maker. This latter power exists only where:

5   Section 31 of the Senior Courts Act 1981.
6   Section 31(2) of the Senior Courts Act 1981.

- the decision in question was made by a court or tribunal;
- the decision is quashed on the ground that there has been an error of law; and
- without the error, there would have been only one decision which the court or tribunal could have reached.[7]

The limited scope for the court to substitute its own decision reflects the nature of judicial review as a means of ensuring that the process by which decisions are made is conducted properly, not that decisions are made correctly on the merits.

Where a decision is quashed and remitted to a body for reconsideration, a different decision will not necessarily be made. A decision maker who failed to take account of relevant circumstances in his original decision may, upon considering such circumstances, come to the same conclusion. A claimant may even find itself in a worse position – for example, where a decision to charge for advice by a local authority is unlawful, but the local authority is entitled to withhold the advice altogether.[8]

Although it is possible for a claimant to seek damages, restitution or the recovery of a debt in a judicial review claim, this cannot be the only remedy which the claimant seeks. Claims for these remedies require a distinct cause of action. If such an action exists, the money claim can be included in the judicial review. The rationale for this is to avoid the inefficiency of parallel proceedings required essentially to determine the same issues. There is no general right to claim damages for losses caused by unlawful action by bodies exercising public law functions, although a claim for damages may be founded upon a claim in tort (eg, for breach of statutory duty or misfeasance in public office) or under the Human Rights Act 1998, which incorporated the Convention for the Protection of Human Rights and Fundamental Freedoms into UK law. By way of example, in one claim, a developer was able to claim substantial damages as a result of a claim for the tort of deceit following judicial review proceedings.[9]

5. **In what circumstances can a claimant bring a claim for judicial review?**

A claimant must satisfy the following requirements in order to bring a claim for judicial review:

- The claimant must have "sufficient interest" to bring a claim;
- The decision or act must be amenable to judicial review; and
- One of the substantive grounds for judicial review must apply.

5.1 Does the claimant have sufficient interest?

In order to make an application for judicial review, a claimant must be granted permission from the court. The court will grant permission only if the claimant "has a sufficient interest in the matter to which the application relates".[10]

The satisfaction of the sufficient interest test is a matter exclusively for the court.

---

7   Sections 31 (5) and (5A) of the Senior Courts Act 1981.
8   *R v Richmond upon Thames London Borough Council, ex p McCarthy & Stone (Developments) Ltd* [1992] 2 AC 48.
9   *Slough Estates Plc v Welwyn Hatfield District Council* [1996] 2 PLR 50.

The parties to a judicial review claim cannot confer jurisdiction by consent where it would not otherwise exist.[11]

In applying the sufficient interest test, the courts are required to strike a balance. They must prevent frivolous litigation against public bodies, while simultaneously ensuring that valid claims are not cursorily dismissed. In doing so, the courts have adopted an increasingly relaxed approach when assessing the standing of claimants. The bar has been described as having been set "at a low level".[12]

In line with this approach, respected pressure groups raising genuine matters of public concern have typically been permitted to apply for judicial review. Thus, Greenpeace has received permission to challenge various decisions, including a 2010 claim arising from the consideration of licence applications for the exploitation of North Sea oil reserves located in deep water, in the wake of the BP Deepwater Horizon disaster in the Gulf of Mexico.[13]

In *R (Greenpeace) v HM Inspectorate of Pollution and Ministry of Agriculture, Fisheries and Food*[14] the court looked at the role played by pressure groups in judicial review. This case concerned variations permitted to the authorisation granted for emission of radioactive waste from the thermal oxide reprocessing plant at Sellafield in Cumbria. Greenpeace brought the judicial review to challenge the variations. The court considered that Greenpeace had standing owing to its size and support base, its accreditation by the United Nations and the fact that if permission had not been granted, Greenpeace's members would not have had an effective way of bringing the issues raised before the court. If Greenpeace's application were to be refused, "a less well-informed challenge might be mounted which would stretch unnecessarily the court's resources and which would not afford the court the assistance it requires in order to do justice between the parties". Greenpeace was described as "eminently respectable and responsible", with "genuine interest in the issues raised".

This approach reflects the willingness of the courts to countenance applications made by pressure groups which will assist the court in discharging its duty to hold public bodies accountable.

The factors which weighed in favour of holding that Greenpeace had sufficient interest reflect the matters which the court will consider when applying the test. These include the following:

- Availability of alternative remedy – judicial review is available only where the claimant has no alternative recourse or right of appeal. A claimant will be obliged to have exhausted all other possible routes to obtain redress prior to commencing a judicial review claim. Thus, where there is a potential claim under a statutory complaints procedure[15] or the possibility of commencing a private prosecution,[16] these avenues should be explored prior to judicial review.
- Strength and importance of the grounds of challenge – in 1994 World

---

10   Section 31(3) of the Senior Courts Act 1981.
11   *R v Secretary of State for Social Services, ex p Child Poverty Action Group* [1990] 2 QB 540.
12   *R (on the Application of Bulger) v Secretary of State for the Home Department* [2001] *The Times* March 7 2001.
13   http://www.greenpeace.org.uk/blog/climate/we-get-green-light-high-court-20110224.
14   [1994] 4 All ER 329.
15   *R v East Sussex County Council, ex p W (A Minor)* [1998] 2 FLR 1082.
16   *R v DPP, ex p Camelot Group Plc* [1998] 10 Admin LR 93.

Development Movement (an environmental pressure group) brought a claim regarding the decision of the government to approve funding for the construction of the Pergau dam and hydroelectric power station in northern Malaysia. The government alleged that the claimant lacked sufficient interest to bring the claim. However, the court found that "the merits of the challenge are an important, if not dominant, factor when considering standing".[17] The claim was permitted to proceed.

- Proximity of the decision to the claimant – a claimant need not have a direct financial or legal interest in a claim in order to satisfy the sufficient interest test. A claimant may be able to bring a claim on the basis that it would be indirectly affected by a proposed course of action. Thus, in one case ICI was found to have standing to seek judicial review of a proposal by the Inland Revenue to value business goods used by Shell, Esso and BP. ICI sought review on the basis that the proposal would have afforded its competitors an artificially favourable taxation regime.[18]
- Claim in the public interest – if an application for judicial review can be shown to be in the public interest, then it will usually be permitted by the courts to proceed. Where an application "raises public law issues which are of general importance, where the [claimant] has no private interest in the outcome of the case", it may be considered to be in the public interest.[19] However, "where a claimant is acting out of ill-will or for some other improper purpose", the court will be unlikely to permit the claim.[20]
- No other challenger – where a refusal to grant permission for a claim would result in no other means of challenging a decision, this is likely to militate in favour of permission being granted. However, it has been stated that it is not "essential, in order for the claimant to have...standing, that there be no one else who could bring such proceedings", on the basis that this is "a relevant factor...but... not an essential requisite".[21]

Where breach of the Human Rights Act is alleged, the jurisdictional threshold for a claimant is modified. The claimant must be a "a victim of the unlawful act".[22]

5.2 Is the decision or act amenable to judicial review?

Judicial review has no application in the absence of a public law element. The definition of 'judicial review' in the Civil Procedure Rules refers to the review of the lawfulness of "an enactment" or "a decision, action or failure to act in relation to the exercise of a public function".[23] It is the character of the function being performed,

---

17 *R v Secretary of State for Foreign Affairs, ex p World Development Movement Ltd* [1995] 1 All ER 611.
18 *R v Attorney General, ex p ICI Plc* [1987] 1 CMLR 72.
   R v Lord Chancellor, ex p Child Poverty Action Group [1998] 2 All ER 755.
   R (Feaskins) v Secretary of State for the Environment, Food and Rural Affairs [2003] EWCA Civ 1546 [2003] All ER 39 (Nov).
19 *R v Lord Chancellor, ex p Child Poverty Action Group* [1998] 2 All ER 755.
20 *R (Feaskins) v Secretary of State for the Environment, Food and Rural Affairs* [2003] EWCA Civ 1546 [2003] All ER 39 (Nov).
21 *R (Hammerton) v London Underground Ltd* [2002] EWHC 2307 (Admin) [2002] All ER 141 (Nov).
22 Section 7 of the Human Rights Act 1998

rather than the body performing it, which determines whether a "decision, action or failure to act" may be reviewed.

It would be unhelpful to seek to set out in prescriptive terms the tests which the court will apply in determining whether a public law function has been exercised. As was stated in one case, "the boundary between public law and private law is not capable of precise definition, and whether a decision has a sufficient public law element to justify the intervention of the Administrative Court by judicial review is often as much a matter of feel, as deciding whether any particular criteria are met".[24] Thus, the decisions of governmental departments, public bodies and, in certain circumstances, private parties may be reviewable.

The characteristics which a court may consider when determining whether a function may be reviewed include the following:

- The 'source of power' test – the court will look at the legal source of the power being exercised by the body facing challenge. Where the source of power is a statute or subordinate legislation made under a statute, the body will be subject to judicial review.[25]

- The 'but for' test – the court will consider whether the functions exercised by the body in question would inevitably be regulated by statute but for the existence of a non-statutory body performing them. The 'but for' test has led to decisions of the Advertising Standards Authority being reviewed (as it was held that, in its absence, its functions would have been performed by a statutory body).[26] Conversely, the Football Association's decisions were not subject to judicial review, as the court found no evidence to suggest that the state would have found it necessary to perform its function if it did not exist.[27] The 'but for' test is not always conclusive – although it was held that the government would have carried out the Jockey Club's functions in its absence, the club was "not in its origin, its history, its constitution...a public body".[28]

- Extensive or monopolistic powers – it may be relevant that a body exercises extensive or exclusive functions. The Takeover Panel, for example, was described as having "a giant's strength".[29] Nevertheless, it is not necessarily enough that a body exercises extensive power in the private sector;[30] and likewise, it is not conclusive that a large number of people are affected, or that the impact of a decision is serious.[31]

- Submission does not result from parties' agreement or consent – where parties have submitted to the decision-making powers of a body voluntarily

---

23   Civil Procedure Rule 54.1(2).
24   *R (on the application of Tucker) v Director General of the National Crime Squad* [2003] EWCA Civ 03 [2003] IRLR 439 at 441.
25   *R v Panel on Takeovers and Mergers, ex p Datafin Plc* [1987] QB 815.
26   *R v Advertising Standards Authority, ex p the Insurance Service Plc* [1990] 2 Admin LR 77.
27   *R v Football Association Ltd, ex p Football League Ltd* [1993] 2 All ER 833.
28   *R v Disciplinary Committee of the Jockey Club, ex p Aga Khan* [1993] 2 All ER 853.
29   *R v Panel on Takeovers and Mergers, ex p Datafin Plc* [1987] QB 815.
30   See *ex p Aga Khan* at 875: "the mere fact of power, even over a substantial area of economic activity, is not enough. In a mixed economy, power may be private as well as public."
31   *Ex p Football League Ltd* at 841: "[the] FA's powers extend beyond contract to affect the lives of many hundreds of thousands who are not in any contractual relationship though...the same could be said about large public companies."

and in circumstances where there was no requirement for them to do so, the acts of such a body are unlikely to be reviewable. Thus, it was emphasised that the City of London is not a club which a party can join or not join at will: "The [Takeover] Panel regulates not only itself, but all others who have no alternative but to come to the market in a case to which the code applies."[32] The decisions of the Takeover Panel were reviewable. By contrast, the decisions of the Association of British Travel Agents (ABTA) were not; ABTA's powers were derived from contractual relationships.[33]

The multiple tests employed and the flexible approach taken mean that the courts have reviewed certain decisions which might not necessarily be considered appropriate for judicial review. For instance, the courts reviewed the decision of a privatised water company exercising statutory powers[34] and an airport operator in relation to noise pollution and vibrations experienced by local residents.[35]

Just as the decisions of bodies that are not patently 'public' may face review, not every act or decision of a public authority will constitute a public function and so attract the scrutiny of the court.

Thus, disputes as to the employment of individuals by public bodies have been found to be excluded from review. In the absence of any further element of public law, they are private law matters.[36] When a public body enters into a commercial contract – for example, for the provision of utilities – this is likely to be outside the remit of judicial review. It is a matter of private law. However, if the services contract is put out to tender, this may characterise it as a public law matter. The Privy Council in *Mercury Energy Ltd v Electricity Corporation of New Zealand Ltd*, a claim arising from the cancellation of a contract for electricity, held that that it was not likely that "a decision by a state enterprise to enter into or determine a commercial contract to supply goods or services will ever be the subject of judicial review in the absence of fraud, corruption or bad faith".[37]

Two cases brought by disappointed tenderers demonstrate the distinction between public and private functions exercised by public bodies. In *Mass Energy Ltd v Birmingham City Council*[38] the claimant objected to the local authority's acceptance of a tender which differed from the original contract specifications. The court held that it was open to the authority to commence the tender process and then negotiate improved terms with a successful tenderer. The authority was entitled to "act as a commercial animal at the stage when it was considering the tenders...received", even in circumstances where this did not "guarantee complete fairness".

Second, in *R (on the application of Gamesa Energy UK Ltd) v National Assembly for Wales*,[39] a claim related to a tender process for the construction of wind farms, the

32   *R v Panel on Takeovers and Mergers, ex p Datafin Plc* [1987] QB 815 at 846.
33   *R v Association of British Travel Agents, ex p Sunspell Ltd* [2001] ACD 16.
34   *R v Northumbrian Water Ltd, ex p Newcastle and Tyneside Health Authority* [1999] Env LR 715.
35   *R v Fairoaks Airport Ltd, ex p Roads* [1999] COD 168.
36   *R v BBC, ex p Lavelle* [1983] 1 WLR 23.
37   [1994] 1 WLR 521 at 529.
38   [1994] Env LR 298.
39   [2006] EWHC 2167 (Admin).

court found that there was not a sufficient element of public law in the claimant's claim – the claimant's objections related to the "nuts and bolts of parts of the exercise and their effect on the individual bid" of the claimant. The decision was not susceptible to judicial review, although the court noted that it was not the case "that a public law challenge to a tendering or pre-qualification process on the basis of irrationality could never be entertained [although] the circumstances under which it could be entertained must be rare".

5.3   Has there been a decision, action or failure to act?

Judicial review claims usually arise from 'decisions' (eg, DECC's decision to launch a fast-track review of feed-in tariffs mentioned at the beginning of the chapter). Typically, a decision will be notified to those affected by it. They will object and, in the absence of any reconsideration, consider the commencement of proceedings.

However, as the definition found in the Civil Procedure Rules states, a claim may arise against any "decision, action or failure to act in relation to the exercise of a public function".

There have been successful applications for permission to review:

- primary legislation/European legislation;[40]
- subordinate legislation;[41]
- policies and schemes;[42]
- proposals and draft schemes;[43]
- directions and instructions;[44]
- opinions and publications;[45] and
- guidance.[46]

However, the breadth of acts which may be challenged is qualified by the reluctance of the courts to inquire into the exercise of public law powers in certain circumstances.

Thus, the courts will not allow a claim to go ahead if it lacks substance or materiality. Proceedings should also be proportionate to the issues involved and the remedy sought,[47] and the courts are disinclined to consider cases which raise questions of only academic interest.[48] Determination of such claims is not in the public interest, which lies at the heart of the function of judicial review.

The courts are unlikely to allow challenges concerning decisions relating to the internal procedures of the UK Parliament and decisions of superior courts of England and Wales (eg, the High Court, Court of Appeal and Supreme Court). Decisions relating to the validity of acts of Parliament have traditionally been beyond the scope

---

40   *R v Secretary of State for Health, ex p Imperial Tobacco Ltd* [1999] EU LR582.
41   *R v Secretary of State for Trade and Industry, ex p Orange Personal Communications Ltd The Times* November 15 2000.
42   *R v Secretary of State for the Home Department, ex p Simms* [2000] 2 AC 115.
43   *R v Chief Constable of Kent Constabulary, ex p Kent Police Federation Joint Branch Board* [2000] COD 169.
44   *R (London and Continental Stations and Property Ltd) v The Rail Regulator* [2003] EWHC 2607.
45   *R (Mowlem Plc) v HM Assistant Deputy Coroner for Avon* [2005] EWHC 1359 (Admin).
46   *R (A) v Secretary of State for Health* [2008] EWHC 855 (Admin).
47   *R (Fudge) v South West Strategic Health Authority* [2007] EWCA Civ 803 [2007] 98 BMLR 112.
48   *Rushbridger v HM Attorney-General* [2003] UKHL 38 [2004] 1 AC 357.

of judicial review, although there are certain areas – such as conformity with EU law – which the courts may investigate.

The courts are also wary of passing judgement on certain issues, such as national security and economic policy. This was illustrated by *R (on the Application of People and Planet) v HM Treasury*.[49] Permission was sought to judicially review the government's policy towards its 70% shareholding in the Royal Bank of Scotland (RBS). An environmental action group wanted the government to impose its influence on RBS to prevent it lending to companies which might be harmful to the environment by reason of their business activities. Permission for judicial review was refused, the court deferring to the government's discretion as to which factors it treated as relevant for the purposes of formulating policy.

Similarly, the courts have been reluctant to review decisions which have a substantial policy element to them,[50] or to consider complex, specialised matters upon which the relevant decision makers may be better suited to make determinations than the court. Inevitably, there is a tension in the jurisprudence between vigilance (ie, the courts' need to protect against abuses of power) and restraint (ie, the responsibility of the courts to allow public bodies to exercise their own judgement and discretion in respect of administrative matters).

5.4 Does one of the grounds for judicial review apply?

The substantive grounds for judicial review are commonly listed as:

- illegality;
- irrationality; and
- procedural impropriety.

This triad was laid down in a seminal 1985 case, the judge cautioning that "further development on a case by case basis may...in course of time add further grounds".[51] This observation is valuable. Subsequent cases have made clear that the grounds for judicial review continue to evolve and overlap. The exercise of seeking to squeeze a factual set of circumstances within one or more of the grounds is rarely of benefit.

For convenience of analysis, however, the following paragraphs start by considering each of the traditional grounds for judicial review in turn.

(a) Is the decision illegal?

In broad terms, a decision or act will be illegal if it occurs:

- in contravention, or in excess, of the powers available to the decision maker;
- in pursuit of a purpose other than that for which the power has been bestowed; or
- in circumstances where there has been an impermissible fettering or delegation of power.

---

49   [2009] EWHC 3020 (Admin).
50   *R v Secretary of State for the Home Department, ex p Launder* [1997] 1 WLR 839.
51   *Council of Civil Service Unions v Minister for the Civil Service* [1985] AC 374 at 410.

Where a body contravenes or goes beyond the powers available to it, it will have acted illegally. In terms familiar to company lawyers, it will have acted *ultra vires*. Illegality may occur where a source of law is inconsistent with a source of law superior to it. Thus, primary legislation inconsistent with European legislation, subordinate legislation inconsistent with primary legislation or acts inconsistent with subordinate legislation are *prima facie* illegal. A claim for illegality permits the court to probe the validity of primary legislation. So, for example, provisions of the Finance Act 1997 applicable to insurance premium tax on travel insurance were considered to amount to illegal state aid under European legislation by the Court of Appeal.[52]

In *R (on the application of Teesside Power Ltd) v Gas and Electricity Market Authority*[53] (a claim related to proposed modifications concerning how electricity transmission losses on the national grid should be treated) the claimant sought review of the decision of the Gas and Electricity Market Authority (Ofgem) that it had the power to approve a modification to an industry code which departed from a timetable for implementation previously set. The court held that Ofgem had no general power to approve proposed modifications outside of the prescribed timetable. It was acting *ultra vires*.

Illegality may also arise where decisions are taken for purposes other than those for which the relevant power has been bestowed. So, for example, in *R v Lewisham London Borough Council, ex parte Shell UK Ltd*[54] the decision of Lewisham London Borough Council to avoid contracting with Shell in the 1980s as a form of protest against Shell's operations in apartheid South Africa was held to be unlawful. The court concluded that it would have been legitimate for the decision to have been taken merely on the basis that it would improve race relations in Lewisham; however, the decision had been taken to exert pressure on Shell to withdraw from South Africa. This constituted an improper purpose and thus was illegal.

A body will also be acting unlawfully if it abdicates or delegates responsibility for a decision or fetters its discretion in circumstances where it is not permitted to do so. Responsibility may be devolved (rather than delegated) in certain cases (known as the 'Carltona doctrine').[55] The Carltona doctrine ensures the efficient administration of public affairs: civil servants may discharge duties on behalf of their ministers. However, a body may not transfer its decision-making responsibilities to another body. A body is also not permitted to follow policy guidelines without further consideration where it is required to exercise its discretion. It must consider each matter with an open mind.

Under the Human Rights Act, it is unlawful for a public authority to act in a way which is incompatible with a European Convention on Human Rights right.[56] This prohibition does not apply if, as the result of one or more provisions of primary legislation, the authority could not have acted differently or acted so as to give effect to provisions which could not be interpreted in a manner compatible with convention rights.

---

52 *R v Commissioners of Customs and Excise, ex p Lunn Poly Ltd* [1999] EU LR 653.
53 [2008] EWHC 1415 (Admin).
54 [1988] 1 All ER 938.
55 *Carltona Ltd v Commissioner of Works* [1943] 2 All ER 560.
56 Section 6 of the Human Rights Act 1998.

(b) **Is the decision unreasonable?**

Unreasonableness or irrationality lies at the heart of judicial review. It reflects the necessity that parties not be subject to acts or decisions which are inexplicable or incomprehensible. So influential has been the leading case concerned with unreasonableness that claims under this ground are often referred to as alleging 'Wednesbury unreasonableness'.

The facts of *Associated Provincial Picture Houses Ltd v Wednesbury Corporation*[57] were as follows. A local authority granted a cinema licence pursuant to legislation which permitted it discretion to impose such conditions as it saw fit. A licence was granted subject to the proviso that no children under 15 years of age should be admitted to Sunday performances with or without an adult. The court held that the authority had not acted unreasonably. The court was entitled to investigate only whether the authority had taken into account matters that it ought not to have, or had disregarded matters that it ought to have, taken into account.

As judicial review is not a process through which the courts review the merits of decisions, the bar for irrational or unreasonable behaviour has been set high. In *Council of Civil Service Unions v Minister for Civil Service*[58] it was said that an irrational or unreasonable decision must be "so outrageous in its defiance of logic or accepted moral standards that no sensible person who had applied his mind to the question to be decided could have arrived at it".

The courts have stated that a reasonable decision is one which was "within the range of reasonable decisions open to a decision-maker".[59] Other cases have described "perversity",[60] a decision maker "taking leave of its senses"[61] and "something overwhelming"[62] as necessary for a successful claim for Wednesbury unreasonableness.

Such judicial formulations give a flavour of the approach of the courts to unreasonableness/irrationality. Evidence of a high standard of misconduct is required in order for a claim under this ground to have any prospect of success. This is unsurprising. As has been repeated throughout this chapter, the courts are extremely wary of 'second guessing' the decisions of officials and administrators. Generally, something must have gone dramatically awry before the courts will be prepared to impugn a decision or act on the basis of a want of reason or rationality.

(c) **Has there been procedural impropriety?**

Procedural impropriety or 'unfairness' often occurs where a decision maker has failed to comply with procedures prescribed for the exercise of its decision-making authority. Thus, a decision maker might be obliged to consult with interested parties prior to reaching a decision. A failure to do so would give rise to a claim for procedural impropriety.

Also underlying the ground of procedural impropriety is the obligation on

---

57   [1948] 1 KB 223.
58   [1984] 3 All ER 935.
59   *Boddington v British Transport Police* [1998] 2 All ER 203.
60   *Reid v Secretary of State for Scotland* [1999] 2 AC 512.
61   *R v Secretary of State for the Environment, ex p Nottinghamshire County Council* [1986] AC 240.
62   *Associated Provincial Picture Houses Ltd v Wednesbury Corporation* [1948] 1 KB 223.

decision makers to comply with the rules of natural justice. This involves ensuring that any process is free of actual or apparent bias, and providing that affected parties have the opportunity to have their views heard.

Claims involving actual bias are rare. It is more common for a claimant to allege apparent bias; where this happens, the courts will assess whether "the fair-minded and informed observer, having considered the facts, would conclude that there was a real possibility that the [decision] was biased".[63]

R (Walker) v Secretary of State for Energy and Climate Change[64] related to the secretary of state for energy's decision that the design of two new types of nuclear reactor was justified under the Euratom Directive. The claimant argued that apparent bias existed in light of the secretary of state's support for nuclear power, and that there should have been a separation between the secretary of state and the justifying authority. The claim was rejected as there was no requirement for independent justification under the directive and the secretary of state had applied the relevant test properly.

Claims for procedural impropriety often arise where one party considers that it is being treated unfairly, by contrast with other commercial actors or competitors.

In *R (on the application of Tate & Lyle Industries Ltd) v Secretary of State for Energy and Climate Change*,[65] a claim was brought in relation to the government's allocation of renewable obligation certificates. The claimant alleged that the government should not have taken account of new data when determining the renewable obligation certificates available for technology used by the claimant, as such data had not been applied to other technologies. The court concluded that although consistency of approach to different technologies was important, if, on the basis of new data, the government concluded that a particular technology would be over-compensated if the allocation of renewable obligation certificates were increased, it was not obliged to ignore that data, with the result that such technology received excessive subsidies. The government's approach had not been unfair. Thus, when considering issues of procedural impropriety, broader considerations of fairness may take precedence over adopting a consistent approach to all affected parties.

With regard to consultation, the courts have also laid down guidance on the manner in which consultations must be carried out in order to be fair:

whether or not consultation of interested parties and the public is a legal requirement, if it is embarked upon it must be carried out properly. To be proper, consultation must be undertaken at a time when proposals are still at a formative stage; it must include sufficient reasons for particular proposals to allow those consulted to give intelligent consideration and an intelligent response; adequate time must be given for this purpose; and the product of consultation must be conscientiously taken into account when the ultimate decision is taken.[66]

63   *Magill v Porter* [2001] UKHL 67.
64   [2011] EWHC 2048 (Admin) (May 12 2011).
65   [2011] EWCA Civ 664.
66   *R v North and East Devon Health Authority, ex p Coughlan* [2001] QB 213.

(d)   Has there been breach of a legitimate expectation?

The ground of legitimate expectation has evolved from the broader ground of procedural impropriety. It is closely linked to its parent ground. It arises where a claimant has had a legitimate belief or expectation that a body will act in a certain way, either because of express statements from the authority or from prior conduct.

There is a distinction between substantive legitimate expectation (ie, the claimant had a legitimate expectation that there would be afforded to it a substantive benefit) and procedural legitimate expectation (ie, the claimant had an expectation that it would be treated fairly or that a particular procedure would be followed as a result of a specific promise or practice). With regard to substantive legitimate expectation, the authorities speak of "a clear and unambiguous representation upon which it was reasonable for [the claimant] to rely".[67] The test is onerous and reflects a recognition by the courts that public bodies must be at liberty to revise policies and practices as circumstances dictate.

In respect of procedural legitimate expectation, in 2007 Greenpeace brought a claim regarding the government's decision that nuclear had a "role to play" in the United Kingdom's energy mix. Greenpeace challenged the government's decision on the basis that it had been reached without adequate consultation, with the result that the process was procedurally unfair and that Greenpeace's legitimate expectation of a full public consultation regarding nuclear new build had been breached. The court found that the government's approach had been "very seriously flawed", and that Greenpeace's legitimate expectation that there would be "the fullest public consultation" before a decision was taken to support new nuclear build had been breached.[68]

(e)   Has there been a breach of the Human Rights Act 1998?

In the late 1990s the traditional grounds for judicial review were supplemented by a new ground: breach of the Human Rights Act. The Human Rights Act permitted standalone claims for breach of the European Convention on Human Rights (as incorporated into English law via the Human Rights Act) to be brought in UK courts. Alleged breaches of the Human Rights Act may also form the basis for judicial reviews.

It might be thought that the Human Rights Act had application only in judicial review claims of the sort which have proliferated in the realms of immigration and asylum. However, reliance is increasingly being placed on the act in commercial judicial review claims.

Save as explained previously, the extent to which the Human Rights Act modifies the law and the applicable tests for judicial review explored above are beyond the scope of this chapter. An example of the Human Rights Act being used in energy sector judicial review proceedings is found in *R (Infinis Plc and Infinis (Re-Gen) Ltd) v Gas & Electricity Markets Authority*,[69] where Infinis Plc brought a claim to judicially review Ofgem's refusal to find that its electricity generators qualified for renewable

---

67   *R v Devon County Council, ex p Baker; R v Durham County Council, ex p Curtis* [1995] 1 All ER 73.
68   *R (on the application of Greenpeace Ltd) v Secretary of State for Trade and Industry* [2007] EWHC 311.
69   [2011] EWHC 1873 (Admin).

obligation certificates The court upheld Infinis's claim that Ofgem's decision breached its right to property under Article 1 of the First Protocol of the European Convention on Human Rights and awarded Infinis damages under Section 8 of the Human Rights Act.

6. The role of third parties in judicial review

Judicial review frequently raises issues of wide public interest which go beyond the confines of a dispute between a private party and a public body. The archetypal situation in the energy sector would be a claim brought by a concerned resident against an authority discharging planning or other approval functions. Commercial parties affected by the claim (eg, a company proposing to construct a nuclear power station) would want to ensure that their plans were not frustrated by a court which had failed to appreciate the nature of their proposals.

Consistent with the nature of judicial review as a means of ensuring that public functions are exercised properly in the public interest, the judicial review procedure allows for the intervention of parties other than the claimant and the defendant.

Two principal categories of third party may participate in judicial review:

- Interested party – an 'interested party' can be "any person (other than the claimant and defendant) who is directly affected by the claim",[70] as long as that party is "affected without the intervention of any intermediate agency".[71] In a case relating to consent granted by the secretary of state for energy and climate change to Helius Energy plc for a biomass power station, a claim was brought by a private company set up in order to conserve and protect the Gwendraeth Valley. Helius participated as an interested party.[72] Interested parties are parties to the claim and may therefore appeal any judgment of the court.

- Intervener – an 'intervener' is anyone granted permission to file evidence or to make representations at the hearing of the judicial review. Interventions in judicial review have been increasing and have included campaign groups, government departments and companies indirectly affected by the outcome of the review. The intervening party should be aware that their intervention may have costs consequences. In *R v Central Criminal Court, ex p Francis & Francis*,[73] the Law Society intervened on a question regarding legal professional privilege. The court ordered that it pay the extra costs arising from its intervention.

7. When must a judicial review claim be brought?

This chapter is not concerned with the procedural aspects of judicial review. However, it is important that practitioners are aware of the importance of commencing judicial review proceedings promptly.

---

70   CPR 54.1.
71   *R v Liverpool City Council Ex p Muldoon* [1996] 1 WLR 1103; [1996] 3 All ER 498.
72   *Coedbach Action Team Ltd v Secretary of State for Energy and Climate Change* [2010] EWHC 2312 (Admin) [2010] EWHC 2312 (Admin).
73   [1989] AC 346; [1988] 3 WLR 989 HL.

The Civil Procedure Rules stipulate that a judicial review claim must be brought "promptly" and "in any event not later than 3 months after the grounds to make the claim first arose".[74] Although the court has the inherent discretion to extend or shorten the time for compliance with any rule, courts have tended to apply strictly the promptness requirement. Where the court considers that there has been undue delay in commencing a judicial review claim, the court may refuse to grant permission for the claim or may refuse any relief sought where it considers that granting such relief would "be likely to cause substantial hardship to, or substantially prejudice the rights of, any person or would be detrimental to good administration".[75]

However, following *Uniplex (UK) Limited v NHS Business Services Authority*[76] and the subsequent cases of *R (Buglife) v Natural England*[77] and *R (on the application of U & Partners (East Anglia) Ltd) v Broads Authority*,[78] the requirement of promptness is not applicable in applications which seek to enforce legal rights arising from EU directives. That is because requiring a claim to be commenced promptly is inconsistent with the EU requirement for legal certainty.

8.   Conclusion

Commercial judicial review is likely to continue to increase in popularity as businesses navigate the regulatory waters within which they operate. The energy industry is no exception. How the United Kingdom sources energy to meet its needs in the decades ahead is a controversial political issue. Pressure groups hostile to exploitation of hydrocarbon reserves and construction of power infrastructure are well versed in using judicial review to further their ends. Private individuals are also becoming increasingly conscious of the benefits which a well-publicised judicial review application may bring. Energy companies may find, as pressure is placed on the national finances, that financial support for certain technologies and energy sources is subject to review. Claims for judicial review of decisions are likely only to increase. In this environment, practitioners in energy disputes would be well advised to ensure that they are familiar with potential avenues of challenge under public administrative law.

---

74   CPR 54.5(1)
75   Section 31(6) of the Senior Courts Act 1981.
76   Case C-406/08.
77   [2011] EWHC 746 (Admin).
78   [2011] EWHC 1824 (Admin).

Disputes in the nuclear industry

Fiona Reilly
Philip Roche
Norton Rose LLP

1.   Introduction

Disputes and claims in the nuclear industry are rich and varied, ranging from criminal prosecutions for illegal attempts to procure nuclear materials, disputes between nations, international sanctions and standard contractual claims through to tortious claims arising from nuclear incidents. However, for an industry which has been operating commercially in the power sector since the 1950s, there are surprisingly few reported disputes.

In this chapter we consider the international regulatory framework in which the nuclear power sector operates and why that framework means that fewer formal claims arise than one might expect, and examine some of the claims that have been made.

2.   International regulatory framework

Uranium was discovered in 1789, but it was not until the late 1800s and early 1900s that radioactivity and its potential uses began to be discovered. From that time until the mid-20th century, the development of nuclear power went hand in hand with the development of nuclear weapons. The potential for nuclear energy to be misused, together with the potentially catastrophic effects of a large nuclear incident such as Chernobyl,[1] means that the industry has developed in a very different way from almost any other industry.

The nuclear industry is regulated by a number of treaties, conventions and bilateral and multilateral agreements. The International Atomic Energy Agency (IAEA) has 19 international treaties under its auspices and there are 13 IAEA-related treaties. In addition, there are nine treaties or international agreements concluded under the Nuclear Energy Agency (NEA) of the Organisation for Economic Cooperation and Development (OECD),[2] plus the Euratom Treaty.[3] In addition to these multi-party agreements, a number of bilateral and multilateral agreements between governments establish how countries can work together in the nuclear industry – the most famous being the US 123 Agreements, which are based on Section 123 of the US Atomic Energy Act 1954.

---

1   Which remains the world's worst civil nuclear incident.
2   Some of which are also IAEA-related treaties.
3   "The Euratom Treaty establishing the European Atomic Energy Community (Euratom) was initially created to coordinate the behaviour of the Member States' research programmes for the peaceful use of nuclear energy. The Euratom Treaty today helps to pool knowledge, infrastructure and funding of nuclear energy. It ensures the security of atomic energy supply within the framework of a centralised monitoring system." European Commission website.

While dealing with different issues, these treaties, conventions and agreements contain a number of common themes and overriding principles:

- non-proliferation;
- safety (including the obligations to have suitably qualified and experienced personnel to operate nuclear sites);
- security and safeguarding;
- corporate responsibility; and
- liability of nuclear plant operators for third-party damage caused by a nuclear incident.

It is within these principles that the nuclear industry operates, placing higher standards on those working in the industry than perhaps other energy industries.

3. Liability conventions

One of the most important overriding principles, when considering claims and disputes in the nuclear industry, is that of the strict liability of a nuclear operator for third-party nuclear damage. This principle is contained in a number of conventions (and the amendments to those conventions):

- the Convention on Third-Party Liability in the Field of Nuclear Energy of July 29 1960, as amended by the Additional Protocol of January 28 1964 and by the Protocol of November 16 1982 (together, the Paris Convention);
- the Brussels Convention Supplementary Convention on Third-Party Liability for Nuclear Damage 1963;
- the Vienna Convention on Civil Liability for Nuclear Damage 1963 and the Protocol to Amend the Vienna Convention on Civil Liability for Nuclear Damage 1997 (together, the Vienna Convention); and
- the Joint Protocol Relating to the Application of the Vienna Convention and the Paris Convention.

At the time of writing, 45 countries are signatories to one or more of these liability conventions.

Under the liability conventions, the operator of a nuclear plant has strict liability for any nuclear damage caused by a nuclear event, whether that be a major release of radioactivity or a minor leak causing harm to third parties or their property or requiring clean-up. This concept is referred to as 'channelling provisions'. The scope and extent of an operator's liability vary under the various liability conventions and the interpretation of those conventions under the domestic law of the relevant jurisdiction. However, the overriding principle remains. This principle is particularly important because unless channelling provisions are in place, the operator of a nuclear plant will not have access to the nuclear insurance market through the nuclear insurance pools[4] which provide insurance for nuclear damage.

---

4   The nuclear insurance pools were first developed in the 1950s in response to pressure from governments and the industry to provide specific insurance for the industry. The pools were needed as the potential risks associated with nuclear were seen to be too great for one insurer to cover.

There are a number of notable exceptions to the countries which are party to the liability conventions, the most prominent being the United States. While the United States is not a party to any of the liability conventions, it does have domestic legislation in place – the Price Anderson Act 1957 – which was brought in as an amendment to the Atomic Energy Act 1946. This enactment is a forerunner to the liability conventions and establishes channelling provisions which channel liability for a nuclear incident to the operator of the nuclear station.[5] Other countries which are not party to the liability conventions, but which do have domestic laws in place incorporating channelling provisions, include Japan and, more recently, India.

The liability conventions contain provisions for the presentation of convention claims for nuclear damage following a nuclear incident: they are to be brought in the courts of the country where the nuclear incident occurred (except as otherwise provided). So, for example, if the Soviet Union had been a party to the Vienna Convention at the time, the courts of the Soviet Union would have had jurisdiction over claims brought in connection with the Chernobyl disaster, as Chernobyl is in Ukraine, which was part of the Soviet Union at that time.

Not all claims from all jurisdictions can be brought under the liability conventions. The liability conventions are reciprocal; they apply cross border, but only to the extent that the other country is party to the same convention or the Joint Protocol which links the Vienna and Paris Conventions. Therefore, even if the Soviet Union had been a party to the Vienna Convention in 1986[6] at the time of the Chernobyl incident, the claims brought by Welsh sheep farmers would not have been settled in the courts of the Soviet Union; but, as happened (£14.3 million was paid out between 1986 and 2009),[7] they would have been paid for from government compensation schemes established in the United Kingdom, since the Soviet Union would have been a party to the Vienna Convention and the UK party to the Paris Convention, and hence there would have been no reciprocity.[8] [9]

The liability conventions and domestic legislation, although together an imperfect regime, do at least provide the basis for claims by victims in the country where the nuclear incident occurred.

Japan is not currently a party to the liability conventions, but does have

---

5   The Price Anderson Act channels economic liability rather than legal liability to the operator of the nuclear station – that is, the operator bears all of the economic consequences of a nuclear incident even though legal liability may rest with others. In the United States, following the Three Mile Island incident in 1979, claims were brought against the operator (the Metropolitan Edison General Public Utilities) Babcock and Wilcox (the designers) and the engineering, procurement and construction contractor. Therefore, while third parties will channel any claims to the operator, the operator itself has a right of recourse against the contractor and technology provider, subject to the normal laws and principles, which is not automatically available under the liability conventions.

6   The Russian Federation signed the Vienna Convention 1963 in 1996, but did not ratify the convention until 2005.

7   Financial Services Authority estimates.

8   There has been an attempt to bring in a global regime through the Convention on Supplementary Convention for Nuclear Damage for countries whether they are parties to the liability conventions or not, but insufficient countries have signed this convention to make it effective at the date of writing.

9   The Joint Protocol was introduced following the Chernobyl incident to begin addressing the lack of reciprocity. If a country is a party to either the Vienna Convention or the Paris Convention and the Joint Protocol, then that country has the benefit of the Vienna and Paris Conventions. However, few Paris Convention countries have signed the Joint Protocol due to the disparity between the provisions in the Vienna and Paris Conventions.

legislation in place channelling liability to the operator. Following the Fukushima incident in March 2011, Tokyo Electric Power Company (TEPCO), as the operator of the Fukushima Daiichi plant, made provisional compensation payments to a number of those who were evacuated from their homes as a result of the incident. In September 2011 TEPCO instigated a claims procedure. Shortly afterwards, it was estimated that TEPCO would pay out $762 million[10] in compensation. The Japanese government approved plans for compensation and provided financial support to TEPCO for this purpose. However, liability for loss and damage remains with TEPCO. In addition, the Japan Federation of Bar Associations agreed to assign approximately 100 lawyers to mediate settlements and to handle compensation claims. Fortunately, the Fukushima incident appears to have had no transboundary effects (which is true of all nuclear incidents to date, with the exception of Chernobyl), and therefore Japan's position in not adopting any of the liability conventions has not had to be addressed.

While the compensation figures are huge and the procedure for providing compensation on such a large scale difficult and complex, one can see why there are few formal disputes in relation to third-party damage following a nuclear incident. The international third-party liability regime provides a clear procedure for bringing and settling claims. Moreover, the political repercussions of failing to settle claims associated with radioactivity contamination under the liability conventions and regime are very serious, and this is well understood within the industry.

The claims that do appear tend to relate either to the scope of the compensation regime or to the interpretation of domestic legislation. Examples of such cases, taken from English (or Scottish) law, include *Merlin v British Nuclear Fuels plc*,[11] which provides that damage to property under the Nuclear Installation Act 1965[12] must be physical damage to tangible property and does not include pure economic loss or damage to intangible property. In that case, although there was radioactive contamination present, it was not sufficient to cause physical damage – the perceived risk or increased risk of damage to property and any consequent increase of the risk of injury to health does not amount to an "injury to any person or damage to any property" within Section 7 of the Nuclear Installations Act 1965.

The *Merlin* decision is to be distinguished from cases in which the radioactive contamination actually alters the physical characteristics of the property and renders it less useful or less valuable. In *Blue Circle Industries plc v Ministry of Defence*[13] plutonium mixed with topsoil on an estate rendered the topsoil 'radioactive waste' within the definition in the Radioactive Substances Act 1960. The physical damage depressed the value of the land for which compensation was recoverable, along with the cost of reinstatement, subject to the usual principles of reasonable foreseeability and remoteness. Similarly, in *Magnohard Ltd v UKAEA*[14] radioactive particles which were discovered on Sandside Beach, adjacent to Dounreay Nuclear Power Station,

10   AsiaOne.
11   [1990] 2 QB 557.
12   The Nuclear Installation Act 1965 implements the Paris and Brussels Conventions into English law.
13   [1998] EWLA Civ 945.
14   [2003] SLT 1983.

were found to have rendered the beach less useful or less valuable, by reason of the sporadic and unpredictable deposit of tiny radioactive particles without any visible sign that would alert a user of the beach as to which parts might contain radioactive particles. Magnohard owns the Sandside Estate, including the beach, together with fishing rights extending 22.2 kilometres out to sea. The other petitioners were family members of the Minter family who owned Magnohard. On judicial review, the court granted a declaration to Maghohard that the UK Atomic Energy Authority (UKAEA) had failed and continued to fail to perform its statutory duty under Section 7 of the Nuclear Installation Act 1965 and to secure that no occurrence of nuclear matter caused damage to any property of any person other than UKAEA, being damage arising out of, or resulting from, the radioactive properties of that nuclear matter. The court remitted the claim to the court for the assessment of damages (together with a claim under the Human Rights Act 1998).

More remote causes of action are often difficult to prove. In *Reay v British Nuclear Fuel plc*[15] the claimant alleged that his sperm had been mutated by radiation which resulted in his daughter's cancer. The court was not convinced by the arguments that any radioactivity had caused paternal preconception irradiation. This can be contrasted with the known link between radioactivity and thyroid cancer where iodine is not prescribed in sufficient time.

4.   Contractual liability

The liability conventions and the relevant domestic legislation provide that the operator of a nuclear power plant has strict liability for a nuclear incident. The operator may have rights of recourse if this is expressly provided for by a contract in writing or if the nuclear incident results from an act or omission with intent to cause damage.

Individuals rarely intend to cause damage to nuclear stations. The assumption is that security and safeguarding measures which operators must have in place to protect nuclear stations and radioactive and fissionable material on station or being transported to or from station should effectively prevent damage being done intentionally.

The question of whether an operator has a right of recourse against a contractor is generally a commercial one. Historically, contractors in the nuclear industry have assumed no liability for nuclear damage; contracts often contain nuclear indemnity provisions in their favour which protect the contractor from not only third-party claims (liability convention claims), but also claims arising from nuclear damage to the station itself. As the industry becomes more international, with more cross-border movement of goods and services, contractors are becoming ever more wary of assuming any liability for nuclear damage. There have been, and there will probably continue to be, relatively few claims where the operator seeks to recover from the contractor for third-party liability or any other damage associated with a nuclear incident.

This is to be contrasted with the position taken in the Indian nuclear liability

---

15   [1994] Enr LR 320; [1994] IMCR1.

legislation, passed in August 2010, which gives an operator a right of recourse against suppliers if it has paid compensation for an accident that is deemed to have been caused by defective equipment or services. In December 2010 lawyers for the US, French and Russian governments were holding intensive talks with Indian authorities in an attempt to draft implementing rules that would reduce the potential impact of liability legislation on international suppliers. The greatest concern about the Indian legislation has been expressed by representatives of the US government and US suppliers, which say that they cannot supply any nuclear technology or equipment to India unless the law is amended to remove supplier liability. However, it was suggested that Areva of France and Atomstroyexport of Russia (as wholly or partly state-owned entities) were in a more powerful position to negotiate a settlement with the Indian government than a private supplier might be. This might put French and Russian suppliers in a more favourable position than their US competitors. The NEA officials did not agree with the opinion that French and Russian suppliers were inherently better protected against Indian claims, because their governments would apply the doctrine of sovereign immunity. The sensitivity in India over accidents caused by large US corporations is not difficult to understand in light of the 1984 Bhopal pesticide plant leak, where large numbers of injured victims were left uncompensated.

The liability conventions and related legislation do not extend to liability for damage to the power station itself or to any property on the site which is used in connection with that installation. The ability of the operator to bring a claim for damage to its nuclear plant is subject to normal legal requirements in the particular jurisdiction. Thus, in the United Kingdom, an operator can bring contractual or tortious claims against contractors or others in the same way as it can in other industries. Again, however, contractors often seek to exclude liability for nuclear damage in their contracts and as a result there are very few claims of this nature.

5. Contractual claims

Where dispute resolution clauses are written into contracts, arbitration is the preferred form of dispute resolution in the international nuclear industry. Some countries, such as the Russian Federation, which historically have had a large domestic nuclear market, in the past provided for dispute resolution in the courts. By contrast, countries which have always been more reliant on foreign suppliers have opted for arbitration. As the nuclear market becomes more international, arbitration becomes more popular as the final dispute resolution procedure of choice. This is unsurprising, as the industry requires its commercial disputes to remain private and confidential and to be more widely enforceable than is the case with court judgments.

As in any other large industry, contractual claims are often brought for breaches of contractual terms and conditions, including material failure, defects, variations, failure to meet design criteria, delay and cost overruns. Damages awarded for such claims are often limited by the terms of the contract.

Delay to the construction period and cost overruns are claims which are often seen in infrastructure and energy projects, and the nuclear industry faces many of the same problems. At the time of writing, a dispute is ongoing between Teollisuuden Voima (TVO) and Areva/Siemens in relation to delay and associated costs caused to the construction of the Okiluoto 3 nuclear plant in Finland. The dispute is being determined by arbitration under the International Chamber of Commerce rules. The Okiluoto 3 project was due to be commissioned in 2009 and is now due to start operations in 2013. Arbitration proceedings were initiated in 2008 concerning the delay to the plant and the cost resulting from the delay, as well as the costs of a technological solution of an issue concerning the construction works.[16]

A more unusual and perhaps more specific nuclear dispute is that between the Tennessee Valley Authority (TVA) and Areva brought by Areva after TVA failed to purchase nuclear fuel for the Bellefonte nuclear power plant following termination of the Bellefonte project.

One of the interesting points to note about this case is the timing of the contract and the dispute. TVA signed a contract with Areva in 1970 for the supply of fuel for the Bellefonte plant near Scottsboro, Alabama. Construction of the two 1200 megawatt electrical pressurised water reactors started in 1974. However, TVA deferred construction of Bellefonte in 1988 after some $2.5 billion had already been spent. At that time, Unit 1 was some 88% complete, while Unit 2 was approximately 58% complete. Areva filed a lawsuit in 2005 claiming that TVA owed Areva $47 million for fuel that the utility contracted to buy for the plant. In 2007 TVA, in consortium with NuStart Consortium, applied to the Nuclear Regulatory Commission (NRC) for a construction and operating licence for the plant, although the construction has yet to be finalised, despite a vote by the TVA board to continue construction of Unit 1 in August 2011. In 2009 the TVA approved a settlement of the lawsuit. Under the settlement, TVA was to make payments of up to $18 million over six years, and the payments may be reduced based on the amount of work performed by Areva for TVA.[17]

This long timescale is historically not unusual because of the downturn in the nuclear market followed by the current so-called 'nuclear renaissance'.[18] In addition, there is the long construction period for nuclear power plants (compared to other thermal plants), although this is usually around five years and not the 40-plus years seen at the Bellefonte plant.

6. Intellectual property

The nuclear industry is highly specialised in many respects. The specialist knowledge resides in the nuclear island and the fuel supply chain. This chapter does not discuss IP issues arising from the balance of plant (which are no different from any other industry) and concentrates on the unique aspects of the nuclear industry.

The Treaty on the Non-proliferation of Nuclear Weapons (NPT) is the cornerstone of the civil nuclear industry: "The NPT aims to prevent the spread of nuclear weapons and weapons technology, to foster the peaceful uses of nuclear energy, and

---

16   www.tvo.fi/www/page/3576/.
17   http://nuclearsteet.com and www.world-nuclear-news.org.
18   The renewed interest in nuclear power has arisen from countries' increased need to meet their climate change commitments, increases in oil prices and other difficulties in the energy market.

to further the goal of disarmament. The Treaty establishes a safeguards system under the responsibility of the IAEA, which also plays a central role under the Treaty in areas of technology transfer for peaceful purposes."[19]

Currently, six reactor suppliers are seeking to sell into the international market: Areva, Atomstroyexport, KEPCO, GE-Hitachi, Toshiba-Westinghouse and Atomic Energy of Canada Limited (AECL). In addition, the Chinese and Indian markets are developing their own technology and other nations intend to do the same over the next decade.

Technology transfer in the nuclear industry is common practice. It usually relates to reactor technology, but may also relate to mixed oxide fuel plants, fuel assembly plants and other nuclear-specific technologies. Areva's EPR and KEPCO's APR1400 reactor technology was derived from Westinghouse's PWR design.[20] To facilitate technology transfers, licensing and joint venture arrangements are agreed, but these are often also backed by intergovernmental agreements. In 2003 the United States and China entered into a bilateral technology transfer agreement. Under this agreement, the Chinese market was opened up to US companies, while China agreed to comply with the NPT and not to on-transfer the technology received from the US companies to other countries.

Within this environment of intergovernmental agreements overlaid with commercial agreements, there are few formal disputes on IP issues. However, they do arise. An example is the Canadian Federal Court decision in *Atomic Energy of Canada Ltd. V AREVA NP Canada Ltd.*[21] AECL commenced an action against Areva on the grounds of trademark infringement, passing off and copyright infringement in relation to Areva's 'A' design mark, which AECL claimed was very similar to its own 'Flying A' design mark. The Federal Court of Canada dismissed the claims of trademark infringement and passing off on the basis that the highly regulated nuclear industry consists of sophisticated customers and thorough and detailed procurement processes, such that there was no real risk of confusion.

7.   Regulatory

The nuclear industry is a highly political and intensively regulated industry. The regulators in each country have significant powers of enforcement (although the courts are sometimes used to question those powers). Each country has a different system of regulation, but the regulators largely apply the same principles to safety, security and safeguarding. In addition, there are the international regulators – primarily Euratom and the IAEA; but they do not have the same enforcement powers as the domestic regulators.[22]

The domestic regulators have a number of powers, including the power to bring criminal prosecutions for breach of environmental standards and the power to

---

19   IAEA.
20   The Rolls-Royce PWR was also derived from the Westinghouse design which was used in UK nuclear submarines.
21   (September 30 2009) 2009 FC 980.
22   Domestic regulators have higher power of enforcement as countries wish to retain their own powers of enforcement.

impose fines on operators for breach of legislation and licence conditions. Prosecutions and fines for discharging radioactive material are reasonably common.

In October 2006 the British Energy Group, being at the time the operator of the Sellafield nuclear site in the United Kingdom, was facing a criminal prosecution in relation to an accident that led to the shutdown of the THORP nuclear fuel reprocessing plant. The case was brought by the Health and Safety Executive for actions which resulted in 83,000 litres of high radioactive dissolved spent fuel leaking into an area beneath a tank in the reprocessing facility. The leak went undetected for eight months as a result of operator and technical failures going back to the 1990s. British Energy pleaded guilty to three offences contrary to Section 4.6 of the Nuclear Installation Act 1965. The judge referred to the fact that there was no chance of the leaked material reaching criticality and there was no evidence of escape of radioactive material into the atmosphere or the ground. Further, no one was injured and no one was exposed to radioactive material. However, the judge considered the defendants guilty of serious faults and failings, and fined British Energy £750,000, reduced to £500,000 in light of British Energy's plea.

UKAEA[23] was prosecuted and fined £140,000 by the Scottish Environmental Protection Agency at the beginning of 2007 for four breaches of the Radioactive Substances Act 1960 for historic unauthorised discharges of radioactive particles, which came to light only in 2007. UKAEA admitted to a single charge of disposing of radioactive waste at a landfill site on a nuclear site between 1963 and 1975 (£40,000 fine). It also pleaded guilty to three charges of allowing nuclear fuel particles to be released through drains into the Pentland Firth between 1963 and 1984 (£100,000 fine). UKAEA submitted that there was only a small amount of material and a minimal possibility of a member of the public coming into contact with a particle. The sheriff gave credit to UKAEA for acknowledging its errors and noted that UKAEA is a public authority, and therefore any fines would ultimately be borne by the taxpayer. Both parties said that they felt the fine was significant.[24]

The courts are often asked to consider the power of governments and regulators to ensure that they are working within their jurisdiction. This tactic is often employed by pressure groups to disrupt the industry. There have been a number of challenges in the last few years as the nuclear renaissance has taken shape. Some of these challenges are highlighted below.

In *Greenpeace Ltd, R (on the application of) v Secretary of State for Trade and Industry*[25] the court had to consider whether the UK Department of Trade and Industry had undertaken a proper consultation before publishing a report to conclude an energy review in July 2006. The report announced the UK government's decision to support nuclear new build as part of the UK's future energy mix. The court found that the consultation was flawed and awarded 'declaratory relief' on the basis that there had been a breach of the "legitimate expectation to fullest public consultation", the consultation process was procedurally unfair and therefore the decision in the

---

23   The United Kingdom Atomic Energy Authority.
24   www.martrifrost.ws.
25   [2007] EWHC 311.

Energy Review that nuclear new-build "has a role to play" was unlawful. This resulted in a delay to the Energy Review and a further public consultation being required.

In 2009 the US Court of Appeals considered the environmental impact of the risk of spent fuel pool fires. The NRC's finding that there was a low risk of spent fuel pool fires at nuclear power plants was challenged by rulemaking petitions from the states. The states argued that licence renewal did not currently consider the proper environmental impact of spent fuel pool fires based on new information, and that the NRC's denial of the rulemaking petition was arbitrary as it relied on plant-specific mitigation. The court held that not only had the NRC not considered most of the studies submitted by the states, but that the study previously considered was unreliable. The court also held that while the NRC had relied on mitigation strategies at particular plants, the NRC had mandated that such mitigation tactics and heightened security be implemented at all nuclear power plants.

In 2005 the NRC discovered that a particular type of fire barrier did not conform to the NRC safety requirement that a barrier be capable of withstanding fire for at least one hour. Indian Point Energy Centre had had the fire barrier installed. The plant's licensee requested a revised exemption from this requirement in 2006. The NRC granted the exemption in 2007. The plaintiff filed a complaint before the US district court challenging the validity of the exemption. It argued that there was a legal requirement to hold public hearings on exemptions. The US district court in 2011 ruled that the NRC had the dual authority to establish rules and grant exemptions on a case-by-case basis, and that a hearing is not mandatory for challenges to exemptions. The district court also concluded that the NRC satisfied its National Environmental Policy Act obligations by taking the requisite 'hard look' at the environmental impact of its decision, and that in granting the exemption the NRC had not acted capriciously. Finally, the US district court refused to determine the issue by substituting its own judgement for the NRC's, extending deference to the NRC's substantive decision on nuclear safety.

In 2009, in Brazil, the public prosecutor filed a public claim against the National Nuclear Energy Commission in Brazil (CNEN) on the grounds that its grant of a partial construction licence for Angra III was not within its regulatory powers. The public prosecutor argued that by granting a partial licence for which there was no explicit mention in the existing law, CNEN had effectively created a new category of licence. CNEN argued that the law did allow for a licence under specific conditions, so long as CNEN standards were met. Evidence was submitted that safety analysis had been conducted by CNEN during the Angra III licensing phase. Further, CNEN argued that as the regulatory body, it possessed powers to supervise each step in the construction of the nuclear power plant. The First Federal Court ruled that CNEN had acted within the legal and technical parameters of its discretionary power as a regulator.

The European Court of Justice (ECJ) in *Land Oberosterreich v CEZ*[26] considered a dispute concerning actual or potential nuisance arising from ionising radiation from

---

26   [2010] All ER (EC) 901.

CEZ's nuclear plant in the Czech Republic and damaging land in Austria. The ECJ held that under Austrian law, an entity such as CEZ operating a nuclear installation in a member state outside Austria, with all the necessary authorisation required in that state, could be the subject of an injunction to prevent nuisance in Austria; whereas if the nuclear installation was in Austria, then it could not, and only damages would be awarded. The ECJ concluded that Austria could not justify the discrimination practised in respect of the official authorisation granted in the Czech Republic for the operation of the nuclear power plant on the grounds that it was necessary to protect life, public health, the environment or property rights. The ECJ pointed out that the existing EU legislative framework, of which that authorisation formed a part, contributed towards the protection of those values.

As these cases demonstrate, the range of claims brought by and against regulators is wide and varied. The regulators have the power to bring criminal prosecution for breaches of licence conditions, but their powers can be challenged in the civil courts.

8.   Military

The courts' ability to review the actions of governments and regulators in some jurisdictions extends to considering the actions of governments in the 1950s in testing nuclear weapons. In 2009 a landmark UK decision allowed Maralinga Australian veterans to claim damages. Australians exposed to deadly radiation in the Maralinga nuclear tests of the 1950s and 1960s had abandoned plans to sue in Australia and instead joined a UK class action seeking compensation for damage to their health. A 2007 New Zealand study found that New Zealand sailors exposed to the nuclear testing had three times the level of genetic abnormality and higher rates of cancer than the general population. A landmark UK court ruling giving UK Maralinga veterans the right to sue their government opened the door for the Australians, who faced statutes of limitations in several states in Australia. In 2010 this ruling was overturned and the Court of Appeal in London threw out the case, resulting in the 2,000 or so remaining Australian veterans of the United Kingdom's outback nuclear weapons testing who had hoped to join a class action against the UK Ministry of Defence (MoD) being left with no further chance of compensation. The appeals court said that illnesses could have been caused by old age and there was no evidence linking sickness to radiation.

In 2011 over 1,000 ex-servicemen from Coventry and Warwickshire in the United Kingdom brought a claim against the MoD for exposure to radiation during tests in the Pacific 50 years previously which caused cancer and other illnesses. At the time of writing, the case is in the Supreme Court. A High Court judge initially approved 10 test cases, but the MoD convinced the Court of Appeal to throw out nine of those cases in November 2010. Only one was allowed to proceed. The MoD claims that the veterans began legal proceedings too late, as claims such as this must be made within three years of any injury being suffered. However, the veterans say that they should be allowed to proceed, because evidence linking the radiation to cancer emerged only in 2007.

This approach taken against nuclear weapons testing can be contrasted with the approach taken by the civil nuclear industry in the United Kingdom in the 1980s.

Following a number of claims for compensation being brought against British Nuclear Fuels Limited (BNFL) by its previous employees, BNFL and the trade unions representing the claimants established the Compensation Scheme for Radiation Linked Diseases. The scheme was intended to be an alternative to more formal legal proceedings, and to be quicker and cheaper and provide more generous awards. UKAEA (along with other companies) joined the scheme in 1987 and further companies have joined since. The scheme awards compensation for mortality or morbidity claims, and is monitored by the BNFL/UKAEA Civil Service Management Board. The scheme also provides free advice to workers who might not otherwise be able to afford it. Around 1,200 claims/750 cases have been made in total from the time the scheme was established until 2009. Over £5 million worth of compensation payments have been made. Most of these cases were not straightforward and were likely to fail if they had proceeded to court, but the claimants were nonetheless partially compensated; such is the generosity of the scheme set up by the industry to provide support to its workers.

9. Sanctions

Much is done by governments and international institutions to prevent the misuse of nuclear materials and to ensure compliance with the NPT. The export controls and sanctions rules of each country generally have specific sections on dual-use materials – that is, materials which could be used in weapons as well as the civil industry – and also on specific nuclear materials.

Criminal prosecutions can be brought if individuals attempt to misappropriate materials. In 2010 in the Canadian case of *Her Majesty the Queen v Yadegari*[27] a Canadian citizen, Mr Yadegari, was convicted for knowingly attempting to bypass the regulatory requirements to obtain a permit and a licence to export pressure transducers to Iran. Pressure transducers are used in the uranium enrichment process and hence are subject to regulatory control. This conviction was the first of its kind under the United Nations Act.[28] The judge ruled that Yadegari knew that he needed paperwork – for example, an end-use certificate – to obtain the products from Germany and the United States. The judge also maintained that there was sufficient evidence to suggest that Yadegari had attempted to forge these documents to conceal his attempts to export the nuclear-related dual-use items. He concluded that Yadegari had ignored all of the controlling regulations for the export of the pressure transducers to Iran because he was motivated by money (rather than ideology). Yadegari was sentenced to six and a half years in prison.

Prosecutions and sanctions are rare in this highly regulated industry, but on occasion the courts are asked to determine whether sanctions are appropriate. The courts will err on the side of caution in this politically sensitive environment. In the English case of *Bank Mellat v HM Treasury*[29] an Iranian bank appealed against a decision upholding the validity of the Financial Restrictions (Iran) Order 2009. The

27 2010 Ontario Court of Justice.
28 Canadian legislation which implements UN resolutions.
29 [2011] 2 All ER 802.

2009 order was made by the Treasury pursuant to powers conferred by the Counter-Terrorism Act 2008 Schedule 7 on the basis that the Treasury reasonably believed, as required by Paragraph 1(4) of Schedule 7, that the development or production of nuclear weapons in Iran or the doing in Iran of anything that facilitated the development or production of any such weapons posed a significant risk to the national interests of the United Kingdom. The effect of the order was to exclude the bank from the UK financial market. The bank challenged the order on the grounds that it was not proportionate. It also challenged the order on procedural grounds, the essential complaint being that it had not been given an opportunity to make representations prior to the making of the order. The appeal was dismissed as the Treasury did not have to prove that the bank had provided trade finance for a nuclear proliferation transaction. The fundamental justification for the order was that, even as an unknowing and unwilling actor, the bank was well placed to assist entities to facilitate the development of nuclear weapons by providing them with banking facilities, in particular trade finance.

10. Conclusion

This is an overview of a highly regulated and politically driven industry. Claims that are brought, while diverse in nature, often seek to achieve one or more common goals – namely, the protection of people, property and the environment and the compensation of people adversely affected by radioactivity. Many people may find it surprising how few formal claims are brought, particularly considering that this is a controversial industry which continues to divide public and political opinion.

Investment treaty arbitration

Tom Cummins
Ben Giaretta
Ashurst LLP

1. Introduction

Another chapter of this book is devoted to international commercial arbitration in the energy sector. The purpose of this chapter is to examine another type of arbitration that impacts on the sector – investment treaty arbitration.

Investment treaties are entered into between states. They give investors from one state protection for their investments in the territory of other states. So, for example, an investment treaty between the United Kingdom and Argentina would oblige Argentina to afford investors from the United Kingdom certain minimum standards of treatment. Likewise, the United Kingdom would be obliged to provide the same standards of treatment to Argentine investors in the United Kingdom.

Investment treaty arbitration is the process whereby a dispute relating to this protection between an investor and a host state is determined by neutral arbitrators. It would be of little benefit to investors if they were obliged to enforce their rights under investment treaties in the courts of the host state responsible for their mistreatment, since often the action complained of is a change in the local law which the relevant court is obliged to uphold. Instead, investment treaties provide for international arbitration outside the national court system.

This chapter explores the distinction between commercial arbitration and treaty arbitration, the availability and scope of the latter, and the opportunities that treaty arbitration may provide for investors. To begin with, we explain the concepts which underlie the investment treaty arbitration regime and briefly describe their evolution.

2. The development of investment treaties

Initially, powerful states protected the commercial interests of their nationals overseas by so-called 'gunboat diplomacy', ensuring satisfactory treatment through conspicuous military power. However, in the first half of the 20th century, with the internationalisation of trade and commerce, attempts were made to protect investment through legal principles.

Following World War II, wealthier states started to enter into treaties on friendship, commerce and navigation with states into which their investment capital was exported. These guaranteed certain standards of treatment for investors of one state in the territory of another. Such treaties gradually evolved into more sophisticated instruments for protection of investors and their investments, and in 1959 the first modern bilateral investment treaty (BIT) was entered into between Germany and Pakistan.

In 1965 an international treaty on the protection of foreign investments, the Washington Convention, was opened for signature. It established the International Centre for Settlement of Investment Disputes (ICSID), which is dedicated to the resolution of international investment disputes, under the auspices of the World Bank, and has created its own arbitration rules for this purpose (the ICSID Rules).

The creation of ICSID led to increasing numbers of BITs being entered into, which provided for direct arbitration proceedings between investors and host states. The United Kingdom concluded its first BIT on this model in 1975, agreeing to reciprocal protection of investments with Egypt and investor-state arbitration in the event that such protection was not forthcoming.[1]

The 1990s saw a surge in the popularity of BITs. During this period the number of BITs increased fivefold, as foreign direct investment boomed.[2] The clamour for sophisticated investment protection instruments to accompany huge inflows of investment into developing countries meant that there were over 1,800 BITs at the end of the decade; as of 2010, there were over 2,800 BITs in force.[3]

Accompanying this trend was another phenomenon – multilateral investment treaties (MITs). These operate in essentially the same way as BITs, except that instead of one bilateral relationship between two states, MITs involve a group of states agreeing to provide investment protection to investors from each other's jurisdictions. In the energy sector, the most prominent MIT is the Energy Charter Treaty (ECT). This was established in 1994 and provides for multilateral cooperation on energy transit, trade and investment protection. To date, 51 countries have signed the ECT, and it has been signed collectively by the European Union and the European Atomic Energy Community.

3. Investment treaty arbitration in the energy sector

Despite this growth in investment treaties, it was not until 1987 that the first arbitration arising exclusively from an investor-state arbitration clause in a BIT was referred to ICSID.[4] A UK investor sought $8 million in damages from the government of Sri Lanka following the destruction of its shrimp farming enterprise (it prevailed, but was awarded significantly reduced damages).[5]

The number of investment treaty arbitrations has increased steadily since then, and it is believed that by the end of 2010 there had been 390 investment treaty arbitrations, with the overwhelming majority referred to ICSID for determination.[6]

1   The Agreement between the Government of the United Kingdom of Great Britain and Northern Ireland and the Government of the Arab Republic of Egypt for the Promotion and Protection of Investments (June 1975).
2   "Bilateral Investment Treaties Quintupled During the 1990s", United Nations Conference on Trade and Development (UNCTAD) Press Release (December 15 2005).
3   World Investment Report 2011 UNCTAD (July 26 2011).
4   As opposed to ICSID cases arising from specific consent to arbitration. See paragraph 18 of the award: "The present case is the first instance in which the Centre has been seized by an arbitration request exclusively based on a treaty provision and not in implementation of a freely negotiated arbitration agreement directly concluded between the Parties among whom the dispute has arisen."
5   *Asian Agricultural Products Ltd v Sri Lanka*, (ICSID Case ARB/87/3).
6   World Investment Report 2011 UNCTAD (July 26 2011).
7   Statistics published by ICSID show that 38% of ICSID arbitrations have arisen from the oil, gas, mining, electric power or other energy sectors. See *The ICSID Caseload – Statistics* (Issue 2011-2).

The energy industry has given rise to the highest proportion of ICSID disputes.[7] This is a reflection of the scale of overseas investment in the sector and the economic pressures faced by host states to achieve a 'fair take' from energy projects as oil (and other commodity) prices rise. In particular, the increase in commodity prices since the start of the 21st century has stimulated a spate of unilateral actions by host states from South America to Central and Eastern Europe, which in turn has generated investment treaty claims.

High-profile investment treaty proceedings in the energy industry in recent years include:

- Chevron's claim against Ecuador arising from Chevron's allegations that it had been deprived of an effective means of asserting claims and enforcing rights in Ecuador under the Ecuador-US BIT;
- Exxon Mobil's claim against Venezuela arising from Exxon Mobil's allegations that its oil assets had been nationalised in Venezuela contrary to the Netherlands-US BIT;
- Saipem's claim against Bangladesh arising from Saipem's allegations that Bangladesh had expropriated its rights contrary to the Italy-Bangladesh BIT in relation to a gas pipeline construction contract after the Bangladeshi courts had overturned a commercial arbitration award;
- claims by certain former shareholders of Yukos against the Russian Federation that Russia had expropriated their investments in Yukos contrary to the ECT; and
- Occidental Petroleum's claim against Ecuador arising from Occidental's allegations of various breaches of the Ecuador-US BIT.

Such claims would suggest that investment treaty arbitration is invariably brought by companies from developed economies against developing economies. However, while there are many that fall into this category, that is not always the case. In 2009 Swedish utility Vattenfall commenced proceedings against Germany alleging breach of the ECT in the manner in which environmental restrictions had been placed on Vattenfall's coal-fired power plant. This case, subsequently settled, demonstrates that investment treaty claims may fall outside the usual paradigms. There are likely to be more such cases in future.

4. Differences between investment treaty arbitration and commercial arbitration

Investment treaty arbitration differs from commercial arbitration in the following ways:

- Political dynamic – treaty arbitrations are between states and investors. The decisions of tribunals may have far-reaching consequences for government policy and finances, and may address issues of wide public interest. For example, there may be tensions between the legitimate demands of the people of host nations for development or environmental protection on the one hand and the legal rights of investors for the preservation of their investments on the other. The stakes may often be higher in treaty arbitrations than in conventional commercial disputes, engaging the attention of the media, the business community and non-governmental organisations.

- Consent to arbitration – party consent is the foundation of the commercial arbitration process. The parties agree to have their dispute determined by an independent tribunal rather than by the courts of any state. This agreement gives the arbitral tribunal the authority to determine the dispute. By contrast, in treaty arbitration the agreement to arbitrate arises from the host state unilaterally consenting to arbitration with any investor which falls within the protections contained within the BIT or MIT, and the investor providing its consent by commencing arbitration proceedings. This has led some commentators to refer to investment treaty arbitration as arbitration 'without privity' (ie, arbitration where there is no direct contractual relationship between host state and investor).
- Frequency of jurisdictional disputes – states which are recipients of investment treaty claims often seek to raise arguments of jurisdiction. They argue, in particular, that the investor is not entitled to the protection of the applicable BIT or MIT, or contend that the relevant investment does not fall within the scope of the BIT or MIT. Such preliminary issues add to the length and cost of treaty arbitration proceedings. We consider this further below.
- Importance of international law principles and experts in this subject – an understanding of the principles of international investment law is fundamental to treaty arbitration. For this reason, arbitrators and counsel with legal expertise in the field are in great demand. The universe of treaty arbitration specialists is relatively small, with the discipline crystallising around a small number of international law firms.
- Publicity – unlike commercial arbitration, the existence of investment treaty arbitration proceedings is often made public. Many awards come onto the public record. The exposure of proceedings to public scrutiny may give rise to controversy and criticism, of both the parties and the arbitral process.

5. Availability of investment treaty arbitration to claimants

The first question for an investor considering a treaty claim is whether there exists a treaty that gives appropriate protection. This is likely to depend on two principal issues:

- whether the investor falls within the protections offered by a BIT or MIT; and
- whether the investment is protected under the BIT or MIT.

5.1 Who is an 'investor' under a BIT or MIT?

BITs protect only investments made by investors of one state party to the BIT in the territory of the other state party to the BIT. Many jurisdictional disputes have arisen regarding the definition of 'investor' in BITs.

Different BITs adopt different criteria for determining whether an investor is protected. Often a broad definition is adopted. 'Individual investors' might be defined in terms of "physical persons deriving their status as [contracting state] nationals from the law in force in the [contracting state]".[8] 'Corporate investors' might be defined as "corporations, firms and associations incorporated or constituted under the law in force in any part of the [contracting state]".[9] This incorporation test is common in BITs concluded in recent decades.

Other treaties adopt more restrictive language. Thus, a corporate investor might need to have a head office in the territory of the contracting state. Other treaties require that an investor carry out "effective economic activities" in the territory of the state whose nationality it claims. Some definitions focus on the underlying control of the investor, with wording defining a 'corporate investor' as a company "effectively controlled, directly or indirectly, by nationals of one of the Contracting Parties".[10] Many BITs adopt a combination of tests to determine nationality.

The nature of control or ownership can be significant in the context of defining an 'investor' claimant. Host states often require that project companies be incorporated within their jurisdictions. The nationality of such project companies is from the host state, and they would therefore not be entitled to the protection of the BIT without express provision. For this reason, many treaties contain wording such as that above so that a project company that is incorporated in the state in which the investment is made, but is controlled by overseas investors, would be entitled to the protection of any relevant BIT.

On the other hand, many BITs also contain so-called 'denial of benefits' provisions. These permit a host state to deny the benefits of a treaty to a company that is controlled by investors of a non-party to the treaty. These provisions are aimed at precluding so-called 'letterbox companies', which have no substantial business activities in a contracting state, from taking advantage of treaty provisions.

The ECT adopts a broad definition of 'investor':

(a) with respect to a Contracting Party:

    (i) a natural person having the citizenship or nationality of or who is permanently residing in that Contracting Party in accordance with its applicable law;

    (ii) a company or other organization organized in accordance with the law applicable in that Contracting Party.[11]

In the claims brought by former shareholders in Yukos against the Russian Federation alleging expropriation of their shareholdings, the Russian Federation argued that the claimants did not fall within definition (ii) above because they were not truly nationals of another contracting party to the ECT, but were ultimately Russian nationals.[12] The tribunal disagreed, observing that the ECT requires only that

---

8   See, for example, the Agreement between the Government of the United Kingdom of Great Britain and Northern Ireland and the Government of the State of Bahrain for the Promotion and Protection of Investments (October 1991).

9   See, for example, the Agreement between the Government of the United Kingdom of Great Britain and Northern Ireland and the Government of the Republic of India for the Promotion and Protection of Investments (March 1994).

10   The Agreement between the Government of the Republic of Peru and the Government of the Republic of Venezuela concerning the Promotion and Protection of Investments (unofficial translation).

11   Article 1(7). The concept of 'control' or 'ownership' of assets is addressed by the definition of 'investment' (see below).

12   *Hulley Enterprises Limited v The Russian Federation* (PCA Case AA 226); *Yukos Universal Limited v The Russian Federation* (PCA Case AA 227); *Veteran Petroleum Trust v The Russian Federation* (PCA Case AA 228).

a claimant be organised in accordance with the law applicable in the contracting state through which it claims the jurisdiction of the ECT, "regardless of the nationality of shareholders, the origin of investment capital or nationality of the directors or management". The claimants satisfied this test.

Accompanying the ECT's definition of 'investor' is 'denial of benefits' wording entitling the host state to exercise its right to "deny the advantage of [the investment protection provisions of the ECT] to a legal entity if citizens or nationals of a third state own or control such entity and if that entity has no substantial business activities in the Areas of the Contracting Party in which it is organized" (Article 17). Arbitral tribunals in ECT cases have consistently taken the view that host states must actively exercise their rights to deny advantages under the ECT under this provision. Those rights cannot merely be denied automatically.[13] The exercise of the right to deny benefits to an investor has no retrospective effect, meaning that a respondent state could not deny the benefits of the ECT to an investor as a defence to an arbitration claim.[14]

5.2   What is an 'investment' under a BIT or MIT?

It is a misconception that investment treaties commonly protect only a narrow category of investments and transactions. 'Investment' is often defined broadly. Frequently, the definition will take the form of an asset-based formulation, referring to "every kind of asset" and then setting out a non-exhaustive list of categories, such as:

- movable and immovable property and any other property rights;
- shares in and stocks and debentures of a company;
- claims to money or to any performance under a contract having financial value;
- IP rights, goodwill, technical processes and know-how and similar rights; and
- business concessions conferred by law or under contract, including concessions to search for, cultivate, extract or exploit natural resources.[15]

This list makes it clear that the definition includes both the more obvious categories of investment asset (eg, ownership of physical property) and contractual rights (eg, those for the exploration and development of oil and gas reserves).

Some treaties define 'investments' more restrictively by:

- requiring that the investment be made in accordance with the laws and regulations of the host state, which effectively imposes an obligation on an investor to comply with domestic legislation rather than seeking to benefit from a more favourable regime for overseas investors;
- requiring that the investment be made in the territory of the host state. This may raise issues where the investment is intangible (eg, a contractual right) and is not obviously made within the host state;

---

13   See *Plama Consortium Ltd v Bulgaria*, Award on Jurisdiction (ICSID Case ARB/03/24); *Yukos Universal Ltd v Russian Federation*.

14   See *Plama Consortium Ltd v Bulgaria*, Award on Jurisdiction.

15   See, for example, Agreement between the Government of the Republic of Ghana and the Government of the Republic of Guinea for the Promotion and Protection of Investments.

- requiring that the investment have the characteristics of an investment. The US Model BIT requires that an investment be one that "an investor owns or controls, directly or indirectly, that has the characteristics of an investment, including such characteristics as the commitment of capital or other resources, the expectation of gain or profit, or the assumption of risk";
- defining 'investment' exhaustively such that the investment must fall within the finite categories specified in the definition; or
- excluding certain 'investments', such as those made other than for business purposes (in order to prevent assets such as holiday homes from attracting protection).

Tribunals have distinguished between investments which receive protection under BITs and ordinary commercial transactions which do not.[16] In doing so they have adopted tests similar to those used to determine whether an investment exists for the purposes of the Washington Convention (see below). For example, in *Romak SA v Republic of Uzbekistan* (PCA Case AA280), a tribunal found that "rights... embodied in and [that] arise out of a sales contract, a one-off commercial transaction pursuant to which [the claimant] undertook to deliver wheat against a price to be paid by the Uzbek parties" did not constitute an investment for the purposes of the applicable BIT.

One issue which has been considered is the extent to which the costs of making an abortive investment can qualify for BIT protection. In *Mihaly International Corporation v Democratic Socialist Republic of Sri Lanka* (ICSID Case ARB/00/2) expenditure incurred before an investment in the development of a power station in Sri Lanka was held not to be an investment. The power station development never proceeded and the tribunal stated that it could find no evidence in investment treaty practice that "pre-investment and development expenditures... could automatically be admitted as 'investment' in the absence of the consent of the host State to the implementation of the project".

Although the definition of 'investment' may extend to contracts entered into directly between two private parties, rather than between an investor and the host state, any such transaction which does not have the necessary characteristics of an investment (see below) will not be afforded protection.[17]

The ECT sets out a non-exhaustive list of investment categories that again recalls wording found in many BITs, and refers to "every kind of asset owned or controlled directly or indirectly by an Investor", including tangible and intangible property, shares, claims to money, intellectual property and returns (Article 1(6)).

However, as the ECT is concerned only with the energy industry, protected investments are those associated with economic activity in the energy sector relating to certain energy materials and products. The definition of 'economic activity in the energy sector' comprises any economic activity concerning the exploration,

---

16 See, for example, the decision of an *ad hoc* committee (a body convened to review an award) in *Mitchell v Democratic Republic of Congo* (ICSID Case ARB/99/7 (decision on annulment)).
17 See, for example, *Alps Finance and Trade AG v The Slovak Republic* (UNCITRAL award).

extraction, refining, production, storage, land transport, transmission, distribution, trade marketing or sale of "energy materials and products" (Article 1(5)). This latter phrase encompasses materials and products in the nuclear, coal, natural gas, petroleum and electrical industries.

The text of the ECT is accompanied by a number of understandings agreed by the contracting states with regard to interpretation of the ECT. One understanding clarifies that direct or indirect control by an investor, for the purposes of the definition of 'investment', means "control in fact, determined following consideration of the investor's financial interest in the investment, and its ability to exercise substantial influence over the investment and its management" (Understanding 3). Another understanding specifies illustrative "economic activities in the energy sector", which include exploration and extraction operations, construction and operation of power generation facilities (including wind and renewable sources), removal and disposal of waste (including radioactive waste), decommissioning of facilities and research, consulting, planning, management and design activities (Understanding 2).

5.3   Can an investor participate in ICSID arbitration?

ICSID remains the preferred choice for investment treaty arbitration claimants because of the involvement of the World Bank and the restricted grounds on which a losing party may resist enforcement of an ICSID award, leading to greater chances of successful enforcement. Claimants considering proceedings must establish that they are able to take advantage of the Washington Convention.

Nearly 150 states have signed and ratified the Washington Convention.[18] States which have not signed the convention include Brazil, Mexico, South Africa, Poland and India. Equally significant are a small number of countries which have signed the convention, but have not ratified it, such as Canada and Russia, meaning that claims under the Washington Convention cannot be brought against those states and investors from those states cannot bring ICSID arbitration against other states.

In addition, a number of states have notified ICSID of exemptions from the convention under Article 25(4). Thus:

- China has consented to ICSID arbitration only in respect of "disputes over compensation resulting from expropriation and nationalisation";
- Saudi Arabia "reserves the right of not submitting all questions pertaining to oil and pertaining to acts of sovereignty" to ICSID arbitration; and
- Turkey has notified ICSID that "disputes, related to the property and real rights upon the real estates are totally under the jurisdiction of the Turkish courts" and not subject to ICSID arbitration.

Even if an investor identifies a BIT or MIT under which it might be able to pursue an ICSID claim, in order to participate in ICSID arbitration it must satisfy the test set out in Article 25 of the Washington Convention. Pursuant to Article 25, the principal requirements for ICSID arbitration are that:

---

18   ICSID, List of Contracting States and other Signatories of the Convention.

- the parties consent to ICSID arbitration in writing; and
- there exists a legal dispute arising directly from an investment between two ICSID contracting states (ie, states that have ratified the Washington Convention).

There are different ways in which parties may consent to ICSID arbitration. A contracting state and an investor may agree to ICSID arbitration in an investment contract, such as a production sharing agreement. Alternatively, a contracting state may consent to ICSID arbitration in its domestic investment legislation. More commonly, a BIT or MIT will contain the contracting state's unilateral consent to arbitrate disputes arising thereunder at ICSID. As described above, the investor then provides its consent by commencing arbitration proceedings.

The nature of an 'investment' and whether an 'investor' is a national of another ICSID contracting state has given rise to controversy. These tests frequently generate jurisdiction objections by respondent states and there is overlap here with the jurisdictional arguments under investment treaties that have been referred to above.

The Washington Convention does not define an 'investment'. Tribunals considering the issue have tended to use as a starting point the decision in *Salini Costruttori SpA v Kingdom of Morocco* (ICSID Case ARB/00/4), which involved claims arising from a Moroccan construction project. The tribunal held that an investment must involve:

- contributions by the investor;
- a certain duration of performance of the contract;
- a participation in the risks of the transaction; and
- a contribution to the development of the host state.

However, in recent years tribunals have moved away from adopting an exclusive set of criteria. In *Biwater Gauff (Tanzania) Ltd v United Republic of Tanzania* (ICSID Case ARB/05/22), a case involving sanitation facilities in Tanzania, the tribunal favoured "a flexible and pragmatic approach".

In *Phoenix Action v The Czech Republic* (ICSID Case ARB/06/5) the tribunal reconsidered the approach of the *Salini* case and noted that an investment made either in bad faith or illegally cannot fall within the scope of ICSID. In *Saba Fakes v Republic of Turkey* (ICSID Case ARB/07/20), a case involving alleged expropriation of telecommunications assets, the tribunal considered the approaches adopted by tribunals and noted that some tribunals had added, to the four *Salini* criteria, the "requirement of a regularity of profit and return". However, the tribunal concluded that "the criteria of (i) a contribution, (ii) a certain duration, and (iii) an element of risk, are both necessary and sufficient to define an investment within the framework of the Washington Convention".

An investor seeking to bring a treaty claim to ICSID will need to satisfy the definition of 'investment' both in the applicable treaty and in Article 25 of the Washington Convention. The tests are separate, although satisfaction of the treaty test may well, in practice, satisfy the ICSID test. In *Malaysian Historical Salvors, SDN, BHD v Malaysia* (ICSID Case ARB/05/10), a claim arising from operations to salvage a historical wreck, an ICSID annulment committee rejected a restrictive interpretation of 'investment' under the Washington Convention in circumstances where the BIT pursuant to which the claim was commenced defined 'investment' broadly. The committee concluded that the definition of 'investment' under the Washington Convention had to be interpreted by reference to the definition of 'investment' in the BIT.

ICSID arbitration is available only to nationals of a contracting state other than the contracting state in which the investment is made. However, parties to a dispute can agree that a national of a contracting state in which an investment is made shall be considered a national of another contracting state by virtue of foreign control (Article 25(2)(b)). This is intended to apply where a host state requires that a project company be incorporated within its jurisdiction. If the project company is controlled by nationals of a different contracting state, the parties can agree that it will be entitled to participate in ICSID arbitration, notwithstanding its nationality.

The approaches of tribunals to the ICSID nationality requirement have varied. In *TSA Spectrum de Argentina SA v Argentine Republic* (ICSID Case ARB/05/5), which involved the privatisation of the Argentinian radio spectrum, the claimant argued that it should be treated as Dutch because its immediate parent company was Dutch. The tribunal concluded that even though the claimant's immediate parent company was Dutch, the ultimate owner was an Argentine national; consequently, jurisdiction was denied. However, in *Tokios Tokelės v Ukraine* (ICSID Case ARB/02/18) the tribunal took a different approach. Even though nationals of Ukraine owned 99% of the claimant's shares and made up two-thirds of its management, the tribunal considered the claimant to be Lithuanian because it was incorporated there.

Other cases have adopted similarly differing approaches, which have tended to turn on the precise facts in dispute. As a result, it is difficult to formulate clear principles on which investors can rely as to when an investor will be considered to satisfy the nationality test.

As the requirements of Article 25 of the Washington Convention are restrictive, in 1978 ICSID introduced the Additional Facility Rules. These authorise the ICSID Secretariat to administer certain proceedings which do not fall within Article 25. Such proceedings include arbitration proceedings for the settlement of investment disputes between parties, one of which is not a contracting state or a national of a contracting state, and arbitration proceedings that do not arise directly out of an investment, "provided that the underlying transaction is not an ordinary commercial transaction" (Article 4(3) of the Additional Facility Rules). The Additional Facility Rules enable parties which do not satisfy the requirements of the Washington Convention to resolve their disputes using rules tailored to investment disputes. However, such arbitrations do not lead to awards which can be enforced under the Washington Convention, but instead must be enforced under the New York Convention (ie, they are treated as commercial arbitration awards).

6. Which law governs the substance of the dispute?

Investment treaties often make express provision for the substantive law which is to govern any dispute between an investor and a host state. Frequently this is expressed to be the treaty itself and the applicable rules and principles of international law. Reference may also be made to the laws of the host state. The ECT provides that any arbitral tribunal appointed thereunder shall "decide the issues in dispute in accordance with this Treaty and applicable rules and principles of international law" (Article 26(6)).

The Vienna Convention on the Law of Treaties provides that "a treaty shall be interpreted in good faith in accordance with the ordinary meaning to be given to the terms of the treaty in their context and in the light of its object and purpose" (Article 31(1)), and by reference to "any relevant rules of international law applicable in the relations between the parties" (Article 31(3)).

In the absence of express choice of governing law, if ICSID arbitration is chosen, guidance is given by Article 42(1), which provides that "the Tribunal shall decide a dispute in accordance with such rules of law as may be agreed by the parties. In the absence of such agreement, the Tribunal shall apply the law of the Contracting State party to the dispute (including its rules on the conflict of laws) and such rules of international law as may be applicable".

The modern approach to BITs and MITs is to interpret them in accordance with principles of international law, as informed by the law of the host state. This ensures that international minimum standards apply to treaty interpretation and prevent host states from relying exclusively on their own laws in order to prejudice investors.[19]

7. What claims may be available to an investor?

Many investment treaties offer substantially the same protections. Treaties are usually short and contain around 10 key provisions.

For example, the 1995 UK-Kazakhstan BIT comprises the following articles:

- definitions;
- promotion and protection of investment, including the obligation to accord fair and equitable treatment to investors;
- national treatment and most favoured nation (MFN) provisions;
- compensation for losses (eg, upon the occurrence of war, riots or emergency);
- regulation of expropriation;[20]
- repatriation of investment and returns;
- exceptions;
- settlement of disputes between an investor and a host state;
- disputes between the state parties;
- subrogation;
- application of other rules;
- territorial extension;
- entry into force; and
- duration and termination (providing that the BIT shall remain in force for 10 years and continuously thereafter, unless notice is given to terminate).

---

19   "A party may not invoke the provisions of its internal law as justification for its failure to perform a treaty" (Vienna Convention on the Law of Treaties, Article 27).
20   That is, not without suitable compensation (see further below).

Investment treaty claims have produced a substantial body of case law. Significant awards are briefly discussed below. However, the wording of treaties and the extent of the protections offered do differ. Decisions of tribunals are influential, but not binding on subsequent tribunals, and a variety of approaches is a feature of investment treaty case law.

7.1 Fair and equitable treatment

Providing fair and equitable treatment to investors is one of the fundamental obligations found in investment treaties and is a cornerstone of investment protection. However, there have been difficulties defining precisely what this is in particular circumstances. For this reason, investors often include claims for breaches of the duty of fair and equitable treatment in disputes under investment treaties in addition to claims brought under other provisions. The outcome of arbitration claims on the basis of breaches of the duty of fair and equitable treatment can sometimes be unpredictable.

Claims for breach of the obligation to provide fair and equitable treatment often arise where investors allege that the courts of a host state have treated them unjustly. This may involve a court failing to consider adequately claims brought by investors or by dispensing justice in a discriminatory way. In *Mondev International Ltd v United States of America* (ICSID Case ARB(AF)99/2), a claim brought by Canadian investors under the North American Free Trade Agreement, the tribunal stated that "the test is not whether a particular result is surprising, but whether the shock or surprise occasioned to an impartial tribunal leads, on reflection, to justified concerns as to the judicial propriety of the outcome ... In the end the question is whether... a tribunal can conclude in the light of all the available facts that the impugned decision was clearly improper and discreditable, with the result that the investment has been subjected to unfair and inequitable treatment".

Unfair administrative decisions by authorities in host states have also been advanced as the basis for investment claims. These may arise where the legitimate expectations of investors have not been met or the host state has acted inconsistently. In *Saluka Investments BV v The Czech Republic* (United Nations Commission on International Trade Law (UNCITRAL) arbitration) the tribunal held that the protection of legitimate expectations was the "dominant element" of fair and equitable treatment. However, the tribunal observed that "no investor may reasonably expect that the circumstances prevailing at the time the investment is made remain totally unchanged. In order to determine whether frustration of the foreign investor's expectations was justified and reasonable, the host State's legitimate right subsequently to regulate domestic matters in the public interest must be taken into consideration as well".

Host states are entitled to make changes to the business environment within which an investor operates. However, if investors have received specific representations, legislative or regulatory changes should not be made contrary to these representations.

In *Plama Consortium Limited v Bulgaria* (ICSID Case ARB/03/24), an investor claimed breach of the fair and equitable treatment obligation in Article 10(1) of the

ECT on the grounds that it had a legitimate expectation that it would not be liable for environmental damage occurring prior to its acquisition of a Bulgarian oil refinery. The tribunal disagreed, noting that "the ECT does not protect investors against any and all changes in the host country's laws. Under the fair and equitable treatment standard the investor is only protected if (at least) reasonable and justifiable expectations were created in that regard".

In *Petrobart v Krygyzstan* (Stockholm Chamber of Commerce (SCC) Award) the tribunal concluded that Krygyzstan had failed to accord Petrobart fair and equitable treatment under the ECT by transferring assets from a state-owned company which owed Petrobart money to another company, and by intervening in court proceedings to the detriment of Petrobart.

7.2   Most favoured nation/national treatment

A fair and equitable treatment provision places an absolute obligation on the host state. It must treat its investors fairly and equitably. Investment treaties also often provide for relative standards of treatment for investors. An MFN provision ensures that an investor is treated no less favourably than other overseas investors. National treatment provisions ensure that investors are treated no less favourably than nationals of the host state.

An MFN provision enables investors to take advantage of favourable provisions in other investment treaties entered into by the host state. In *MTD Equity Sdn Bhd v Republic of Chile* (ICSID Case ARB/01/7) Malaysian investors seeking to establish a planned community in Chile incurred significant expenditure on the project. Following the subsequent refusal of permits, the investors relied on provisions in the Chile-Croatia and Chile-Denmark BITs that were more extensive than those found in the Chile-Malaysia BIT.

Debate has been provoked with regard to the extent to which investors can use MFN provisions to 'import' procedural rights from other investment treaties into treaties on which they rely. In *Maffezini v The Kingdom of Spain* (ICSID Case ARB/97/7), there was a complicated dispute resolution clause in the Argentina-Spain BIT. An Argentine investor failed to comply with the requirement that disputes be submitted to Spanish courts before arbitration. Instead, the investor relied on the simpler procedure in the Chile-Spain BIT. The tribunal held that he was entitled to do so. This decision has been criticised and tribunals have adopted differing approaches to whether procedural rights, as distinct from substantive rights, in other BITs can be invoked under MFN provisions.

7.3   Regulation of expropriation

There is a perception that investment treaties forbid expropriation. In fact, they typically recognise that expropriation may occur, but provide for the level of compensation to which the investor is then entitled. Expropriation will often be permissible if it is justified and non-discriminatory, and if prompt, adequate and effective compensation is paid to the investor.

Expropriation is a broad concept which may take different forms. 'Direct expropriation' might involve the seizure of an asset by the host state. 'Indirect expropriation' might involve measures by a state depriving the investor of the economic benefit of its investment. Another example of indirect expropriation might be amendments to the fiscal terms governing a transaction. In recent years there has been a trend towards so-called 'creeping expropriation', where states gradually introduce measures that have the effect of depriving the investor of the benefit of its investment over time.

In *Generation Ukraine Inc v Ukraine* (ICSID Case ARB/00/9) the tribunal stated that "creeping expropriation is a form of indirect expropriation with a distinctive temporal quality in the sense that it encapsulates the situation whereby a series of acts attributable to the State over a period of time culminate in the expropriatory taking of such property". In *Walter Bau AG v The Kingdom of Thailand* (UNCITRAL arbitration) the tribunal stated that "a strong interference with contractual rights needs to be shown". No creeping expropriation was found to have occurred in a claim brought by a shareholder in a tollroad, noting that the host state's "alleged misdeeds… were inaction rather than affirmative action".

Article 13 of the ECT prohibits expropriation save where it is in the public interest, non-discriminatory, carried out under due process of law and accompanied by the payment of "prompt, adequate and effective compensation" calculated on the basis of "fair market value".

In *Ioannis Kardassopoulos v Georgia* (ICSID Case ARB/05/18) the Greek claimant argued that Georgia had expropriated his investment in pipeline facilities by a series of governmental decrees. The tribunal concluded that this represented a "classic case" of direct expropriation and rejected Georgia's contentions that it had acted in the public interest by transferring pipeline rights to companies better able to develop necessary infrastructure, and that its acts had been non-discriminatory.

In *Nykomb Synergetics v The Republic of Lativa* (SCC Award) a tribunal considered a claim arising from the tariff to be paid for electrical power in Latvia to an investor. The investor claimed that the refusal by the state to pay the full tariff constituted creeping expropriation such that the enterprise was no longer economically viable. The tribunal concluded that so-called 'regulatory takings' may amount to expropriation. It stated that "the decisive factor for drawing the border line towards expropriation must primarily be the degree of possession taking or control over the enterprise the disputed measures entail". However, in the circumstances it concluded that there was no taking of possession over the investor's assets or interference with the investor's rights or control over the investment.

7.4   Protection of investments

Investment treaties usually require host states to offer full security and protection to investors. This is usually treated as a separate and distinct standard to fair and equitable treatment. Although the precise formulations differ, tribunals have found that host states are obliged to exercise due diligence and to be vigilant with regard to the physical protection of investments.

Tribunals have taken different approaches as to whether a protective obligation extends to legal protection as opposed to physical safeguarding. In *Azurix Corporation v The Argentine Republic* (ICSID Case ARB/01/12) the tribunal noted that full protection and security "is not only a matter of physical security; the stability afforded by a secure investment environment is as important from an investor's point of view". It found that Argentina had failed to protect adequately Azurix's investment in water and sewerage assets.

7.5 Free transfer of funds

The ability to transfer returns made from their investments to bank accounts outside the host state is important to investors. Most investment treaties address this. In some treaties, this protection is qualified by the application of the laws of the host state for the purposes of protecting creditors' rights (eg, on insolvency of an investor), enforcement and satisfaction of judgments and the collection of taxes. For example, the ECT states that the obligation to guarantee the freedom of transfer of funds is subject to the host state's right to "protect the rights of creditors, or ensure compliance with laws on the issuing, trading and dealing in securities and the satisfaction of judgments in civil, administrative and criminal adjudicatory proceedings" (Article 14).

7.6 Umbrella clauses

In many investment treaties the host state agrees to observe any obligation that it has entered into with regard to investments in its territory. Provisions to this effect are known as 'umbrella' (or 'observance of undertaking') clauses. Such clauses can radically broaden the scope of what can be claimed under an investment treaty. If a host state has entered into a contract with an investor and then breaches that agreement, an umbrella clause may have the effect of elevating a contractual claim into a BIT claim.

Investors frequently argue that umbrella clauses elevate all breaches of contract by a state into breaches of BITs; states argue that they do not. The approach of tribunals to this has not been consistent. In *SGS Société Générale de Surveillance SA v Islamic Republic of Pakistan* (ICSID Case ARB/01/13) a tribunal refused to elevate a breach of contract into a breach of the relevant BIT because to do so would have consequences "so far-reaching in scope, and so automatic and unqualified and sweeping in their operation [and] so burdensome in their potential impact upon a Contracting Party". The tribunal held that "clear and convincing evidence" would have to be adduced to indicate that that was the intention of the parties to the BIT.[21]

Conversely, in *SGS Société Générale de Surveillance SA v Republic of the Philippines* (ICSID Case ARB/02/6) the tribunal took a different view: it considered the wording of the BIT to be sufficiently clear that a failure by the Philippines to observe a contractual commitment amounted to a breach of the treaty.[22]

Subsequent tribunals have variously followed the approach taken in each of these cases. However, some commentators and practitioners consider that

---

[21] The relevant wording in the Switzerland-Pakistan Treaty was: "Either Contracting Party shall constantly guarantee the observance of the commitments it has entered into with respect to the investments of the investors of the other Contracting Party."
[22] The relevant wording in the Switzerland-Philippines Treaty was: "Each Contracting Party shall observe any obligation it has assumed with regard to specific investments in its territory by investors of the other Contracting Party."

interpreting the clear meaning of umbrella clauses in the manner of *SGS v Philippines* case is the more appropriate course. *SGS v Pakistan* has been criticised as being overly restrictive.

In *Sempra Energy International v The Argentine Republic* (ICSID Case ARB/02/16) the tribunal "distinguished breaches of contract from treaty breaches on the basis of whether the breach has arisen from the conduct of an ordinary contract party, or rather involves a kind of conduct that only a sovereign state function or power could effect". The tribunal noted that this distinction may not always be apparent.

Article 10(1) of the ECT contains an obligation on each contracting party to "observe any obligations it has entered into with an Investor". In *Mohammad Ammar Al-Bahloul (Austria) v Tajikistan* (SCC Arbitration) a tribunal found that this obligation had been breached by Tajikistan failing to issue hydrocarbon exploration licences to the claimant investor in breach of contractual obligations to that effect.

8. How is an arbitration commenced and conducted under an investment treaty?

Investment treaties typically set out the procedures to be applied in the event of a dispute. Common practice is for the treaty to require mandatory negotiations between investor and host state before the commencement of any proceedings. This cooling-off period is frequently three to six months from notification of a claim.[23]

Some older BITs require an investor to exhaust local remedies before commencing arbitration proceedings. This approach derives from a time when arbitration was perceived as a dispute resolution mechanism subsidiary to litigation. More commonly, investment treaties offer an investor the choice of litigation in local courts or international arbitration. In such circumstances, if the decision is taken to proceed in the local courts, the right to apply to arbitration may be extinguished. This mechanism is known as a 'fork in the road' provision.

The ECT offers investors the choice of dispute resolution in the courts or administrative tribunals of the host state, by any previously agreed dispute resolution procedure or by international arbitration (Article 26(2)). Certain states have required that where a dispute is submitted to local courts or other agreed procedure, the host state is deemed not to have consented to arbitration (Article 26(3)) (Annex ID).

Recent investment treaties provide investors with a choice of arbitration forum. Investors are often given the option of arbitration under ICSID or the ICSID Additional Facility Rules (where one of the treaty states is not party to the Washington Convention). Arbitration under the Rules of the Court of Arbitration of the International Chamber of Commerce (ICC) or the SCC Rules of Arbitration is often offered. Investment treaties commonly also enable an investor to commence *ad hoc* arbitration proceedings under the UNCITRAL Arbitration Rules. The majority of treaty arbitrations take place under either ICSID or the ICSID Additional Facility Rules, with UNCITRAL arbitration proving the next most popular choice.[24]

---

23   The ECT prescribes a three-month cooling-off period (Article 26(2)).
24   IIA Issues Note 1, March 2011, "Latest Developments in Investor-State Dispute Settlement".

Claimants selecting arbitration under the ECT have a choice of ICSID, ICSID Additional Facility Rules, SCC or *ad hoc* UNCITRAL Rules arbitration (Article 26).

Faced with a choice between ICSID arbitration and arbitration in accordance with other institutional or *ad hoc* rules, the factors that the investor should consider are as follows:

- 'Delocalisation' of proceedings – unlike other forms of arbitration, ICSID arbitration is regulated exclusively by the Washington Convention. It is not dependent on national legal systems and there is no scope for the supervision or interference of national courts in the conduct of the arbitral proceedings.

- Enforcement of awards – enforcement is not by means of the New York Convention. The Washington Convention regulates enforcement of ICSID awards, requiring contracting states to treat them as if they were judgments of a court of such state. ICSID awards are often considered to be more enforceable than awards where enforcement is sought under the New York Convention. This may be because of ICSID's association with the World Bank and the reluctance of states to be seen to defy an ICSID award. There are also fewer grounds to resist enforcement. Nevertheless, the Washington Convention does not prevent a state from invoking sovereign immunity to prevent the execution of any ICSID award (Article 54(3)) over its assets.[25]

- Scope for jurisdiction disputes – as explained above, ICSID arbitration frequently gives rise to disputes as to whether the ICSID arbitral tribunal has jurisdiction. The requirement of ICSID that there exist "a legal dispute arising from an investment between two ICSID Contracting States" gives scope for differing interpretations. Host states invariably object to the jurisdiction of ICSID, resulting in increased costs and length of ICSID proceedings. Such jurisdiction disputes can be avoided if non-ICSID arbitration is adopted.

- Confidentiality – confidentiality is often associated with arbitration proceedings as a distinguishing factor from court litigation (although commercial arbitration is often less confidential than parties may assume). However, the existence and progress of an ICSID arbitration are matters of public record, published on ICSID's website. There is also provision under the ICSID Rules for non-parties to file written submissions in respect of the issues in dispute (Arbitration Rule 37). The ICSID Rules impose no obligation on the parties to keep awards confidential and a large number of ICSID awards are available online. By contrast, non-ICSID arbitrations are more likely to remain confidential, although non-ICSID awards are frequently published or made available online. The likelihood of publicity of proceedings may be attractive to an investor, as a means of increasing the pressure on a host state; on the other hand, such publicity may prove distracting or disruptive, particularly if it results in criticism of the investor by the media.

- Availability of provisional measures –the arbitral rules most commonly used in investment arbitration (ICSID, ICSID Additional Facility, ICC, SCC and

---

25 Awards rendered pursuant to the ICSID Additional Facility Rules must be enforced pursuant to the New York Convention.

UNCITRAL) each provide that provisional measures can be sought pending determination of the dispute. However, whereas recourse may be made to a national court in non-ICSID arbitration prior to the formation of the arbitral tribunal,[26] the ICSID Rules empower only the tribunal to recommend provisional measures unless the parties have agreed that they may apply elsewhere. Given the time which it may take in order to appoint a tribunal and the potential urgency of provisional measures, this may be a significant factor in directing an investor away from ICSID to an alternative form of arbitration. Further, while in some states provisional measures during non-ICSID arbitration may be enforced through the courts, provisional measures in ICSID proceedings are merely 'recommendations' requiring the goodwill of the party against which the measures are granted (although the prevailing trend is to consider such recommendations to constitute binding obligations).

- Annulment/challenge of awards – the Washington Convention provides for annulment of awards where:

    (a) the Tribunal was not properly constituted;

    (b) the Tribunal has manifestly exceeded its powers;

    (c) there was corruption on the part of a member of the Tribunal;

    (d) there has been a serious departure from a fundamental rule of procedure; or

    (e) the award has failed to state the reasons on which it is based.

    (Article 52)

Annulment applications are considered by a panel of three arbitrators unconnected with the original award. Such applications must be brought within 120 days of the award or, in the case of corruption, within 120 days of discovery of the corruption and in any event within three years of the date of the award (Article 52(2)). By contrast, challenges to non-ICSID awards are considered by the courts and governed by the laws of the seat of the arbitration. There is a general perception that the ICSID annulment mechanism is unpredictable, with an increasing number of awards being fully or partially annulled. The approach of courts in arbitration-friendly jurisdictions such as Singapore, France and Sweden is viewed as more consistent.

9. Current trends in investment treaty arbitration

Before the late 1990s there were relatively few investment treaty arbitrations (fewer than 150 known claims). Since then, as cross-border investment flows have increased and more investment treaties have been entered into, the number of arbitrations has increased enormously, reaching an annual high in 2003, when over 40 reported cases were commenced. There has been some decline since then and 2010 saw the lowest number of known arbitrations commenced since 2001. By 2010, 83 countries had received claims, with Argentina,[27] Mexico, Czech Republic and Ecuador facing the most.[28]

---

26   Including pursuant to the ICSID Additional Facility Rules (Article 46(4)).

The boom in investment treaty arbitration in the 21st century has focused attention on its practice, drawing comment and criticism. In August 2010 a group of academics issued a public statement expressing a "shared concern for the harm done to the public welfare by the international investment regime as currently structured, especially its hampering of the ability of governments to act for their people in response to the concerns of human development and environmental sustainability".[29] They advocated the withdrawal from or renegotiation of investment treaties.

Criticisms of treaty arbitration tend to focus on:

- the perceived favour shown by tribunals to investors;
- the emphasis on protecting commercial concerns over the public interest; and
- the failure by tribunals to respect defences advanced by states that actions taken were required by necessity or otherwise justified by the public interest.

In this climate, Ecuador and Bolivia have withdrawn from ICSID and Venezuela has indicated that it favours taking a similar route.[30] Australia has also announced that it no longer proposes to include investor/state arbitration provisions in its investment treaties, citing concerns regarding the conferral of greater legal rights on overseas investors in preference to domestic businesses and constraints on Australia's ability to enact social and environmental legislation.[31]

Substantive criticisms aside, the costs and length of treaty arbitrations have also raised concerns. Legal costs routinely run into the many millions of US dollars – for example, the parties to a notorious ECT claim in 2011, which did not even proceed to a substantive hearing but failed on jurisdictional grounds, together claimed $60 million in costs.[32] There is also a perception that the duration of treaty cases have increased significantly in recent years, not least because of the proliferation of jurisdiction objections. It has been calculated that the average length of a treaty case is between three and four years.[33]

10. Conclusion

It is the nature of the energy industry that investors are often reliant on the protection and cooperation of host states. In the oil and gas industries, resources are often found in politically unstable jurisdictions with relatively undeveloped legal systems. Power sector investors which have invested heavily in immovable and long-term infrastructure find themselves vulnerable to aggressive host states seeking to

27   Argentina has faced many claims arising from the emergency measures implemented with regard to its 1999 to 2002 financial crisis. It is not uncommon for one act of a host state, or series of acts, to generate a multitude of treaty claims. Single projects can also result in multiple claims. The failed Dabhol power project in India led to a slew of claims by both the major shareholders (GE and Bechtel) and the commercial lenders (all of which subsequently settled).
28   IIA Issues Note 1, March 2011, "Latest Developments in Investor-State Dispute Settlement".
29   See Public Statement on the International Investment Regime (August 31 2010).
30   "Chávez Takes Steps to Exit Global Forum" (*Wall Street Journal*, September 13 2011).
31   *Gillard Government Trade Policy Statement: Trading our way to more jobs and prosperity* (April 2011).
32   *Libananco Holdings Co Limited v Republic of Turkey* (ICSID Case ARB/06/8).
33   Investor-State Disputes: Prevention and Alternatives to Arbitration (UNCTAD 2010).

redefine investment bargains. Investors reliant on subsidies and favourable taxation regimes to justify their investments may be obvious targets for host states struggling with financial downturns. Finally, as commodity prices increase there may be political pressure on governments to try to recover more from a project than a foreign investor had previously bargained for.

A familiarity with investment treaties and the protections which they offer can be invaluable for investors negotiating with host states. Investment treaty arbitration is often at best undesirable and frequently unthinkable in practical terms for investors, which work hard to retain the favour of host governments. Divisive arbitration proceedings are rarely anything other than measures of last resort. However, the prospect, and perhaps the threat, of arbitration can serve to focus minds. Investment treaty arbitration is an important part of the international investor's armoury.

International boundary disputes

Drazen Petkovich
Crescent Petroleum

Energy is at the heart of modern life. Industry, agriculture, transport, home light, and heat, cannot function without it. The industrial revolution was fuelled by coal, which remains a vital if polluting resource. Since petroleum displaced whale oil in the 19th century, it has been the energy source of choice. Investments in the finding, production, transport, refining, and marketing of petroleum ... remain huge. [These] complex and expensive arrangements require contracts and concessions.
– Judge Stephen Schwebel[1]

1.   Introduction – why boundary disputes matter to the energy sector

At first blush, a chapter on international boundary disputes in a book entitled *Dispute Resolution in the Energy Sector*, forming part of a practical business series, may seem something of an anomaly. We all know that, by their very nature, boundary disputes involve states and their respective borders – not private parties, their investments, projects and contracts, with which the preceding chapters are concerned. This is surely the stuff of public international law: the self-determination of peoples, politics, high diplomacy and, when that fails, the law of war.

But upon further reflection, it is actually quite fitting that this chapter should conclude the book. The connection is articulated in the quotation from Judge Schwebel above: petroleum literally powers the world today. Hydrocarbons remain the primary source of fuel for transportation and the generation of electricity for light, heat and cooling (particularly in the Gulf States), despite efforts to increase reliance on renewable sources.[2] Many commentators (and the International Energy Agency) expect that trend to continue following the Fukushima incident of 2011, in particular heralding a new 'golden age' of natural gas.

In a world where the bulk of our energy continues to be derived from hydrocarbons lying beneath the earth's surface, control of the territory in which these resources are located is clearly axiomatic, underpinning the upstream operations[3] from which everything else in the energy value chain flows. In the case of international oil companies (IOCs), such control dictates the nature of the host government instruments to be negotiated, which in turn shape joint operating agreements, sale and

---

1   Judge Stephen Schwebel, Foreword to PD Cameron, *International Energy Investment Law – The Pursuit of Stability* (Oxford University Press: 2010).
2   Aside from fuel, the products of petroleum include various everyday goods such as carpets, curtains, plastic toys, drip-dry fabrics, fertilisers, grease and even cosmetics and toothpaste.
3   That is, exploration for, and extraction and production of, oil and gas.

purchase agreements, agreements for the processing, transmission and/or distribution of hydrocarbons and, perhaps, distribution of the energy produced from them. In the case of states, sovereignty over prospective hydrocarbon territory brings with it, among other things, the potential for immense transformational wealth via licensing fees from exploration, then development, followed by production share, royalties and taxes upon successful production on a recurring basis over what is hoped to be a relatively long term. For example, the fields offshore Cyprus are said to be worth up to €100 million[4] and up to $167 billion of taxes and revenues is said to be at stake in relation to fields offshore the islands the subject of dispute between Argentina and the United Kingdom,[5] both of which are discussed below.

The importance to states of controlling exploration acreage may also be observed in the rise of the national oil companies (NOCs) over the last 30 years. Whereas the "Seven Sisters"[6] dominated control of oil resources from the early to mid 20th century, the position changed dramatically in the mid to late part of the millennium. In 1970, IOCs had full access to 85% of the world's resources and NOCs just 1%; however, in just 10 years the situation was almost the converse: by 1980 the IOCs' share had shrunk to 12% and the NOCs' grown to 59%.[7] Today, NOCs own 73% of the world's oil reserves and 61% of production.[8] Added to this is the phenomenon Professor Cameron calls the "Millennium Wave" – a pattern of unilateral host state actions against IOCs which began early this century and was provoked by dramatically rising oil prices,[9] starting with Venezuela's 2005 announcement that it was nationalising 32 private oil fields.[10]

2. The prevalence of border disputes: *oceans et mers sans frontiers*?

Subject to a few notable exceptions,[11] most of the world's onshore acreage has been, or is in the process of being, explored or exploited for conventional hydrocarbons. This has driven IOCs to move offshore, in ever deeper waters – a phenomenon made

---

4   "Gas find 'a gift from God' " by Evripidou, *The Cyprus Mail*, December 30 2011 (http://www.cyprus-mail.com/cyprus-eez/gas-find-gift-god/20111230); *The World Tonight* News Programme on BBC Radio 4, broadcast January 16 2012.

5   With $10.5 billion estimated from the Sea Lion Field alone – see "Britain accuses Argentina of 'harassing' Falklands" by A Croft, *Reuters*, March 16 2012 (http://uk.reuters.com/article/2012/03/16/argentina-falklands-idUKL5E8EG2GF20120316; "Offshore oil a 'game-changer' for Falkland Islands", by M Warren, *Associated Press*, March 16 2012 (http://www.sfgate.com/cgi-bin/article.cgi?file=/n/a/2012/03/16/international/i031514D95.DTL).

6   Royal Dutch Shell, Texaco and Standard Oil of California (now Chevron), Gulf Oil, British Petroleum (formerly Anglo-Iranian Oil Company), Standard Oil of New York (Mobil) and Standard Oil of New Jersey (Esso, then Exxon), the latter two who became ExxonMobil.

7   Diwan, R, "The Current Implications of the World Energy Situation for United States Energy Supplies" (2007), cited in *Oil and Governance – State-owned Enterprises and the World Energy Supply*, eds DG Victor, DR Hults & M Thurber (Cambridge University Press, NY: 2012), p 6.

8   The picture as regards natural gas is similar: 68% of reserves and 52% of production, "Introduction and overview" in *Oil and Governance – State-owned Enterprises and the World Energy Supply*, eds DG Victor, DR Hults & M Thurber (Cambridge University Press, NY: 2012).

9   According to the chief economist of the International Energy Agency, the price of oil is overtaking the sovereign debt crisis as the dominant concern of governments and industry around the world because high benchmark oil prices tend to presage economic recession. See comments by Mr Fatih Bitol, quoted in in the *Financial Times*, March 25 2012 on p 1 (G Chazan "Fears for recovery as oil costs soar" & p 6 (E Crooles, G Chazan and A Beattie, "Once more over a barrel").

10 PD Cameron, op cit, at para 1.10 and appendix 1 (p 429).

11 The Kurdistan Region of Iraq, the Antarctic, the Arctic (if large tracts of ice are treated as land), Central Africa and possibly Sudan and the new Republic of Sudan.

possible by recent advances in technology, which in turn makes maritime boundaries very relevant for the oil and gas business.

As it happens, offshore maritime boundaries constitute the great majority of contentious inter-state boundaries. As at December 2007, there were more than 430 maritime boundaries around the world. Less than half of them have been agreed.[12] Just over four years later – at the time of writing – a perusal of the resources made available by Durham University's International Boundaries Research Unit[13] together with cases lists/reported decisions of the relevant international tribunals[14] reveals that the situation has not materially changed.

This relatively high level of boundary uncertainty is perhaps less surprising if one takes into account that a comprehensive legal regime for settling borders was lacking until the United Nations Convention on the Law of the Sea (UNCLOS) was created in 1982. Moreover, it took another 11 years for UNCLOS to come into force (on November 16 1994, when the ratification threshold was reached). One might also postulate that coastal states tend not to be proactive when it comes to delimiting or resolving maritime boundaries, unless there is some catalyst. While it is certainly true that not all border disputes involve the discovery of hydrocarbons,[15] it is undoubtedly the case that there is nothing like the discovery of oil or gas to pique the interest of states in previously inconspicuous areas and/or to revive dormant quarrels in relation to unresolved borders.

The purpose of this chapter, then, is to provide an overview of the legal framework for maritime border delimitation, including the kinds of dispute that occur and the mechanisms available to resolve them.[16] Having outlined these factors and the key concepts, we turn to two very topical disputed maritime areas – both involving the discovery of hydrocarbons – as interesting case studies of how these concepts apply and to consider whether any themes emerge.

3. Offshore boundary delimitation – legal framework and key concepts

3.1 Territorial sea, exclusive economic zone and continental shelf[17]

As mentioned above, the key international instrument governing maritime boundaries is UNCLOS.[18] Although, like any treaty, UNCLOS formally binds only

---

12 Pratt, M & Smith, D "How to Deal with Maritime Boundary Uncertainty in Oil and Gas Exploration and Production Areas", paper prepared for the Association of International Petroleum Negotiators (AIPN, December 2007).

13 Hereafter, "IBRU". See http://www.dur.ac.uk/ibru/.

14 Namely, the International Tribunal for the Law of the Sea (www.itlos.org), the International Court of Justice (http://www.icj-cij.org) and arbitrations administered under the auspices of the Permanent Court of Arbitration (http://www.pca-cpa.org/).

15 In the case of Croatia and Slovenia, for example, their dispute relates to shipping lanes in the Bay of Piran. The impetus was Croatia's accession to the European Union.

16 For detailed and comprehensive analysis of the legal framework concerning maritime boundary delimitation and dispute resolution, the technical methods of delimitation and issues likely to be encountered by IOCs, the reader is referred to Garcia, MM, "Territorial delimitation and hydrocarbon resources", in *Oil and Gas: A Practical Handbook* (Globe Law and Business: 2009); and to Pratt M & Smith, D, *op cit.*

17 A table showing the status of claims to maritime jurisdiction as at July 15 2011 can be accessed at http://www.un.org/depts/los/LEGISLATIONANDTREATIES/PDFFILES/table_summary_of_claims.pdf.

18 See http://www.un.org/depts/los/convention_agreements/texts/unclos/closindx.htm.

those states which have ratified it,[19] many of its provisions are now generally considered to embody customary international law, which is binding on all states, irrespective of whether they are signatories.

The regime of UNCLOS is that all coastal states are entitled to a territorial sea, extending up to 12 nautical miles from the relevant baseline.[20] The coastal state enjoys full territorial sovereignty over the territorial sea, including the seabed, subsoil and the supervening airspace. In addition, a coastal state is entitled to an 'exclusive economic zone' (EEZ) extending up to 200 nautical miles from the baseline. The EEZ is a very important concept under UNCLOS, because coastal states have sovereign rights over the sea and seabed within their EEZ, specifically including rights to conduct oil and gas activities,[21] subject to foreign ships being allowed to pass through those waters protected by the doctrine of innocent passage.[22]

If the coastal state has a continental shelf, then it may exercise sovereignty up to the limit of that continental shelf[23] – beyond its EEZ – up to the prescribed limits of 350 nautical miles from the baseline or a depth of 2,500 metres.

Article 76 of UNCLOS defines the 'continental shelf' as "the seabed and subsoil of the submarine areas that extend beyond its territorial sea throughout the natural prolongation of its land territory to the outer edge of the continental margin, or to a distance of 200 nautical miles from the baselines from which the breadth of the territorial sea is measured where the outer edge of the continental margin does not extend up to that distance".

In order to claim a continental shelf beyond its EEZ, a state must lodge a submission to the UN Commission on the Limits of the Continental Shelf (a body created under UNCLOS), which is accompanied by detailed scientific data proving the existence and extent of this subsea geography. The commission's role is a technical one, and it does not rule on the merits of overlapping claims. Following the recent International Tribunal for the Law of the Sea (ITLOS) award in *Bangladesh v Myanmar*, it has been established that the absence of a ruling by the commission is not a jurisdictional bar to binding determination under one of the UNCLOS dispute resolution mechanisms (discussed below).[24]

Whereas states have previously shown little appetite for establishing claims beyond the 200 nautical mile limit of their EEZs, technological advances in the past decade or so have made exploration and production in deeper waters possible, and increasing energy scarcity has incentivised states to explore the potential of claims on the 'natural prolongation' basis.

---

19   Article 18 of the Vienna Convention on the Law of Treaties, 1969 obliges states which have signed a treaty to refrain from acts which would defeat the object and purpose of a treaty prior to its entry into force.
20   Article 2 of UNCLOS.
21   Articles 60 and 80 of UNCLOS relate to installations and structures (eg, offshore platforms); Article 79 deals with pipelines and Article 81 concerns the exclusive right to control drilling.
22   That is, passage which is "not prejudicial to the peace, good order or security of the coastal state": see Articles 17 and 19 of UNCLOS.
23   Subject to Article 79 of UNCLOS, which permits other states to lay subsea cables and pipelines on the continental shelf of a coastal state, subject to that coastal state's right to take reasonable measures, among other things, for the exploration of its continental shelf and the exploitation of resources contained within it. The coastal state's consent is required for cables and/or pipeline to be laid across its continental shelf.
24   See notes 33 and 34.

Diagram 1 – key concepts under UNCLOS[25]

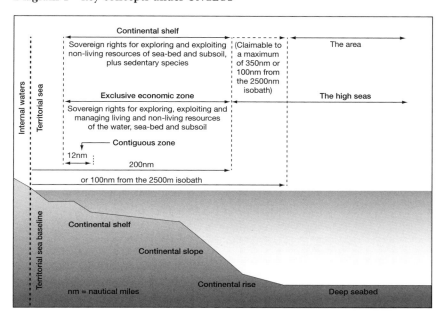

(a)   *Principles of delimitation – baselines, the median line and equitable solutions*
Measurement of a distance for any purpose obviously requires the setting of a
baseline from which to start. Article 5 of UNCLOS defines the normal baseline as
"the low-water line along the coast as marked on large-scale charts officially
recognized by the coastal State". This creates a default baseline tracking the contours
of the coastline at the relevant distance out to sea. However, in certain
circumstances, straight baselines will be adopted instead of this (to even things out)
– for example, where a coastline is deeply indented or where there is a cluster of
islands along the coast in its immediate vicinity. Accordingly, in relation to baselines,
there is ample room for dispute as to whether the correct charts are being employed
or whether the coastal geography is such as to warrant the use of a straight baseline.
        Where neighbouring states have overlapping claims in relation to the territorial
sea, EEZ and/or continental shelf, absent an agreement, the starting point for
delimitating any of these boundaries is the 'median' or 'equidistance line'. This is the
line between them along which every point is equidistant from the nearest points on
the opposing baselines from which the length of the territorial seas of the two states
is measured. Having established a median line, there then follows enquiry as to
whether any special circumstances necessitate a modification in order to address
particular features in the coastline, such as length, shape and/or the effects of islands
or rocks. The International Court of Justice (ICJ) has, in several decisions, explained

---

25   Source: http://www.dfo-mpo.gc.ca/oceans/canadasoceans-oceansducanada/marinezones-zonesmarines-
       eng.htm.

the rationale of UNCLOS in this regard as the need to eliminate the "disproportionate effect" of islets, rocks and minor coastal projections and thereby produce an "equitable solution". In the *North Sea Continental Shelf* cases the court stated that an equitable delineation requires "a reasonable degree of proportionality".[26] The need for, and extent of, such equitable modifications (and proportionality) present fertile ground for disputes, given the vague and open-textured nature of these concepts.

However, the most fertile area for dispute in the delimitation process is whether a natural offshore land mass is merely a 'rock' (simply affecting the shape of the coastline) or attracts the privileged status of 'island' (capable of generating its own territorial sea, EEZ and/or continental shelf).

(b)   Dispute resolution – interim options

In the absence of an agreement on boundary delimitation, UNCLOS mandates[27] neighbouring coastal states to make good-faith efforts to enter into "provisional arrangements of a practical nature". In practice, this often results in the creation of 'joint cooperation zones' or 'joint development zones' to share control of the disputed area and any resources in it. These may be temporary or longer term, and range from very simple arrangements[28] to highly complex affairs featuring various joint committees to make operational decisions in specified geographical sectors and/or including their own dispute resolution provisions.[29] Depending on the strategic objectives of the states concerned, these arrangements can serve as a blueprint for an eventual delimitation (and/or cooperation) agreement or defer the need to strike any permanent agreement.

(c)   Dispute resolution mechanisms – binding options

Should states wish to submit themselves to a binding maritime determination process, UNCLOS provides for three options: judicial settlement by ITLOS,[30] the ICJ[31] or *ad hoc* arbitration (the default option absent an agreed choice of forum).[32]

UNCLOS established ITLOS as a special tribunal dedicated to resolving maritime boundary disputes and disputes generally arising in relation to the interpretation and application of UNCLOS. ITLOS is based in Hamburg and, like the ICJ, its proceedings are public. On March 1 2012, ITLOS delivered judgment in the first-ever delimitation

---

26   *North Sea Continental Shelf (Federal Republic of Germany/Denmark; Federal Republic of Germany/Netherlands)*, Judgment, 1969, para 98.
27   Specifically, Articles 74(3) and 83(3) of UNCLOS. The scope of the obligation was explored by the tribunal in the *Guyana v Suriname* arbitration, award dated September 17 2007, available at http://www.pca-cpa.org/upload/files/Guyana-Suriname%20Award.pdf.
28   For example, the agreement between Sharjah and Iran concerning the Abu Musa area is a single page: "Sharjah-Iran, Memorandum of Understanding, signed in November 1971", *Middle East Economic Survey*, Vol XV, No 28, May 5 1972, Supplement.
29   The Timor Gap Treaty between Australia and Indonesia provides for three zones of cooperation, two decision-making organs (Ministerial Council; Joint Authority), various rules and regulations, including a petroleum mining code, a model production-sharing contract and a taxation code (see http://www.austlii.edu.au/au/other/dfat/treaties/1991/9.html).
30   Annex VI of UNCLOS.
31   Part XV of UNCLOS.
32   Annex VII of UNCLOS.

dispute submitted to it (in December 2009) by Bangladesh in relation to its boundary with Myanmar.[33] Not only was this ITLOS's first-ever delimitation case; it was also the first instance of a tribunal ruling on the boundary of two states' outer continental shelf.[34]

The ICJ – also known as the 'World Court' – is the principal judicial organ of the United Nations, established in 1945 under the UN Charter. Based in the Peace Palace in The Hague, the ICJ's role is to determine legal disputes (and give advisory opinions on questions) referred to it by states in accordance with international law. ICJ proceedings and awards are public, and the ICJ's jurisdiction over states is consent based. Almost all of the jurisprudence on boundary disputes emanates from this court and, since UNCLOS came into effect in 1994, the ICJ has considered at least seven cases concerning maritime boundary disputes.[35]

Ad hoc arbitration of maritime boundary disputes has usually been administered by the Permanent Court of Arbitration (PCA), an intergovernmental organisation established in 1899 to facilitate peaceful dispute resolution between states,[36] also based in the Peace Palace in The Hague. The advantage of *ad hoc* arbitration is that proceedings may remain confidential and the parties may select their tribunal, have greater control over the procedure and generally obtain a faster determination.[37] Since UNCLOS came into effect in 1994, five out of the six arbitrations have been held under the auspices of the PCA.[38]

The number of maritime border disputes resolved pursuant to these binding mechanisms is minuscule against the backdrop of approximately 400 maritime borders which remain totally unresolved to date. This indicates that states tend to be very reluctant to submit high-stakes and sensitive issues of sovereignty to the vagaries of third-party decision making, especially where the inherent vagueness of concepts such as 'equitable solutions' and 'proportionality' confer very wide discretion on a tribunal empowered to fix a boundary. Such lack of predictability acts as an incentive to avoid formal dispute resolution processes in favour of negotiated outcomes, which may take anywhere from years to decades to resolve. That said,

---

33   A summary of the decision is contained in the press release available at http://www.itlos.org/ fileadmin/itlos/documents/press_releases_english/pr_175_engf_02.pdf. The text of the full decision is available at: http://www.itlos.org/fileadmin/itlos/documents/cases/case_no_16/1-C16_Judgment_14_ 02_2012.pdf.
34   The dispute concerned the delimitation of the maritime boundary between Bangladesh and Myanmar in the Bay of Bengal with respect to the territorial sea, the EEZ and the continental shelf. The tribunal addressed a number of issues raised by the parties, including Bangladesh's claim that the delimitation of the territorial sea had already been agreed by the parties in 1974 and the delimitation of the EEZ and continental shelf within 200 nautical miles of the baselines from which the breadth of the territorial sea is measured. In addition, the tribunal had to deal with Bangladesh's claim that the continental shelf beyond the 200 nautical mile limit should be delimited (a request which was opposed by Myanmar), which entailed considering whether ITLOS could and should exercise its jurisdiction in respect of the delimitation of the continental shelf beyond 200 nautical miles.
35   The count is nine cases if proceedings relating to sovereignty over islands are included – namely, the matters of *Sovereignty over Pulau Ligitan and Pulau Sipadan (Indonesia/Malaysia) (1998)* and *Sovereignty over Pedra Branca/Pulau Batu Puteh, Middle Rocks and South Ledge (Malaysia/Singapore)*(2003); see case list at http://www.icj-cij.org/docket/index.php?p1=3&p2=2.
36   The PCA's mandate has since been widened to accommodate disputes involving non-state parties.
37   On the assumption that potential delays due to non-availability of multiple arbitrators are still less than delays due to a full court docket.
38   See http://www.pca-cpa.org/showpage.asp?pag_id=1288.

there may come a point where state parties desirous of a conclusion have no option but to refer their dispute for binding determination because of prolonged and unfruitful negotiations. For example, the dispute between Singapore and Malaysia over Pedra Branca was submitted to the ICJ in 2003, following over 20 years of inconclusive diplomatic discussions. Likewise, Bangladesh welcomed the recent ITLOS determination against Myanmar as "a victory for both states because it finally resolves … a problem that had hampered the economic development of both states for more than three decades".[39]

(d)   *Dispute resolution mechanisms – non-binding options*

UNCLOS also provides two non-binding dispute resolution options: mediation and conciliation. Mediation involves the appointment of a neutral third party to act as facilitator of the states' negotiations. The third party can be an individual, another state or an international organisation. The most famous example of a successful mediation is the Argentina/Chile maritime boundary dispute mediated by Pope John Paul II, whose intervention led to the 1984 Treaty of Peace and Friendship between the disputants. Conciliation is similar, in that the result is not binding on the parties; however, the process is more structured, involving the appointment of a 'conciliation commission' charged with producing a recommended solution, as opposed to the 'shuttle-diplomacy' approach of a mediator. In the dispute between Iceland and Norway over Jan Mayen, the conciliation commission's recommendation of a joint development zone was adopted by the states as a formal agreement.[40]

Diagram 2 – UN Map of the Eastern Mediterranean Region[41]

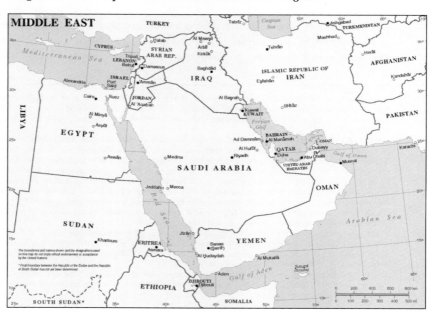

4. The Eastern Mediterranean

The island of Cyprus lies in the Eastern Mediterranean Sea, neighbouring the coastal states of (and overlapping EEZs with) mainland Turkey in the north, then (moving clockwise), Syria, Lebanon, Israel and the Gaza Strip in the east and Egypt to the south. Only two (perhaps three)[42] of these six boundaries have been finally delimited: the EEZ boundaries with Egypt[43] and Israel[44] agreed in February 2003 and December 2010, respectively. An EEZ delimitation agreement was entered into with Lebanon in January 2007, but has not yet been ratified and therefore has not entered into force.

While the coastal geography of the region is rather simple, the area is extremely complex from a legal perspective, due to the existence of at least two[45] unresolved and longstanding land border disputes. Since 1974, the island of Cyprus has been divided into a Greek southern half, which is an independent EU member state; and northern half, which is part of Turkey. The Greek Cypriot South does not have diplomatic relations with Turkey, which still lays claim to the rest of the island (and its waters). Accordingly, Turkey rejects any assertion of maritime territory by Cyprus or agreed delimitations with neighbouring coastal states. Moving ashore, Lebanon and Israel remain officially at war and their land border remains disputed. Since 2000, the countries have been committed to a ceasefire along a UN designated and patrolled line of withdrawal known as the 'Blue Line'.[46] The lack of an official land border between them means that even the starting point for a maritime border baseline is contentious.

Earlier, it was mentioned that the discovery of hydrocarbons may act as a catalyst for either clarifying maritime boundaries or awakening and exacerbating dormant

---

39   Bangladesh Foreign Minister Dipu Moni, quoted in A Ross, "Tribunal explores the outer waters of its jurisdiction", *Global Arbitration Review*, March 16 2012.

40   *Agreement on the Continental Shelf between Iceland and Jan Mayen, Iceland v Norway*, October 22 1981, 21 ILM 122 (1982).

41   http://www.un.org/Depts/Cartographic/map/profile/mideastr.pdf.

42   The Syrian Arab Republic has asserted an EEZ (see http://www.un.org/depts/los/LEGISLATIONANDTREATIES/STATEFILES/SYR.htm), but it is unclear whether any delimitation agreements exist between Syria and its coastal neighbours, Turkey, Cyprus and Lebanon. The literature is silent on whether any agreement exists between Cyprus and Syria in particular, except for a passing reference in a Lebanese newspaper (www.nowlebanon.com/Print.aspx?ID=229427). One commentator describes Syria as something of a "black box", on account of difficulties encountered with gathering consistent and reliable data: see A Cleary, "The Mashreq, Israel, and the Palestinian Territories" in *Natural Gas Markets in the Middle East and North Africa* (B Fattouh & J Stern Eds), (Oxford University Press, New York: 2011).

43   Agreement between the Republic of Cyprus and the Arab Republic of Egypt on the Delimitation of the Exclusive Economic Zone, February 17 2003 (entry into force: March 7 2004; Registration #: I-44649; registration date: January 14 2008; link to UNTS): http://www.un.org/depts/los/LEGISLATIONAND TREATIES/PDFFILES/TREATIES/EGY-CYP2003EZ.pdf.
In May 2006 Cyprus and Egypt signed another treaty concerning the joint development of hydrocarbon resources straddling the demarcation line. Turkey objected to this in the *Law of the Sea Bulletin* No 57: Information note concerning Turkey's objection to the Agreement between the Republic of Cyprus and the Arab Republic of Egypt on the Delimitation of the Exclusive Economic Zone, February 17 2003 (available at http://www.un.org/Depts/los/doalos_publications/LOSBulletins/bulletinpdf/bulletin57e.pdf).

44   Agreement between the Government of the State of Israel and the Government of the Republic of Cyprus on the Delimitation of the Exclusive Economic Zone, signed in Nicosia on December 17 2010 (entry into force: February 25 2011; Registration #:I-48387; Registration date: March 9 2011: http://www.un.org/depts/los/LEGISLATIONANDTREATIES/PDFFILES/TREATIES/cyp_isr_eez_2010.pdf; Annex II; http://www.un.org/depts/los/LEGISLATIONANDTREATIES/PDFFILES/TREATIES/cyp_isr_eez_ 2010annex.jpg).

45   As regards Israel and the Palestinian Territories, it does not appear to be suggested that the Gaza/Israel land border is itself in doubt, as opposed to being part of a wider dispute.

46   See http://www.un.org/Depts/Cartographic/map/profile/blueline.pdf.

disputes. Both of these tendencies are evident in the developments in the Eastern Mediterranean over the past decade.

The discovery of hydrocarbons in the region dates back to 1999, when the Palestinian Authority awarded the BG Group[47] a licence to explore the Gaza Marine block offshore the Gaza Strip.[48] BG had been exploring offshore Algeria and Egypt and decided to follow some promising geology northwards, leading it to the Gaza Strip and Israeli territorial waters. BG reported a discovery of 28 billion cubic metres (bcm) of natural gas in Gaza Marine; however, the field was never developed due to inconclusive pricing negotiations and the inability to find a suitable market in Egypt or Israel.[49] About the same time, BG was exploring Gaza Marine,[50] it was also exploring the adjoining Israeli block, Med Yavne, which produced a modest natural gas find in November 1999.

These initial discoveries sparked great interest in Israel and, shortly afterwards, in 2000 Noble Energy discovered the Mari-B Field offshore Israel, very close to the Gaza Marine Block. Exploration continued apace, with a string of successful discoveries during the decade: the Tamar and Dalit Fields in 2009, and the aptly named Leviathan Field the following year.[51] This success did not go unnoticed in Cyprus, which soon began its own exploration activity. In 2006 Cyprus began offshore seismic surveys,[52] which were sufficiently positive to impel the state to enact a new Hydrocarbons Law the following year, governing the issue of authorisations for upstream operations and reasserting a claim to Cyprus' EEZ in accordance with UNCLOS.[53] Also in 2007 came the announcement that Cyprus would be holding its first licensing round of offshore acreage.

In March 2010 the US Geological Survey published the results of a now oft-cited study into the natural gas reserves on the Levant Basin region – the sea area in the southeast of Cyprus and west of Lebanon and Israel. The amount of gas estimated was 122 trillion cubic feet (tcf) of recoverable gas and 1.7 billion barrels of recoverable oil.[54]

In the meantime, Noble Energy had expanded its operations in the area, acquiring a licence to explore offshore Cyprus, which was logical given the proximity of the Israeli finds to the EEZ claimed by Cyprus. In particular, Noble Energy acquired

---

47 And their 10% partners in the block, Consolidated Contractors Company: see A Cleary, "The Mashreq, Israel, and the Palestinian Territories" in *Natural Gas Markets in the Middle East and North Africa* (B Fattouh & J Stern eds), (Oxford University Press, New York: 2011).

48 See http://www.un.org/Depts/Cartographic/map/profile/semedite.pdf and http://www.un.org/Depts/Cartographic/map/profile/israel.pdf.

49 Later, political complications with the Hamas takeover of the Gaza strip in 2007 are said to have impeded further progress.

50 As operator with a 50% share, together with Isramco Group 42% and Delek Drilling (8%).

51 See www.nobleenergyinc.com/operations/Eastern-Mediterranean-128.html.

52 Neocleous, P & Stamatiou, C, "Ready, Steady, Drill: the Legislation Governing the Race for Cyprus's Offshore Hydrocarbon Resources" [2007] (12) *International Company and Commercial Law Review* 417.

53 The purpose of the new law was to make Cypriot law compliant with EU Directive 94/22/EC regarding the conditions for the exploration, utilisation and management of all natural resources, the waters, the seabed and subsoil; the production of energy; the utilisation of installations and structures; and all rights and duties under UNCLOS. See Neocleous, P & Stamatiou, C, *op cit*, at 417.

54 Schenk, CJ, Kirschbaum, MA, Charpentier, RR, Klett, TR, Brownfield, ME, Pitman, JK, Cook, TA, and Tennyson, ME, 2010, Assessment of undiscovered oil and gas resources of the Levant Basin Province, Eastern Mediterranean: US Geological Survey Fact Sheet 2010-3014 (available at http://pubs.usgs.gov/fs/2010/3014/pdf/FS10-3014.pdf).

licences from both Cyprus and Israel to facilitate exploration of the Leviathan Field.[55] Noble Energy's exploration of the Levantine Basin appears to have provided the impetus for a delimitation agreement between Cyprus and Israel, which was signed on December 17 2010[56] and came into force on February 18 2011,[57] nine months before the IOC's next major discovery was announced – this time in Cypriot waters.[58]

Although the precise details of the Cyprus/Israel treaty are not known, it is thought that the delimitation of the respective EEZs occurred along the median line, and that the treaty contemplates cooperation and joint development of hydrocarbon-bearing reservoirs extending beyond one EEZ into the other via subsequent framework agreements for sharing and developing such resources. The Cyprus/Israel Treaty was roundly criticised by both Turkey and Lebanon. Turkey rejected the new boundary, since it was agreed without the participation of the Turkish-supported government in Northern Cyprus, which also claims rights to resources in the area. Lebanon lodged a formal objection with the United Nations on June 20 2011, on the basis that Israel was an occupying power and therefore subject to the applicable legal rules and international resolutions, which forbid any measure taken by an occupying power with a view to seizing, administering or annexing part of the territory that it occupies.[59]

The next major development involving maritime borders in the Levantine Basin came in July 2011, when Israel deposited a claim to the northern limit of its maritime area with the United Nations – the area bordering Lebanon. The asserted boundary was based on the terminus of the Blue Line, extending outwards to meet the eastern endpoint of Israel's agreed maritime boundary with Cyprus.[60] Unsurprisingly, Lebanon lodged a strident objection to Israel's submission, having previously asserted its own claim to an EEZ[61] and seeking to delineate the boundaries. By letters

55 IBRU Boundary News Headline "Cyprus an Israel reach agreement for maritime delimitation"; see http://www.dur.ac.uk/ibru/news/boundary_news/?itemno=11350&rehref=%2Fibru%2Fnews%2F&resubj =Boundary+news%20Headlines and the sources quoted therein: 'Maritime delineation completed between Israel and Cyprus', Catherine Hunter, *IHS Global Insight*, December 20 2010; 'Turkey criticizes Cyprus-Israel maritime border deal', *IHS Global Insight*, December 22 2010; "Cyprus, Israel sign accord demarcating maritime borders with eye on offshore gas search", M Hadjicostis, *Associated Press*, December 17 2010. Clearly, it is not always practicable for an IOC to secure a licence from each of the states claiming ownership over a certain area.
56 *Ibid.*
57 "Cyprus Parliament unanimously ratified an agreement between Cyprus and Israel", news release by Cyprus Law firm CD Messios LLC, dated February 2011.
58 The Aphrodite Field in Block 12 offshore Cyprus (located some 200 kilometres south of Cyprus) is estimated to contain 3 to 9 tcf of natural gas (*Middle East Economic Survey*, September 26). See also www.nobleenergyinc.com/operations/Eastern-Mediterranean-128.html.
59 A letter dated June 20 2011 from the minister for foreign affairs and emigrants of Lebanon addressed to the secretary general of the United Nations concerning the Agreement between the Government of the State of Israel and the Government of the Republic of Cyprus on the Delimitation of the Exclusive Economic Zone, signed in Nicosia on December 17 2010 (see http://www.un.org/depts/los/ LEGISLATIONANDTREATIES/PDFFILES/communications/lbn_re_cyp_isr_agreement2010.pdf).
60 IBRU Boundary News Headline, "Israel unilaterally defines the northern limit of its maritime space" dated July 14 2011, available at http://www.dur.ac.uk/ibru/news/boundary_news/?itemno=12445 &rehref=%2Fibru%2Fnews%2F&resubj=Boundary+news%20Headlines, and sources quoted therein: 'Lebanese President warns Israel over maritime border' *BBC Monitoring Middle East*, 14 July 2011; "List of Geographic Coordinates for the Delimitation of the Northern Limit of the Territorial Sea and Exclusive Economic Zone of the State of Israel in WGS84", Permanent Mission of Israel to the United Nations, July 12 2011. See also "Israel-Lebanon gas rivalry heats up", available at http://www.upi.com/ Business_News/Energy-Resources/2011/08/17/Israel-Lebanon-gas-rivalry-heats-up/UPI-35571313605665; and http://www.bbc.co.uk/news/world-middle-east-14104695.

dated July 9 2010 and October 11 2010, Lebanon deposited the geographical coordinates of, respectively, the southern and southwestern borders of its EEZ.[62] Lebanon had previously also expressed concern at Israel potentially using the Blue Line as a basis for delimiting its borders. This was because Israel had installed a line of buoys extending out to sea for two miles from the Blue Line for 'security reasons' shortly upon withdrawing from Lebanon in 2003.[63] The Lebanese concern that this floating line of markers may be prejudicial and possibly encroach upon its own maritime territory was heightened following Noble Energy announcing a large discovery in the Leviathan Field. Specifically, Lebanon contends that the Leviathan Field may extend into Lebanon's claimed EEZ and hence Israeli-licensed exploration may illegally remove natural gas from across the undefined area.

To date, the position between Lebanon and Israel remains unresolved. However, this state of affairs has provided the impetus for Lebanon to press on with promulgating an offshore hydrocarbons law and launching its first offshore licensing round (it is currently in the preliminary stages of inviting IOCs to pre-qualify).[64] As one government representative put it: "We are in a hurry because Israel is in a hurry and is exploring near our border."[65]

Returning to Cyprus, the exploration activities of Noble Energy in late 2011 stoked tensions with Turkey. Following the Greek Cypriot government's announcement in September 2011 that it intended to resume exploratory offshore drilling operations in its asserted EEZ, the Turkish government responded angrily, threatening that "frigates, gunboats and its air force will constantly monitor developments in the area",[66] and began its own gas exploration activities offshore Cyprus. According to some accounts, this entailed seismic vessels escorted by Turkish navy warships into Cyprus's EEZ and threats to drill in areas overlapping with Cyprus' 13 blocks in its EEZ.[67]

Despite the tension in the region, the drilling programme continued and, in early 2012, Noble Energy announced a large discovery (5 to 8 tcf) of natural gas in the Block 12 Aphrodite Field, which was hailed by one Cypriot as "a gift from god" that may have a profoundly transformational effect on the Cypriot economy, potentially paving the way for collaboration between Cyprus and Turkey – perhaps even leading to a resolution of the Cyprus issue.[68]

---

61 And warning Noble Energy not to work near Lebanon's EEZ: N Razzouk, "Lebanon May Auction Oil, Natural Gas Exploration Contracts Within a Year", Bloomberg, August 16 2010: http://www.bloomberg.com/news/2010-08-16/lebanon-may-auction-oil-natural-gas-exploration-contracts-within-a-year.html.

62 Details of the Lebanese claim are available at http://www.un.org/depts/los/LEGISLATIONANDTREATIES/PDFFILES/mzn_s/mzn85ef.pdf; http://www.un.org/depts/los/LEGISLATIONANDTREATIES/PDFFILES/lbn_2011decree6433.pdf.

63 F Biedermann, "Gas field threatens fresh Lebanon-Israel dispute", Financial Times, July 16 2010; available at http://www.ft.com/intl/cms/s/0/f80d4142-90eb-11df-85a7-00144feab49a.html#axzz1jSaqG8hr.

64 See http://www.lebanon-exploration.com/ and the map available at http://www.lebanon-exploration.com/images/Map/Large_Map1.jpg.

65 N Razzouk, op cit.

66 IBRU Boundary News Headline, "Tensions rise between Cyprus and Turkey over proposed drilling", (September 21 2011), available at http://www.dur.ac.uk/ibru/news/boundary_news/?itemno=12830&rehref=%2Fibru%2Fnews%2F&resubj=Boundary+news%20Headlines.

67 D Dombey, "Ankara gas hunt angers Cyprus", Financial Times, September 28 2011; N Razzouk, op cit.

68 Note 4 supra.

5. Competing claims over the Falkland Islands/Las Malvinas

The dispute between the United Kingdom and Argentina over who enjoys sovereignty over the small archipelago just off the tip of Tierra Del Fuego known as the Falkland Islands, or alternatively Las Malvinas, stretches back to the 18th century.

In short, the basis of the Argentine claim is succession: that Argentina inherited the islands from Spain upon gaining independence. The UK claim is based on long-term administration of the islands and the self-determination of the islands' residents. The United Kingdom also disputes that Argentina inherited the islands on the basis that they were abandoned by Spain in the early 19th century before the putative time of inheritance.[69] Both claims are complex, involving international law principles which do not point clearly in any one direction, as well as factual determinations stretching over a long period of time. It is presumably this complexity and uncertainty that has hitherto dissuaded either state from submitting its claims for adjudication.

Following a short conflict in 1982, it took approximately 11 years for a rapprochement to develop, which included discussions concerning a regime for the effective exploration for and exploitation of hydrocarbon resources believed to lie in surrounding waters.[70] The proximity of the islands to mainland Argentina makes it the sensible option for piping any oil or gas onshore for processing, storage and distribution, and South America likewise makes for an obvious market for ultimate sales.

Despite some initial exploration in the early 1990s, the exploration activity remained relatively dormant until February 2010 (as did political activity between the disputant states), when the IOCs Desire Petroleum and Rockhopper Exploration started exploratory drilling offshore the islands, which resulted in significant oil finds.[71] Tensions between Argentina and the United Kingdom then rose steadily over the course of 2011 following the announcement that the IOCs were about to embark upon an extensive appraisal programme, intensifying as the 30th anniversary of the Falklands war on April 2 2012 drew closer.

In the ensuing months there was increasing press coverage of Argentina's criticism of the United Kingdom for "militarising" the islands and escalating tensions by seeking to mark its territory by deploying the prince of Wales on a (search and rescue) mission to the islands and sending a UK destroyer to the region.[72] This included official protests to the United Nations. Other developments included a show of solidarity with Argentina by South American trading bloc Mercosur in denying port access to any ships flying the Falkland Islands flag,[73] and Peru cancelling a planned visit by British Royal Navy frigate HMS Montrose, as well as

---

69 For a helpful summary of the competing claims, see http://www.bbc.co.uk/news/magazine-17045169. The UK position is articulated by the Foreign Office at http://www.fco.gov.uk/en/travel-and-living-abroad/travel-advice-by-country/country-profile/south-america/falkland-islands/?profile=history.
70 P Armstrong, "Falklands Oil", *IBRU Boundary and Security Bulletin*, July 1994.
71 See http://www.desireplc.co.uk/; http://www.rockhopperexploration.co.uk/.
72 http://www.bbc.co.uk/news/uk-16864318; http://www.bbc.co.uk/news/world-latin-america-16939043; http://www.bbc.co.uk/news/world-latin-america-16940313.
73 N Cecil, "Call to send N-sub after ban on Falklands ships", *Evening Standard*, December 21 2011.

Argentine authorities detaining any ship suspected of delivering operations materiel to the islands.

At the time of writing (early April 2012), Argentina has threatened civil and criminal legal action against IOCs operating in the region, as well as companies providing them with financial and logistical support, having already implemented a regime of special permits and inspections of any ships leaving the mainland for the islands.[74] In response, the United Kingdom has defended the rights of the islanders to develop their petroleum resources without interference and accused Argentina of harassing the Falkland Islands. Against this backdrop of legal and political uncertainty, it is interesting to note that the IOCs intent on drilling operations are also assuming massive commercial risk, reportedly incurring $1.3 million per day with less than a 25% chance of success for two planned exploratory wells.[75]

6. Other areas of interest

Very briefly, there are two other regions where actual or anticipated discovery of hydrocarbons have recently triggered border disputes: the Arctic region and the Caspian region.

6.1 The Arctic Circle

The gradual melting of ice caps has made this area a place of great interest to national oil companies and IOCs.[76] Canada, Denmark, Iceland, Norway, Sweden, Russia and the United States all lay claim to territory in the Arctic Circle. As present, the main bone of contention in the area is the Lomonsov Ridge, a subsea ridge that runs under the North Pole from Greenland to Russia.[77] Both Canada and Russia claim that this structure is a natural prolongation of their respective continental shelf, and are currently engaged in the process of collecting seabed data to support their claims, at the same time sending armed forces to the area to demonstrate effective control.[78]

---

74 "Falkland Islands oil dispute: UK hits back at Argentina", *BBC News*, March 16 2012: http://www.bbc.co.uk/news/world-latin-america-17395537; http://uk.reuters.com/article/ 2012/03/16/argentina-falklands-idUKL5E8EG2GF20120316.

75 "Offshore oil a 'game-changer' for Falkland Islands", by M Warren, *Associated Press*, March 16 2012: http://www.sfgate.com/cgi-bin/article.cgi?file=/n/a/2012/03/16/international/i031514D95.DTL.

76 Indeed, the right to cooperate with state-owned Rosneft in the exploration of the Russian zone of this area was the subject of arbitration before the Stockholm Chamber of Commerce between TNK-BP and its joint venture partners Alfa Access Renova in early 2011. An injunction ordered by the tribunal against BP eventually led to Rosneft dropping BP from the project in favour of ExxonMobil later that year. See T Toulson, *Global Arbitration Review*, "BREAKING NEWS: Tribunal blocks BP-Rosneft deal", March 24 2011; S Pfeifer & I Gorst, "BP blow as Rosneft tie-up is blocked", *FT.com*, March 24 2011; T Bergin & D Busvine, "No breakthrough seen in BP-Rosneft-TNK talks", *Reuters*, May 16 2011: http://uk.reuters.com/article/2011/05/16/tnk-bp-idUKLDE74F22C20110516; "Exxon Mobil clinches Arctic oil deal with Rosneft", BBC News, August 30 2011: http://www.bbc.co.uk/news/business-14720830; and K Karadelis, "Second arbitration over BP Arctic deal?", *Global Arbitration Review*, October 26 2011.

77 Norway and Russia signed a delimitation agreement including the Arctic Ocean on September 15 2010. They also agreed to negotiate a unitisation agreement if any hydrocarbon-bearing structures are found to straddle the (maritime) boundary.

78 C Cummins, "Canada presses Arctic claims", *The Wall Street Journal*, September 29 2011; see also the special edition of the *Oil, Gas & Energy Law Intelligence (OGEL) Journal*: OGEL 2 (2012) – Arctic Region: Boundaries, Resources and the Promise of Cooperation.

6.2   The Caspian

The Caspian Sea is the largest enclosed body of water on Earth by area, variously classed as the world's largest lake or a fully fledged sea. It is bounded to the north by Russia, to the south by Iran, to the west by Azerbaijan and to the east by Kazakhstan and Turkmenistan.[79] These littoral states have been debating their share of the Caspian Sea maritime area since the collapse of the Soviet Union in 1991. The extant Caspian Sea legal regime is based on two agreements signed between Iran and the former Soviet Union in 1921 and 1940. The three new littoral states of Azerbaijan, Kazakhstan and Turkmenistan, established after the collapse of the Soviet Union, do not recognise the prior treaties, triggering a debate on the future status of the sea. There is also a substantive debate on the criteria for delimitation of the waters and seabed of the Caspian Sea.[80]

Iranian officials have recently declared that huge new reserves of natural gas – in the vicinity of 50 tcf – have been discovered in the 'Iranian sector' of the Caspian Sea. Since it is not clear who owns what in the Caspian Sea, the legal status of the newly discovered sources is unclear and the announcement has prompted Iran's neighbours to ask for clarification as to what that 'Iranian sector' is. Iran claims approximately 20% of the area, whereas its Iran's coastal neighbours consider its share of the Caspian as less than 12%. Any opposition to Iranian operations is unlikely to pose a problem for IOCs in this case, given that the operations are conducted by the state-owned National Iranian Oil Company through its various subsidiaries.

7.   Conclusion

It is difficult to discern whether the presence of hydrocarbons makes it easier or harder to resolve a maritime dispute. As with many legal problems, it all depends on the circumstances, and underlying sovereignty claims make quite powerful confounding variables.

In the case of the Falkland Islands/Las Malvinas, the geography presents logistical and commercial incentives to resolve matters, negotiations appear to have reached an impasse, but neither side has suggested referring the dispute for judicial or arbitral determination. In the case of the Levantine Basin, Cyprus had made good progress with its neighbours, Egypt, Israel and perhaps Lebanon, but the difficulties with Turkey remain despite geographic and commercial imperatives militating in favour of a resolution. The difficulties between Lebanon and Israel involve a range of issues, and it remains to be seen whether the clear benefits to having defined borders and certainty in offshore operations produce a beneficial effect on the relationship between them.[81]

---

79   See http://www.un.org/Depts/Cartographic/map/profile/centrasia.pdf.

80   See G Englefield, "A Spider's Web: Jurisdictional Problems in the Caspian Sea", *IBRU Boundary and Security Bulletin Autumn 1995*, p 30; http://english.farsnews.com/newstext.php?nn=9010170137; http://www.payvand.com/news/11/dec/1297.html.

81   According to recent press reports, Israeli Energy Minister Uzi Landau has indicated that Israel is willing to sell some of its natural gas finds to Arab neighbours, in the hope this will improve relations in the troubled region, with Jordan and the Palestinian Territories to be among the first customers. See, for example, "Israel ready to sell gas to Arab neighbours", *Oman Tribune*, March 29 2012.

What can be deduced with some degree of confidence is that states generally prefer to try to negotiate their border disputes instead of submitting themselves to third-party determination, although the commencement of a formal process may well be the catalyst for a negotiated outcome. That said, the claims lodged by Bangladesh mentioned earlier are an example of the opposite situation – where the desire for clarity following a prolonged period of inconclusive negotiations has prompted proceedings (against both Myanmar and India). Also, the dispute between Bangladesh and Myanmar concerned the oil and gas-rich Bay of Bengal, with the former state having awarded a concession to ConocoPhillips.[82] According to a member of Bangladesh's counsel team in the ITLOS proceedings, the relatively speedy determination by the tribunal (27 months) may encourage more states to file ITLOS proceedings.[83]

While states are the formal actors in the border disputes discussed above, IOCs are never far away from the action. Indeed, often it is an IOC's discovery that generates interest in the disputed area, and sometimes provides the catalyst for states to clarify their borders. It is also apparent that IOCs – especially smaller, independent IOCs – are risk takers by nature: the business of petroleum exploration and production involves a number of inherent risks being assumed. There is uncertainty in relation to geology, technical efficacy and economics. Viewed in this context, uncertainty in relation to an unsettled maritime boundary (or other aspects of a state's petroleum regime) is just another risk factor to be weighed in the balance against the potential rewards, and does not appear to be a deterrent where a prospective area is concerned (ie, an area of promising geology) and the fiscal terms are satisfactory. This trait, which impels IOCs forward into areas of uncertain borders, is a necessary one because it is not always realistic for IOCs to hedge their bets and apply for petroleum licences from all states claiming sovereignty over a particular area.

The examples discussed in this chapter show that independent IOCs appear to be more willing to conduct operations in frontier regions where maritime boundaries are unclear, and that fortune tends to favour the brave. The best example of this is the leading role taken by Noble Energy in the Levantine Region, establishing itself as an incumbent in the main fields and moving from Israeli to Cypriot acreage, evidently undeterred by threats of force from neighbouring states (or forces acting on their behalf)[84] disputing the legality of its operations. Indeed, the uncertainty as regards Lebanon's borders with Cyprus and Israel has failed to deter other IOCs from expressing their interest in the forthcoming Lebanese offshore licensing round. To the contrary, at the Lebanon International Petroleum Exploration Forum held last June, one of the attendees gave a presentation on "The Role of Smaller Oil and Gas Companies in Global Exploration",[85] extolling the virtues of smaller, independent

---

82   A Ross, *op cit.*
83   *Ibid.*
84   In response to threats by Hezbollah to attack Israeli energy installations on behalf of Lebanon, the Israeli authorities deployed unmanned aerial drones to provide around-the-clock surveillance: "Israel-Lebanon gas rivalry heats up", available athttp://www.upi.com/Business_News/Energy-Resources/2011/08/17/Israel-Lebanon-gas-rivalry-heats-up/UPI-35571313605665.
85   See: http://www.lebanon-exploration.com/DownLoads/Forum_Presentations/P16_LIPE_PetCeltic_Corcoran.pdf.

IOCs with greater risk appetites responsible for the most significant discoveries worldwide in recent years. In the case of Cyprus, the border issues with Turkey and Lebanon have likewise failed to dampen enthusiasm for Cyprus' second offshore licensing round, which has generated unprecedented interest. Over 70 companies have subscribed for seismic data upon which to base their applications to acquire one of the 12 remaining blocks in Cyprus' EEZ.[86]

86   "70 companies seek data for 2nd Cyprus natgas round", *Financial Mirror*, March 30 2012.

About the authors

Helen Clark
Solicitor, Ashurst LLP
helen.clark@ashurst.com

Helen Clark is a solicitor in Ashurst's dispute resolution department in London. She has experience in commercial litigation, with a particular focus on the energy, transport and infrastructure sectors. Ms Clark also has experience of other forms of dispute resolution, including arbitration, mediation and adjudication.

Mark Clarke
Partner, Ashurst LLP
mark.clarke@ashurst.com

Mark Clarke is a partner in the dispute resolution department at Ashurst in London. He has extensive experience in complex commercial disputes in the English High Court, in particular in the energy sector. He has advised in litigation, arbitration and expert determinations regarding a wide range of matters, including disputes arising under production sharing agreements and farm-in agreements; exploration disputes; regulatory investigations concerning the reclassification of oil and gas reserves; disputes concerning the construction of drilling rigs; disputes concerning the price and quality of gas supplied under long-term gas sales contracts; and criminal investigations concerning allegations of bribery and corruption in the oil and gas sector. He also has experience advising on disputes arising in the nuclear sector.

Tom Cummins
Senior associate, Ashurst LLP
tom.cummins@ashurst.com

Tom Cummins is a senior associate in Ashurst's dispute resolution department in London and a member of the firm's international arbitration group. He has advised clients on a range of disputes with an emphasis on the energy and mining sectors. Mr Cummins has experience of a number of different forums, including English court litigation, expert determination and international arbitration.

Peter Edworthy
Associate, Ashurst LLP
peter.edworthy@ashurst.com

Peter Edworthy is an associate in Ashurst's dispute resolution department in London and a member of the firm's international arbitration group.

Jeremy Farr
Partner, Ince & Co LLP
jeremy.farr@incelaw.com

Jeremy Farr is a partner and the global head of energy and offshore at Ince & Co, based in London. Having joined Ince & Co in 1985, he has been a partner for the past 18 years. He advises construction, drilling and other oilfield services contractors in support of their worldwide activities.

His experience covers the full lifecycle of engineering, procurement and construction and similar projects in the energy sector from tender through to project completion, including working with project teams in order to prevent issues from escalating into disputes.

On the dispute side, he has many years' experience of leading teams running major domestic and international arbitrations and litigation concerning all aspects of such projects. Notable among these are projects involving the construction or conversion of floating production units, mobile offshore drilling units, mooring systems, pipelines, jackets and process facilities.

James Farrell
Partner, Herbert Smith LLP
james.farrell@herbertsmith.com

James Farrell is a partner in the litigation and arbitration division of Herbert Smith LLP in London. He has 20 years' experience of disputes in the energy sector. Mr Farrell has been involved in disputes in a wide range of oil, gas and power matters, in a variety of jurisdictions. He has experience before the High Court and appellate courts, as well as in arbitration, and in particular expert determination.

Mr Farrell lectures regularly on a range of legal topics, and is the co-author of *Expert Determination* (4th Edition) by Kendall, Freedman and Farrell.

Ben Giaretta
Partner, Ashurst LLP
ben.giaretta@ashurst.com

Ben Giaretta is a partner in Ashurst's dispute resolution department and is based in Singapore. He heads Ashurst's dispute resolution group in Asia, focusing on the energy and infrastructure sectors. A specialist in international arbitration, Mr Giaretta is a fellow of the Chartered Institute of Arbitrators and a fellow of the Singapore Institute of Arbitrators, and is on the arbitrator panels of the Singapore International Arbitration Centre, the Kuala Lumpur Regional Centre for Arbitration and the Singapore Institute of

Arbitrators. He has extensive experience in other forms of dispute resolution, including court litigation, mediation and expert determination.

Ted Greeno
Partner, Herbert Smith LLP
ted.greeno@herbertsmith.com

Ted Greeno joined Herbert Smith in 1981 and has been a partner since 1989, specialising in oil and gas and other energy industry disputes.

During this period, he has advised on disputes all over the world involving a wide range of matters, including disputes relating to the price of oil and gas; production sharing contracts; concession agreements; joint operating agreements; farm-in agreements; joint study and bidding agreements; drilling contracts; long-term gas sales and transportation agreements; allocation agreements; power purchase agreements; and gas and electricity trading agreements.

Mr Greeno has conducted international arbitrations involving oil, gas and power industry disputes in Africa, the Middle East, Indonesia, the Philippines, China, India, North America, South America, the United Kingdom and continental Europe. He also sits as an arbitrator and has lectured and written on various aspects of arbitration and expert determination in the oil and gas industry.

Simon Hems
Partner, Ince & Co LLP
simon.hems@incelaw.com

Simon Hems is a partner in the energy and offshore group at Ince & Co in London. He handles all forms of dispute resolution, including both litigation and arbitration, in respect of claims arising out of energy construction and installation projects. These matters typically involve pursuing or defending technically complex and high-value claims on behalf of contractors involved in, for example, the construction of pipelines, offshore units/vessels and power plants, and the provision of offshore services.

He represents some of the largest contractors in the oil and gas industry and has handled matters arising out of projects all over the world, with particular experience of the US, Latin American, Russian and former Soviet states and West African markets.

Ben Holland
Partner, CMS Cameron McKenna LLP
ben.holland@cms-cmck.com

Ben Holland is a solicitor advocate working exclusively on energy-related disputes, with particular emphasis on the oil and gas, power and mining sectors. He handles large-scale commercial dispute resolution for UK and international clients. Much of his work involves multi-jurisdictional disputes under long-term, high-value contracts disrupted by volatile oil prices and the consequential price impact on natural gas, coal and commodities. Mr Holland also advises on disputes concerning the construction and operation of oil and gas production facilities and equipment, pipelines, onshore and offshore engineering and power stations. He advises on, among other things, contractual disputes under joint operating agreements, production sharing agreements, power purchase agreements, and gas and liquefied natural gas sales agreements, both in the United Kingdom and internationally.

David Isenegger
General counsel, Centrica Energy
David.Isenegger@centrica.com

David Isenegger is general counsel of Centrica Energy, based in Windsor, United Kingdom. Prior to joining Centrica, he was head of legal for Shell's upstream business in the United Kingdom. Before this, he was the lawyer responsible for major Shell oil and gas projects and interests in Iran and Kazakhstan. Previously, he had a senior legal role with the Sasol Group, where he was involved in developing gas to liquids projects in the Middle East and West Africa. He also spent two years as a team leader with the United Nations Security Council in Geneva, working to resolve energy sector claims against Iraq arising from the first Gulf War. Mr Isenegger is a graduate of the University of Alberta and began his legal career in private practice in Calgary. While at university, he served as an officer in the Royal Canadian Navy.

Caroline Kehoe
Partner, Herbert Smith LLP
caroline.kehoe@herbertsmith.com

Caroline Kehoe is a partner in the dispute resolution division of Herbert Smith in London. She has specialised in disputes within the oil and gas industry for more than 20 years.

Ms Kehoe has experience of High Court and Commercial Court litigation, expert determination and arbitration. Many of her cases in the energy sector have involved complex, technical engineering disputes, and she has advised on a variety of matters, including disputes relating to joint ventures, unitisation/equity redeterminations, pre-emption rights, drilling rig contracts and disputes under long-term gas sales agreements, including take-or-pay, gas pricing and quality disputes.

Recent high-profile cases include acting for Chevron UK in relation to the civil proceedings arising out of the explosion at the Buncefield Terminal in December 2005, which involved not only claims from 4,000 claimants suffering damages in excess of £1 billion, but also complex issues arising out of the joint venture arrangements.

Ronnie King
Partner, Ashurst LLP
Ronnie.king@ashurst.com

Ronnie King is a partner in the dispute resolution department of Ashurst LLP and heads the international arbitration group. He has considerable experience of multi-jurisdictional litigation and arbitration in the power and energy sectors.

Mr King is a fellow of the Chartered Institute of Arbitrators and is recognised as a leading practitioner in the field of arbitration, commercial litigation and energy law in the *Chambers* and *Legal 500* independent guides, which have described him as "a leader in energy litigation" and "almost peerless" for energy disputes.

Elie Kleiman
Partner, Freshfields Bruckhaus Deringer LLP
elie.kleiman@freshfields.com

Elie Kleiman is a member of the international arbitration practice group of Freshfields in Paris, and managing partner of the Paris office. He holds degrees in private and international law.

His practice focuses on international arbitration and related court proceedings. Mr Kleiman's work covers a variety of areas, including joint venture contracts, gas pricing, mergers and acquisitions and shareholder disputes in the energy sector. His practice also extends to aeronautics, chemicals, biotechnology, transportation and logistics, financial institutions, construction and engineering, telecommunications and media.

Mr Kleiman is a native French speaker and is fluent in English. He teaches at his alma mater, the *Université de Paris II – Panthéon-Assas*, and is widely published in his area of practice.

Charles Lockwood
Partner, Ince & Co LLP
charles.lockwood@incelaw.com

Charles Lockwood is a partner in the energy and offshore group at Ince & Co in London. He advises clients in relation to both onshore and offshore energy operations, including drilling and other offshore services, construction, engineering and installation contracts and floating production, storage and offloading units.

Mr Lockwood drafts, negotiates and advises on proposed contracts, and has a wealth of

experience of dispute resolution in these areas, with significant expertise in large-scale, often technical international arbitrations and litigation. His client base includes major energy and offshore industry contractors and insurance providers.

Tim Martin
Principal, adrgovernanceinc
tim@timmartin.ca

Tim Martin has over 30 years' experience in the international oil and gas industry in more than 50 countries. He has been president of the Association of International Petroleum Negotiators and other industry organisations. Mr Martin's peers have selected him for the *International Who's Who of Oil and Gas Lawyers* and the *International Who's Who of Commercial Arbitrators*, where he has been described as the "best around for energy disputes" and "a true expert in the [oil and gas] sector".

Mr Martin has extensive experience as an arbitrator and expert, and has acted as counsel in international arbitrations, cross-border litigation and boundary disputes. He has written and spoken extensively on dispute resolution and energy-related matters. Mr Martin is a chartered arbitrator and is on the arbitrator panels of many of the leading international arbitration institutions.

Further details on Mr Martin's career and expertise can be found on his websites www.timmartin.ca and www.adrgovernance.com.

Jessica Neuberger
Senior associate, Ashurst LLP
jessica.neuberger@ashurst.com

Jessica Neuberger is a senior associate in the dispute resolution department of Ashurst in London. She has considerable experience of advising on disputes arising from a broad range of sectors, principally real estate, construction and energy. She has advised in relation to litigation, arbitration and various forms of alternative dispute resolution, and frequently assists with the drafting of dispute resolution provisions in complex cross-border transactions.

Drazen Petkovich
Legal director, Crescent Petroleum
dpetkovich@crescent.ae

Drazen Petkovich heads the legal department of Crescent Petroleum. Based in Sharjah, United Arab Emirates, Crescent Petroleum is the first and oldest private exploration and production company in the Middle East. Over the past 40 years, Crescent Petroleum has operated in numerous countries, including Egypt, Pakistan, Yemen, Canada, the former Yugoslavia, Tunisia and Argentina. At present, its main projects are in the Kurdistan Region of Iraq and the United Arab Emirates. Crescent Petroleum is also the largest shareholder in Dana Gas, the Middle East's first and largest regional private-sector natural gas company.

Before joining Crescent Petroleum, Mr Petkovich was a member of the litigation and international arbitration team of Ashurst LLP, London, where he specialised in energy disputes as well as banking and finance litigation.

Georgia Quick
Partner, Ashurst Australia
georgia.quick@ashurst.com

Georgia Quick specialises in dispute resolution and risk management in respect of energy and resources, construction and major projects, and is head of the Ashurst Australian international arbitration practice. She is admitted to practise in Australia and England and Wales, and worked in London for seven years, practising primarily in international arbitration for energy clients.

Ms Quick has been involved in disputes in respect of commercial developments such as power plants, offshore platforms, rolling stock, port and airport facilities in a number of foreign jurisdictions. She is also involved in the litigation of complex construction and infrastructure matters in Australia and has considerable adjudication and mediation experience.

Ms Quick regularly advises in respect of dispute resolution clauses and provides strategic advice in relation to cross-border dispute resolution and investor-state arbitrations. She is a director of the Australian Resources and Energy Law Association and the Australian Centre for International Commercial Arbitration, and a director and fellow of the Chartered Institute of Arbitrators Australia.

Tim Reid
Partner, Ashurst LLP
tim.reid@ashurst.com

Tim Reid is a partner at Ashurst specialising in the resolution of disputes in the energy sector. His experience has been built up over 25 years and ranges from resolving disputes relating to the construction of floating production, storage and offloading units, to disputes under take-or-pay contracts and other gas sales contracts, and disputes arising under production sharing agreements and farm-in agreements.

He has practised in England and Hong Kong and is experienced in all forms of dispute resolution, both formal and informal, including High Court litigation, international arbitration and early neutral evaluation.

Fiona Reilly
Partner, Norton Rose LLP
fiona.reilly@nortonrose.com

For more than 15 years Fiona Reilly has worked on all aspects of the nuclear cycle. She advises on liability regimes, insurance, licensing, regulatory regimes and reporting requirements, feasibility studies and structuring, as well as contracts relating to the financing, development, construction, operation, maintenance and decommissioning of nuclear stations and the fabrication, reprocessing and storage of nuclear fuel and waste.

Before joining Norton Rose, Ms Reilly worked for Alstom, where she managed multimillion-pound international disputes and negotiated contracts for nuclear, defence and airport-related projects. She was also seconded to Sizewell B nuclear power station and spent time working on nuclear projects at Wylfa.

Ms Reilly is a solicitor advocate (civil) and is a member of the Technology and Construction Solicitors Association, the Chartered Institute of Arbitrators, the International Bar Association, the Energy Institute, the International Nuclear Lawyers Association and Women in Nuclear.

Philip Roche
Partner, Norton Rose LLP
philip.roche@nortonrose.com

Philip Roche is a partner in the transport, energy and trade dispute resolution group at Norton Rose in London. Before joining Norton Rose, Mr Roche served in the Royal Navy as a deck officer for 11 years.

Mr Roche is a disputes and legal risk lawyer. In addition to handling all types of dispute, including international arbitrations, he advises ship owners and operators, insurers and energy companies on the legal, commercial and environmental risks of owning and operating ships and the carriage of cargo, including pollution risks. Among other things, he advises clients on other issues such as the International Ship and Port Facility Security Code, container security and the carriage of hazardous goods, including cargo relating to the nuclear industry. He also advises on piracy matters, including the arming of guards and sanctions relating to Libya and Iran that affect shipping, insurance and financial transactions.

Deborah Tomkinson
Senior associate, Ashurst Australia
deborah.tomkinson@ashurst.com

Deborah Tomkinson's experience centres on dispute resolution in the energy, major projects, construction and infrastructure industries. She is a member of the Ashurst Australia international arbitration practice and of the Chartered Institute of Arbitrators.

Ms Tomkinson regularly advises clients on issues of liability and procedure, as well as providing strategic advice with respect to the drafting of appropriate dispute resolution clauses. She has acted for clients in litigation proceedings ranging from district court matters to special leave applications in the High Court of Australia. She has also represented clients in various forms of alternative dispute resolution, including arbitration, mediation, facilitation, expert determination and adjudication.

Ms Tomkinson practised for a number of years in the United Arab Emirates, acting for clients in relation to litigation conducted in the courts of Dubai and the Dubai International Financial Centre, as well as in arbitral proceedings conducted both in the United Arab Emirates and abroad, pursuant to various institutional rules.

Joanna Wallis
Associate, Ashurst LLP
joanna.wallis@ashurst.com

Joanna Wallis is an associate at Ashurst. She read philosophy, politics and economics at Oxford University before pursuing a career in law. Ms Wallis practises commercial litigation and has been involved in a number of complex and high-value disputes in the energy sector in particular.